RESEARCH
MADE
SIMPLE

To the men and women brave enough
to imagine a world with fresh air, clean water,
healthy land, sustainable living, and nonviolence.

RESEARCH MADE SIMPLE

A HANDBOOK FOR SOCIAL WORKERS

RAYMOND MARK

SAGE Publications
International Educational and Professional Publisher
Thousand Oaks London New Delhi

For information address:

SAGE Publications, Inc.
2455 Teller Road
Thousand Oaks, California 91320
E-mail: order@sagepub.com

SAGE Publications Ltd.
6 Bonhill Street
London EC2A 4PU
United Kingdom

SAGE Publications India Pvt. Ltd.
M-32 Market
Greater Kailash I
New Delhi 110 048 India

Printed in the United States of America

Library of Congress Cataloging-in-Publication Data

Mark, Raymond.
    Research made simple: A handbook for the human services / Raymond Mark.
       p.   cm.
    Includes bibliographical references and index.
    ISBN 0-8039-7426-4 (alk. paper).—ISBN 0-8039-7427-2 (pbk.: alk. paper)
    1. Human services—Research. 2. Social service—Research.
I. Title.
HV11.B44   1996
361.3′2′072—dc20   95-41740

This book is printed on acid-free paper.

    97 98 99 10 9 8 7 6 5 4 3

Sage Production Editor: Diane S. Foster
Sage Typesetter: Andrea D. Swanson

Contents

Foreword

So you have to take a research class? Or check on how to sample a large group? Or develop understanding of a social service phenomenon that requires qualitative research?

Well, you have come to the right place! That unconscious antipathy to statistics that most Americans carry around as a result of the way we learned mathematics will fade if you try "Dr. Mark's Balm for the Baffled."

Just as a little time with this book will change your perspective, Professor Raymond Mark's intellectual gifts have amplified their user-friendly attributes from the therapeutic *Research Guides for the Helping Professions of 1988.*

The helpful addition of two chapters, the politically correct "Culture- and Gender-Sensitive Research" (Chapter 4) and the empathetic "Defining a Research Problem and Using the Library to Search the Literature" (Chapter 5), will help bring the calming effect of knowledge acquisition.

This prompts me to repeat and amplify my 1988 Foreword to give glimpses of the struggle of the practitioners of applied social sciences, the social workers, to bring scientific rigor and human caring together:

> What a peculiar minuet social work practice and social work research have danced, sometimes reservedly bowing at a distance, occasionally joining hands in ardor, as they execute their assigned functions.

Since the meetings of the Section on Social Economy (1874-1879) of the American Social Science Association, research and practice in social work have been trying to make a fit in the applied science of social work. Early demonstrations of the peaks of that periodic practice-research courtship were displayed with Dr. Amos Griswold Warner's *A Study in Philanthropy and Economics* of 1894, the Pittsburgh Survey of 1909, and Mary Richmond's *Social Diagnosis* in 1917.

The necessity for this relationship gained increasing intellectual recognition in social work over the years. It was evidenced in the organization of the Social Work Research Group of 1949, the Hollis-Taylor (1951) report on *Social Work Education in the United States,* the comprehensive *Curriculum Study* (1959, Vol. 9) of the Council on Social Work Education, and the National Association of Social Worker's [NASW's] periodic research review volumes from 1959 through 1978, each step enhancing the quality of the practice-research relationship.

But organic integration has never been consummated. The flirtation was interrupted by the intervention of the anti-intellectualism and the professional masochism of the 1960s. The dichotomous argument regarding social work as an art versus a science obscures honest intentions. The emphasis on clinical training for privatization of social services tends to squeeze out the research ideology in the educational curricula. Underlying these barriers is the traditional dependence on research from other disciplines and the social sciences.

Fortunately, the NASW publication of *Social Work Abstracts* since 1965, its expansion into the *Social Work Research and Abstracts* in 1977, and its bipolar separation into *Abstracts* and *Research* in 1994 have been supported by a cadre of dedicated researchers who have kept aflame the practice-research romance.

One minimilestone was the 1978 National Conference on Social Work Research, which charted a future betrothal for the social work profession in NASW's publication the *Future of Social Work Research.* Another was the NASW's Harriett Bartlett Practice Effectiveness Project in the early 1980s, which uncovered more than 1,800 research studies on social work practice in the United States.

These peaks of research choreography surfaced through three decades: (a) the rock and roll period of the 1960s that struggled over individual treatment and social action, or between so-called micro and macro practice; (b) the 1970s, when the attacks on social services and the defensive battles to protect them brought the research introspection into whether our methods were really effective in helping clients; and (c) the 1980s accommodation period to the Reagan reactionaries with deeper interest in qualitative designs—single subject, ethnographies, and others—which looked to heuristic methods.

So the Apache dancing of quantitative and qualitative research advocates continues in the 1990s, and the practice dominion struggles with public and voluntary constrictions under the onslaught of conservative public policy and privatization of social services. Raymond Mark's new chapters "An Alternative to Group Research Designs: The Logic of Elaboration" (Chapter 8) and "Qualitative Research" (Chapter 10) guide the reader's steps on the latest postmodernist approach.

Unfortunately, most of the social work researchers continue to be isolated in academic settings, a commentary on the scientific knowledge commitment of social agencies. Also, fundamental to the oscillations in our profession has been the problem of how, and to what degree, to inculcate research attitudes and knowledge into the beings of developing social work professionals. The academicians, fortunately, continue to serenade the practitioners with the reproductive advantages of a research liaison, but they retreat from thesis requirements in the schools of social work.

Often, the literal translation of the methodology and techniques of the social sciences into the relationship methodology of social work, the misapplication of conventional physical sciences techniques to the studies of moving human targets, and the complexities of social phenomena have created unscalable barriers for students. Even more saddening, they have tended to fixate previous mathematical and methodological traumas.

In research methodology, the social work profession faces the future with blunted instruments, only occasionally sharpened for battle on behalf of the social services, and certainly with no academic divisions to wield them. Psychological research explores the capabilities of the individual and sociology explores facts of societal function, but too little exploration has taken place in the interaction between those two, the complications of cause and effect in the person-societal interactions.

Raymond Mark has extended his choreography of a modern ballet of social work research, continuing to combine the classical integrity of statistical techniques with the latest problems of planning and implementation, a kind of researcher's "rodeo."

One hopes this book's use as a teaching instrument and its application as a research stimulus and guide will encourage both students and practitioners to work harder at achieving a sounder integration of theory and practice in social work. Just do it!

—Chauncey A. Alexander, ACSW, LCSW, CAE
Huntington Beach, California

Preface

Before you begin to read this book you might ask yourself why you have decided to read it at all.

Most likely, you are an undergraduate or graduate student in social work taking a required course in social work research. Or you are a practicing social worker needing to review your research knowledge or to learn more about research methods so that you can improve your performance as a social worker.

Like most social workers, you may approach the task of learning about research methods with less than complete enthusiasm. That is understandable. It is no secret that of all the courses in the social work curriculum, the research methods course is one of the least popular. There are two reasons for this: anxiety about the unknown and the erroneous belief that research methods are irrelevant to practice.

In the 15 years that I taught research methods to social workers, I was struck by the high level of anxiety experienced by many beginning students. That students should feel this way is understandable. After all, this course uses a specialized vocabulary that is unfamiliar to the layperson, and at least some of the material is quite technical. Still, it is useful to enter this course with some perspective about anxiety.

Anxiety is not entirely bad. Scientists who have studied human learning (using the same methods that you will learn in this book) have discovered an interesting phenomenon: Very low levels of anxiety interfere with learning as do very high levels. A moderate level of "arousal" facilitates learning, perhaps by getting you motivated and oriented to the task at hand. So as a seasoned instructor, my advice to you is to draw on your anxiety to help you get through the course. Stay motivated, ask questions, and keep to a regular schedule of study. Don't panic if understanding doesn't come right away. Calm down and keep at it until you thoroughly understand the material.

I read a study recently that showed that most social workers still believe they can evaluate their practice using nonresearch methods, such as worker intuition and subjective judgments about clients. But as you will see in the pages that follow, these unsystematic methods are fraught with danger: Without the guidance of systematic methods, we are likely to simply confirm what we want to believe. No social worker is truly able to do the best for clients without knowledge of research methods.

Social work research methods *are* relevant to practice. Consider two examples. Since the beginning of the Reagan era—with its cutbacks in spending for social services and its emphasis on "trickle-down" economics—national attention has turned to the problem of homelessness. Many social workers have been involved in the debate about this problem. They have had to rely on the results of research studies to answer the many questions that arise. To serve clients and shape social policies that make sense, good answers to these questions are necessary.

For example, research studies have addressed questions such as these: How many homeless people are there? What events precipitate homelessness? What are the characteristics of homeless people—how many are children, mentally ill, employed persons, single adult males? Where do homeless people spend their time? Which interventions and programs have been helpful in solving this problem, and which have not?

Spousal abuse is another pressing social problem that has involved the attention of many social workers. Again, social workers have relied on research studies to inform them about the nature and scope of the problem: What are the different types of abuse—physical, sexual, and psychological? How widespread is the problem—how many husbands abuse wives and how many wives abuse their husbands? To what extent is this a problem among nonmarried couples and same-sex couples? What conditions—such as job loss and substance abuse—are associated with spouse abuse? What reasons do abused spouses give for staying in abusive relationships? What services are available for abused spouses? What interventions are most successful in getting perpetrators to stop their abuse?

No matter what your field of practice, knowledge of social work research methods is essential to designing studies that provide answers to critical questions that shape your knowledge about social problems and determine how you go about addressing them.

This brings me to another point. Some research methods texts prepare you to be a *producer* of research. That is, they provide information in great detail, enabling you to design research studies, carry them out, and report their results. This handbook has a more modest goal: to enable you to be an informed *consumer* of research studies carried out by others. *Research Made Simple* gives you the raw materials that will allow you to read a research report, understand its findings, and judge the accuracy of its conclusions and its application to your own situation. (For readers who do want to know how to write a research report, I have provided guidelines in Appendix D at the end of the book.)

However, this handbook will also give you a solid foundation if you decide to pursue advanced study of research methods. Although you may not plan to become a researcher, the increasing number of social work research roles, nevertheless, may propel you into a research career in the future. For example, you may need to become a researcher if you plan to (a) write proposals or grants to foundations or government funding sources (increasingly these sources require that you include a research plan in your proposal); (b) work for a policy or research institute, such as the Institute for Research on Poverty at the University of Wisconsin—Madison or the Alcohol and Drug Abuse Institute at the University of Washington; (c) become an administrator of an agency (requiring you to assess service needs and evaluate the services provided); or (d) become a social work instructor in a school of social work (in most cases, this will require a doctorate with advanced research training and publication of your own research studies).

In the unlikely event that you still believe that research methods are irrelevant to social work practice, I want you to consider my favorite reason for learning these methods: I guarantee they will help you to think more effectively. The way in which you evaluate evidence of all kinds will become more clear and logical. This will become evident as you read *Research Made Simple*. For example, in the chapter on sampling, you will learn how to avoid erroneous conclusions based on nonrepresentative samples—a common fallacy in much thinking, including the thinking of social workers. The chapters on research design will show you how to figure out alternative explanations for why things work out the way they do.

Chapter 1 defines the scientific method, which forms the philosophical base of social work research, and Chapter 2 establishes a basic research vocabulary that will be used throughout the rest of the book. I discuss ethics early on, in Chapter 3, to stress the importance of respecting the rights of research participants and to allow you to consider the design and conduct of research in light of ethical requirements. In a similar vein, Chapter 4 sensitizes you to the need to design and evaluate research studies so as to take account of the unique perspectives of women and cultural and ethnic minorities. As the population of the United States becomes more diverse, this will continue to be an important prerequisite for effective social work.

Every researcher must be well-grounded in the literature and must define clear and specific questions that are amenable to study. These topics are covered in Chapter 5. Chapter 6 outlines methods for selecting individuals for study. The next three chapters—7, 8, and 9—present traditional and alternative research designs—the plans followed by researchers to obtain answers to the research questions defined earlier. The methods presented in *Research Made Simple* up to this point have been dubbed *quantitative,* in contrast to the more subjective *qualitative* methods (covered in Chapter 10) that rely on understanding people from within their own views of a situation.

Chapter 11 is a brief primer on the methods typically used by agencies to evaluate social service needs and programs. The nitty-gritty of obtaining data from various sources is outlined in Chapter 12. Chapters 13, 14, and 15 address these questions: How good or accurate is the information I have collected? How do I analyze my data in the most valid and appropriate ways to answer my research questions? In Chapter 16, you will learn how to use statistics to test hypotheses—that is, statements about how variables are related to one another. Chapter 17 presents an overview of the most common types of computer applications used by social work researchers. Finally, a series of appendixes addresses practical issues, such as how to write a research proposal and how to present data in tables and figures.

A final word. I have learned after many years of teaching that students who have confidence in their ability to master new material will have the best experience in their research course.

A positive attitude will also help if you are a practicing professional using this handbook to refresh old learning or to guide you in evaluating or conducting a research study. If you are like the many practitioners to whom I have spoken, you may think, "I can't remember anything I learned about research back in school." If that is the case, this handbook will be especially valuable to you.

You may feel at times that the understanding simply won't come. Just remember, if you have been admitted to a research course, if you are a practicing professional—in short, if you've come this far—that is proof positive you've got what it takes to learn everything in this handbook. So don't be discouraged if at first the concepts appear strange or confusing. Some of them are. Know that this handbook and a good dose of patience are all you need to accomplish the task.

—Raymond Mark

Acknowledgments

I would like to thank Bill Cohen for his encouragement and his wise advice—he helped make this book possible. It has been a pleasure to work with the dedicated and caring staff at Sage Publications: I owe a special thanks to Jim Nageotte, whose faith in this book kept it alive during the ups and downs of its birth. I am also grateful to Terry Hendrix, Linda Gray, and Nancy Hale for their continuing support and help.

1 Research and the Scientific Method

S ocial workers have developed programs for and provided services to the poor, mentally ill, and handicapped; children; the elderly; and many others in need. Great strides have been made in the development and delivery of services, yet most would argue that much remains to be done. We need to know more about individuals, families, groups, and communities to meet their needs effectively.

Research has made a significant contribution in addressing a variety of human problems. For example, a number of research studies have shown that many persons institutionalized for mental illness can live and function well in the community, provided that adequate mental health and support services are available to them (Joint Commission, 1961; President's Commission, 1978). Research has also demonstrated that prenatal care is vital to the health and well-being of newborn babies (Schuster & Ashburn, 1980).

Many societal myths have been challenged by research. For example, it was generally believed that old people become senile. But research has demonstrated that senility is not an inevitable part of growing older (Baltes & Labouvie, 1973).

In another instance, society believed that nearly all people on welfare were cheaters. Again, research has shown that only a small minority of public aid recipients deliberately cheat (Julian & Kornblum, 1983; Stein, 1969; U.S. Congress, 1972).

These examples illustrate a few of the many important contributions that have been made by social work research.

WHAT IS RESEARCH?

Every specialized endeavor is characterized by a particular view of the world and a specialized vocabulary. Because social work research is based on methodologies developed for research in the social sciences and because these methodologies use language in new and unfamiliar ways, social workers are sometimes bewildered by the world of research.

The purpose of Chapters 1 and 2 is to help you (a) understand the assumptions and worldview that form the basis for social science research, (b) appreciate the value of research for social work professionals, and (c) become familiar with some special vocabulary that will be used throughout the rest of the book. Once you understand these, social work research will seem less bewildering.

Research can be defined as "a systematic way of asking questions, a systematic method of inquiry" (Drew, 1980, p. 4). Research involves a quest for knowledge, one that is conducted in a rational way using scientific methodology. Its purpose is to discover answers to questions and to accumulate dependable knowledge. Thus social work research is a method for gaining new knowledge about the world.

WHY DO RESEARCH?

Although there are many reasons for doing research, the primary one is that there is a need to further the knowledge of the profession. Thus, if research was never done, the social work profession would be based merely on guesswork and speculation. Research must continually be conducted to provide answers to complex questions related to understanding human behavior and establishing effective social work programs and practices.

Many students and professionals in social work are reluctant to engage in research. They are apprehensive about research courses that they feel are far removed from the real world. Research seems dull compared to the exciting practice of their profession. They believe that their practice skills are sufficient to intervene successfully with individuals, groups, families, organizations, and communities. Despite all of these reservations, knowing about research—from either a consumer's or an investigator's perspective—is vital for social workers.

Atherton and Klemmack (1982) described four important reasons for social workers to be involved in research:

1. Social workers who are knowledgeable about research are able to use research techniques for analyzing and processing data, which leads to better practice and policy decisions.
2. Social workers who have developed some sophistication in research are less likely to be deceived by poorly done research.
3. Social workers with research skills are able to evaluate the usefulness of research from other disciplines.
4. Social workers who can participate in research are able to demonstrate accountability to their various constituencies—boards, legislators, and citizens, especially clients. (p. 10)

CONCEPTS

Now that you have an understanding of what is meant by research and the value of doing research, let's begin to discuss the vocabulary that will be used throughout the rest of this book.

Let's start with the most basic research term: *concept.* We use concepts all the time. Every word in this book is a concept. What is a concept?

Definition: A *concept* is a word, term, or symbol that tells us what otherwise different things have in common.

I can illustrate this definition by defining the concept *red.* To understand this notion of a concept, we have to look at the world with a new perspective. So imagine that you are entertaining a visitor from another planet. Your visitor does not have eyes but, rather, a technical device that attaches to her head and functions something like a television set. But all the television set devices on your friend's planet are tuned to black and white reception only. Therefore, the notion of color is alien to your visitor (so to speak).

Over dinner one evening, you notice your visitor pouring catsup into her soup, and someone at the table remarks at how red this year's tomato crop has

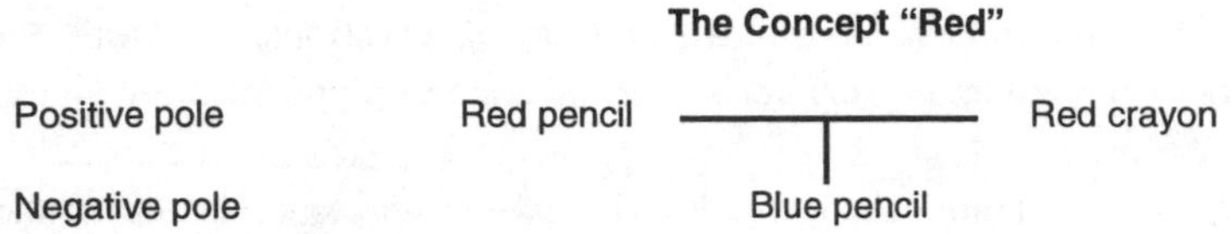

The Concept "Red"

Positive pole   Red pencil ━━━━━━┳━━━━━━ Red crayon

Negative pole   Blue pencil

Figure 1.1. Defining the Concept *Red.*

been. Your visitor looks up and, with a quizzical look on her screen and a tilt of her antennae, says, "Define red."

What's an earthling to do?

Your explanation might sound something like this: "Well, red is something that different objects or ideas have in common. For instance, here is a red pencil, and here is a red crayon. Red is the thing they have in common."

Your friend's screen clears for a moment and she remarks, "I get it, red is something earthlings use to draw."

Obviously, you haven't been clear enough. To define red or any other concept, you must provide not two, but three, examples at a minimum. To show that the concept represents something similar in different objects, you must provide at least two examples of things that embody the concept.

You did that when you showed your visitor the red pencil and the red crayon. (These objects are said to form the positive pole of the concept red.) But you also need to show at least one object that is exactly the same as one of the objects you used for the positive pole of the concept, but it must *not* embody the concept. For example, you can show a blue pencil. (This object is said to form the negative pole of the concept red.)

The model in Figure 1.1 can be used to define any other concept. For example, how would you define the concept of *aggression?* Your two examples of aggression might be "Jimmy hitting Joey" and "Ms. Grumpy screaming at Mr. Grumpy." Then your example of something that is not aggression might be "Mary sitting quietly reading a novel."

If you think about it, it is just about impossible to come up with an example of something that is not a concept: Our thoughts are formed in terms of words or language, and our language is conceptual. Concepts help us to bring order into the world.

Can you think of something that is not a concept? To do that we need a term or symbol that does *not* tell us what otherwise different things have in common. For this, we turn to very young children in their preconceptual stage of development and not yet using language. As an example, the child may know that *chair* refers to the rocker in the living room at home, but he or she doesn't yet understand that the term *chair* also refers to other objects that are used for a similar purpose. So you can see how important concepts are to thinking and hence to research.

Think about the many concepts you use in other settings: age, ethnicity, social welfare program, income, interaction, cognition, services, evaluation, social class, and so on. Try to apply the positive-negative pole definition illustrated in Figure 1.1 to some of these concepts.

Definition: A *conceptual scheme* is a collection of concepts that are related in some way.

For example, the "systems approach" (Pincus & Minahan, 1973) is a conceptual scheme. It is a way of understanding social work practice by categorizing people into groups such as "change agent system," "client system," and "target system" and categorizing worker relationships into those involving "collaboration," "bargaining," or "conflict." These are, of course, all concepts. Conceptual schemes tie concepts together with assumptions and propositions such as, "The client system is different from the target system" and "Where there are shared goals, influence can be more easily achieved in a collaborative or bargaining relationship than in a conflictual relationship."

Conceptual schemes—when they are well developed through reasoning, logic, or research—can also be called *theories*. Theories will be discussed in the next chapter.

THE SCIENTIFIC METHOD

I said earlier that social work research, like every specialized endeavor, has a particular view of the world. All social science research is based on the scientific method. This method is a type of philosophy: It makes certain assumptions and holds certain beliefs about the nature of the world. These assumptions and beliefs can be quite different from our ordinary way of thinking.

The scientific method and our ordinary way of thinking are similar in that they both attempt to order events and explain our world by using concepts and conceptual schemes. But that is where the similarity ends. These two methods can give very different results. For instance, although ordinary thinking leads us to believe that psychiatric patients are violent, if we apply the scientific method, we find that psychiatric patients, on the average, are less likely than others to be violent. How do we get two such different conclusions?

Kerlinger (1973) described four ways in which the scientific method differs from what he calls "common sense." The first way explains our troubling discrepancy about psychiatric patients. The scientist is *systematic,* whereas the ordinary person is unsystematic. As nonscientists, we allow our bias to color our perceptions. If we believe that psychiatric patients are violent, then we tend to take notice whenever we hear of a John Hinckley or a Charles Manson. The media encourage this because they give full coverage to the Hinckleys and Mansons but never mention when a psychiatric patient is *not* violent. That is understandable, but it leads to a wrong conclusion.

Scientists on the other hand, are systematic about the way they collect data. Aware that personal biases color our openness to new evidence, scientists will carefully and systematically collect evidence about the relationship between violence and psychiatric status from all sources. They won't rely on newspaper accounts or personal recollection alone but will insist on statistics and other consistent sources of information.

This systematic approach is not limited to collecting evidence. Scientists will also be systematic in the way they build conceptual schemes and theories: Are the underlying propositions clear and consistent? Can the theory be tested in ways that meet acceptable standards of social science research?

Scientists' use of *control* is the second way in which they differ from the ordinary person. Scientists try to understand relationships between events. For instance, as a scientist, you may want to understand what factors lead to a serious problem among young people: acne.

Common sense has it that eating chocolate causes acne, and there may be some evidence for this. But as a scientist, you don't take this presumed relationship between chocolate and acne at face value! You know that many other factors may lead to acne and that eating chocolate may or may not be one of them. So you use control. You know that to show unequivocally that chocolate leads to acne, you need to rule out all other factors that could possibly lead to development of acne. It may be, for instance, that the highest levels of chocolate consumption occur among young people, and that it is really youth—with its flush of hormones—that is the culprit in causing acne.

The point is that scientists look carefully at all possible events that can lead to a particular outcome before they jump to conclusions. As another example of the idea of control, consider how scientists determine whether a social service program—such as counseling, job training, or child care—is effective in making clients happier or more productive. If we find at the end of the program that the client is happier or more productive, we might like to say that this result was due to the program. But before we can do that, we have to rule out other possible causes for our success. For example, was it simply the fact that the client got some attention that made him or her feel better, and would any program have worked as well? Did the program seem to work because we picked only those clients who were going to improve even without the program? In Chapters 7, 8, and 9 on research designs, I will show you exactly how these kinds of questions are answered.

The third way in which the scientific method differs from common sense is that the scientist looks for *relationships* between events or factors. It is true that sometimes the scientist is interested only in describing things: Of the clients served by this agency, how many are African American, Latino, Asian, and White? What is the average age? How many elderly persons on the east side of town would use the services of a low-cost community health center?

But the real work of the scientist is discovering relationships between events or factors: What factors encourage and what factors discourage potential clients from using the services of this agency? What types of health care services are most likely to maintain or improve the health of elderly people?

The fourth characteristic of the scientific method is that the scientist *avoids metaphysical explanations.* A metaphysical explanation is one that cannot be tested. Usually, it is based on faith, the opinion of others, or "wisdom" passed down through generations. Examples of metaphysical explanations include these: "Mary's children are all in trouble with the law because they are 'bad seed,' " "A little suffering is good for the soul," "Mr. Smith didn't survive the accident because his number was called."

The scientist does not claim that such explanations are false but, rather, that they fall outside the scope of the scientific method. They are better addressed by religion or other spiritual means. The scientific method is not able to address metaphysical explanations because it is limited to testing only those explanations that have the potential of being shown false. As scientists, we never stack the deck in our favor. We set up our explanations and our methods so that we can be shown wrong or right. We also make sure that our evidence is available for anyone to judge. Any other person should be able to look at our evidence and come up with the same conclusion.

So we do not deal with the explanation that Mary's children are "bad seed." But we might want to test this notion: "Poor economic opportunity and peer relationships with delinquents are likely to lead a teenager into trouble with the law." We can never say what is "good for the soul." But we can find out if experiencing pain early in life helps a person to adapt to painful experiences in adulthood.

ARE SCIENTISTS ALWAYS SCIENTIFIC?

It should be clear that the scientific method is very different from common sense. But do scientists really follow our idealized view of them? Are scientists always scientific?

For the most part they are. But scientists are people too, and sometimes they allow their biases, prejudices, sloppiness, or pride to influence their work. Scientists have been known to falsify their results to achieve a prized research grant or recognition from their peers. This dishonesty is rare.

A more serious problem is the distortion of results that happens when we deviate from the scientific method. This is much more common than outright fraud, and is one of the reasons for you, as a social worker, to learn about research—to be a critical consumer of research reports so that you can judge the accuracy of the writer's conclusions. Being knowledgeable can also alert you to questions that should have been asked by the researcher but were not or to data that should have been collected or presented but were not.

What are some ways in which scientists can violate the scientific method? First, they can be so attached to a preferred view (perhaps because they have spent years defending it and building their careers on it) that they ignore or discount evidence that contradicts their view. They can even become illogical or devise elaborate explanations to discount the new evidence so that their preferred view is defended. For example, one of Sigmund Freud's pet theories held that certain effects in his patients were due to seduction by an adult during childhood. When evidence became available that these seductions had not occurred, Freud argued that his patients had imagined these events and that their belief in them caused the same effects (Freud, 1920). He clung to his theory even in the face of contradictory evidence.

Second, to support their personal views, scientists can distort the way the research is done or how the data are collected or presented. Because scientists can be more passionate than objective in their work, these distortions can work in subtle ways.

An example of the way in which personal views can influence outcomes is provided by Rosenthal and Jacobson (1968). The researchers randomly selected a number of children in an elementary classroom. Although the children had been randomly selected, their teachers were told that on the basis of extensive testing, these children showed unusual promise for outstanding academic achievement. Testing at the end of the school year showed that these children did actually achieve at higher levels than their classroom peers. The power of suggestion on the teachers was so strong that they actually influenced the results. Their beliefs turned these average children into high achievers.

Another example of the effect of scientist bias is illustrated by a study of male homosexuals. Bieber (1965) held to the traditional psychoanalytic view that homosexuals are emotionally disturbed and have distorted family relationships. Not surprisingly, his study of homosexuals confirmed this view. His subjects had many emotional problems and were likely to have a pathological mother who was described as "close-binding intimate," an undesirable characteristic, according to the researchers.

Other researchers criticized Bieber for being biased. They pointed out that all of Bieber's subjects were men who had entered therapy, people who were likely to have emotional problems regardless of their sexual orientation. In addition, the interview data were judged by individuals who supported the psychoanalytic-pathology view of homosexuality, so it was not surprising that they found pathology. These researchers had violated a major feature of the scientific method that we mentioned earlier: Their method did not allow for the possibility that their view could be shown to be incorrect.

A third way in which scientists are sometimes unscientific is the way in which some scientists fail to open their data to public inspection by other scientists. Some of this is due to the way in which scientific knowledge is usually shared: in professional journals. Journals do not generally publish negative results (i.e., results in which the researcher's contentions were not supported), and therefore much valuable knowledge about what didn't work never sees the light of public scrutiny. Some of it is due to the unwillingness of researchers to present *all* their data. For instance, if four of five graphs confirm the researcher's contentions, it is all too easy to decide that the fifth graph was unrepresentative and to leave it out. It is not uncommon for individuals whose scores differed greatly from the norm to be dropped from the analysis.

In addition, researchers may be secretive about data that could be used for the personal gain of competing colleagues. They may want to squeeze that last article out of the data set before making it available to others, or they may want to ensure that competitors cannot use the data to offer competing explanations. Some years ago, two social workers were criticized when they used a prominent researcher's data to present a new interpretation of the researcher's well-known study (Berger & Piliavin, 1976a, 1976b).

A fourth and final way in which scientists may be unscientific is the way in which they may rush to support a hypothesis or create a theory in the absence of supporting data. This is especially true in social work where a number of intervention models have been popularized with little support from research (Berger, 1986). Simon (1970), commenting on the nature of social casework, noted that casework is very rich in theory (abstract models) but poor in technology (procedures validated by research). Validating procedures by research is a long and painstaking process. Creating a theory is more fun, less work, and, if successful, may attract a lot of attention that is often not forthcoming to the meticulous researcher.

WHAT THE SCIENTIFIC METHOD IS AND IS NOT

I have said that the scientific method is systematic, uses control, looks for relationships among variables, and sets up propositions so that they can be tested objectively. We have also seen that there are many pitfalls on the road to being a truly scientific researcher.

Many people have misunderstandings about science, so it is also important to understand what the scientific method is not (see McCain & Segal, 1969, p. 244 ff).

Many people believe that scientists are concerned mostly with practical questions that affect our day-to-day lives. In this age of high technology it is no wonder that when people think of scientists they think of engineers and other technicians who create bridges, computers, and other useful devices. It is true that these *applied* sciences are vital. But much, perhaps most, of science is *basic* rather than applied—that is, it focuses on the discovery of new knowledge that has no immediate application in the real world.

Most research in social work is applied. This is due to the nature of our field, which is oriented to meeting practical human needs. But it is important to remember that basic science is as important as applied science and often has long-term real-world applications that may not be apparent immediately. Sometimes these applications take many years. In the physical sciences for instance, Einstein's discovery of the relationship between energy and matter $(E = mc^2)$ eventually led to the development of nuclear power. This development could not have been foreseen at the time of Einstein's discovery.

In the same way, Ivan Pavlov, in his work with the salivary response of dogs in the earlier part of the 20th century, established laws of human behavior that today are considered basic. It is not likely that he foresaw the development of psychological techniques that are widely used today to treat anxiety. But these psychological techniques would not have been possible without Pavlov's basic research into behavior.

Another common misunderstanding is that the primary goal of science is the collection of facts and information about the world. But as we saw earlier, although scientists do collect data, the primary purpose of science is to increase knowledge of how our world operates. This is done by discovering how various events and factors affect each other and by creating theories to explain and predict. Without theories and propositions to explain why the data are the way they are, the information we collect would be of little use.

Yet another misunderstanding about science is the belief that science is exact. Although some believe that this is true of the physical but not the social sciences, in fact, it is true of neither. All scientific propositions are probability statements. For instance, in descriptions of the atom, the exact location of electrons can never be determined; we can state only the probability that an electron will be in a given place at a given time. In the same way, we know that the incidence of infant mortality among lower-class African American mothers is higher than among other groups. We can even specify how much higher that probability is. But we cannot predict exactly which mothers will lose their infants. We can make only probability statements about groups of people.

Finally, it is often said that science distorts reality, that it gives a very incomplete picture or understanding of the world. This is perhaps true. Early theories of human behavior, such as psychoanalysis and ego psychology, provided a very broad understanding of human behavior. Such theories were indeed used to explain a wide variety of phenomenon from personal motivation, to humor, to politics. But these theories were not scientific.

It is in the nature of scientific theory that it encapsulates and focuses on a very small aspect of the world. In doing so, it predicts and explains, but it may fail to capture the essence of the world as we know it. For example, the germ theory of disease was very effective in explaining and controlling one limited type of health problem (infectious disease), but it told us very little about why and how people stay healthy. Given our current state of knowledge, we have to settle for highly specific but limited theories that explain only small portions of the world but that do so well.

SUMMARY

Social work research is a method of gaining new knowledge about the world. Research has made a significant contribution in addressing a variety of human needs and has great value for social workers.

Research, like other specialized endeavors, uses a special vocabulary. A concept is a word, term, or symbol that tells us what otherwise different things have in common. The scientific method, like common sense, uses concepts but is also characterized by systematic inquiry, use of control, the search for relationships between factors, and the avoidance of metaphysical explanations.

Because scientists are fallible, they are sometimes unscientific in their work. Good scientific practice is possible when we are open to new interpretations, present our data as completely and objectively as possible, open our work to public scrutiny, and form conclusions based on ample evidence.

Much of science is devoted to generating new knowledge that may not have immediate real-world applications. The goal of science is to generate principles that will help us to understand the world. Scientific statements generally focus on events that are limited and specifically defined, and they are usually expressed in terms of probabilities rather than certainties.

DISCUSSION QUESTIONS

    1. What is research?
    2. Name at least four reasons why research is helpful to social workers.
    3. Name four ways in which the scientific method differs from common sense.
    4. Name four ways in which scientists may be unscientific in their work.
    5. Explain the difference between basic and applied research.
    6. What is wrong with the following statement? "The major purpose of science is to collect facts about the world."

SHORT ASSIGNMENTS

    1. Metaphysical explanations are propositions that cannot be tested. Transform the following metaphysical explanations into specific propositions that can be tested:

"The good die young."

"Cindy is a natural born healer."

"Too many cooks spoil the brew."

"Johnny will quit drinking when he makes up his mind to stop."

"Spare the rod and spoil the child."

Here is an example:

- *Metaphysical explanation:* "Those people will never amount to anything because a rolling stone gathers no moss."
- *Proposition that can be tested:* "Children who come from families that move frequently are likely to do poorly in school."

2a. Define the following concepts using the model illustrated in Figure 1.1. That is, define each of the following concepts by naming two examples that embody the concept (the positive pole) and one example that does not (the negative pole):

Income

Social class

Race

Frail elderly person

Juvenile offender

Poverty

Sexism

2b. Name three concepts that apply to your area of social work practice or interest (for example, child protective services, income maintenance, home health care, hospital social work). Use the model in Figure 1.1 to define each of these concepts.

Here is an example:

The concept "client" can be defined as follows:

Positive pole   Mr. A., who receives counseling ————┬———— Mr. B., a participant in
                        from my agency   │   a work training program

Negative pole   Mr. C., who currently
                                           receives no services

FURTHER READING

Butterfield, H. (1960). *The origins of modern science.* New York: Macmillan.
Kuhn, T. (1970). *The structure of scientific revolution.* Chicago: University of Chicago Press.
Mahoney, M. (1976). *The scientist as subject: The psychological imperative.* Cambridge, MA: Ballinger.

2 Understanding Research Vocabulary

A s I mentioned in the previous chapter, every specialized endeavor uses a special vocabulary. Social work research is no different, so for you to understand the material in later chapters of this book, I need to define a number of terms. We can think of these as building blocks. In this chapter, I will define the following terms: *variable, theory, problem statement, hypothesis, operational definition, independent variable, dependent variable, experimental research,* and *nonexperimental research.*

WHAT IS A VARIABLE?

In Chapter 1, we learned about concepts. Variables are a special type of concept. As Figure 2.1 shows, not all concepts are variables, but all variables are concepts.

Definition: A *variable* is a concept that varies. It can take on two or more values.

For example, among college students the variable *class standing* can take on the values *freshman, sophomore, junior,* and *senior.* The variable *family income* can take on the values *low, medium,* and *high;* or if we want to be

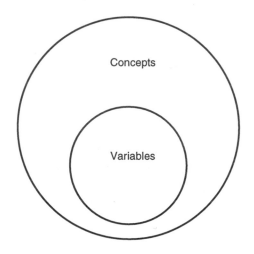

Figure 2.1. Relationship Between Concepts and Variables

more precise, it can take on any dollar value. It can have literally thousands of different values.

So for a concept to be a variable, we must be able to classify it into different categories, such as low, medium, and high, and these categories must meet two criteria: they must be *exhaustive* and *mutually exclusive.*

Definition: A *variable* is a concept that may be classified into two or more exhaustive and mutually exclusive categories.

To understand what I mean by exhaustive and mutually exclusive, we need to play a game of marbles. Imagine that we have a bowl of marbles of various colors: red, green, yellow, and blue. Tomorrow is the big marble swap down at the playground, and in preparation for trading we need to sort our marbles into piles, each pile representing a different color. If we are able to create a pile for each color represented in our marble collection, then we should be able to find a pile for every one of our marbles. If at the end of our sorting, we find that every single marble has been taken out of the bowl and put into its correct color pile, we can say we have exhausted our marbles. (If any marble had been left over, say, if we found a chartreuse marble and didn't have a pile or color category to put it into, then our system would not be exhaustive.)

Definition: Categories are *exhaustive* if every object can be placed in a category.

For a variable to be a concept, its categories or values must not only be exhaustive; they also must be mutually exclusive. Imagine that in the process of sorting our bowl of marbles we come across a "swirly," a marble that is a mix of different colors. If all our piles or categories are for a single color, we won't be sure where to put our swirly. Does it belong in the blue pile, the green pile, the yellow pile, or in all of them?

We can't physically place a marble in more than one pile, and we don't want to double count marbles anyway, because at the end we would like to get a count of how many marbles we have of each color. What we want is a way of categorizing marbles that allows each marble to be put into one and only one category.

Definition: Categories are *mutually exclusive* if each object can be placed in one and only one category.

How do we solve the problem of the swirly marble? Probably, the easiest way is to create a pile called "mixed colors," or perhaps we could call it, simply, "other." Then it would be clear where each marble in our collection belonged. Our categories would then be both exhaustive and mutually exclusive.

When researchers create variables for their studies, they play a game similar to our marble game. For example, in a study of the effects of income maintenance programs on different racial groups, we face the task of measuring the race of our participants or clients. Consider the following item on a questionnaire:

PLEASE INDICATE YOUR RACE BY CHECKING
THE APPROPRIATE CATEGORY:

_____Caucasian (white)
_____Black
_____Native American
_____Asian

Race is the variable being measured here. But is this really a variable—are the categories both exhaustive and mutually exclusive? Not really. If I can show that at least one person in my study is not included in these categories, then the categories are not exhaustive. Someone of East Asian descent who does not consider himself or herself a member of the above groups would be such a person. Also, if I can show that at least one person could be included in more than one group, then the categories are not mutually exclusive. This might be someone of mixed race.

There is no simple solution to the problem of wording the question in such a way that the categories are exhaustive and mutually exclusive—that is, so that the concept *race* is truly a variable. The best solution is to figure out all the possibilities that are likely to occur in the persons to be studied. Sometimes we can look at census data or earlier research to get some idea of the group's demographic profile—its composition in terms of variables such as race, age, income, and so on.

It will also be important to use wording that is as specific and detailed as possible, to give examples for each category, and to include an "other" category for someone who might not fit. As long as only a few people check the "other" category, we can use it without sacrificing too much information about the racial makeup of our group. The following is an example of how one researcher defined race as a variable:

PLEASE CHECK THE ONE CATEGORY
THAT DESCRIBES YOUR RACIAL IDENTITY:

_____Asian (includes Japanese, Chinese, Korean, and Filipino descent)

_____Black, non-Hispanic (includes Afro-American, Jamaican, Trinidadian, West Indian, and African descent)

_____Hispanic (includes Mexican, Puerto Rican, Cuban, Latin American, or Spanish descent regardless of race)

_____Indian, American

_____White, non-Hispanic

_____Other (includes others not covered above and should include Pakistani and East Indian, Aleut, Eskimo, Malayan, Thai, and Vietnamese descent)

It is important to remember that variables *vary*. If a concept cannot take on at least two values, it is not a variable. For instance, the following concepts are not variables: family, bureaucracy, urban, and young. Presumably these concepts do not vary, and in fact they might actually represent *values* of variables. *Family* might be one value of the variable *type of social organiza-*

TABLE 2.1 Illustration of Values and Variables

Values	*Variables*
Family	Type of social organization
	Type of dispute
	Type of film
Urban	Type of residence
	Type of lifestyle
Bright	Level of intelligence
	Level of achievement
Young	Age (number of years)
Poor	Health status
	Quality of performance
	Level of achievement

tion, with other values being *friendship network, social club, church group,* and so on. *Urban* might be one value of the variable *type of residence,* with the other values being *rural* and *suburban.* Table 2.1 summarizes several values and associated variables.

Notice that the variables in Table 2.1 have prefixes indicating that these are concepts that vary: "type of," "level of," and so on. Variables are not always stated with such prefixes, but the prefixes are implied. For instance, when researchers use the variable *age* they really mean *level of age* or *number of years*; when they use the variable *race* they mean *type of race.* It is good to keep this in mind. When you are first learning to identify variables it might be handy to attach prefixes to them to remind you that they vary.

Concepts and variables give us a way to identify aspects of the world that we are interested in studying. They are the building blocks of theories.

WHAT IS A THEORY?

Definition: A *theory* is an explanation.

We observe something in the world around us and come up with an explanation for what we have observed. For example, if we observe that older persons who seem to have the best adjustment are those who have extensive social networks—family and friends—then we might devise a theory that explains why, how, or under what conditions older people become well-adjusted. The theory would include an explanation of the ways in which having friends and family helps in adjustment. Perhaps having close ties makes the older person feel more useful, allows for the exchange of services that makes people feel good, and provides a source of support in times of need or crisis.

A theory, then, is made up of concepts and variables. A successful theory of aging might be made up of concepts and variables such as social network, peer relationship, life satisfaction, self-esteem, and independence. These will then be joined together to explain successful aging. Kerlinger (1973) provides a more complete definition of a theory.

Definition: "A theory is a set of inter-related constructs (concepts), definitions, and propositions that presents a systematic view of phenomena by specifying relations among variables, with the purpose of explaining and predicting the phenomena" (p. 11).

Ideally, a theory will both predict phenomena and explain why they occur. Some researchers, however, feel that prediction is sufficient. For example, basic reinforcement theory (also called operant theory) is very useful because it predicts responses even though it doesn't explain why they occur. Reinforcement theory tells us, for example, that when Johnny's hand raising in class is reinforced by attention from the teacher, that response will tend to be repeated. This is useful because it gives us some control over Johnny's behavior: If we want him to raise his hand in class, we can increase that response by reinforcing it—that is, following it with attention from the teacher. If we want to extinguish Johnny's hand raising, we can do so by not following it with reinforcement—that is, by ignoring it.

But notice that reinforcement theory does not explain why reinforcement increases Johnny's response. Researchers who were not satisfied with the poor *explanatory* power of reinforcement theory came up with an alternative theory that not only predicts but also explains why reinforcement leads to an increase in responding. Drive-reduction theory explains that when a response is rewarded, some basic drive is reduced. For example, a laboratory rat who is reinforced with a drink of water for pressing a bar is likely to increase its pressing of the bar because that response results in a reduction of a physiological drive: thirst. In the same way, teacher attention may be reinforcing for Johnny because it satisfies a desire for recognition or accomplishment.

TABLE 2.2 Steps in the Research Process

Theory
↓
Identify Concepts and Variables
↓
Generate Hypotheses

Theories that not only predict but also explain why events occur are more satisfying than theories that only predict. Ultimately, our curiosity leads us to want to understand not only *what* but *how*. Nevertheless, both types of theory are useful in social work research.

It is often said that researchers devise theories and then test them. In a sense that is true. But because theories are made up of abstract concepts and variables and because it is impossible to measure abstractions, theories are never tested directly. In addition, theories tend to explain a number of different phenomena, and generally, we can test only one or a few specific phenomena at a time.

In effect, the researcher uses theory to generate specific guesses about how variables are related to one another. Rather than test the theory directly, the researcher tests these guesses, which are called hypotheses. To the extent that these hypotheses are confirmed, the researcher can say that the theory is valid.

Table 2.2 summarizes the steps of the research process that we have discussed so far.

WHAT IS A HYPOTHESIS AND HOW IS IT TESTED?

Definition: A *hypothesis* is a guess about the nature of the relationship between two or more variables.

For every hypothesis, we must be able clearly to identify two or more variables. The hypothesis should also make clear how the researcher believes the variables are related to one another.

Consider the following hypothesis: "Individuals from lower social classes are less likely to use mental health services than are those from higher social classes."

Can you identify the two variables in this hypothesis? Figure 2.2 lists these variables and their possible values.

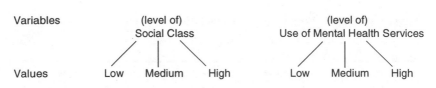

Figure 2.2. Illustration of Two Variables in a Hypothesis

TABLE 2.3 A Handy-Dandy Recipe for Writing and Analyzing Hypotheses

As Variable 1	*Variable 2*
Increases	Increases
Decreases	Decreases
Stays the same	Stays the same
Changes	Changes

Writing hypotheses and identifying the variables in hypotheses are skills, and just as with learning any other skills, it takes time to feel comfortable with them. Until that happens, we can rely on the handy-dandy recipe in Table 2.3, which can be used both for writing hypotheses and for identifying the variables in them. When we become more comfortable with this skill, we can throw away the recipe, just as we threw away those trainer wheels when we first learned how to ride a bicycle.

If we apply this recipe to the hypothesis just mentioned, we should get something like this: "As social class decreases, the use of mental health services decreases." This makes it easy to identify the two variables in the hypothesis: *social class* and *use of mental health services*.

Here are some additional hypotheses. Identify the variables in each of them:

As the size of workers' caseloads increases, client satisfaction with agency services decreases.

As availability of day care services increases, the proportion of mothers who work outside the home increases.

Poorly assimilated ethnic groups are less likely to use services than are well-assimilated ethnic groups.

Older persons with few leisure interests will have greater difficulty adjusting to retirement than will older persons with many leisure interests.

Clients in short-term treatment show greater clinical improvement than do clients in long-term treatment.

A well-constructed hypothesis will meet two criteria:

1. It will clearly state the relationship between two or more variables.
2. It will use variables that potentially can be measured. (For instance, in our first hypothesis, there are ways to measure individuals' social class and use of mental health services.)

There will, of course, be times when our handy-dandy recipe for hypotheses will not be "up to snuff"—in the same way that those training wheels can hold us back in a very fast bike race. One example is when the relationship between variables is more complex. For example, what if use of mental health services decreases as social class decreases for those in the middle classes? But for those of very low social class, use might actually increase because of a higher use of public institutions. Under these circumstances, the hypothesis should state, "As social class decreases, use of mental health services initially decreases and then increases as social class falls below the middle-class level."

What about hypotheses that state the relationships between more than two variables? Three-variable hypotheses can be helpful in giving us a better picture of how groups of variables affect one another. For example, staff members of a local community mental health center may find when they study all their clients that use of services does in fact decrease consistently as the social class of those in its service area decreases.

But a knowledgeable agency staff member may suggest a more detailed hypothesis: "For those under 65 years of age, as social class decreases, use decreases. For those 65 and older, there is no difference in use as social class changes." For the agency to test this refined hypothesis, it will have to look at the relationship between social class and use it twice: once for those under 65 and again for those 65 and older. To the two original variables in our hypothesis (social class and use of services), we have added a third variable (age).

Here is another example of a three-variable hypothesis: "For elementary school children, tangible rewards (e.g., gifts) are more effective than praise in increasing academic performance, whereas for high school children praise is more effective."

Can you identify the three variables? (They are *type of reward, level of academic performance,* and *grade level.*)

Are four- and five-variable (or even more) hypotheses possible? Yes, but they are not desirable because they are difficult to understand and therefore cause confusion. There are, of course, many situations in which we want to know how several variables affect one another. And there are statistical techniques suited to such analyses.

For example, a well-known study found that frail elderly clients who received casework services died sooner than did those who were not served (Blenkner, Bloom, & Nielsen, 1971). In an attempt to figure out the reasons for this disturbing result, Berger and Piliavin (1976a, 1976b) looked at the simultaneous effect of a number of variables operating together and their effect on survival of clients. These variables included the older person's age, mental status, and physical abilities. In situations such as this, which involve groups of variables, it is often best to simplify: State your hunches as a *series* of two- or three-variable hypotheses. For example,

H1: Elderly clients who have poor mental status (i.e., who are disoriented) are less likely than clients with good mental status to survive for 5 years.

H2: Elderly clients who have poor physical ability (e.g., have difficulty feeding themselves) are less likely than clients with good physical ability to survive for 5 years.

H3: Compared with elderly clients who live with family members, those who live alone are less likely to survive for 5 years.

As we have seen, hypotheses can be classified into two-variable and three-variable hypotheses. There is one other way in which hypotheses are classified and that is according to the nature of the relationship that is stated. There are three possibilities:

1. The hypothesis states that there is no relationship between variables (as one changes, the other one stays the same) or that there is no difference between groups (say, between those who received services and those who did not). This is called the *null hypothesis.*

2. The hypothesis states that there is a relationship between variables or a difference between groups. There are two possibilities in this instance:

   a. The hypothesis states the direction of the relationship or difference—for example, "Social work students are more intelligent than business students" or "Social work students are less intelligent [sorry!] than business students." This is called a *directional* hypothesis.

   b. The hypothesis does not state the direction of the relationship or it does not say how the groups will differ (which one will be better)—for example, "Social work students differ from business students in level of intelligence." This is called a *nondirectional* hypothesis.

These distinctions between hypotheses are important because they have implications for how we interpret our data. This is discussed further in Chapter 16, "Statistical Hypothesis Testing."

DESCRIPTIVE RESEARCH

As I said earlier, the scientist studies relationships between variables, and this is done by testing hypotheses derived from theories. Most social work research follows this pattern.

There is an important type of research, however, called descriptive research, which does not use hypotheses. In some instances, rather than studying relationships between variables, we are simply interested in describing a group of persons, families, organizations, or communities. We describe each of these entities one variable at a time.

For example, if I am interested in studying the social service needs of an underserved neighborhood, I might want to begin by doing a survey to get a description of the types of people who live in that neighborhood: What is the age distribution? How many live in families and how many live alone? What kind of incomes do people have? and so on. In my survey, I might ask questions to find out what services, if any, are needed: What medical facilities are used? Is day care available? What do residents do for recreation? What services would they use if available? and so on.

When is descriptive research used? It is used any time we are interested in describing an individual, group, organization, or community. Descriptive research is used, for example, when we are assessing needs, such as the need for a day care center in a neighborhood. It is often used when we have no theory to work from or when we are beginning to explore a new area that has not been researched before. In these situations, there is no body of knowledge to guide us in formulating hypotheses. The purpose of our research, then, may be simply to describe a phenomenon so that we will be better able to study it in the future. Our descriptive research will help us to better understand what we are studying so that later we may be able to create theories and hypotheses for future research.

Despite the importance of descriptive research, our research efforts are most worthwhile when we work from theories and hypotheses. We make guesses about how variables are related to one another, and we study these relationships. This is done by testing hypotheses. Because hypotheses are made up of variables, we will need some way of measuring variables to test our hypotheses. And to measure our variables, we need to *operationally define* them.

OPERATIONAL DEFINITIONS

Definition: An *operational definition* tells us what activities or operations we need to perform to measure a concept or variable.

Assume that our hypothesis is this: "As the level of income increases, the use of psychotherapy increases." To test this hypothesis, we will need some way of measuring each of its variables: level of income and (level of) use of psychotherapy.

The operational definition for level of income might be "gross income as reported on Line 32 of the individual's latest federal income tax form."

The operational definition for use of psychotherapy might be "the individual's response to the interview question, 'Within the past six months how many hours of service did you receive from a psychotherapist? Indicate the number of hours, such as 0 for no visits, 3 for three hours of service, and so on.' "

Creating operational definitions for concepts and variables allows us to be creative because there is often no one correct way to operationally define them. The operational definitions just mentioned may not be the best way to measure the variables of concern. For example, among homemakers a better approximation of income might be Line 32 of their spouses' tax forms. If it is available, should income reported on a joint return be used as the best operational definition of level of income? What if the couple filed a joint return but are currently separated? These are the kinds of issues we will need to handle in devising the best operational definitions for our concepts and variables.

At first, it is difficult to think in terms of operational definitions because they are very different from the kinds of definitions we are used to. Operational definitions are different from dictionary definitions. Consider the dictionary definition of the variable we operationally defined earlier: income. According to the dictionary, income is "the money or other gain periodically received by an individual, corporation, etc., for labor or services, or from property, investments, operations, etc." (*Webster's New World Dictionary,* 1964).

The dictionary definition for psychotherapy is "the application of various forms of mental treatment, as hypnosis, suggestion, psychoanalysis, etc., to nervous and mental disorders" (*Webster's New World Dictionary,* 1964). This definition does not tell us what steps we must take to identify the concept *psychotherapy.* An operational definition of psychotherapy might be, "Professional services rendered by any individual currently listed in the Registry of Clinical Psychologists or the Academy of Certified Social Workers or anyone licensed as a clinical psychologist, social worker, or marriage and family counselor in this state." This operational definition is useful to the researcher because it specifies what must be done to measure the concept— that is, the researcher must find the individual on one of the relevant lists. All such individuals are to be considered psychotherapists.

Dictionary definitions are useful in helping us to understand what concepts mean. Generally, they provide synonyms or examples of the concept. But they are useless for research because they fail to tell us how to measure our concepts and variables.

Operational definitions are also different from attribute definitions. Attribute definitions define concepts by specifying what they consist of. For instance, an attribute definition of apple pie might be, "A dessert prepared from flour, water, apples, and sugar." But if I actually wanted to make an apple pie, an operational definition would be more useful: "An apple pie is a food item prepared according to the recipe for apple pie that appears on page 56 of the *American Desserts Cookbook.*"

As I said earlier, there is some creativity in coming up with good operational definitions. But what makes for a good operational definition? Two criteria should be met.

First, the operational definition should be *reliable* or *replicable.* Good operational definitions are so clearly stated that two independent researchers, following the same operational definition, will measure the same concept or variable in exactly the same way. For example, if I define income as individuals' gross income as reported in their latest federal tax return, there should be no trouble in coming up with consistent figures, even if I send different researchers to collect the information. If my instructions are clear enough, anyone should be able to arrive at the same figures.

Second, the operational definition should be *valid.* Validity is more difficult to achieve than reliability. An operational definition is valid to the extent that it measures the variable or concept in such a way that it reflects its "true" meaning.

It is possible for an operational definition to be reliable but not valid. Suppose, for example, that a naive anthropologist from another culture decided that he would identify Americans who are "in love" by observing whether they held hands with another person. With a little work, we could probably come up with a reliable definition of holding hands that would be consistent enough so that it could be used with the same results by independent observers strategically placed in city parks on warm summer afternoons. That is, our observers would agree most of the time on which individuals fell into the two categories of "holding hands" and "not holding hands."

But we would question the validity of this operational definition as a measure of being in love. Holding hands may be a reliable, but it is not a valid, definition of being in love, because many people who hold hands are not in love and vice versa.

A more realistic example of an operational definition that is reliable but possibly not valid concerns the use of standardized intelligence tests with cultural and racial minorities. Tests such as the Wechsler Adult Intelligence Scale are reliable: They will yield the same or similar IQ scores when repeatedly used on the same individuals, and they are consistent over time as well. But critics of these tests argue that they are culture bound. For individuals who are not familiar with white middle-class terms and concepts these tests may not be valid measures of native intelligence (Bourne & Ekstrand, 1982, pp. 201-210; *New Republic,* 1994). (See Chapter 4 for a more detailed discussion of cultural bias in research.)

To avoid confusion later, it is useful to point out that reliability and validity are characteristics that are applied to at least three different aspects of research methods. We have just discussed the reliability and validity of operational definitions. Two separate issues that we will discuss in later chapters are the reliability and validity of research designs (Chapter 7) and the reliability and validity of measuring instruments, such as questionnaires and interview schedules (Chapter 14).

So far we have learned about theories, concepts, variables, hypotheses, and operational definitions. Table 2.2 illustrated that research proceeds according to a certain order: Theory comes first. Concepts and variables are then used to construct hypotheses derived from theory. The remaining steps are shown in Table 2.4. The concepts and variables in the hypotheses are operationally defined. By providing directions for measuring these concepts and variables, operational definitions allow us to collect data that are later analyzed and interpreted. In Chapters 12 through 17, I will discuss data collection, analysis and interpretation, and the presentation of results.

TABLE 2.4 Steps in the Research Process

Theory
↓
Identify Concepts and Variables
↓
Generate Hypotheses
↓
Operationally Define Concepts and Variables
↓
Collect Data
↓
Analyze Data
↓
Interpret Data and Present Findings

Interpretation of data and presentation of results is never the final step in the research process. Our findings continually lead us to modify, expand, or even abandon our theories, so when the steps in Table 2.4 have been completed, we can think of them recycling over and over again.

There is, however, one caution that we must observe. When we use our data to modify or create theory, we must confirm that theory with an *independent* set of data. In other words, we should not use data to create a theory and then use those same data to argue that our theory is correct. Why not?

If we use the same data to create a theory *and* to confirm it, we have violated one of the rules of the scientific method, discussed in Chapter 1. When we use the same data to both create a theory and confirm it, we are stacking the deck in our favor: We are creating a situation in which our propositions cannot be shown to be false. That does not mean that we should not look to our results to modify or create theory. We *should* do that. But to confirm that modification or that new theory, we need to use an independently collected set of data.

EXPERIMENTAL AND NONEXPERIMENTAL RESEARCH

We have now defined most of the concepts we will need to get into the "meat" of research: stating research questions and getting answers to them. But first, we need to establish some additional research vocabulary.

As I said earlier, the scientist looks for relationships between variables. In this process, we usually need to distinguish between two types of variables.

Definition: In a two-variable relationship, the *independent variable* is the one that comes first. The *dependent variable* comes second.

We can think of the independent variable as the presumed "cause" and the dependent variable as the presumed "effect." (Note that I use the word *presumed.* Just because two variables are related does not mean that one causes the other. This is discussed further on page 336 in Chapter 16.)

For example, when we evaluate the effect of social work programs on clients, participation in the program is generally the independent variable, and the intended change in the client is the dependent variable. Consider this hypothesis: "Participation of preschool children in the Head Start Program enhances their academic performance in grade school." *Participation in Head Start* is the independent variable because it comes first. *Level of academic performance* in grade school comes later: It is the dependent variable.

Demographic variables, such as race, age, occupational status, and social class, are generally independent variables. Typically, we look at the effects of these independent variables on outcomes, or dependent variables. For example, we might be interested in studying the effect of race (independent variable) on attitudes toward the use of birth control by teenagers (dependent variable).

The situation is not always clear-cut, however. There are situations in which it is difficult to tell which is the independent and which the dependent variable. For example, it has been known that the incidence of severe mental illness is higher among the lower socioeconomic classes. For a long time, it was assumed that socioeconomic status was the independent variable. That is, researchers believed that lower-class status, with its economic deprivation and lack of resources, led to stress, which in turn led to a higher incidence of mental illness.

But it may be the other way around: Mental illness may lead to low socioeconomic status. That is, the mental illness may prevent the person from functioning in social and occupational roles, and that may cause the person to remain in or drop to a lower socioeconomic class. In this view, mental illness is the independent variable.

There are plenty of examples of situations in which it is difficult or impossible to distinguish between the independent and dependent variables. We know that intelligent people also tend to be creative. But which one came first—the intelligence or the creativity? It is also true that people who like each other tend to have similar interests. But do they like each other because they have similar interests, or have they developed similar interests because they like each other? One of the functions of theory is to explain such relationships so that we can identify which are the independent and which are the dependent variables.

Is it always important to distinguish between independent and dependent variables? When we study relationships between variables, it *is* important. Differentiating between variables helps us to better understand how they are related, and it determines the way we present our data and interpret our results. This will become more clear after reading the rest of this book.

Differentiating between independent and dependent variables also helps us to distinguish between two types of research that we will be studying in more detail in Chapter 7. I define them here:

Definition: *Experimental research* is research in which the independent variable is manipulated by the researcher. In *nonexperimental research*, the researcher has no control over the independent variable.

One type of experimental research is often used to evaluate the effectiveness of social work programs. In this type of study, the researcher assigns one group of individuals to participate in a program; another group of individuals does not. The researcher can then compare the two groups to see if the program worked. This is a case of experimental research because the researcher manipulated the independent variable of *participation in the program*—that is, the researcher determined who was going to participate and who was not going to participate in the program. So when the researcher controls who will receive the different levels of the independent variable (in this case, participation versus no participation in the program), then we say that the researcher manipulated the independent variable. This means that the research was experimental.

In many situations, the researcher cannot manipulate the independent variable. That is, the researcher cannot determine who will be in one group or the other. Let's say, for example, that the researcher wanted to study the level of job satisfaction among different types of social workers. The researcher may hypothesize that those who work in public welfare agencies are less satisfied with their jobs than those who work for private agencies. The independent variable here is *type of agency,* and its values are *public welfare agency* and *private agency.*

Because the researcher does not have the power to assign some workers to work in public agencies and others to work in private agencies, all that can be done is to locate workers in the two types of agencies and ask them about their job satisfaction. In other words, it wasn't the researcher who manipulated the independent variable. It was already "manipulated" by nature, circumstance, or fate, and the researcher merely came onto the scene after the fact. Therefore, this type of study is nonexperimental.

Although it is often desirable for the researcher to manipulate the independent variable (we'll learn why in Chapter 7), in most situations in social work research this is not possible. Here are some examples of research hypotheses that would be studied using nonexperimental research. See if you can identify the independent and dependent variables and explain why these questions would have to be studied using nonexperimental research.

> Older persons have more positive attitudes about aging than do younger persons.
>
> Social work students are more altruistic than business administration students.
>
> Families with a developmentally disabled child are more likely than other families to be involved in community activities.
>
> As level of family income increases, willingness to contribute to the United Way increases.

In the case of each of these hypotheses, the researcher is not able to manipulate the independent variable. Therefore, each hypothesis would have to be tested using a nonexperimental study.

SUMMARY

This chapter completes the presentation of the basic language of social work research. We saw that variables are special types of concepts and that theories, which serve as explanations, are constructed from concepts, variables, and propositions. To see if our theories are valid, we derive hypotheses from them and then test these hypotheses. But first, we must operationally define the concepts and variables in our hypotheses. Social work researchers also distinguish between independent and dependent variables and between experimental and nonexperimental research. It will be useful to remember these terms as we continue our study of social work research.

DISCUSSION QUESTIONS

1. Define and give an example of each of the following terms:

   Variable
   Mutually exclusive categories
   Exhaustive categories
   Theory
   Hypothesis
   Operational definition
   Experimental research
   Nonexperimental research

2. Which of the following statements is true?

   All concepts are variables.
   All variables are concepts.

3. The following is a list of variables and values (of variables). Identify which ones are values and which are variables.

   Poor
   Age
   Group membership
   Single-parent household
   Socioeconomic status
   Level of participation
   High academic achievement

4. Older people live in a variety of different settings. These may include their own home, the home of a relative, a retirement center, a boarding home, a nursing home, or a hospital. Imagine that you are going to conduct an interview of older persons. Design a question that will be included in the interview to determine the type of living arrangement. Make sure that the question has categories that are both mutually exclusive and exhaustive.

5. State two criteria that characterize good hypotheses.

6. Explain the difference between *descriptive research* and *research that employs hypotheses.*

7. Explain the difference between *operational definitions* and *dictionary definitions.*

8. *Demographic variables* are characteristics of study participants, such as age, race, and income. Why are demographic variables classified as *independent variables?*

SHORT ASSIGNMENTS

1. In the list that follows, I have defined a number of concepts. Which of the following are *reliable* operational definitions—regardless of their validity? That is, identify the reliable operational definitions, whether or not you agree with the accuracy of the definition.

   a. A successfully treated psychiatric patient is one who adjusts to a normal life in the community.
   b. A successfully treated psychiatric patient is one who is not rehospitalized in a psychiatric facility for at least 2 years after being released.
   c. An intelligent student is one whose grade point average is above 3.5 points.
   d. An intelligent student is one who possesses superior intellectual ability.
   e. A well-functioning family is one in which all members communicate freely.
   f. A well-functioning family is one in which all adult members score above average on the Family Assessment Device (a rating scale that measures family functioning).

2. For each of the reliable operational definitions above, critique the validity of the definition.

3. Research studies often begin with an observation or general statement that is then converted into one or more testable hypotheses. Consider each of the general statements that follow. Then, convert each statement into one or more hypotheses.

You will need to do the following (in order):

Identify the variables of interest.
Provide an operational definition for each variable.
Determine if your operational definitions are both reliable and valid.
Combine the variables into one or more hypotheses (statements of the relationship between two or more variables).

   a. Adequate child care facilities should be available to all working mothers.
   b. To adapt well to the aging process, older persons need to maintain their social ties.
   c. Housing vouchers are the most effective means of reducing homelessness in urban communities.

   4. Select one social problem area of concern to you. This might be substance abuse, domestic violence, developmental disabilities, homelessness, aging, child abuse and neglect, or some other area.

   a. On the basis of your knowledge of the social problem, state two hypotheses that might be of concern to social work researchers in that area. (Your hypotheses should meet the criteria for good hypotheses—see page 23 in this chapter.)
   b. For each hypothesis, list the variables in the hypothesis.
   c. For each variable in your hypotheses, provide a reliable and valid operational definition.

FURTHER READING

Chavetz, J. (1978). *A primer on the construction and testing of theories in sociology.* Itasca, IL: F. E. Peacock.

3 Ethics

Ethics refers to standards of conduct to ensure moral behavior. Ethical systems help to answer the age-old question, In our dealings with other persons, what constitutes right and wrong behavior?

Much of biblical writing has to do with ethics—setting standards of moral behavior toward our parents, other family members, neighbors, and strangers. For centuries, philosophers have struggled with ethical standards, and more recently, they have been of concern to lawyers, physicians, scientists, and other professionals.

ETHICS IN RESEARCII

Since social work's beginnings at the start of the 20th century, social workers have been motivated by ethical concerns. Initially, these involved society's ethical responsibility to the poor and vulnerable. The notion that ethical standards ought to apply to social science researchers is a more recent idea, one that originated only after World War II. This was probably due to a naïveté—among laypersons and professionals alike—about the role of researchers.

As highly trained professionals, social science researchers could be trusted to conduct their studies in a responsible manner, free from harm to individuals or communities—or so the argument went. They were in the best position to decide how, and to what purpose, research should be conducted. Their goal of enhanced knowledge was not in conflict with the needs of society or individuals.

In recent decades, it has become apparent that this view—although comforting—was too simplistic. In truth, the researcher's "need to know" can conflict with the rights of research participants to be free from harm. This is perhaps most evident in biomedical research.

For example, when medical researchers evaluate the effectiveness and safety of a new drug, they administer the drug to a group of individuals and then observe the outcome. To evaluate the effects of the drug on this treatment group, a placebo—an inert substance—is administered to a second group of research participants, and the two groups are compared. Neither the physicians administering the test substance—drug or placebo—nor the individuals receiving it are informed as to whether participants are receiving the drug or the placebo. This is the *double-blind* method of drug evaluation, and it is a standard requirement for federal approval of new drugs.

In this situation—one that is repeated in clinics every day across the United States—the rights of researchers to test their drugs outweigh the rights of those research participants who inadvertently find themselves in the placebo group. We can justify withholding the "real" treatment from the placebo group by weighing the benefits to society of having a fully tested and effective drug against the rights of research participants to have the best and latest treatment available. But what if these individuals are in a terminal stage of illness or in pain or deteriorating? Waiting to receive the drug until after the study may be clearly against the interests of placebo group participants.

The issue is really no different in social work research studies that use control groups to evaluate the effectiveness of psychosocial treatments. For example, is it ethical to use control groups to test the effectiveness of a program to treat spouse abuse, eliminate smoking, or help clients develop job skills?

Sometimes social work researchers place participants on a waiting list for a program and then use them as a control group to compare with a treated group. Is this ethical?

If social work researchers are studying a method to get autistic children to stop their self-injury behavior, is it ethical for them to stop treatment for a while to see if it is working?

If a social work researcher poses as a citizen to observe and record a meeting of the board of directors of a community agency—has the researcher violated the rights of those who are being observed without their permission?

In studies that examine socially disapproved behavior—such as drug abuse or extramarital sex—research participants may also be harmed by the probing of researchers or the disclosure of their participation in the research.

These examples illustrate a basic tenet underlying all human subjects research: Because the interests of participants may conflict with the interests of researchers, there is a need for universally recognized standards of ethics to protect research participants.

HISTORICAL BACKGROUND AND ETHICAL CODES

At the conclusion of World War II, the Allied countries tried Nazi war criminals in the much publicized Nuremberg Trials. Among those tried for crimes against humanity were physicians and scientists who had subjected concentration camp inmates to biomedical experiments.

Although these experiments were highly unusual, the experts who conducted them were not. They were ordinary physicians and scientists, recruited from civilian life to take advantage of the "opportunity" that presented itself when innocent people were put into concentration camps and thereby lost all their rights. But with a Nazi ideology that portrayed the inmates as "subhuman," and with no formal ethical standards, terrible experiments were undertaken. For example, inmates were subjected to extremes of heat and cold to determine how long they could survive. Other inmates were burned, poisoned, or subjected to gruesome surgeries.

In conjunction with the Nuremberg trials, the Allied countries drafted what became known as the Nuremberg Code—a set of standards for ethical behavior in the conduct of biomedical research (Annas & Grodin, 1992). The Nuremberg Code was the first of its kind, and it set the standard for later research ethics codes. It established two important principles. First, the participation of individuals in any biomedical research should always be *voluntary.* Second, the risk of harm to research participants should be weighed against the potential benefits to society of new knowledge from the study. Therefore, research procedures that place individuals at risk can be justified only if the researcher can show that there are potential benefits of the research to others.

The Belmont Report, drafted by the National Commission for the Protection of Human Subjects in Biomedical and Behavioral Research, extended the Nuremberg Code (*Belmont Report,* 1987; National Commission for the Protection of Human Subjects, 1978a). It set out three broad principles to govern the ethical conduct of research:

1. *Respect for persons.* Researchers must treat participants as autonomous persons and must respect their decisions, including the decision not to participate. Those participants with diminished autonomy—for example, children, the mentally ill, and the retarded—need special protection.
2. *Beneficence.* The researcher has an ethical obligation to cause no harm. Where harm is possible, the researcher must work to maximize benefits to the individual and society and minimize harm to participants.
3. *Justice.* Certain groups in society have little power. This may include the impoverished, racial and ethnic minorities, and persons in institutions such as prisons. Although members of these groups are often easily available to researchers, it is unjust for these groups to bear the brunt of research risks because of their powerless position in society. This principle is particularly important for social work research, because, commonly, social work clients and research participants are members of powerless or oppressed groups.

The Nuremberg Code and the Belmont Report established a basis for codes of ethics used today by social work researchers. By the 1960s, much of the biomedical and social science research done in the United States was funded directly or indirectly by the government. In 1974, the U.S. Congress established the National Commission for the Protection of Human Subjects of Biomedical and Behavioral Research. The commission created a series of guidelines (National Commission for the Protection of Human Subjects, 1978a, 1978b) that, with some revision, are still in use today in research studies conducted by the federal government or studies conducted in agencies or institutions supported by federal funds. This includes almost all universities and many research centers and other institutions.

Although the commission was disbanded in 1978, the ethical guidelines it developed were adopted by various federal agencies and private organizations. In social work, ethical research conduct is governed by regulations issued by the Department of Health and Human Services (DHHS). At universities, research centers, hospitals, and other institutions that receive federal funds, an institutional review board (IRB) receives study proposals from researchers (Penslar, 1993). These proposals must describe the research and its purpose in some detail. They must describe procedures that will be used to protect the rights of participants. If there are any risks to participants, the researcher must explain the nature of these risks and show that the research is justified because of potential benefits of the study to society.

Many social work research studies are routine, or they place participants at virtually no risk. As a result, the DHHS developed a set of criteria for research that does not require prior review by the institution's IRB. For example, research that involves routine testing in educational settings does not have to be reviewed by the IRB.

Most social work studies involve collection of data by surveys, interviews, or observations. Generally, these studies do not require prior IRB review unless they record data in such a way that participants can be identified (for example, by name or appearance) and the behavior under study could harm the participant if it became known to others (illegal conduct or sensitive behaviors, such as sexual behavior or alcohol use, fall into this category).

In many institutions, however, it is routine for social work researchers to submit all research studies for IRB review. The review process is a good way to ensure that researchers adhere to ethical research conduct. The process of review by other researchers and professionals helps researchers to consider the anticipated and unanticipated consequences to participants. It ensures that the researchers have designed their study in the most ethical way possible, while preserving the study's scientific merit. Finally, securing IRB approval helps to protect the researcher in the event that a participant or member of the community challenges the ethical conduct of the researchers.

INFORMED CONSENT

The principle of voluntary participation was formalized in the Nuremberg Code and the Belmont Report and later incorporated into the guidelines of the National Commission for the Protection of Human Subjects and the regulations of the DHHS.

The principle of *informed consent* is at the heart of efforts to ensure that all participation is truly voluntary. Ethical social work researchers design their studies to include informed consent procedures. According to the guidelines of the National Commission for the Protection of Human Subjects (1978a) a research study must meet three conditions to satisfy the requirement for informed consent. First, research participants must be competent to give informed consent. Second, researchers must provide sufficient information about the study to allow potential participants to decide for or against their participation. Third, individuals' consent to participate must be truly voluntary. It must not be coerced in any way.

Federal regulations issued by the DHHS set out the basic elements of informed consent. In general, social work researchers must provide the following information—usually in writing—to all potential research participants:

- They must be told the purpose of the research, the procedures that will be followed, and an estimate of the amount of time that will be required.
- They must be told of any possible risks or discomfort that may be experienced.
- They must be given a description of any benefits to them or to society that may result from the research.
- If relevant, they must be given a list of alternative procedures or treatments that may be beneficial to them.
- They must be given a description of procedures, if any, that will be used by the researchers to ensure that their participation and responses will be kept confidential.
- They must be given information about whom to contact if they later have questions or concerns about the study or if they feel they have been harmed.
- They must be given a statement that their participation is completely voluntary. Participants must be told that they can withdraw at any time without consequences. In addition, their refusal to participate will not affect any benefits they may be entitled to. For example, if the research study takes place in an agency where the potential participant is receiving service, that service will in no way be affected by the participant's decision to refuse or withdraw from participation.
- If the research involves more than "minimal risk"—that is, risk greater than what one would encounter in normal life or from routine physical or psychological tests—the informed consent procedure must also include an explanation as to whether any compensation or treatment is available in the event of an injury and where the participant may obtain this.

Box 3.1 presents an informed consent form that I used in a study of the effectiveness of a communication training program for elderly nursing home residents.

DEPARTURES FROM INFORMED CONSENT

The DHHS regulations recognize that it is not always possible to provide all these elements of informed consent to participants. Researchers may omit some or all of this information in certain research situations. Specifically, this is justified if there is no more than minimal risk to participants, if withholding this information will not violate the rights of participants, and if the study would be impractical or impossible if all this information were provided. In these types of studies, the researchers must show that these conditions are true.

**BOX 3.1. INFORMED CONSENT FORM:
COMMUNICATION TRAINING PROGRAM
FOR NURSING HOME RESIDENTS**

[Instructions to research staff: Read and discuss all of the following with each participant. After obtaining resident's signature, make a duplicate copy of this form and give it to the resident.]

The communication training program is sponsored by the Group Behavioral Training Unit of the School of Social Work at the University of Wisconsin.

You are being asked to participate in a research study. The purpose of the study is to develop an effective way to train older nursing home residents to handle social situations—for example, situations involving other residents, staff, and doctors.

If you agree to participate, you will receive six sessions of communication training. Each session will last an hour or less.

The communication training program was developed from research conducted at the County Nursing Home over the past 6 months.

We would like to have your consent to participate in this program. This is what you will be asked to do. You will meet individually with an instructor for six sessions. At these sessions, you will discuss common social situations that often occur at the home. These sessions include brief procedures to see if the training has been effective.

If you agree to participate, in the next 2 weeks you will be told exactly when these sessions will occur. Read or listen to the following statements before giving your consent by signing this form:

There are instances in social work research studies when it would not be practical—or even possible—to provide all of this information to participants. For example, if a researcher distributes a very brief and anonymous questionnaire to persons in a public setting, such as a shopping center, it may not be reasonable to assume that participants will take the time to listen to or read a

**BOX 3.1. INFORMED CONSENT FORM:
CONTINUED**

I understand that my participation in this program is voluntary and that I may withdraw my consent to participate at any time, without any consequences to me.

I understand that this program will contribute to scientific knowledge that will be used to help other older persons.

I understand that there are no foreseeable risks to me.

I understand that all information collected will be confidential. In all probability, there will be publications or other educational uses based on the information collected from me. These publications will present group results only. They will not include any material that is identified with me or with my name.

I understand that I may ask questions about any aspect of the program at any time. Should I have any questions or concerns I may contact

Dr. [name]
[address and phone number]

I have read the above and give my consent to participate in this program.

_____   _____
Signature of participant   Date

list containing all informed consent information. Another researcher might set out to observe the behavior of community members at a public meeting. This is another situation in which it may not be practical to provide informed consent information to the many persons who may be observed at the meeting.

A thornier situation arises when the research study requires the researcher to withhold complete information about the study's existence or its purpose. A study, for example, to determine fair housing practices in a community may send mixed-race couples to apply to rent apartments. To achieve its aims, the couple must pose as potential renters rather than research staff. This procedure is routinely used by local equal opportunity agencies.

In another instance, a social work researcher may want to learn how a group of people respond to an ambiguous or stressful situation in the laboratory. But to get a valid measure of participant behavior, it is necessary to obscure the true purpose of the study. For example, a group of research participants may be placed in a room and told simply that they are participating in a study of "problem solving" and then be given an insoluble puzzle to solve. If they were told the true purpose of the study their responses might not accurately reflect their real-world response to an ambiguous and stressful situation.

With modern advances in recording technology, social work researchers face a new ethical research challenge in the field of *unobtrusive measures.* These are techniques for recording real-world or simulated behavior in a wide range of settings. Recording devices such as audio- and videocassette recorders and microphones have become very sensitive and miniaturized. As a result, they can be concealed and used with ease in homes, work sites, schools, institutions, and other natural settings.

From the researcher's point of view, it is desirable to use these unobtrusive measures without the knowledge of those being observed. In this way researchers can get an accurate view of real-life behavior. For example, in one controversial study, researchers placed hidden microphones in a jury deliberation room to study the interactions of jury members.

Unobtrusive measures raise troubling ethical issues. In the jury example, did the researchers tamper with a valued democratic institution? If future jurors feel they may be monitored without their permission—or awareness— will this affect their ability to judge defendants?

There are many ways in which researchers might use unobtrusive measures. Corporations have come under fire from workers for surreptitiously monitoring office telephone conversations. As increasing numbers of workers use computers, managers can obtain complete records of workers' activities by monitoring computer logs. It may be possible to use new technologies to monitor many behaviors, such as patient compliance with medical regimens, personal lifestyles of welfare recipients, or the behavior of parents being investigated for child abuse or neglect.

In general, the ethical guidelines reviewed in this chapter prohibit this type of unobtrusive observation because it does not meet basic requirements for informed consent. Unless the researcher can show that the benefits of a proposed study—for example, the prevention of child abuse—are so great that the requirement for informed consent can be waived—few social workers would accept unobtrusive measures as ethical.

Nevertheless, there are situations where full informed consent is not practical—for example, in the anonymous shopping center survey. In these instances, it is important to provide at least some of the elements of informed consent. Participants, for example, can be told the purpose of the study and they can be assured that their responses will be anonymous.

In studies that involve deception, and after individuals' participation, researchers may provide some explanation of the true purpose of the study. They should also offer an opportunity for participants to express any concerns they might have about the effects of their participation. In this situation, it is often necessary for the researcher to wait until the entire study is completed so that "debriefed" participants do not share information with potential new participants and thereby compromise the study. A practical way to do this is to record participants' names and addresses (separately from their responses so that participants cannot be associated with their responses to the researcher's questions). Then at the conclusion of the study, researchers can mail a brief report of the results to all those who participated as research participants. This procedure is often used by social work researchers.

OBTAINING INFORMED CONSENT

In practice, few social work research studies involve deception. Most social work researchers collect data by using straightforward interviews, questionnaires, and observations. With few exceptions, these studies allow researchers to provide full informed consent to all participants. This is usually done by asking participants to read an informed consent form.

Presenting this information in written form protects both respondents and researchers. It ensures that all participants will receive complete and consistent information. Individuals can be provided with a copy of the form to take with them, allowing them to review their experience as research participants and to voice concerns later if they arise. The form is a convenient place to provide information about the procedure for contacting researchers should the need arise.

Although it is not required in most social work studies, it is a good idea to get the participant's signature on the informed consent form. This provides evidence that the participant has read and understood the informed consent information.

ANONYMITY AND CONFIDENTIALITY

Individuals who participate in social work research studies have a right to know that all information about them will be treated in a responsible manner. It is a simple matter to assure clients of confidentiality. But in reality, the issue of confidentiality is not a simple one. There are many different ways in which information about research participants can be handled, and there are many ways in which a research participant or a client may be harmed by release of information.

It is important for the social work researcher to recognize the difference between anonymity and confidentiality. Research participants are *anonymous* when their study responses cannot in any way be identified with them—by the researcher or by anyone else. For example, in many questionnaire surveys, it is impossible to identify the person who completed any particular questionnaire. This assumes, of course, that the participants did not put their names on the questionnaire and that any other personal information—such as sex and age—could not be used to identify a given individual.

Many public health departments collect research information from individuals who seek testing for the human immunodeficiency virus (HIV) at anonymous test sites. At these sites, individuals do not provide their names. They receive a code number that is known only to themselves. This code number is attached to their blood sample without any other identifying information. Results of the testing are provided only to the person who can provide the code number. This testing situation meets the basic requirement of anonymity—those tested cannot be identified. They cannot be linked with the test results or even with the fact that they were tested.

Individuals who seek HIV testing from a personal physician or from a clinic that is not an anonymous test site can be assured of *confidentiality*, but not anonymity. In such confidential test sites, those tested do give their names, and a record is kept of the testing and its results. The difference between anonymous and confidential testing is that in a confidential situation, the participant's identity is written into a record. Because these records are confidential, clinic staff may not reveal information in the record (without the participant's permission) to anyone other than the participant, other clinic staff, or public health officials. Most social work research studies that use interviews, and many that use questionnaires, offer participants confidentiality, but not anonymity.

In many situations, neither anonymity nor confidentiality is absolute. For example, in an anonymous HIV testing clinic, the individuals who draw test blood and those who report the results see the person being tested face to face. They may know that person's identity. These individuals are bound by law not to reveal the identity of anyone tested. In sites where only HIV testing takes place, other individuals may see the participant. In a small town, it is especially likely that the person being tested will be known to staff or other patients, and there is always the possibility that anonymity will be breached.

In nonanonymous test sites, clinic staff are required by law to report to the public health department the identities of persons who test positive for one of several "reportable" diseases. It is also possible for a court order to require that testing information be revealed to a third party, such as a law enforcement agency.

In many social work research studies, the researcher records the participant's name, address, and phone number, often to allow for follow-up contacts. This information is filed with the participant's responses to the test, questionnaire, or interview. Researchers need to limit the number of personnel who have access to these records and to ensure that none of these personnel knows the participant or the participant's significant others. Some social work researchers require research personnel to sign a pledge of confidentiality, in which the personnel agree not to disclose any information about research participants to anyone other than research staff. It is also useful to include confidentiality procedures in staff training.

When social work researchers study illegal behavior—such as drug abuse or parental neglect—it is possible that law enforcement agencies will want information about participants that they can use in an investigation or prosecution. This is a sensitive area in which the rights of research participants have to be balanced against the rights of society.

Research studies conducted in agencies or institutions that receive federal funds (and that are reviewed and approved by the appropriate IRB, as described earlier) are protected by federal law. In these studies, a law enforcement agency cannot compel a researcher to reveal any information about research participants. For those many studies sponsored outside of federally funded institutions, the law is unclear. A court may require a researcher to breach confidentiality and reveal the identity of participants or information about them. Social work researchers who study sensitive or illegal behavior should consider this possibility when they plan their study.

In general, researchers will want to adhere to the following guidelines to ensure confidentiality for research participants. (These guidelines are a summary of those in use at a major university.)

- Whenever researchers study human subjects, they should keep all information about participants confidential, unless participants have given them written permission to reveal such information.
- Researchers should solicit and record only personal information that is necessary for the study to achieve its purpose.
- All study information that could reveal a participant's identity should be stored in a safe place. Only the researcher and study staff should have access to this information.
- Questionnaires, interviews, tests, and observational recording may have the participant's name or identifying information attached to them. As soon as possible after these data are collected, they should be coded, and the participants' identifying information should be removed, if possible. After all analyses are completed, the original data should be destroyed. Or if the original data are to be retained, the researchers should plan their long-term storage in a safe place.
- In some situations, researchers seek access to data that were originally collected for some other purpose. (This does not apply to information in the public domain, such as the voting records of elected officials.) If participants could be identified by these data, the researchers should examine potential risk to these participants and determine if it is appropriate and feasible to obtain additional informed consent.

NATIONAL ASSOCIATION OF
SOCIAL WORKERS (NASW) CODE OF ETHICS

Professional associations publish codes of ethics to ensure that their members—including researchers—treat others in an ethical manner. These codes include many of the ethical principles discussed in this chapter. Members of these associations may be censured or even expelled for violating these codes. Although very few professionals are ever investigated for code violations (and fewer still are disciplined), these codes are nevertheless important

**BOX 3.2. EXCERPT ON "SCHOLARSHIP AND RESEARCH"
FROM THE NATIONAL ASSOCIATION OF
SOCIAL WORKERS (NASW) CODE OF ETHICS**

Scholarship and Research—The social worker engaged in study and research should be guided by the conventions of scholarly inquiry.

1. The social worker engaged in research should consider carefully its possible consequences for human beings.

2. The social worker engaged in research should ascertain that the consent of participants in the research is voluntary and informed, without any implied deprivation or penalty for refusal to participate, and with due regard for participants' privacy and dignity.

3. The social worker engaged in research should protect participants from unwarranted physical or mental discomfort, distress, harm, danger, or deprivation.

4. The social worker who engages in the evaluation of services or cases should discuss them only for professional purposes and only with persons directly and professionally concerned with them.

5. Information obtained about participants in research should be treated as confidential.

6. The social worker should take credit only for work actually done in connection with scholarly and research endeavors and credit contributions made by others.

SOURCE: NASW (1994, p. 4). Used with permission.

in regulating the behavior of all professionals. They serve as a guide for professionals in difficult ethical situations and as a learning resource in schools and training programs. They represent a commitment on the part of professionals to respect the rights of others.

The NASW Code of Ethics (1994) includes a separate section devoted to standards for social work researchers. This section is reproduced in Box 3.2.

SUMMARY

Ethics refers to standards of conduct. Since World War II, various governments and professional groups have published ethical standards to guide the activities of researchers who study human subjects. These standards were developed by medical and social scientists primarily to protect the rights of research participants. Human subjects research conducted by institutions such as universities and hospitals is generally subject to prior review by IRBs. Commonly accepted principles of research ethics include voluntary participation of individuals, balancing risks to participants against potential benefits to society of new knowledge, informed consent, and responsible treatment of information collected about participants.

CASE STUDIES

One of the best ways to learn about the ethical conduct of research is to consider research studies that pose ethical dilemmas because of harm or potential harm to research participants or to others. Consider the following studies.

LIFE IN A SMALL TOWN

In the 1950s, Cornell University sponsored a research project to study the social and political behavior of individuals in a typical small town. Arthur Vidich, the project director, used participant observation to study village officials and others (Vidich & Bensman, 1960). That is, he lived in the town for over 2 years, got to know its citizens and politicians, and participated in its social and political life. After Vidich left the university, he published a book that gave a detailed account of life in the town.

Many people in the town and the university felt that Vidich had violated their rights. Had he? Although he disguised the names of the individuals he had observed, to anyone familiar with this town, the identities of these people were obvious. In describing these individuals and in reviewing the events he had observed, it was impossible to disguise the information so completely that the research participants could remain anonymous.

This study raised another ethical issue. Did Vidich have the right to publish the findings of a study that had been sponsored by a university? Although he took sole authorship for his book, there were other individuals involved in the project, and the whole enterprise was paid for by the university. Which members of the research team have the right to "use" the data from a study sponsored by an institution? Who "owns" the data? Because there are few guidelines to answer these questions, social workers who are involved in research studies sponsored by groups or institutions should have clear agreements at the start about how the data from the study are to be used.

THE TUSKEGEE SYPHILIS STUDY

In 1932, the U.S. Public Health Service (PHS) began a study of untreated syphilis in black men that eventually became "the longest nontherapeutic experiment on human beings in medical history" (Thomas & Quinn, 1991). This was at a time when rates of syphilis among black men in the rural South were very high. In the years leading up to the study, the PHS had been active in syphilis treatment and control demonstration projects in Macon County, Alabama, and across the rural South. As a result, local agencies, physicians, and citizens had developed a high degree of trust in federal health programs. The PHS decided to take advantage of this opportunity to study the disease.

In its original design, the PHS planned to study the course of untreated syphilis for only a short period—6 to 9 months. PHS researchers recruited 399 black men who were infected with the bacterium that causes syphilis and 201 uninfected controls—all from Macon County. As the study proceeded, the researchers' curiosity about what would happen to these men, if untreated, led to the continuation of the research for four decades.

The Tuskegee Study could never have happened had the researchers followed even the most rudimentary requirements of informed consent. Deception was built into the study from the start. PHS researchers obtained the cooperation of a wide range of agencies and community institutions—the Macon County Medical Society, state and local health boards, public schools, black churches, and the operators of farms where many of these men worked as field laborers. State and county health officials were told by the PHS that all the men who were found to test positive for syphilis would be treated with one important proviso: The treatment would be less than that required to cure the disease.

At the same time, research participants never knew they were in an experiment. In fact, the researchers went to great lengths to conceal the true nature of the intervention. They employed a black public health nurse, who formed trusting relationships with the participants, reassured them, and arranged for medical exams and transportation. These men were extremely poor and had no access to any other medical care; many had never seen a physician before. Clinic staff deliberately refrained from educating the men about syphilis—the men never knew, for example, that they had a disease they could transmit to others through sexual intercourse. Instead, the men were told that they were being tested for "bad blood." They were given incentives that included free medical exams, transportation, and food. When some of the men died, researchers offered burial stipends to induce families to allow the researchers to conduct autopsies.

The researchers went to great lengths to preserve the "scientific merit" of the study, which required that the men remain untreated. For example, during World War II, about 50 study participants who were tested for syphilis by the local draft board were identified as positive and ordered, by the draft board, to come in for treatment. PHS researchers intervened with the draft board to prevent these men from being treated. Later, when penicillin was introduced as the first effective treatment for syphilis, the PHS continued to withhold treatment. In 1969, a federal review panel decided to continue the study. It was not until a PHS official—concerned with the ethics of the study—leaked the story to an Associated Press journalist in 1972 that the full details were published in newspapers. This raised a storm of controversy among the public and in federal agencies, and the study was finally halted.

The shocking revelations of the Tuskegee Study raise troubling ethical concerns. This study violated ethical standards first established in the Nuremberg Code and the Belmont Report (discussed earlier in this chapter) as well as later federal guidelines. These men did not participate voluntarily because they were never aware that they were part of an experiment. They were never given the opportunity to give informed consent. Researchers violated the notion of respect for persons by choosing a highly vulnerable group: extremely poor, uneducated minority men. Later commentators have noted that it is unlikely this study would have been attempted among educated nonminority people.

In retrospect, it is hard to see how the terrible harm that resulted to many of these men from untreated syphilis was outweighed by the benefit to society of knowing about the long-term effects on the body of the untreated disease. Certainly by 1951, when the widely available drug penicillin became the standard of treatment for syphilis, it should have been clear to researchers that there was no longer a compelling medical need to determine the long-term effects of syphilis.

That this study could continue for so long—despite harm to participants and little scientific merit—is a reminder of the dangers of unethical research.

THE GOLDZIEHER STUDY OF BIRTH CONTROL PILLS

This controversial study shows that research participants may be harmed even in studies that follow recognized standards of ethical conduct in research ("Goldzieher Case Raises Ethical Storm," 1971).

By the late 1960s, many women were using birth control pills licensed by the Food and Drug Administration (FDA). Many of these drugs, however, caused side effects that were poorly understood. To determine which of these side effects were caused by the drug—and which were "psychosomatic"—it would be necessary to conduct a "blind" study: Researchers would need to administer approved birth control drugs to some women and a placebo (an inert substance) to others. To control for psychosomatic effects, none of the women could know, until after the study, which type of pill she received. Researchers could then compare side effects between the groups of women.

Joseph Goldzieher, a physician from San Antonio, Texas, obtained approval from the FDA to do such a study. His experiment included 398 women who had come to a clinic for birth control. These women were primarily low-income Mexican Americans with little education. Goldzieher randomly assigned each woman to one of five groups. In three of these groups, women received one of three FDA-approved birth control pills—these drugs had been approved as safe and effective. In another group, women received a new experimental birth control pill. The last group of women served as a control: They received a placebo. All study participants believed they were taking birth control pills.

In carrying out his study, Dr. Goldzieher followed standard federal guidelines for ethical research—those established by the then Department of Health, Education, and Welfare. All women signed consent forms. These forms described the risks of the research and advised study participants to use a backup contraceptive to prevent pregnancies.

When the study ended in its second year, there were seven unwanted pregnancies among study participants. One woman taking the experimental pill and six women taking the placebo had become pregnant. Several review teams concluded that this study was ethical. Dr. Goldzieher believed that the seven pregnant women were at fault because they failed to use backup contraceptives as instructed.

Were the rights of these women violated? Did the researcher take advantage of the vulnerable status of uneducated minority women—women who had few resources to purchase family planning services and contraceptives and who were unlikely to question medical procedures? Even though the informed consent forms explained the need for backup contraception, did these women truly understand this advisory? Were they given sufficient opportunity to discuss and question the details of their treatment?

This study was ended prematurely when the FDA determined that the new experimental pill that some of these women received was unsafe. This is an ever-present danger in research on new treatments—when do we have enough information about the treatment to determine that the risk of harm is low enough to warrant administering the treatment to a large group of study participants? And in this case, did the benefit to society of knowledge about drug side effects outweigh the risk to these women of unwanted pregnancies and possible drug injury?

TEAROOM TRADE

Until the 1960s, almost all research about gay men was based on studies of men in trouble: those who were receiving psychological treatment and those in institutions such as prisons. As sexual attitudes became more liberal in the 1960s and 1970s, researchers began to study the social and psychological adjustment of gay men in natural, community settings.

Because, however, most gay men remained "in the closet"—that is, they did not reveal their sexual orientation to others—these studies relied on just one segment of the gay community: those men who were recruited through gay bars and social and political organizations. Men who had sex with men—but who did not participate in any part of the gay community—remained hidden. Few social scientists even knew of the existence of this group.

In a fascinating and creative study, Laud Humphreys (1970) gained access to just such a group of men. The means he employed to do so, however, have remained controversial to this day.

Humphreys became aware that certain public restrooms in a city park served as the setting for a group of men to come together for anonymous sex. To gain the trust of the men, he spent time in these restrooms and facilitated interactions between the men by serving as a "lookout" to warn of intruders. Because the men did not speak or get to know one another, Humphreys knew nothing about their lives outside this setting. For example, did these men identify themselves as gay? What kinds of social and work lives did they lead?

To answer these questions, Humphreys needed some way to gain access to these men in a setting in which they could be interviewed. The procedure he chose to accomplish this was simple. After individuals left the restroom area to return to their cars, Humphreys recorded their license plate numbers. With the help of Department of Motor Vehicle records, he was able to obtain their names, addresses, and phone numbers. He later sent university staff members to interview these men in their homes. The men were not aware that they had been identified by their restroom activities, and their interviewers provided a fictional pretext for the research study.

Understandably, these men kept their public sex behavior secret from their families and others. Remarkably, many of these men lived mainstream lifestyles in every respect other than their restroom activities: They lived in suburban homes, often with a wife and children, and held middle-class occupations. Many of these men did not consider themselves to be gay.

Humphreys used a controversial procedure to gain access to a group that otherwise would be impossible to study. By doing so, he enlarged social science knowledge about an important aspect of human sexuality.

But did he violate the rights of these participants by deceiving them? Certainly, there was potential for great harm to these men—to their marriages, family, and work relationships—if their activities became known. This example illustrates a research study that could not have obtained informed consent from study participants and still achieve its goals of learning about these men. It also highlights the importance of ensuring the anonymity of research participants when information about their behavior could cause personal harm.

DISCUSSION QUESTIONS

1. The Nuremberg Code established two principles to govern the ethical conduct of biomedical research. What were these principles?
2. What is an institutional review board, and what is its role in social work research?
3. What is informed consent? What three conditions must be met by a research study for it to meet the requirements of informed consent?
4a. What is the difference between anonymity and confidentiality?
4b. Why is anonymity not always possible in social work research studies?
4c. What steps can a researcher take to ensure that research participants' confidentiality will be maintained?

SHORT ASSIGNMENT

Tom Smith is a social work consultant at a local nursing home. Tom has designed a program to increase the social skills of residents. Through discussion, modeling, and role play of hypothetical situations, residents who participate in this program are to be taught useful interactional skills. For example, they will be taught how to communicate more effectively with their doctors, how to request the help of nursing home staff members, and how to respond to requests from family members and unreasonable behavior from other residents.

The nursing home administrator is in favor of Tom's program. But he has asked Tom to draw up a plan that describes how patients are to be recruited for the skill training program. In addition, Tom is expected to have a plan to evaluate the program. Tom knows that participation in any new skills program is likely to lead to at least some improvement in interpersonal skills. Therefore, Tom plans to randomly assign one group of patients to the skill training program and another group to a discussion-only control. Patients in the latter group will discuss general topics unrelated to interpersonal skills and receive no specific training. Yet another group of patients will be assigned to a control group that will not receive any intervention. The social skills of patients in all groups will be evaluated before and after the skill training program, using an interview to assess their skill in handling difficult interpersonal situations.

The design of Tom's study looks like this:

	Time 1	*Time 2*	*Time 3*
Group 1	Pretest	Skill Training	Posttest
Group 2	Pretest	Discussion-Only Control	Posttest
Group 3	Pretest	No Contact	Posttest

1. Identify as many ethical concerns as you can in Tom's plan. Consider issues of recruitment, informed consent, potential risk, and confidentiality.

2. Make specific suggestions for procedures that will help to ensure that this research study follows accepted principles of ethical research conduct.

FURTHER READING

Kimmel, A. J. (1988). *Ethics and values in applied social research.* Newbury Park, CA: Sage.
Lee, R. M. (1993). *Doing research on sensitive topics.* Newbury Park, CA: Sage.

4 Culture- and Gender-Sensitive Research

When I received my training in social work research in the 1970s, like most other students, I believed that the methods I was learning were applicable to all types of people. Our instructors taught us that if we used standard social science research methods we would be unbiased in the way we studied our clients, their families, and their communities.

Today that view seems naive. We know now that much existing social work research failed to take into account the unique perspectives of various racial and ethnic groups. Even worse, these studies were often biased in favor of the perspectives of the primarily white male researchers who did most of the research.

In this chapter, I will review the many pitfalls that may cause research studies to be insensitive to women, ethnic and racial groups, and others. I will present guidelines for overcoming this problem and a detailed example of a study that employed culture- and gender-sensitive research methods.

DEFINITIONS

In preindustrial times, people lived together in homogeneous groups. That is, all the people with whom we interacted shared similar physical features, language, history, and social customs. In the modern world, that is no longer true. Most of us interact daily with people who look different from us and who come from groups that have a wide variety of different customs and histories. One result has been a lot of discussion about human differences. We regularly use the terms *race, ethnicity, culture,* and *gender.* In daily speech, however, these terms are often used in vague or inaccurate ways. Because accurate use of these terms is important to a discussion of culture- and gender-sensitive research, it is important to define these terms.

Definition: *Culture* refers to people's "learned ways of life, which are modified and passed on from one generation to the next" (Robertson, 1981, p. 53).

According to Robertson (1981), the term culture refers to the entire way of life of a society. Culture includes both material aspects (the physical objects we create, such as our homes, clothing, and implements) and nonmaterial aspects. In this chapter, I am most concerned with the nonmaterial aspects of culture, that is, society's "languages, ideas, beliefs, rules, customs, myths, skills, family patterns, [and] political systems" (Robertson, 1981, p. 53).

Some commentators use the term culture inaccurately to refer to a set of persons. In this chapter, however, culture refers to a set of abstract ideas that shapes a group of people organized into a society.

Race and ethnicity are also used to refer to characteristics of groups of people. There is a good deal of confusion about the meaning of these terms, and they often are used interchangeably, although they refer to different things. Race refers to "the genetically transmitted physical characteristics of different human groups." Ethnicity refers to "culturally acquired differences" (Robertson, 1981, p. 281).

As humans have developed in a variety of climates over the past 2 million years, they have taken on various physical characteristics that have helped them adapt to their locales. For example, humans who have developed in areas along the equator have dark skin to protect them from the harsh sunlight common in this locale.

There has been a lot of confusion about the concept of race. Some anthropologists believe there are only a few races, whereas others have identified over 100. As groups of people have intermarried, there has been so much mixture that it is difficult to identify "pure" racial groups. Biologically, the concept of race has little meaning.

Social beliefs about race, however, have great importance (Robertson, 1981). Many believe that persons with particular physical features (say, dark skin) also share particular characteristics; and historical and social customs have reinforced centuries-long treatment of persons based on their race. Witness the long-term effects on black Africans of slavery and later discriminatory practices against them. For these reasons, social work researchers cannot ignore differences based on race.

Definition: "A *race* is a large number of people who, for social or geographical reasons, have interbred over a long period of time; as a result, they have developed identifiable physical characteristics and regard themselves, and are regarded by others, as a biological unity" (Robertson, 1981, p. 281).

Although ethnicity is often confused with race, these terms refer to different characteristics of groups of people.

Definition: *Ethnicity* refers to the cultural characteristics of a group. These characteristics include "language, religion, national origin, dietary practices, [and] a sense of common historical heritage" (Robertson, 1981, p. 282).

Definition: "An *ethnic group* is a large number of people who, as a result of their shared cultural traits and high level of mutual interaction, come to regard themselves, and to be regarded, as a cultural unity" (Robertson, 1981, p. 282).

Some groups of people are defined in such a way that they are distinguished by both race and ethnicity. For example, African Americans share both a distinct race and an ethnic group. Even here, however, there are important cultural and physical differences in that blacks from different areas of Africa may differ from one another in physical appearance, language, customs, and so on.

Other groups are distinguished by ethnicity but share a common racial group. For example, German Americans, Swedish Americans, and British Americans come from different cultures but share common physical characteristics.

As I said earlier, social work research has often been biased in favor of the perspectives of men over women.

Definition: *Gender* refers to the characteristic of being male or female.

Today's social work researchers are also concerned about bias related to *gender identity* and *sexual orientation.*

Definition: *Gender identity* is the self-perception of being male or female (Berger & Kelly, 1995).

It is important to distinguish between gender and gender identity because there are in every society a small number of individuals whose gender identity differs from their biological gender. These individuals are called *transsexuals.* They are biological males who view themselves as women, biological women who view themselves as men, and such persons who have artificially altered their gender by sex reassignment surgery.

Definition: *Sexual orientation* refers to an individual's preference for sexual and affectional relationships with persons of the same sex, opposite sex, or both sexes (Berger & Kelly, 1995).

Although most people are heterosexual (they prefer sexual and affectional relationships with members of the opposite sex), a significant number of people in every society are gay men or lesbians (they prefer sexual and affectional relationships with members of the same sex). Some individuals are bisexual.

The purpose of this chapter is to sensitize you to the need to make social work research unbiased and relevant to all the groups covered by the preceding definitions: cultural groups, racial and ethnic groups, transsexuals, gays, lesbians, and bisexuals.

In recent years, social work research has been criticized for its historical bias against the groups just mentioned. Sohng (1994) has summarized these criticisms. At times, researchers have asked questions that imply that the group being studied is responsible for its own problems or questions that are culturally inappropriate. They have used measures that are culturally biased, drawn stereotypical interpretations, ignored the effects of a group's history or tradition, discounted the effects of institutional discrimination, and have not been accountable to the communities they studied (Sohng, 1994).

Although researchers have claimed to be neutral, "detached observers," in fact they often imposed the views of the dominant society and did not bother to get the view of the people they studied (Sohng, 1994). Much study has been directed at identifying differences between minority groups and the larger culture, with little attention devoted to why these differences exist. The implication is often made that any negative differences—for example, the poverty of certain ethnic groups—are due to a lack of motivation or other deficits of the individual rather than to the society (Sohng, 1994). Ethnic behavior may be misunderstood because researchers fail to explain it within the context of the unique values of the ethnic group.

QUANTITATIVE VERSUS QUALITATIVE METHODS

Some researchers have argued that certain types of research methods are inherently biased against women and cultural groups. Researchers who feel this way generally favor qualitative over quantitative research methods.

Quantitative research methods assume that there is a single objective reality. According to this view, two independent researchers can use standard research methods to study a particular problem, and both will arrive at the same conclusion. To avoid imposing the researcher's bias on the observations, the researcher must remain separate and detached from and emotionally uninvolved with the study participants. In quantitative research, researchers emphasize careful control and measurement using quantitative means—that is, the assigning of numbers to measurements.

Qualitative research methods assume that there is no single reality. Rather, the nature of reality is defined by the interaction of the researcher with the phenomenon under study. Researchers should take advantage of, rather than avoid, applying their own perceptions and assumptions to the research study. To accurately represent that which is studied, researchers must also enter into the participant's world. Therefore, qualitative researchers stress intensive, real-world interaction with study participants, using methods such as participant observation, in-depth interviews, and immersion in the culture or group (although they may also analyze existing materials, such as personal documents). Because the data collected by these methods are "rich," researchers using them favor qualitative methods—narrative or lengthy descriptions rather than numbers. (Qualitative research is discussed in greater detail in Chapter 10.)

Are qualitative research methods truly less biased against women and cultural groups? It is true that qualitative methods—because they incorporate the views of study participants and because they collect a great deal of information about participants' lives—are better at describing social problems as seen by people actually experiencing them. Qualitative methods have been used recently and successfully by women and minority researchers to study social problems without stigmatizing or ignoring these groups, a problem in earlier quantitative studies.

Qualitative methods, however, are not inherently better suited to the study of women and cultural groups. Unlike more carefully controlled quantitative methods, qualitative methods allow the values and perceptions of researchers—including all their biases—to color the data and their interpretation. This is obvious in early studies in which anthropologists used qualitative methods (for example, living among natives) to study preindustrial cultures. Their conclusions were often highly critical of these people who were described as "primitive" or "unintelligent." In retrospect, these negative characterizations were due to the researchers' bias in favor of dominant Western values and customs.

Ashford (1994) argued that neither the quantitative nor the qualitative method is inherently biased against cultural groups. (His argument also applies to research on women and the other groups mentioned earlier.) Rather, the concepts and ideas that researchers bring to their research determine if it will be culture-sensitive. According to this view, researchers should use *all* available methods to study women and cultural groups.

ENTRY POINTS FOR BIAS IN RESEARCH

To ensure that their studies are gender- and culture-sensitive, researchers need to guard against the entry of bias in every step of the research process. This includes theory formulation, research questions, operational definitions, assessment measures, study methodology, data collection, selection of individuals for study, and reporting of results.

THEORY FORMULATION

Schizophrenia is a severe mental disorder in which the individual suffers from delusions, thought disorder, hallucinations, and bizarre behavior. Early theoretical explanations for the cause of schizophrenia blamed this disorder on the effects of disturbed family environments. It was believed that adults became schizophrenic because they were raised by disturbed parents (Coon, 1983).

One popular theory was that the disorder was caused by a psychologically disturbed mother. This theory illustrates a common bias in psychological theories that explain behavior of children that does not fit the norm. Mothers are more likely than fathers to be identified as the culprit. This was also true in some psychoanalytic theories that attributed the homosexuality of sons primarily to an overly possessive and intimate mother (Bieber, 1965). Perhaps because the originators of these theories were themselves fathers, they tended to focus on the problematic behavior of mothers rather than on fathers.

Because they were biased toward psychological explanations, these theorists also ignored genetic and other biological factors to explain adult behavior. Today, most scientists recognize a strong biological basis for schizophrenia. This is also true for homosexuality.

Another example of biased theorizing is the "culture of poverty" theory promoted by anthropologist Oscar Lewis (1968). Lewis studied poor, urban, Puerto Rican families in the United States and Puerto Rico. The culture-of-poverty theory claimed to explain why Puerto Ricans were the most impoverished of all Latino groups and why their poverty persisted from generation to generation. Although Lewis mentioned poor economic conditions, for the most part, his theory cited the individual characteristics of those caught in the culture of poverty. For example, the culture-of-poverty theory stated that poor urban Puerto Ricans lacked impulse control, held a fatalistic attitude toward life, were unable to delay gratification, did not adhere to the norms of marriage, and were concerned only with the present rather than the future.

The behavior of poor urban Puerto Ricans also could have been explained by referring to limited educational opportunities, societal discrimination, marginal employment, and other harsh economic conditions. By highlighting individual characteristics, however, Lewis's theory could be seen as racist. His theory blamed this cultural group for its own problems and implied that social programs and enhanced economic opportunities would not have helped. In this way, his theory justified the continued economic exploitation of low-wage labor that this group provided to the larger society. The culture of poverty theory also encouraged social welfare policies that were ineffective with and demeaning to poor ethnic groups.

RESEARCH QUESTIONS

From the 1950s through the 1970s, a number of research studies sought to determine the "causes" of homosexuality. This research agenda reflected the view of the presumably heterosexual researchers that heterosexuality was "normal"; all that was left to explain was the puzzling question as to why some people chose to be homosexual. Significantly, no one proposed to study the causes of heterosexuality.

Heterosexual bias was also evident in other aspects of research on homo-sexuality. For example, Weinberg and Williams (1975) conducted an exten-sive interview and questionnaire study of homosexual males. To assess the nature of homosexual relationships, they asked respondents about their sexual activity and whether there was another homosexual man with whom they primarily had sexual relations. As heterosexual researchers, they seemed to be unaware of the well-established role of "lover" in the gay community, a role that involves both affectional as well as sexual commitment. The result was that their large-scale and expensive survey failed to provide an accurate description of homosexual relationships.

Similar problems have affected research among other groups. For example, generally, poverty researchers study poor people. That is where they believe the problem of poverty resides, and that is where the government and foun-dation money leads them. Some radical social workers have suggested, however, that poverty researchers should study rich people. These social workers argue that if we understand the economic conditions that lead to an uneven distribution of wealth—hence, how rich people become rich—we will understand poverty as well. (I am sure this is why a student with the Institute for Research on Poverty, where I also studied, tagged a sign to his door that read, "Institute for Research on Wealth.")

OPERATIONAL DEFINITIONS

Assumptions about differences between men and women can creep into the way we define the concepts under study. For example, in a study of the career concerns of men and women, women were asked what effect their child care responsibilities had on their work experiences. Researchers did not ask this question of the men. The assumption that having children affects the work experience of women but not men—did the researchers believe that fathers do not have child care responsibilities?—prevented the researchers from gaining a complete picture of the work experience of men.

In another study—of low-income African Americans—researchers de-fined an "intact family" using white, middle-class norms that require the presence of both a mother and father and include only parents and children. But in the African American community, the normative family may be headed by a single mother; in addition, extended kin, such as aunts, uncles, and cousins, may be included in the family unit. Suggesting that this type of family is incomplete, and ignoring extended kin, prevented the researchers from gaining an accurate picture of African American family life.

In California at the time of this writing, there is a heated debate about the economic costs and benefits of undocumented aliens (persons from other countries who have come to the United States illegally). Two well-publicized studies came to opposite conclusions about economic impact. One concluded that illegal aliens cost the state millions in welfare and education services; the other concluded that, on the whole, the net economic contribution of illegal aliens was greater than the amount paid by the state for their support. How did two studies reach such differing conclusions?

In conducting these cost-benefit studies, researchers made many decisions about how to operationally define both costs and benefits. Costs include expenditures for Medicaid and Medicare, long-term care, public education, and police services. Economic benefits include taxes paid on wages earned by illegal workers and sales taxes paid on goods and services purchased by them.

The results of the cost-benefit analysis depend, in large measure, on how the researcher chooses to operationally define costs and benefits. For example, in a cost-benefit analysis, one researcher may decide to include as a benefit to society the savings that accrue to employers as a result of being able to hire illegal workers at very low wages to provide child care, care for the handicapped, and agricultural work. Another researcher may not include these savings in the operational definition of benefits. This illustrates how our biases can affect how we define our variables and determine the results of our studies.

ASSESSMENT MEASURES

One of the most controversial areas of research has been the use of intelligence tests to compare racial and ethnic groups (*New Republic,* 1994). A few researchers have argued that some racial minorities have, on the average, lower intelligence (although they all recognize that there is great overlap among groups) (Murray & Herrnstein, 1994). This conclusion is based on average differences between groups on standardized intelligence tests. A number of commentators in social work and other fields have argued vigorously against this conclusion. They have noted that intelligence tests are developed on the basis of white, middle-class concepts and are standardized primarily on white, middle-class groups. As such, they may not be valid when used with other groups.

Language differences may also affect the validity of assessment measures when the measure is written in one language and then applied in another. For example, Rubin and Babbie (1993, p. 161) described a study of Korean immigrants in the United States. Researchers had a difficult time designing a question about retirement. In Korean, there is no equivalent for the English word *retirement*. For example, one term refers to retirement from a government position with a pension; another term refers to retirement from self-employment.

There is an established procedure for ensuring that an interview schedule, questionnaire, or test developed in one language is translated correctly into another language, so as to ensure valid responses. *Back translation* works as follows. The original instrument is translated into the new language. Then a separate group of translators who have not seen the original measure translate the instrument back into the original language. The original and back-translated instruments are then compared and discrepancies resolved.

Language differences may also affect the use of assessment measures when applied to different social class or cultural groups that use the same language. For example, in a study of poor rural whites in the southern United States, interviewers asked, "Do you think profits should be regulated by the government?" Most respondents said "no" because they believed that the work of prophets—and other religious activities—was best left unregulated by government (Selltiz, Wrightsman, & Cook, 1976).

Researchers should also take account of differing cultural norms when studying groups other than their own. For example, Asian Americans and some Native American groups follow a cultural norm of modesty. Boasting is considered poor behavior. When asked a question such as, "How successful would you say you are economically?" most members of these groups will describe themselves as not too successful. In this situation, getting answers that accurately reflect study participants' situations and feelings will require in-depth interviewing and possibly the use of an interviewer from the same cultural group as the participant.

STUDY METHODOLOGY

The particular methods used by researchers can also lead to inaccurate results that reflect the biases of the researcher. For example, on the basis of intensive interviews with female clients, Freud (1933) concluded that mature women were able to experience what he called a "vaginal orgasm" that was different from a presumably less desirable "clitoral orgasm." Although this conclusion was based on a limited methodology that provided only indirect evidence—verbal self-report—it was accepted by mental health professionals for many years. It was accepted, that is, until sex researchers Masters and Johnson (1966) observed and recorded couples having sex in their laboratory. Masters and Johnson's instruments told a different story: Physiologically, there was no difference between vaginal and clitoral orgasms.

Anthropologist Tobias Schneebaum (1988) lived with and studied natives in a remote area of Papua New Guinea. These natives had been studied by Christian missionaries who had described their behavior in some detail. According to the missionaries, homosexual behavior was unknown in this culture, and cannibalism was a practice that had been long abandoned. Unlike the missionaries who preceded him, Schneebaum lived with these people day and night and was initiated into their society as a "blood brother." He observed that the natives hid some behaviors from outsiders, including the missionaries, because they knew these behaviors were censured. Schneebaum, however, was able to observe that sexual relations between men were commonplace (these men also engaged in sexual relations with their wives and did not adopt the social role of "homosexual"). He also learned of a recent incident of cannibalism. Clearly, Schneebaum's method of total immersion in the culture yielded more accurate results than those of other observers.

DATA COLLECTION

Marlow (1993, p. 95) suggested that when researchers are socially distant from study participants they should use in-depth interviews rather than questionnaires. When the worldviews of the researcher and the participant are wide apart, it is likely that a questionnaire or highly structured interview will not be understood by the participant in the same way as by the researcher. The in-depth interview allows the researcher to amplify the questions and to probe for understanding by the participant. It also allows participants to expound on their answers and to raise additional points that researchers, bound by their own culture, may not have anticipated.

Researchers should also consider that the values of some cultural groups are violated by quick and efficient encounters. Members of these groups respond well only after lengthy social exchanges have allowed the researcher and participant to develop a relationship. Some feminist researchers have argued that women participants respond better when there is a personal connection between researcher and participant and when they explore the topic together in an informal atmosphere (Marlow, 1993, p. 96).

SELECTION OF INDIVIDUALS FOR STUDY (SAMPLE SELECTION)

When recruiting individuals for participation in research studies, researchers often fail to include a representative sampling of members of various cultural groups. The researcher may feel that ethnic and racial group members are difficult to recruit. Potential study participants may live at a distance from the research site or face social and economic barriers that limit their participation. They may feel, with some justification based on past abuses, that researchers are not to be trusted. They may feel less invested in the "system" and perceive that the researcher or the research institution is part of the system.

It is important for researchers to make the effort to include ethnic and racial minorities and women in their research studies as appropriate. When these groups are not sufficiently represented in research studies, researchers should not make the common error of generalizing the study's findings to the general community.

When only a few ethnic and racial minority members are included in a study, any differences based on these characteristics tend to be obscured. The researcher may attempt to repeat the data analyses for subgroups. But if these subgroups contain only a few individuals, subgroup results may not be accurate. Therefore, if subgroups are small and it is important to determine how various cultural groups differ on the variables under study, it may be necessary to "oversample" these groups—that is, to include a greater number of individuals from these groups than we would expect if we were including them in proportion to their representation in the population. This will provide us with subgroups that are large enough to make meaningful comparisons.

An unfortunate example of a historical bias in the selection of study participants is that of biomedical research—research on medical drugs, diagnostic procedures, and treatment. Many of these studies used samples that included few or no women. This bias in biomedical research may have a negative effect on the health care experiences of women, because they often respond to drugs and procedures differently than do men. Recently, the federal government has required that federally funded biomedical research include women.

REPORTING OF RESULTS

Typically, researchers share the results of their studies with the professional community by publishing articles in academic journals. They also may prepare reports for funding agencies or sponsoring groups, such as a university, foundation, or government agency.

Researchers are less likely to share their results with the lay community and often do not share them with the study participants themselves. This is a deficiency that can and should be remedied. There are many ways to do this. For example, when participants complete their questionnaires or interviews, they can make their names and addresses available on a separate list to receive a brief report of results in the mail. (See Chapter 3 on ethics for a description of procedures to ensure participant confidentiality.) The researchers can write an article based on their study for an agency or local community publication. (See Appendix D for guidelines on writing a research report.) They can present their findings to an agency meeting or community forum. Reports to these groups should, of course, be nontechnical so that laypersons can understand them. One way to achieve this is to focus on the conclusions of the study rather than on the more technical aspects of the findings.

Research reports should communicate in language that is free from bias against women, ethnic and racial groups, gays and lesbians, the physically disabled, and other groups. Several professional organizations, including the National Association of Social Workers (NASW) and the American Psychological Association, have published guidelines for unbiased language. According to the official press policies of the NASW,

> In the interest of accurate and unbiased communication, authors should not use language that may imply sexual, ethnic, or other kinds of discrimination, stereotyping, or bias. NASW is committed to the fair and equal treatment of individuals and groups, and material submitted to the NASW Press should not promote stereotypical or discriminatory attitudes and assumptions about people. (Beebe, 1993, p. 303)

NASW Press guidelines for unbiased writing are summarized in Box 4.1.

AVOIDING BIAS AGAINST
CULTURAL GROUPS AND WOMEN

Sohng (1994) proposed a "minority perspective" or framework for conducting culture-sensitive research. These principles apply as well to gender-sensitive research. Sohng (1994) discussed five principles. First, researchers must recognize that it is not possible to study many ethnic issues "objectively" because they represent conflicts in values. Most often, the values of the

**BOX 4.1. GUIDELINES FOR
UNBIASED WRITING OF RESEARCH REPORTS**

1. Avoid exclusive use of male pronouns when referring to both men and women. Use the plural noun *they,* if necessary, to avoid reference to men or women:

> Biased: The client resumed his monitoring.
> Better: Clients resumed their monitoring. *or* Clients resumed monitoring.

2. When referring to adults of both genders, use parallel terms:

> Biased: Men and girls
> Better: Men and women

3. Specify the gender, race, ethnicity, or other group membership of the person only if relevant. Therefore, you should refer to the "social worker" rather than the "female social worker" unless there is some reason to mention the social worker's gender.

4. Avoid occupational descriptions that imply one or the other gender:

> Biased: Stewardess, chairman, fireman
> Better: Flight attendant, chair or chairperson, firefighter

5. Avoid the term *man* or *mankind* when referring to both men and women:

> Biased: Man the agency
> Better: Employ staff at the agency
> Biased: Mankind
> Better: Humankind, humans, people

6. The terms to identify members of particular cultural and other groups may change over time (for example, *Native American* versus *Indian; Black* versus *African American*). Choose the most current usage or the one that is most appropriate to your audience.

SOURCE: Some of the above examples were adapted from the American Psychological Association (1994) and Beebe (1993).

dominant society are recognized as legitimate, and those of the ethnic group are not made explicit. For example, from the perspective of middle-class whites, it may appear that low-income Puerto Rican families care only about immediate needs and do not plan for the future. As a result, there is little educational achievement or economic stability. But from the perspective of these families themselves, it is so difficult and time-consuming to meet everyday needs for food and shelter that planning for the future is impossible.

Second, there is no single explanation or "one story" that will adequately explain the situation of cultural groups. Rather than searching for a single explanation, the researcher should study the divergent perspectives of all the people involved. Third, culture-sensitive research depends on a recognition and critique of the societal institutions and values that affect racial and ethnic minorities. This means that the researcher must study not just the behavior of particular ethnic and racial groups but also how it fits into the rest of society. For example, the health-seeking behavior of poor urban ethnic groups should include attention to the difficulties in getting access to care, the demeaning nature of care in emergency rooms and public clinics, the role of poor patients as a training resource for medical school students and residents, and the exclusion of poor patients and sick persons from private health insurance.

Fourth, researchers should value the diversity and richness of ethnic cultures. To understand the social problems and life situations of cultural groups, researchers should include a study of their popular wisdom, folklore, and informal leaders. Fifth, researchers should use what Sohng (1994) called "ethical reasoning." That is, researchers should make the values underlying the research explicit by asking questions such as, "Who does the content of this research empower?" and "Whose point of view does this research champion?"

In recent years, feminist social workers have introduced the *feminist participatory research model* into social work research methods. This is an orientation to research based on feminist theory and values, and it represents a departure from more traditional methods based on a quantitative approach (see the earlier discussion in this chapter and Chapter 10 for a comparison of quantitative and qualitative research methods).

There is no single, unified feminist research method (Reinharz, 1992). Renzetti (1995), however, has identified five principles that underlie the feminist participatory research model and distinguish it from more traditional quantitative approaches. First, the feminist model focuses on gender and gender inequality. This implies a commitment to reducing inequality between men and women. Although gender is included as a variable in most traditional research, it is not a central focus. At times, women are not included in the sample, or the responses or characteristics of men are accepted as typical or normative. In feminist research, an analysis of the effects of gender is central to the research plan.

Second, feminist research aims to "give voice" to women's everyday experiences. Feminist researchers are particularly interested in the voices of marginalized (for example, poor, oppressed) women whose views and responses typically have not been included in research studies. This emphasis on recording personal experiences has led feminist researchers to prefer convenience and purposive samples (see Chapter 6 for a description of these) and qualitative methods such as in-depth interviews and life histories. Quantitative and statistical analyses are useful to feminist researchers—particularly in documenting discrimination and other social problems—but not to the exclusion of allowing women to "tell their stories."

Third, there is an orientation toward "action research." Feminists engage in research with action or policy implications and pursue the goal of social betterment of the women they study. Fourth, feminist researchers are aware at all times that researchers' gender, race, class, and sexual orientation shape their approach to the research study. Rather than attempt to enforce an artificial objectivity, feminist researchers acknowledge that their values and worldview determine what they will study and how.

Fifth, the feminist research process is participatory. In traditional research, the "expert" researcher selects the problem for study, decides who is to be studied, creates the research instrument, collects the data, and interprets it—all without input from those studied. To maintain objectivity, the researcher remains separate from study participants. Feminist researchers, on the other hand, use a collaborative research strategy, involving participants at every point in the study. For example, study participants have input on deciding what will be studied, how it will be defined, and how data will be collected. They may review or write questionnaires and monitor data collection. They may participate in writing and presenting the results. In addition, the feminist researcher does not stand apart from study participants. Rather, she shares personal information about herself and her motivation for the research study, her opinions and hopes. She may also offer help and advice to participants and potential participants.

Swigonski (1994) has proposed the use of *feminist standpoint theory* as a basis for feminist social work research. Like the feminist participatory model, to which it is closely related, it provides an alternative to traditional quantitative approaches. Its central concern is the life experiences of marginalized groups, such as poor women and poor ethnic and racial minorities.

Feminist standpoint theorists argue that marginalized members of society—the least powerful and most oppressed—are able to provide the most accurate view of society. This is because, to survive, marginalized people must understand the perspective of the dominant culture as well as that of their own group. They therefore have a more complete view of social relations and are in a better position to describe them. Whether or not this is true, feminist standpoint theory encourages researchers to examine social problems from the varying perspectives of different groups in society.

According to Swigonski (1994), feminist standpoint theory is based on the following tenets. First, research must be based on the concrete life experiences of those studied, and the researcher must assume an attitude of caring and responsibility (rather than judgment) toward participants. The *standpoint* adopted by the researcher is the day-to-day experience of the group being studied. As an example, Swigonski cites a study of poor adolescent mothers in which the researcher was able to identify the coping capacities of these mothers, a characteristic that might have been missed by a less involved researcher.

Second, members of the most and least powerful groups in society may have opposite understandings of the world. Because the dominant group has a vested interest in maintaining things the way they are, their view may be less complete than the view of the least powerful persons.

Third, less powerful groups may adopt the dominant view of the most powerful, unless their standpoint is developed through education. For example, ethnic minorities may incorporate beliefs about stereotypical characteristics of their group, thereby developing poor self-esteem and self-blame. Through education, the less powerful can come to understand the nature of their oppression.

Fourth, research studies should focus on the everyday lives of marginalized groups. This reveals the way that public policies and beliefs structure everyday life. It can also reveal the coping capacities and strengths of individuals.

Fifth, members of marginalized groups have the "advantage" of being outsiders to the dominant social order. They thus have a valuable fresh perspective of the social order, and it may be easier for them to see patterns of beliefs and behavior that are not apparent to others.

Sixth, some outsiders, by joining the ranks of professional researchers, have become "outsiders within." An increasing number of social workers and researchers are women or members of ethnic and racial groups. As members of both groups, these professionals may have a clearer vision of social relations between dominant and marginalized members of the community.

Although feminist standpoint theorists rely heavily on the insights of marginalized groups (women, ethnic and racial minorities) the very notion of standpoint implies that there are a variety of perspectives, depending on one's position in society. Different groups see different versions of the world. The implication of this is that to achieve the most complete view of social problems, researchers must study these problems from the standpoints of all members of society.

These alternative models—minority perspective, feminist participatory, and feminist standpoint theory—will help to ensure that future social work research is less biased and more representative of the experiences and views of women, racial and ethnic minorities, and others who have been overlooked in the past. The methods advocated by these models will serve well if they augment rather than replace existing research methods.

SUMMARY

Much of existing social work research has failed to take into account the perspectives of ethnic and racial groups, women, and others such as gays and lesbians. Historically, social work researchers have been white males, and this has biased the research process in favor of their particular way of looking at the world.

Although qualitative methods are sometimes preferred by those who want to include the perspectives of overlooked groups, no single method is inherently biased against women or other groups. Ideally, researchers will use all research methods to gain a better understanding of the realities of all groups. Bias against various groups may enter the research process at any of its steps from theory formulation to reporting the results. In recent years, new models of research have been developed to avoid the racial, ethnic, cultural, and gender biases of the past. These include minority perspective, the feminist participatory research model, and feminist standpoint theory.

CASE STUDY[1]

It is generally recognized that partner abuse is a widespread problem in our society. Partner abuse can take many forms. Battering or physical abuse may range from pushing and shoving to hitting to actually injuring another person with a knife or gunshot. Verbal abuse includes unfounded accusations, threats of harm, humiliation in public, and demeaning comments. Partners may also be sexually abused—forced to have sex against their will or penetrated with foreign objects. Abusers may also threaten the pets, children, or personal property of their partners. These acts of abuse often have a devastating effect on the abuse victim.

Partner abuse between heterosexual (opposite-sex) partners has been widely studied and discussed in the media. Many services exist today for battered and abused women. The phenomenon of lesbian partner abuse, however, has been almost universally ignored by mainstream social work, social service researchers, and the lesbian community itself. The lesbian community has been especially reluctant to uncover this problem because of an unwillingness to shatter the myth that women-only relationships are always supportive. There also has been a reluctance to reveal a problem that conservative forces could use in their attacks against the gay and lesbian community.

This silence, and the resulting lack of supportive services for abused lesbian partners, has made the victims of this type of abuse particularly vulnerable.

Dr. Renzetti, a sociologist, was first alerted to this problem by a student. Although not a member of the lesbian community, Dr. Renzetti was well versed in the feminist participatory research model. A study of lesbian partner abuse seemed an ideal opportunity to apply the model.

In 1985, Dr. Renzetti met with an activist in a battered women's service agency in a large East Coast city. Through this activist, Dr. Renzetti obtained preliminary information about the problem from articles that had been published in local lesbian and gay newspapers. Dr. Renzetti also was put in touch with a number of other activists.

At a meeting with the activists, Dr. Renzetti proposed a research study to determine the nature and extent of lesbian partner abuse in the local community. The activists embraced this idea. They formed a group that met regularly with Dr. Renzetti throughout the project. At various points, Dr. Renzetti also sought the help of representatives of a battered women's group, and of members of the lesbian community.

The activists' extensive experience in providing services to abused lesbian women was essential to the design and execution of the study. The activists were able to educate Dr. Renzetti about the nature of lesbian relationships, the local lesbian community with its particular norms and values, available resources, and characteristics of lesbian battering. Dr. Renzetti contributed her technical expertise: her knowledge of funding sources, grant writing, problem definition, questionnaire design, and data analysis and interpretation.

The activists and the researcher agreed on a number of goals for the study. Bringing a long-hidden problem into the open would empower victims, encourage them to speak out, and encourage them to get help. The study would raise community awareness about the problem, make women's services more aware of this specialized need, and serve notice to the community that abusers will be held accountable. The study would provide information about types of abuse and the prevalence of the problem as well as differences between lesbian and heterosexual partner abuse. It would help determine why lesbian women stayed in abusive relationships and what they did to protect themselves.

This process of goal selection illustrates several key features of the feminist participatory model. The study was designed to "give voice" to a group of women whose needs had been ignored by virtually everyone. It provided a forum for them to "tell their stories," thus empowering them to survive their experiences. This was an action research project with the clear goal of bettering the situation of abused lesbian women. The goal-setting process (and subsequent steps) involved the mutual participation of researcher and participants. It set the tone for a research project in which members of the studied group played a major role in designing every aspect of the study, from start to finish. Finally, rather than discount the importance of her "outsider" status, the researcher self-disclosed her agenda and her heterosexual orientation. Her openness allowed the activist group to assist in the most constructive way possible—by providing expertise about the many aspects of lesbian life with which the researcher was unfamiliar.

A lengthy discussion between Dr. Renzetti and the activists concerned *ownership* of the research project. Dr. Renzetti wanted to ensure that the study results would be shared, through publication, with other researchers in the domestic violence field. The activists were suspicious that social scientists or others might use the findings to damage public perceptions about lesbians. Following the feminist participatory model, the researcher and activists agreed that the project ownership was shared equally by the group and the researcher. Dr. Renzetti agreed to report the study findings to academics and to social service providers, and the activists would disseminate the findings in the local lesbian community. As the work progressed, however, these distinctions became less important. Perhaps more important was the level of mutual trust that developed between the researcher on the one hand and the activists and lesbian community on the other.

Although the feminist participatory model encourages the use of in-depth interviews, Dr. Renzetti and the activists decided that the most efficient way to begin data collection was by distributing a questionnaire. In comparison to time-consuming interviews, questionnaires would allow the research project to survey a much larger number of women, thereby gaining a more accurate estimate of the extent and nature of the problem. A questionnaire would also facilitate honest responses, because it ensured respondents' anonymity and would be less threatening than a face-to-face encounter with an interviewer.

Dr. Renzetti and the activists also collaborated on a plan to recruit respondents. It was decided that respondents would be solicited by print advertisements in newspapers and by public announcements. The activists selected the particular publications and settings for announcements. They designed the advertisements and announcements as well as an informational brochure about lesbian partner abuse. The brochures solicited respondents for the study and provided a mail-in card. Volunteers who mailed the card received a questionnaire in the return mail.

The design of the questionnaire turned out to be a more lengthy process than Dr. Renzetti had imagined. She brought a draft copy of the questionnaire to a meeting of the activists, expecting that it would require only a few revisions. Instead, the draft questionnaire led to extensive group discussions that resulted in several drafts over a 9-month period. This lengthy process, however, produced a high-quality questionnaire that was subsequently well received by respondents.

The questionnaire was distributed to 200 women. Of these, 100 women returned completed questionnaires—a respectable response rate of 50%. The final page of the questionnaire asked respondents to volunteer for an in-depth interview to follow up on the issues covered in the questionnaire. Seventy women volunteered and were interviewed by Dr. Renzetti. In accordance with the feminist participatory model, Dr. Renzetti attempted to break down the distance between herself as a researcher and her respondents. For example, when appropriate, she referred respondents to outside sources of help, such as support groups. As respondents reviewed their painful experiences, she provided advice and emotional support. She also encouraged respondents to ask questions and to provide her with feedback about the interview and the study.

The questionnaire data were analyzed by computer, and the interviews were audiotaped and summarized. After deletion of respondents' names, all these data were shared with the group of activists. Dr. Renzetti explained the technical aspects of the results, such as the interpretation of statistical tests and tables. The activists wrote a report of the questionnaire results and mailed it to respondents, fulfilling their commitment to treat respondents with respect and caring. Dr. Renzetti published her findings in the professional literature, with input and review by individual activists from the group.

Although the purpose of this summary is to illustrate the ways in which Dr. Renzetti's study followed the feminist participatory model, it is also interesting to note some of the findings of the study. Dr. Renzetti (1992) concluded that domestic violence is as prevalent among lesbian couples as it is among heterosexual couples. There is no "typical" form of abuse, with abuse taking a wide variety of forms that vary in severity from verbal threats to stabbing and shootings.

The most significant factor associated with abuse was the partners' mutual dependency. Abusers were "intensely dependent" on their partners, and the greater the dependency, the more severe the abuse. Most abusers succeeded in isolating their partners from family, friends, work associates, and all outside interests and activities that did not involve the abuser directly. This merely worsened the situation and increased the partners' dependency on one another. Typically, abusers showed an obsessive jealousy of their partners, often subjecting them to repeated, lengthy interrogations. Abuse of alcohol and drugs seemed to facilitate the abuse but did not cause it. Sadly, victims found it very difficult to get any kind of help. Lesbian partners who were abused did not perceive existing battered women's services to be appropriate sources for help because these services were exclusively heterosexual. Frequently, friends and others were not supportive. Although these findings are distressing, they provide a powerful first step in naming this problem, empowering its victims, and spurring the development of appropriate services.

DISCUSSION QUESTIONS

1. What are the differences between *culture, race,* and *ethnicity?*
2. What is your culture, race, and ethnicity? Which of these characteristics was passed on to you from the genes of your parents? Which of these characteristics was passed on to you through learning?
3. What is the difference between *gender, gender identity,* and *sexual orientation?*
4. What are quantitative and qualitative research methods? Are qualitative methods better suited to study racial and ethnic minorities and women?
5. The bias of the researcher can affect every step of a research study. For each of the following research steps, give one example of the way in which the researcher's bias might affect that step of the study:

   Creating or modifying a theory
   Specifying the research questions
   Creating operational definitions for concepts or variables
   Creating or using assessment measures, such as tests
   Selecting a research methodology

Collecting the data

Selecting individuals for study

Reporting the results

6. What are five principles that underlie a *minority framework* for conducting research?

7. What are five principles that underlie the *feminist participatory research model?*

SHORT ASSIGNMENT

Visit the section of your library that houses recent periodicals or journals. Review recent issues of social work journals.

Find one article that reports the results of a research study of an ethnic, racial, or cultural minority; women; low-income persons; or gays, lesbians, or bisexuals. Read this article carefully. Critique each step of the research study in terms of the question, How accurate has the researcher been in studying this group in a sensitive way—that is, in a way that takes account of the views and perspectives of the group being studied? In your critique, consider each of the research steps listed in Question 5.

You will find it useful to review recent issues of one or more of the following journals:

Child Welfare
Families in Society: The Journal of Contemporary Human Services
The Gerontologist
Health and Social Work
Journal of Social Service Research
Journal of Social Work Education
Research on Social Work Practice
Social Service Review
Social Work
Social Work Research

You also may want to review the following journals that specialize in topics related to one of the groups discussed in this chapter:

Affilia: The Journal of Women and Social Work
Hispanic Journal of Behavioral Sciences
Journal of Black Studies
Journal of Gay and Lesbian Psychotherapy
Journal of Gay and Lesbian Social Services

Journal of Homosexuality
Journal of Jewish Communal Service
Journal of Multicultural Social Work
Women and Therapy

NOTE

1. See Renzetti (1995) for the complete study in a special issue of the *Journal of Gay and Lesbian Social Services* titled "Lesbian Social Services: Research Issues," edited by C. Tully.

FURTHER READING

Marin, G., & Marin, B. V. (1991). *Research with Hispanic populations.* Newbury Park, CA: Sage.
Reinharz, S. (1992). *Feminist methods in social research.* New York: Oxford University Press.
Renzetti, C. M., & Lee, R. M. (Eds.). (1993). *Researching sensitive topics.* Newbury Park, CA: Sage.

5 Defining a Research Problem and Using the Library to Search the Literature

All social work research begins with a *research problem.* Often, a research problem is stated in the form of a question. For example, a research problem might be, What effect does client resistance have on counseling? If there is a theory or previous research that provides some explanation of the phenomenon under study, the researcher might state the purpose of the study in the form of one or more hypotheses. For example, in a study of client resistance in counseling, the researcher may hypothesize the following:

H1: Clients are most resistant when working with therapists whose characteristics age, gender, and race—are unlike their own.

H2: Clients are more likely to exhibit resistance during the problem definition phase of treatment and less likely to exhibit resistance during later phases.

The following are additional examples of research problems, stated in the form of questions:

What types of education are most effective in inducing adolescents to practice safer sex behaviors?

Are there differences in survival rates and health status between frail older persons cared for in nursing homes compared with those cared for at home?

Do transracially adopted children (those adopted by parents of a different race) have greater adjustment problems during adolescence?

Does participation in a work incentive program lead to greater employment levels among Aid to Families With Dependent Children (AFDC) mothers?

STATING A RESEARCH PROBLEM

Before we can conduct a research study, we must have a clear definition of the research problem. We must know the answer to the question, What exactly do I want to find out? Because a clear statement of the research problem affects all parts of the study, it makes sense to devote time and effort to this task.

Not every problem or question is researchable. As I discussed in Chapter 1, the scientific method can shed light only on questions that can be tested. Questions based on faith, wisdom, values, or "common sense" do not lead to researchable problems. For example, the following questions are not researchable: Should the government ensure that all citizens have health care? What happens to a person's soul after that person dies?

Selltiz et al. (1976) argue that to be researchable, a problem must meet three criteria:

1. The concepts stated in the problem must be clear enough so that we can specify in words exactly what the question is.
2. We must be able to obtain evidence for the concepts stated in the problem. This evidence must be obtainable through direct observation or measurement. In effect, we must be able to translate the concepts into specific variables and operationally define those variables.
3. It must be feasible to carry out the operations necessary to define the variables.

We may have only a general idea about the research topic or problem that we want to pursue. For example, we may be interested in studying the experience of elderly nursing home residents. This is a perfectly valid topic, but before it can serve as the basis for a research study, the topic will have to be narrowed down considerably. As with any large task, we should approach this one in a stepwise fashion. We can formulate researchable questions by following these steps.

1. Select a topic. It makes sense to choose a topic for which we feel a certain passion—or even a personal interest. We may have visited a grandparent in a nursing home and wondered about his or her welfare. Thus we have selected the topic: the experience of elderly nursing home residents. We may want to visit the nursing home again and observe the general environment. Or we may want to talk to nursing home staff members and residents about their experiences. We can also read articles or books about nursing homes.

2. Brainstorm a list of things we might want to know about the topic. Brainstorming is a technique that was developed to allow people to generate new and creative ideas (Haefele, 1962). The only rule is to jot down every conceivable idea or question we have about the topic, without trying to evaluate our ideas. The purpose is not to generate ideas that are all useful but simply to generate as many ideas as possible. For example, in brainstorming ideas for the nursing home topic, we may come up with questions such as the following:

> How is living in a nursing home different from living in one's own home?
> What are some of the easiest and some of the most difficult changes that residents must adjust to when they move to a nursing home?
> How do residents react when confronted with situations they don't like?
> What resources do residents have when they need help with a problem?

3. Select a focus for the problem. We should put the brainstormed list away for a day or two and come back to it when we can read it with a fresh eye. When we do that, we may decide that the greatest difficulty nursing home residents face has to do with their interactions with others. We determine that residents interact with other residents, with nursing home staff members, and with medical personnel. We may decide to focus on interactions with other residents, because these seem to be the most frequent. The focus of the study then becomes this: interpersonal interactions among nursing home residents.

4. Relate the focus of the problem to existing knowledge. Now that we have defined the focus of our study, we should turn to the literature and perhaps talk to experts in the area. We discover that there is a large literature on interpersonal interactions and a somewhat smaller literature devoted to describing procedures to identify interpersonal situations that commonly cause stress or ineffective behavior. There is also a literature on procedures that can be used to train people to identify problematic interpersonal situations and to resolve them in ways that provide effective solutions (Berger & Rose, 1977).

As we continue reading, however, we discover that most of this literature involved studies with young adults. It seems that no one has thought to apply this body of knowledge to older people and certainly not to older people in nursing homes. This presents us with an opportunity to extend an existing body of knowledge—on interpersonal skill training—to older persons living in nursing homes.

5. State the specific research question or problem. What we have learned in Steps 1 through 4 leads us to focus the study on the following question: Can an interpersonal skill training program enable elderly nursing home residents to handle social situations with other residents more effectively?

6. Operationalize the concepts and variables in the research question or problem. We want to define the research question precisely so that we will know how to study the question and so that others can duplicate our work— this is essential to the scientific method. In this example, we may define (a) an "older person" as an individual who is 65 years of age or older, (b) a nursing home as a state-licensed residential facility that provides nursing care to older persons unable to care for themselves at home, and (c) an interpersonal skill training program as a series of meetings with a trained instructor in which the resident gets coaching and role-play practice in responding to social interactions with other residents.

These steps—careful specification of a research problem and operationalization of variables—often suggest the approach that can be used to carry out the research study. In this study, we will probably want to compare two groups of nursing home residents—those who participate in a training program and those who do not—in terms of how well they handle problematic social situations.

Books, journals, and other literature can be useful at every step of the journey toward defining a research problem. Reading up on a general topic area—such as nursing homes—may stimulate thinking and help begin to narrow the focus of the study. Once we have completed the preceding steps—that is, once we have specified our research problem—we will need to return to the literature. This time, we will need to be very thorough in unearthing everything we can find that is relevant to the research problem. This is done by using a research library.

USING THE LIBRARY
TO SEARCH THE LITERATURE

No university or college can function without a library. The library is one of the most important tools for the social work researcher. The library houses materials that will tell all about the particular research problem selected for study. We may learn how earlier researchers defined the problem, how the problem relates to other areas of concern, how researchers have studied the problem, and what conclusions they have drawn. Even if no one has ever researched a particular problem or question, the library will provide information on related problem areas, as well as ideas for our own research.

The bottom line is that our study will be valuable only if it is based on a thorough assessment of what others have done before us. This assessment will aid us in defining the problem in a way that builds on earlier work in the area and avoids duplication. It will also serve as the basis for the literature review, a necessary part of every research report.

The library should be approached in the same manner as a research course: one step at a time. Spending time familiarizing yourself with the library is a good investment that will save time and effort later on. In this section, I will provide an overview of basic library procedures and resources, along with guidelines for using the information collected in the library to write a literature review. You may want to follow a reading of this section with a visit to your local library.

THE BASICS

Modern libraries are complex organizations. Most libraries, however, are organized along similar lines. The greatest amount of space in the library is devoted to "the stacks"—shelves of books organized according to call numbers that appear on the spine of each book. Most college and university libraries use the Library of Congress system of call numbers. In this system, books on the social sciences (including social work) begin with the letter H. With few exceptions, these books can be checked out by presenting a library card or student identification card at the circulation desk near the entrance to the library.

Journals, which contain articles on a wide variety of topics, are bound into hardcover and stored in a section of the stacks. Often, recent issues of journals are placed in a separate section awaiting binding into hardcover. Usually, journals do not circulate—that is, they cannot be checked out and therefore must be used only in the library.

All the books and journals in a library are listed in the library's Online Public Access Catalog (OPAC). "Online" refers to the fact that in today's libraries, card catalog information is computerized. We search the OPAC by entering commands on a keyboard. These systems are user-friendly, but they can be frustrating unless we take the time to read the instructions that usually appear on the computer screen or in a handout near the keyboard. For example, in my university library, users may type the following commands:

( ) indicates information to be entered by the user

To start the search: start cat [prompts the user to enter information about the item to be searched]

To search by title: find xt (exact title) or find tw (selected words in the title)

To search by subject area: find xs (exact subject heading) or find su (selected words in subject heading)

To search by author: find pa (last name, first name) [find personal author] or find ca (corporate author, e.g., U.S. Government)

Reference books are usually placed in a separate Reference section of the library. Reference books provide general information and are often a useful way to gain an understanding of an area that we know little about. Reference books include encyclopedias, dictionaries, directories, and handbooks. These books cannot be checked out from the library.

Public documents also may be placed in a separate section. This is the place to find the many books, reports, and pamphlets published by local, state, and federal governments. Public documents include census data, records of legislative and congressional sessions and hearings, and reports issued by government agencies.

To save space, many libraries also store books, journals, and other materials on microfilm or microfiche. Essentially, these are small photographs that can be read with the use of special machines that are available in the library. Many libraries also house video- and audiotape recordings, compact discs, and laser discs.

Most libraries are connected to a network of other libraries as a way to share their materials. When we locate a book, journal, or document in the OPAC, the listing may indicate that the item is available in another library within the system. Or we may not be able to find a listing for that item. In either case, we may want to visit the interlibrary loan desk, where we can fill out a request to order the item from another library. Materials ordered on interlibrary loan may be available for only short periods of time, and there may be a charge for this service.

The library offers a wide range of resources. In the Reference section, we will find one or more reference librarians, who can help locate the material we are looking for. Large university libraries usually have a reference librarian who is a specialist in an area—say, social work or the social sciences. The reference librarian is the single most important person we will speak to in our literature search. Here are some guidelines for getting the most out of a request of the reference librarian (D. Murphy, reference librarian, University of California, Santa Cruz, personal communication, September 6, 1994):

• Don't hesitate to ask the librarian about the topic of interest, even if it seems very broad or very specific. The first step is to locate and read material that relates to the area of interest. Later, we can modify the interest area or research question.

• Understand that the job of the reference librarian is to direct patrons to the appropriate resources. Our job is to comb through them.

• Understand that the literature search is a process. We should expect to return to the reference librarian one or more times as we consult the various resources to which we have been directed.

• Allow enough time for the literature search. Many of the resources we locate will need to be ordered from another library or retrieved from another patron. So allow plenty of time for obtaining and reading through material.

• The reference librarian will direct us to a variety of resources—for example, directories, encyclopedias, and laser disc readers. As we use each resource, we should take time to read the instructions for the use of that resource.

• Keep a written record of all the steps in the literature search, including full citations for every resource consulted. Also keep track of resources or searches that did not yield the desired information.

• Show the reference librarian what we have done to date, including resources that did not work. This will help the librarian to get us on track.

GETTING STARTED:
FINDING BACKGROUND INFORMATION ON THE TOPIC

Unless we already have some information about the research topic, we will probably want to start the literature search in the Reference section of the library. We need to familiarize ourselves with the general topic area so that we can later narrow the search to a more specific focus. Several types of resources are available in the Reference section (see Box 5.1 for a listing of resources).

Handbooks. A handbook is usually a single volume that provides an overview of a particular area. This may be a basic introduction to an area, or it may be a collection of the latest information. A handbook is useful for gaining an understanding of basic terminology, for a summary of statistics, or for learning about other sources of information on a topic.

For example, The *Handbook of Aging and the Social Sciences* (1990), edited by R. H. Binstock and L. K. George, is a widely used handbook that can help us find a researchable topic in the field of social gerontology. The American Psychiatric Association publishes the *Diagnostic and Statistical Manual of Mental Disorders (DSM-IV)* (1994), a handbook that provides detailed information about psychiatric diagnoses. These diagnoses are widely used in clinical social work settings. The *Clinical Handbook of Psychological Disorders: A Step-by-Step Treatment Manual* (1985), edited by D. A. Barlow, is a good source for learning about treatment approaches for many psychological disorders. Psychotherapists will find a review of current theory and practice of behavioral psychotherapy in *Handbook of Psychotherapy and Behavior Change* (1994), edited by A. E. Bergin and S. L. Garfield. The *Handbook on Mental Health Administration* (1982), edited by M. J. Austin and W. E. Hershey, describes services and programs in mental health. Procedures for evaluation research are summarized in *Handbook of Evaluation Research* (1975), edited by E. L. Struening and M. Guttentag. *The Tenth Mental Measurements Yearbook* (1989), edited by J. C. Conoley and J. J. Kramer, lists assessment instruments for a variety of psychological characteristics. J. Fischer and K. Corcoran, in *Measures for Clinical Practice* (1994), list instruments that can be used to assess clients in clinical social work settings.

Encyclopedias. Encyclopedias are much like handbooks, but generally, they summarize a large body of information in several volumes. Specialized

(text continued on p. 91)

BOX 5.1. SAMPLE OF LIBRARY RESOURCES FOR RESEARCH

Abstracts

Psychological abstracts. Washington, DC: American Psychological Association.
Social work abstracts [Formerly *Social Work Research and Abstracts*]. Washington,
   DC: National Association of Social Workers Press.
Sage family studies abstracts. Thousand Oaks, CA: Sage.
Sociological abstracts. San Diego, CA: Sociological Abstracts.
Women studies abstracts. New York: Women Studies Abstracts.

Bibliographies

Books in print. (Annual.) New York: R. R. Bowker.
Conrad, J. H. (1982). *Reference sources in social work: An annotated bibliography.*
   Metuchen, NJ: Scarecrow.

Dictionary

Barker, R. L. (1987). *The social work dictionary.* Silver Spring, MD: National Association of Social Workers.

Directories

Olson, S. (1994). *Foundation directory* (16th ed.). New York: Foundation Center.
Ulrich's international periodical directory. (Annually with supplements.) New York:
   R. R. Bowker.
U.S. Department of Health and Human Services, National Institute of Mental Health.
   (1985). *Mental health directory.* Washington, DC: Government Printing Office.
Office of the Federal Register, National Archives and Records Administration. (1985).
   United States government manual. Washington, DC: Government Printing
   Office.

Encyclopedia

National Association of Social Workers. (1995). *Encyclopedia of social work* (19th
   ed.). Washington, DC: National Association of Social Workers.

Handbooks

American Psychiatric Association. (1994). *Diagnostic and statistical manual of mental
   disorders* (4th ed.). Washington, DC: Author.
Austin, M. J., & Hershey, W. E. (Eds.). (1982). *Handbook on mental health administration.* San Francisco: Jossey-Bass.
Barlow, D. A. (Ed.). (1985). *Clinical handbook of psychological disorders: A step-by-
   step treatment manual.* New York: Guilford.
Bergin, A. E., & Garfield, S. L. (1994). *Handbook of psychotherapy and behavior
   change* (4th ed.). New York: John Wiley.

(continued)

BOX 5.1. CONTINUED

Binstock, R., & George, L. K. (Eds.). (1990). *Handbook of aging and the social sciences* (3rd ed.). New York: Van Nostrand Reinhold.

Conoley, J. C., & Kramer, J. J. (Eds.). (1989). *Tenth mental measurements yearbook.* Lincoln: University of Nebraska Press.

Fischer, J., & Corcoran, K. (1994). *Measures for clinical practice* (Vols. 1 & 2, 2nd ed.). New York: Free Press.

Struening, E. L., & Guttentag, M. (Eds.). (1975). *Handbook of evaluation research.* Beverly Hills, CA: Sage.

Indexes

Criminal justice periodical index. Ann Arbor, MI: University Microfilms International.

Current contents. Philadelphia: Institute for Scientific Information.

Educational Resources Information Center (ERIC). Available through Bibliographic Retrieval Service (BRS) and Dialog.

National Council on Aging. *Current literature on aging.* Washington, DC: Author.

New York Times index. New York: New York Times.

Public Documents

Andriot, J. (Ed.). (1969 to present). *Guide to United States government serials and periodicals.* McLean, VA: Documents Index.

Commerce Clearing House. (1937 to present.) *Congressional index.* Chicago: Author.

Congressional Information Service. (1974 to present). *American statistics index.* Washington, DC: Author.

Council of State Governments. *Book of the states.* Lexington, KY: Author.

Index to current urban documents. (1972 to present). Westport, CT: Greenwood.

Index to U.S. government periodicals. Chicago: Infordata International.

International Management Association. *Municipal yearbook.* Washington, DC: International City Management Association.

Statistical reference index: A selective guide to American statistical publications from private organizations and state government sources. Washington, DC: Congressional Information Service.

United States. *United States code.* (1925 to present). Washington, DC: Government Printing Office.

U.S. Superintendent of Documents. *U.S. government books.* Washington, DC: Government Printing Office.

U.S. Library of Congress, Processing Services. (1910 to present). *Monthly checklist of state publications.* Washington, DC: Government Printing Office.

U.S. Congress. (1873 to present). *Congressional record.* Washington, DC: Government Printing Office.

BOX 5.1. CONTINUED

U.S. Department of Commerce, Bureau of the Census. (Annual). *Statistical abstract of the United States: National database and guide to sources.* Washington, DC: Government Printing Office.

U.S. Department of Commerce, National Technical Information Service. (1946 to present). *Government reports announcements and index.* Springfield, VA: National Technical Information Service.

Guide to Serials

Mendelsohn, H. N. (1992). *An author's guide to social work journals* (3rd ed.). Washington, DC: National Association of Social Workers.

---

encyclopedias present entries written by authorities in their fields. For social workers, the most useful encyclopedia is the *Encyclopedia of Social Work* (1995), which provides background information covering the entire field of social work. It includes entries such as "Alcohol Use and Addiction" and the "Food Stamp Program." Entries are arranged alphabetically, with a separate section for biographies of individuals important to the social welfare field. The *Encyclopedia of Social Work* also contains useful statistics on social issues. The disciplines of psychology and sociology have similar encyclopedias.

Dictionaries. Dictionaries define the words of a language or of a specialized field. R. L. Barker's *The Social Work Dictionary* (1987) lists over 3,000 terms commonly used in social work.

Bibliographies. Bibliographies are a rich resource because they lead the researcher to other sources of information. A bibliography is a list of books, journals, reports, and other sources all related to a single topic. One of the most useful bibliographies in social work is *Reference Sources in Social Work* (1982) by J. H. Conrad. This bibliography summarizes the major reference resources in social work and related fields. To find complete citation information about a book in any field, we can consult *Books in Print,* an annual summary of all books that are currently available or soon to be published. We can look for a book by consulting separate listings by author, title, or subject. The subject guide is a good way to locate books in the area of our research topic. *Ulrich's International Periodical Directory* lists journals and magazines published all over the world. It is the most comprehensive summary of journals available.

Directories. Directories provide lists of organizations, agencies, or persons. We may consult a directory for a description of an organization as well as its address and phone number. For example, the *Mental Health Directory* (1985) lists mental health facilities in the United States, such as psychiatric hospitals and clinics. The *United States Government Manual* (1985) is a good source for descriptions of and addresses for government agencies and international organizations in which the United States participates. The *Foundation Directory* (1994) provides information about private and public foundations, including the nature and funding priorities of each foundation. It is a good resource for a researcher or practitioner who seeks to obtain funding for a research or service project.

HONING IN ON THE TOPIC

A visit to the Reference section of the library will provide background information on the research topic. As we read about the topic, we will want to keep a record of articles, books, bibliographies, and other sources of information that we may want to consult.

As I discussed in the first part of this chapter, at some point we will narrow the topic and focus on one or several research hypotheses or questions. Once we have done that, we are ready to collect sources of information that relate to the specific research study. We accomplish this through the literature search. It is important to be as thorough as possible, so that the study will reflect the most accurate and recent knowledge available on our research questions or hypotheses.

Next, I have summarized the most common sources of information used for a literature review (see Box 5.1).

Serials. Serials refer to journals, magazines, and newspapers. Professional journals are the best source of the latest information about the topic. The literature search should include relevant articles that have appeared in the most recent issues. H. N. Mendelsohn's *An Author's Guide to Social Work Journals* (1992) lists 138 journals in social work and related fields. These are organized by subject categories such as "Administration," "Health and Health Care," and "Special Populations." Some of the major journals in social work are listed in Box 5.2.

It may be useful to scan the table of contents of recent journal issues to spot articles in our area of interest. When we do find a relevant article, we should take careful note of the list of references at the end of the article. Ideally, the author of the article will have reviewed earlier work in the area so that the references will be a good guide to previous work on this topic.

Many thousands of journals are published in the world each year, and many journals—especially those in emerging fields such as AIDS—may not be reflected in Mendelsohn's *Guide* or in other reference works. Therefore, merely browsing through journals that we happen to find is not enough. A much more efficient method for locating journal articles on our topic is to use an index or abstract.

Index. An index is a list of books, journals, or other sources in a particular area—such as child welfare or psychology—that is arranged so that it is easy to find complete citation information: author, date, title, source, and page and volume numbers. Abstracts are indexes that also provide brief descriptions or summaries about the contents of each article, book, or other source. Some abstracts are particularly useful to social work researchers. For example, *Social Work Abstracts,* published quarterly by the National Association of Social Workers Press, abstracts articles in over 400 journals in social work and related fields. *Sociological Abstracts* and *Psychological Abstracts* perform similar functions in their respective disciplines. There are indexes that will help us to locate newspaper articles, such as the *New York Times Index.* The Educational Resources Information Center system, known as ERIC, abstracts a wide variety of journal articles, research reports, and other materials related to education. Other specialized indexes and abstracts include *Current Literature on Aging,* the *Criminal Justice Periodical Index, Sage Family Studies Abstracts,* and *Women Studies Abstracts.*

Current Contents, an index published by the Institute for Scientific Information, publishes the titles of recent journal articles. Social work researchers may want to refer to its section for the social and behavioral sciences.

Public Documents. Public documents are those produced by federal, state, and local governments. According to Mendelsohn (1987), the "United States government is the largest publisher of information in the world" (p. 71). The

(text continued on p. 96)

**BOX 5.2. SAMPLE OF MAJOR SOCIAL WORK-RELATED
JOURNALS, LISTED BY TOPIC AREA**

Administration

   Administration in Social Work
   Public Administration Review
   Public Welfare

Aging

   The Gerontologist
   Journal of Gerontological Social Work
   Journal of Gerontology

Children and Families

   Child and Youth Care Forum
   Child Welfare
   Journal of Marriage and the Family

Ethnic Studies

   Explorations in Ethnic Studies
   Hispanic Journal of Behavioral Sciences
   Journal of Black Studies
   Journal of Jewish Communal Service
   Journal of Multicultural Social Work

The Field of Social Work

   Families in Society: The Journal of Contemporary Human Services
   Journal of Progressive Human Services
   Journal of Sociology and Social Welfare
   Social Work
   Social Service Review

Health and Health Care

   AIDS Education and Prevention: An Interdisciplinary Journal
   Health and Social Work
   Social Work in Health Care

BOX 5.2. CONTINUED

Mental Health and Psychotherapy

  American Journal of Orthopsychiatry
  Behavior Therapy
  Clinical Social Work Journal
  Community Mental Health Journal
  Psychotherapy in Private Practice
  Smith College Studies in Social Work

Research

  Journal of Social Service Research
  Social Work Research

Sexuality

  Journal of Gay and Lesbian Social Services
  Journal of Homosexuality
  Journal of Social Work and Human Sexuality

Social Issues and Social Policy

  Journal of Social Issues
  Social Policy
  Social Problems

Social Work Education

  Journal of Social Work Education
  Journal of Teaching in Social Work

Women's Issues

  Affilia: The Journal of Women and Social Work
  Women and Therapy

SOURCE: Mendelsohn (1992).

Office of the Superintendent of Documents, a federal agency, provides a large number of documents to regional libraries across the United States, which in turn make these documents available to other libraries through interlibrary loan. *U.S. Government Books* is a quarterly bibliography that lists books published by the federal government. The *Index to U.S. Government Periodicals* and the *Guide to United States Government Serials and Periodicals* are indexes to federal government journals. These indexes are arranged by agency, subject, and title.

The federal government collects many statistics that are of use to social workers in areas such as population trends, social welfare needs, and environmental pollution. We can locate publications with statistical information by using the *American Statistics Index,* a guide to all federal statistical publications. The primary source for statistical information about the United States is the *Statistical Abstract of the United States: National Database and Guide to Sources.* This document provides summaries of statistics in a wide variety of areas, including population data, social welfare needs, and activities of state and local governments.

Government Reports Announcements and Index provides abstracts of the many technical reports summarizing federal research. For information about current federal legislation, we can consult the *Congressional Index* or the *Congressional Record.* Legislation that is enacted into law is summarized in the *United States Code.*

Of particular interest to social work researchers are the many publications of the Department of Health and Human Services and its agencies. For example, useful publications can be obtained from the National Institute of Mental Health, the National Center for Health Statistics, the National Institute on Alcohol Abuse and Alcoholism, the National Institute on Drug Abuse, and the Social Security Administration.

State government publications can be located by consulting an index called the *Monthly Checklist of State Publications,* and city and county publications are listed in the *Index to Current Urban Documents.* The social work researcher may also consult the *Statistical Reference Index: A Selective Guide to American Statistical Publications From Private Organizations and State Government Sources,* an index to statistical publications. For information on municipal government, we may turn to the *Municipal Yearbook,* and for comparable information on states, we can consult the *Book of the States.*

COMPUTERIZED SYSTEMS

Computer systems are ideal for information storage of all kinds. Information can be stored in a very small space; it is easily disseminated to patrons at the storage site or at great distances via telephone or computer networks; and searching is greatly facilitated by computer programs that can search, find, and copy selected items with great speed. It is no surprise then that many of the library resources described earlier are now available on computerized systems.

I have already described the OPAC, a computerized version of the old paper card catalog. Computerized bibliographic searches have also become popular. To use these services, we schedule an appointment with a reference librarian. Using a description of the topic, the librarian enters key words into a computerized database—for example, "elder abuse." The end result is a printout of journal articles, books, and other resources. These computerized bibliographic searches usually require some skill in the proper use of commands, there is usually a fee, and we may have to wait for the printout to be mailed to us. For wide-ranging searches, the cost may run into hundreds of dollars.

In recent years, CD-ROM has replaced the librarian-assisted computerized bibliographic search. Because the CD-ROM is easier to use, generally, students can conduct their own searches. Unlike computerized bibliographic searches that depend on commercially owned databases, CD-ROMs are purchased by the library and housed on-site, so there is usually little or no cost for their use, and printouts are immediately available. Several of the resources mentioned in the previous section are now available on CD-ROM, such as *Sociological Abstracts,* ERIC, U.S. government publications, and *Social Work Abstracts.*

Some libraries, particularly those at large universities, provide patrons with access to the Internet. This is a worldwide system of over 39,000 computer networks with over 5 million individual users (Marine, Kirkpatrick, Neou, & Ward, 1994). The Internet is a wide-ranging system that includes government agencies, universities, research centers, private agencies, and individual users. Through the Internet, it is possible to communicate with other individuals who have done research in our area and to gain access to databases on many topics. Users obtain "addresses" and "mailboxes" that allow them to send and receive "e-mail." They may also participate in "conferences" with others interested in a particular topic.

The Internet is an instant worldwide communications network with almost unlimited possibilities. As just one example, imagine that we are studying foster care practices in our community. Through the Internet, we can communicate with other foster care specialists around the world and obtain access to statistics, government and agency policies, and research data on foster care in other communities and countries.

Some libraries already have integrated information systems. These are computer systems that allow access to all of the library's computerized resources from a single keyboard. This includes all the functions discussed earlier—the OPAC, computerized bibliographic services, CD-ROMs, government indexing services, Internet, and so on. With a personal computer and a modem, it is possible to use this system from the office or home. Eventually, with development of the information superhighway, we will use our computer, telephone, and television set as a single system for gaining access to print and visual data from around the world—and all this without leaving home.

SUMMARY

The first step in the research process is to define a research problem. Research problems often begin with interest in a general topic, but to conduct a research study, the researcher must narrow the topic to one or more specific research questions or hypotheses. It is possible to accomplish this by following a number of steps:

1. *Select a topic*
2. *Brainstorm possible questions related to the selected topic*
3. *Select a focus for the problem*
4. *Relate the focus of the problem to existing knowledge*
5. *State the specific research question or problem*
6. *Operationalize the concepts and variables in the research question or problem.*

The research library is a rich resource for information that is useful in every step of the research study. Once we have selected a research topic, we must use the library to conduct an extensive search for literature on that topic. In doing this, we ensure that the research problem selected for study will build on the work of others.

Sources of information available in the library include handbooks, ency-clopedias, dictionaries, bibliographies, directories, serials, indexes, abstracts, and public documents.

Many of these sources of information are currently accessible via com-puter, enabling us to search quickly for information relevant to our research problem. In the library of the future, we will gain access to all the resources of the library by using an integrated information system.

Case Study

The case study that follows (Rosenblatt & Kirk, 1981) illustrates these concepts: problem definition, use of literature, independent and dependent variables, hypotheses, and operational definitions.

In this research study, the authors collected questionnaire data from under-graduate, master's, and doctoral students in 15 social work programs across the United States. The purpose of the study was to assess the cumulative effect of taking research courses on knowledge (How much did students understand about basic research methods?) and attitudes (Did students think that research was important, useful, and valid?).

To define their research questions and to ensure that their work would add to the existing knowledge base, the authors searched the literature on the research knowledge and attitudes of social work students. Although they found little theory to guide them, there were some interesting findings in the literature.

It seemed that not very much was known about the effectiveness of social work research courses in educating students about research methods. Results of the five or six studies that had been done, however, indicated that master's students did not learn much research, despite the requirement that they take at least one research course. Almost no study had been made of undergraduate and doctoral students. Although these two groups have been small in the past, today they compose a large segment of social work education, so it was important to include them in a study on the effect of research courses.

The researchers defined two independent variables: level of education (which took on the values of bachelor's, master's, and doctoral), and the number of research courses taken. The researchers were wise to measure the independent variable in these two different ways. Because social work pro-grams vary in the number of required research courses, simply measuring the educational level of the student (bachelor's, master's, or doctoral) may not be an accurate indicator of how much research has been taught to them. The purpose of the study, then, was to examine the effect of the level of education and the number of courses on the dependent variables.

The researchers chose to define four dependent variables. They were (a) level of knowledge of research methods, (b) belief that research is important, (c) belief that research is useful, and (d) conviction that existing research is valid.

The hypothesis of this study was that among social work students, as the level of education and number of research courses increase, knowledge of and favorable attitudes toward research will increase. In effect, this study tested eight hypotheses by pairing each of two independent variables with each of four dependent variables:

Independent Variables	Dependent Variables
Level of education	Knowledge of methods
Number of research courses	Belief in importance
	Belief in usefulness
	Conviction of validity

The researchers provided careful and detailed operational definitions for each of the independent and dependent variables. In each case, the variable was defined by some response or set of responses that students made on a 16-page questionnaire that was distributed to the 15 schools of social work. The level of education and the number of research courses were operationalized according to students' responses to two questions soliciting this information.

The researchers developed a 60-item true-and-false inventory to measure knowledge of research. They first collected a pool of 120 knowledge items from existing research inventories, from research exams, and from research instructors. They pretested these items on a group of students. Those items that were answered correctly by over 80% of students were dropped because these items did not do a good job of differentiating knowledgeable students from those who were not. The remaining items were submitted to four research instructors. Items that were not answered correctly by all the instructors were dropped. Some final editing produced the completed knowledge inventory of 60 items. In scoring the inventory, the student received 1 point for each correct item. Each student, then, could receive a score from 0 to 60, with a higher score indicating greater research knowledge.

The three attitude dependent variables were also operationally defined as the sum of students' responses to a series of questions (when answers are summed or averaged across items, the series of questions is referred to as a *scale*). Each attitude variable was measured by using three to seven questionnaire items. Each item was a simple declarative sentence to which the student was asked to respond by indicating a number from 1 to 6, with 1 indicating *strongly agree* and 6 indicating *strongly disagree*. For example, a typical item among those used to measure belief regarding importance of research was this: "Limited agency resources should not be spent to pay for evaluative research." One item to measure belief in the usefulness of research was this: "Generally, a researcher's interests are not related to the practice needs of social work."

These operational definitions illustrate two important features: (a) Often, a great deal of effort is put into operationally defining research variables. The operational definitions must be detailed and specific so that they are valid and reliable—that is, so they measure what they purport to measure and that they do it consistently. (b) In much social work research, we rely on subjects' self-report. The questionnaire is the most common type of self-report, and research variables are often operationally defined as responses to a particular questionnaire item or set of items.

What did the researchers find? Unlike earlier studies, which showed social work education did not lead to greater research knowledge, this study showed significant changes as the result of social work education. As the level and amount of education increased, students' knowledge level and their belief in the importance and usefulness of research increased. Bachelor's, master's, and doctoral students did not differ, however, in the extent to which they believed that currently available research was valid.

DISCUSSION QUESTIONS

1. What are the six steps of identifying a research problem?
2. Think about a social problem in your area of interest. For example, you might be interested in learning why some adolescent mothers neglect their children; or you may want to know what types of intervention are most effective with substance abusers.

   a. Using the guidelines discussed in this chapter, state a research problem.

   b. Identify the variables in the research problem.

   c. Describe how these variables will be operationally defined.

SHORT ASSIGNMENTS

1. Visit your college or university library. Spend time there to become familiar with its resources. If necessary, ask for the help of a reference librarian. Make a written list of the location of each of the following:

a. Books

b. Journals that have been bound in hardcover volumes

c. Recent issues of journals that have not been bound

d. The Reference section

e. The Information Desk

f. Public documents

g. Microfilm library

h. Card catalog or OPAC

i. Computerized bibliography search service

j. Interlibrary loan desk

k. CD-ROM resources

l. Internet (if available)

2. On your visit to the library identify one example of each of the following types of information sources:

a. Handbook

b. Encyclopedia

c. Dictionary

d. Bibliography

e. Directory

f. Abstracts or index

g. Government reports

FURTHER READING

Beasley, D. (1988). *How to use a research library.* Oxford: Oxford University Press.

Creswell, J. W. (1994). *Research design: Qualitative and quantitative approaches.* Thousand Oaks, CA: Sage. Chapter 2: Use of the Literature; Chapter 4: The Purpose Statement.

6 Sampling

S uppose we have defined a problem to be researched. We have looked at the relevant literature to see what theories and data are available to guide us. On the basis of this knowledge we have set out hypotheses to be tested and have operationally defined the concepts and variables in our hypotheses to make this test possible. What next?

Before we can collect data or observations, we need to decide which individuals, families, groups, organizations, communities, or events we will study. In other words, What *sample* will we choose?

In a sense, each of us collects data all the time, data in the form of unsystematic observations about the world. For example, have you ever heard any of the following statements?

Most people on welfare are lazy.
Social workers are "do-gooders."
Old people are rigid.
Adolescents today have no respect for authority.

These statements are conclusions based on a kind of sampling. We observe welfare recipients or social workers or others, and on the basis of our observations, we draw conclusions about these groups. These "commonsense" conclusions are often inaccurate because our samples are too limited or too biased. For instance, our "sample" of welfare recipients may be limited to several recipients who engaged in fraud and were written up in the local newspapers. Newspapers are not systematic or inclusive about which welfare recipients they write stories about. In fact, the sample they present to the public is likely to be limited to those recipients who have done something wrong.

Viewed in this way, it is easy to understand why samples of behavior based on personal experience are not very good for understanding what groups are really like. The purpose of scientific sampling is to generate samples that *do* give us an accurate understanding of what groups and individuals are like.

DEFINING TERMS

Definition: A *population* is the collection of all individuals, families, groups, organizations, communities, events, and so on that we are interested in finding out about.

To define a population, we specify a set of variables or characteristics. For example, I might be interested in studying persons 65 years of age or older. My population would then be all individuals in the United States (or other specified area) who are 65 or older. Or my population might be defined as all females 65 or older currently living in a nursing home facility. Or it might be all mothers with children under the age of 5 and who work at least 10 hours per week outside the home.

Definition: Each member (person, family, organization, event, etc.) of a population is called an *element* of that population.

When data are presented based on a measurement of each population element (say, individual test scores for students in a school population), the element is also referred to as a *unit of analysis.*

Populations tend to be very large. For this reason, researchers rarely study every element in the population. Rather, they select a portion of that population for study.

Definition: A *sample* is a portion of a population selected for study.

Sometimes, populations are defined in very concrete terms, as in the example of all persons 65 and over in the United States. At times, however, researchers are not as clear as they should be about the specific characteristics that define the population. In a study that uses college students to evaluate the effectiveness of an assertiveness training program, what is the population? Is it all students at the researcher's university? All students at the researcher's university who volunteer for a training program? Or is it all college-aged men and women? Most likely, the researcher would like to be able to say that the program was effective for all young adults, so the last definition of the population would be the most appropriate.

It is important to state the specific variables or characteristics that define the population. Even though constraints of time and money prevent us from actually compiling a list of all elements of the population, if we have clearly defined our population, we should be able to describe how this compilation could be done if we had the resources.

Why use samples? In most cases, our interest goes beyond the limited number of elements we are studying. We are really interested in making statements about characteristics of the population or statements about how variables are related in the population. We say that we seek to "generalize our (sample) findings to the population." Is assertiveness training effective with young adults? What effect does availability of in-home care have on older persons in the United States? Are men really more sexist than women? What characteristics do the most effective school teachers have?

If we could measure every element in the population, we would surely have answers to our research questions. But populations are very large. For practical reasons, it is usually impossible to study every element in the population. It would be too costly, and many individuals, groups, and so on would not be available for our interview, questionnaire, or observation.

The researcher resolves this problem by studying a sample and generalizing findings from the sample to the population. This is the most efficient way to do research, because we have methods that allow us to estimate characteristics of populations by measuring only a small sample of population elements. Of course, we have to assume that the sample is representative of the population. Otherwise, what we find in the sample may not be true for the population. Later in this chapter, we will discuss different methods for ensuring that our samples are representative of the populations to which we seek to generalize our findings.

There are, of course, times when we want to sample every element of some population. This will be the case if the population is small enough so that every element can be measured without much additional cost. It will also be the case when we are not interested in generalizing to some larger group. For example, the director of your agency may ask us to study staff morale within our agency. If the purpose of the research is to learn only about the situation in our particular agency (perhaps so that recommendations to improve morale can be drafted), then the collection of all staff members in the agency *is* the population. In this case, the sample and the population are the same.

RANDOMNESS AND REPRESENTATIVENESS

Randomness and representativeness are two characteristics of samples and sampling plans.

Definition: Random sampling is a procedure for drawing a sample from a population so that every element in the population has an equal chance of being selected for the sample.

In most situations, random sampling is the best way to select a sample. By introducing randomness into the selection of elements for the sample, we minimize biases and other systematic factors that may make the sample different from the population from which it was drawn. For example, if we wanted to study public attitudes toward funding of social welfare programs, we might be tempted to interview those people who were most conveniently available—our friends and relatives—rather than individuals randomly selected from the population. But this sample is almost certainly biased. As social workers, our acquaintances are likely to be more educated and more "liberal" on social issues than the population at large. Results based on this sample would be inaccurate for the population.

There is another reason for using random sampling. After data collection, we apply statistical tests to infer the characteristics of a population based on characteristics of the sample. (For example, if the mean income of sample respondents was $12,000, we can infer what the mean income of all persons in the population is likely to be.) To use such statistical tests, we must assume that the sample was randomly selected from the population.

Definition: A *representative sample* is one that is very similar to the population from which it is drawn, on those variables relevant to the study.

Variables relevant to the study include the dependent variable or variables (for instance, assertiveness) and all variables that might be related to the dependent variable (such as age, sex, and race). So in a survey of social science majors, if the population of all currently enrolled social science majors is 55% female, 82% white, and has an average age of 25 years, then a representative sample of social science majors should have approximately the same distribution of these variables.

Are random samples representative of the populations from which they are drawn? It turns out that random sampling is only one way of constructing representative samples, and it does not always produce truly representative samples.

Random samples, however, *tend* to be representative. This is due to a natural process called the "principle of randomization," which can be understood intuitively. Because in random sampling, every element of the population has an equal chance of being selected, elements with certain characteristics—male or female, high or low income, and so on—will, if selected, probably be counterbalanced in the long run by selection of other elements with the opposite quantity or quality of the characteristic. Characteristics that are most typical of the population are those that occur most frequently and are therefore most likely to be selected for the sample. (For example, if I have twice as many female as male students in my class and if I randomly select a sample or subgroup of students from this class, this sample is also likely to have about a 2:1 female-to-male ratio.)

Although random samples tend to be representative and although random sampling is usually the best way to get a representative sample, there is no guarantee that random sampling will produce a representative sample. In the female-dominated classroom, for instance, if my sample is small—say just a few students—the chances that the sample will mirror the 2:1 sex ratio of the class (population) are much smaller than if my sample is large. Large random samples are more likely to be representative than are small samples. Large samples allow the principle of randomization to work. In small samples, a few individuals with nonrepresentative characteristics can make the sample less representative.

(We can verify this principle by repeatedly flipping a coin and noting the proportion of heads and tails. If we flip the coin just 4 or 5 times, the proportion of heads may be quite far from .50. If we flip the coin 25 or 100 times, the proportion of heads is much more likely to be close to the true proportion of .50.)

RANDOM SAMPLING VERSUS RANDOM ASSIGNMENT

Typically, when we study a group of people, we use the process of randomization at two different points in the research. It is important to distinguish between these two independent steps.

The first step is to randomly select those individuals or elements from the population that will be included in the study—that is, to select the sample. The next step is to randomly assign those individuals or elements to different conditions. Some participants may be assigned, for instance, to receive a treatment, and the remaining participants may be placed in a control group. In most situations, it is desirable to use the process of randomization for both sample selection and assignment to comparison conditions. It is not always possible to do this. There are many situations, however, in which you will be able to randomly select a sample and randomly assign individuals to different conditions. Let's see how this is done.

Imagine that the Friendly Family Service Society of North America has decided to hire us as evaluators. Our job is to determine if family therapy is effective. We decide that we want to answer this question by dividing a number of client families into two groups of equal size: Families in one group will receive the Friendly Family Therapy program (treatment group); families in the other group will meet regularly with a therapist, but the therapist will not provide any specific therapy interventions. (This is the control group.) At the end of the 10-week family therapy program, we will evaluate all the families to see how well they are functioning.

We ask directors of all member agencies to submit a list of all families currently on the waiting list for family therapy. When we assemble all the names, we find that we have a computer printout with 5,000 names, but we decide on 40 as our sample size. Half these families will receive Friendly Family Therapy, and half will not. (Because we are ethical social work researchers, we make sure that at the end of the evaluation all families who did not receive therapy will be offered the service.) In other words, our task is to draw a random sample of 40 families from a population of 5,000 families and randomly assign the 40 families in equal numbers to two comparison groups.

Where do we begin? We start by numbering the families on our printout from 0001 to 5,000. To choose 40 randomly selected families, we will have to refer to a random number table (such as the one that appears on page 379 at the end of this book). We have reproduced a portion of such a table here. We begin at a randomly selected point in the table and read off four digits at a time, vertically or horizontally. (We can find a randomly selected point in the table by closing our eyes and stabbing the page at a random point with a pencil. Be careful to keep your hand out of the way!)

```
...   41995   88931   73631   69361   05375   ...
...   10798   86211   36584   67466   69373   ...
```

In this example, we read off four digits at a time horizontally. Note that the grouping of numbers in the table is arbitrary and is done only to make the table easier to read. Each group of four digits represents a family to be selected for our sample. Skipping numbers that are larger than 5,000, we determine that

Family 4,199 is Participant 1.
Family 5,889 is skipped.
Family 3,173 is Participant 2.
Family 6,316 is skipped.
Family 9,361 is skipped.
Family 0,537 is Participant 3, . . . and so on.

We stop when we have selected 40 participants. We now have a random sample of 40 families drawn from a population of 5,000 families. The next step is to randomly assign families, 20 each, to the therapy and control conditions. We could use the four-digit family numbers again, but to make things easier, we renumber the families from 01 to 40. Again, we enter the random number table at another randomly selected point, and this time we read off pairs of digits:

```
...   34803   92479   33399   71160   64777   83378   ...
...   68553   28639   96455   34174   11130   91994   ...
```

Using the same procedure as last time, we select Families 34, 39, 24, 33, and so on, until we have selected 20 of our 40 families. Then we randomly decide if these 20 families will be assigned the therapy or the control condition. We can do this by flipping a coin. Or if we want to be more sophisticated, we can specify that this group will be the treatment group if the first number randomly selected from the table is odd, or it will be the control group if it is even. The remaining 20 families are assigned to the other group. (If we have more than two groups, we could number them 1, 2, 3, and so on and assign them to the conditions in the order in which these numbers appear in the random number table, skipping out-of-range numbers.)

In the discussion of the principle of randomization, I said that random samples tend to be representative of the populations from which they are drawn. The principle of randomization results in a related phenomenon: If sample elements are randomly assigned to groups, the groups will tend to be equivalent. This means that comparison groups formed by random assignment should be very similar to each other on variables such as sex, race, age, and so on.

Just as random sampling does not guarantee a representative sample, random assignment to groups does not *guarantee* equivalent groups. The larger the groups, the more likely they will be similar. The same principle is at work. If the groups are small, a few atypical elements may make a group different from the others. But with large groups, any atypical element assigned to one group is likely to be counterbalanced in the other groups, and population characteristics are more likely to be reflected equally in each of the comparison groups. When we study group research designs in the next chapter, we will see that the equivalence of comparison groups is important in many studies.

TYPES OF SAMPLES

Researchers try to select samples that are representative of the populations from which they are drawn so that they can make statements about those populations on the basis of their study of the samples. In most situations, it would be ideal to draw random samples of sufficient size from our populations because these samples are most likely to be representative. Social work researchers, however, are usually limited by real-world constraints, such as little money, inaccessible or unwilling participants, and lack of information about populations. A number of sampling procedures have been developed to cope with these constraints. We will review here the most common ones.

There are two types of samples:

Definition: *Nonprobability samples* are those that do not use random sampling. *Probability samples* are those that use random sampling in at least one stage of the sampling process.

NONPROBABILITY SAMPLING

Accidental Sampling. This is the weakest form of sampling. In this procedure, participants are recruited as they become available or because they happen to be convenient for the researcher. Such samples are often limited to personal contacts of the researchers or to people who happen to be available at meetings or in organizations or in a particular place and time. A favorite type of sample used by college professors is the professor's own class: It is handy, and the professor has a captive sample, so to speak.

This is a weak form of sampling because it does nothing to control bias. For example, suppose we wanted to study the attitudes of students at the University of Hard Knocks toward a recent proposal to use mandatory student fees to build a campus swimming pool. We decide to distribute a brief questionnaire to students by setting up a booth in the student union and asking passersby to complete and return it to us.

This is an accidental sample because it includes only those students who happen to walk by our booth *and* are willing to fill out a questionnaire. The sample is likely to be biased on certain variables that are related to attitudes toward the swimming pool proposition. It is probably biased against working students and those who live off campus, because these students are less likely to be in the student union. They are also less likely to want to pay for a pool. The sample is probably biased against disabled students for the same reasons. It is also limited to those students with the strongest opinions on the subject, because they are most likely to have the motivation to complete and return the questionnaire. The problem in using this sample is that it is not a good base from which to make generalizations about the attitudes of all students at the university.

Quota Sampling. Quota sampling attempts to avoid at least some of the biases of accidental sampling. In this procedure, the researcher has some knowledge about characteristics of the population likely to affect the dependent variables—

characteristics such as age, race, and sex. This knowledge is then used to establish quotas for the numbers of persons with the relevant characteristics who must be included in the sample. For example, if we want to construct a quota sample of social work students, we begin by looking at national statistics on the characteristics of social work students. If national data tell us that social work students are 65% female and 68% white, and that 58% are 25 years of age and younger, we select students for our sample so that it will have the same proportions of students with these characteristics. Specifically, our data collectors will be instructed to recruit a certain number of white females under 25, a certain number of African American females under 25, and so on.

It is not always necessary to select individuals in numbers proportional to their presence in the population. For example, we may know that there are two females for each male in the population, but we do not have a sufficient number of females available to us to include twice as many females as males in our sample. The sex ratio in our sample may be 1:1. In that case, we can simply weight the females' responses by 2 so that the final result will reflect the correct (population) proportions. The only requirement is that we sample enough of each kind of student so that some confidence can be placed in the results.

Most commonly, there are few restrictions on the particular persons who can be chosen for the sample as long as they fulfill the needed quota. Some public opinion polls use this procedure, setting quotas for the variables most likely to be related to opinions on public issues—age, sex, race, income level, and geographic location.

It is possible, of course, to set certain restrictions on interviewers or other data collectors so that the most obvious biases are avoided. For example, if we survey low-income families, we can require our interviewers to use in-person interviews so that those without a phone are not excluded, to interview a certain number of families who live on upper floors (to counteract interviewers' aversion to climbing stairs), and so on. Other than that, in quota sampling, interviewers are free to choose whomever they wish for the sample, provided that they fulfill the specified quota.

Unfortunately, quota sampling represents only a marginal improvement over accidental sampling. In fact, within each class set up by the quota (e.g., African American females under 25 years of age), we are actually taking an accidental sample. Quota sampling is an improvement over accidental sampling in that its use of quotas "forces" the sample to be representative of the population, at least on a few of the most obvious variables. A limitation of the quota sample, however, is that it is not truly representative. A multitude of other variables may be related to what we are studying, and they may or may not be reflected accurately in the sample. These variables are usually not known.

The Purposive Sample. This is another type of sample that does not use randomization in its selection of elements. It is similar to the quota sample, but it does not use specific predetermined quotas. In this method, study participants are hand-picked by the researchers to serve the purpose of the particular study. For example, suppose I have designed a curriculum for a program to train child welfare workers to detect and treat child abuse. To judge the quality and appropriateness of the curriculum, I want to submit it to a number of child abuse experts and ask them to complete a questionnaire on their opinions of the curriculum. This is a situation in which I may want to handpick the members of my sample. I will use my judgment and knowledge of the field to identify persons whom I feel to be leaders and experts in this area.

Purposive samples also have been used to predict the outcome of elections. In this situation, the researcher handpicks a few key election districts and samples voters in those districts on their anticipated voting behavior. This is sometimes a good method for predicting an election, particularly if the researcher can identify election districts that have consistently mirrored the results for the entire area or state.

From a research point of view, nonprobability samples are less desirable than probability samples. Because they do not use randomization in their selection of elements, they are often seriously biased, many times in ways that make their findings suspect or invalid. Whenever possible, the probability samples described later should be preferred. There are, however, reasons for using nonprobability samples in some situations.

There may simply be no other way to study the phenomenon at hand. For example, a group of researchers studied the norms and behaviors of an urban youth gang. Because these gang members were extremely wary of outsiders, the researchers chose to study only the gangs with which they were involved. In fact, they spent many months interacting with and getting the trust of gang members before they collected any data. Because these were the only gang members available to them, it was simply a question of studying this accidental sample or not studying gangs at all. The anthropologist is often in a similar situation. In studying a dying culture, for instance, the researcher will have to rely on available respondents.

Another situation in which a nonprobability sample is appropriate is one in which the researcher's purpose is not to generalize to a population. That is, the researcher has some purpose other than making accurate statements about the distribution of certain variables in a population. In the discussion of purposive sampling I gave one such example, in which the researcher handpicked a sample of child abuse experts to judge a training curriculum. Here, the purpose was to judge the quality of the curriculum rather than to generalize to a population.

For example, I (Berger, 1984) studied older gay men to determine if they fit the stereotypes that are associated with this group: that they are lonely, isolated, and poorly adjusted. Almost all research on homosexuality must rely on nonprobability samples because it is difficult to define, locate, and recruit this population for study. One social science researcher defended this use of a nonprobability sample on the following grounds. To the extent that the purpose of the study was to refute commonly held stereotypes about older gay men (rather than to describe the characteristics of this population as a whole), the use of a nonprobability sample is appropriate, as long as it is sufficiently large and includes a sufficient diversity of respondents (F. Suppe, Committee on the History and Philosophy of Science, University of Maryland, personal communication, March 1982).

Although researchers usually prefer to use probability samples, much social work research has used nonprobability samples. This research has often added important new knowledge to the literature.

PROBABILITY SAMPLING

Simple Random Sampling. This is the most basic type of probability sampling. In many cases, it is the most desirable, if not the most feasible, form of sampling, and it is used as a component of other probability sampling procedures. In a simple random sample, every element of the population has an equal chance of being selected into the sample. The list of 40 families from the Friendly Family Service Agency that we generated earlier is a simple random sample. Although simple random sampling produces unbiased samples—that is, the samples are likely to be representative of the population—it is not always the most efficient method for our research purpose.

Stratified Sample. In a stratified sample (also called a stratified random sample), the population is divided into subgroups or strata by population

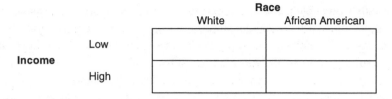

Figure 6.1. Illustration of a Stratified Sample Using the Variables of Race and Income to Define Strata

characteristics, such as race, income, and sex. A simple random sample is then drawn for each subgroup or stratum. For example, if we wanted to stratify the population on the basis of race and income, we would set up the table of cells illustrated in Figure 6.1. We would then draw a simple random sample within each of the cells, that is, from low-income whites, then from low-income African Americans, and so on.

When is a stratified sample preferable to a simple random sample? In general, stratified sampling will be more efficient than simple random sampling when stratifying the sample results in homogeneous subgroups. Homogeneous subgroups occur when, on the dependent variables, there are fewer differences within groups (say, low-income African Americans) than between groups. In other words, in a stratified sample, the differences between subgroups should be large in comparison to differences within subgroups.

Once we have defined our strata, there are two ways in which we can sample. In *proportional stratified sampling* the number of elements sampled in each subgroup is proportional to its representation in the population. For example, if low-income African Americans make up 8% of the population, then 8% of the participants in the total sample will be low-income African Americans. (It is, of course, also possible to select different numbers within subgroups and to weight the scores in the subgroups so that they reflect the relative sizes of subgroups in the population. As in quota sampling, this may be necessary if the researcher cannot get a sufficient number of participants for each of the subgroups so that they reflect the population proportions.)

In *nonproportional stratified sampling* an equal number of elements is selected for each subgroup, or elements are selected in numbers that do not reflect their proportions in the population.

Proportional stratified sampling is used when the researcher wants to generalize the findings to the population as a whole. In this case, the goal is to produce a sample that is as representative of the population as possible. To the extent that we have included important subgroups in the same proportions as in the population, we have guaranteed that our sample is similar to the population, at least on the stratified variables.

There are, however, times when the researcher will want to use nonproportional sampling. One such situation is when the researcher's purpose is not to generalize to the population as a whole but, rather, to make comparisons between subgroups. For example, if the researcher is interested in comparing the job opportunities of African Americans and whites, it makes sense to include an equal number of African Americans and whites in the sample, even though they are not equal in number in the population.

Another situation calling for the use of nonproportional sampling is when the researcher wants to ensure that representatives of an important but very small subgroup within a population are included in the sample. For instance, a simple random sample of refugee families may fail to include Kampuchean refugees. If we want to ensure that this group will be studied, we can do so by including them in numbers greater than their proportional representation in the population.

Finally, nonproportional stratified sampling is also appropriate when the researcher is interested in subdividing cases within strata for further analysis. In Figure 6.1, for example, the researcher may want to do additional analyses to study the differences within the subgroup of low-income African Americans: What are the differences, say, between urban and rural low-income African Americans or between low-income African Americans who live alone versus those who are heads of household? In this case, it would be best to have equal subsamples of sufficient size for each of the strata.

One limitation in the use of stratified samples should be noted. As we increase the number of variables on which we stratify, we increase the number of cells in our sampling design, requiring larger samples to fill up the cells. This is particularly important when we want to compare different subgroups or cells, because cells with very few elements will generally not give good estimates.

As we add variables on which to stratify, the number of cells increases dramatically. In Figure 6.1, for example, if we were to add just one additional stratifying variable with just two values, say, sex of respondent, the number of cells would double. So it is a good idea to remember that we should stratify only on those variables that will result in homogeneous groups. If there is no reason to believe that stratifying will lead to more homogeneous groups, then it is more efficient to use a simple random sample.

Simple random sampling and stratified sampling are usually the best ways to ensure representative samples. But alas, they are not always possible. They were designed to meet the needs of statisticians rather than researchers, who must deal with real-world limitations. For instance, we may not be able to draw a simple random sample because we are unable to generate a list of all the elements in the population. If we were studying elementary school children in North America, for instance, how would we get a list of all school children so that we could draw our random sample from it? We certainly don't have the resources to contact every school district in our population, even assuming they would all cooperate. Even if we did obtain a fairly complete list, it is unlikely we would have the resources to send interviewers to schools scattered all over the country. That wouldn't be efficient, because there might be only one or two respondents in any particular school.

Cluster Sampling. These are some reasons why alternatives to simple random sampling have been developed. The most common alternative, and one used frequently for large-scale surveys, is cluster sampling. In this method, the population is divided into clusters or units and then into successively smaller subunits. At each level, the units and subunits are randomly selected. Clusters are usually defined as geographic or organizational units. For example, in a study of high school students' attitudes toward birth control, I may use cluster sampling to obtain results that I can say are indicative for students in my state. I randomly select a number of state regions, and then within each selected region, I randomly select a number of counties; within each county, I randomly select a number of school districts, and so on. The last cluster level may be the individual classroom.

Within each unit, I may take a simple random sample of subunits, or if the number of elements in a subunit is small, I may include all the elements in my sample. In the birth control study, for example, if there are only one to five high schools in a school district, I may sample all the high schools for each selected school district. Within the classroom, I may ask all or some students to complete a questionnaire.

Although a simple random sample or a stratified sample may yield more precise results, its use must be weighed against its cost. In the birth control study, for example, it would be very expensive to compile a list of all students in the population and to contact the many widely scattered schools that would be reflected in a random selection of students. Once we got access to the classroom, the simple random sample would require that we sample only one or a few students in each classroom, even though we could have easily included the entire class without much additional effort. In fact, administering questionnaires to a few selected students may very well be more disruptive than administering them to the entire class.

Cluster sampling avoids these problems. It limits the number of schools we would have to approach, and it allows us to collect data from all the students who may be conveniently available. The resources we save can then be applied to collecting a larger sample, making cluster sampling a practical alternative to simple random sampling.

Systematic Sampling. In this procedure, the first sample element is randomly chosen from the numbers 1 through K, and subsequent elements are chosen at every Kth interval. For example, a systematic sample of homes may be selected from a suburban neighborhood. If there are 10 houses on each block, I set $K = 10$, and I use a random number table to choose a number between 01 and 10 (by picking the first two digits between 01 and 10 after my pencil lands on a randomly selected point on the page). If $K = 6$, I include the sixth home on each block within my sample; that is, I interview the families in Homes 6, 16, 26, 36, and so on until I reach the desired sample size.

In systematic sampling, it is critical that the first element between 1 and K be chosen randomly. If it is not, then most of the elements in the population have no chance at all for selection into the sample, and the sample cannot be assumed to even approximate a simple random sample.

Systematic samples are used primarily for convenience and simplicity. For instance, I once participated in a telephone survey of community attitudes toward the local United Way. A phone survey, of course, excludes many low-income people who do not have phones, but within that constraint we did have a list of population elements: the telephone directory. It would have been possible, but impractical, to take a simple random sample from the phone book. It would have required numbering tens of thousands of names, and the process of picking out corresponding numbers from a random number table would have been tedious.

We chose a simple alternative. On the basis of the number of telephone listings and the number of respondents we wanted to include, we determined our K. We then randomly selected a number between 1 and K. In this way, we determined that every 16th name in every third column of listings should be included in our sample. By using a specially marked card, it was possible to quickly select the appropriate name on each page. Each of these listings was called, and the first adult to answer was asked to participate in our brief telephone interview.

There is a serious limitation to systematic sampling. If there is any systematic or cyclical bias in the population, a systematic sample may also be seriously biased. In the telephone survey, it didn't seem likely that there were characteristics common to persons whose names were listed in the 16th position in every third column or that these persons differed consistently from the other listings.

But consider the survey of suburban homes. Our sample of every sixth home on each block is seriously biased. This sample excludes homes on corner lots. Although you might not think that this factor is related to what you are studying, consider again. Research studies have shown that families who live in corner homes are different from their neighbors: These homes are more expensive, and their occupants are likely to have higher incomes and more conservative political beliefs. It is easy to imagine a number of phenomena that would be affected by this sample bias: attitudes toward social welfare programs, voting preference, and so on.

It is always possible that a systematic sample may be biased because of this kind of systematic or cyclical characteristic in the population. Because systematic samples are always constructed from lists of elements, whenever a systematic sample is possible, it should also be possible to draw a simple random sample or stratified sample. Therefore, unless the additional work is prohibitive, it is preferable to use the latter types of samples.

SUMMARY

In observing the world around us, we all use a kind of commonsense sampling. But because this sampling is unsystematic, it often results in wrong conclusions. The scientific method relies on the careful selection of elements of populations into samples so that these samples can be used as the basis for generalizations about the populations from which they were drawn. The most basic form of sampling is simple random sampling, in which each element of the population has an equal chance of being selected for the sample. A sample selected in this way will tend to be representative of the population. In addition to the selection of a random sample from a population, many studies also use random assignment to comparison groups. All sampling plans can be divided into nonprobability samples (that do not use random sampling) and probability samples (that do use random sampling in at least one step of the sampling plan).

CASE STUDY

It has been known for some time that family members who provide significant amounts of care to an impaired older person often feel burdened and experience stress. This study (Deimling & Bass, 1986) was designed to examine the causes of stress on caregivers of impaired older persons. Specifically, the study analyzed the effects of the older person's level of social functioning, disruptive behaviors, and cognitive incapacity (e.g., memory loss, forgetfulness, confusion, etc.) on the amount of stress experienced by the caregiver.

The data used in this research came from a study of families who provided care to impaired older persons residing in their own homes in the Cleveland area. From over 2,000 referrals, 614 families were chosen using a stratified random sampling procedure. The sample was stratified into three subgroups: geographic area of residence, racial characteristics, and generational configuration (number of generations living in the household).

The subgroup of geographic area of residence included 40% urban, 40% suburban, and 20% rural; the racial characteristics included 25% African American and 75% white; and the generational configuration included 50% one-generation, 30% two-generation, and 20% three-generation households.

Although the researchers did not state in detail how the original sample was drawn, they probably followed a procedure that resembled the following. On the basis of theory and previous research, the researchers expected that variations in caregiving occurred because of the geographic location (urban, suburban, or rural), race (white or African American), and generational configuration of the family (one-, two-, or three-generational households). Therefore, because these variables were related to caregiver stress, they wanted to ensure that these subgroups would be adequately represented in the sample. In addition, the researchers' ability to generalize their findings based on a sample of the population would be enhanced if the sample resembled the population on the stratified variables: geographic location, race, and generational configuration.

How did the researchers determine the proper proportions for each subgroup? The ideal way would have been to make the size of the sample subgroups proportional to the actual characteristics of caregivers in the Cleveland area population. (That is, if 40% of caregivers in the Cleveland area lived in suburban areas, then the sample would have been chosen so that 40% of caregivers in the sample lived in suburban areas.)

It is unlikely, however, that the researchers had this information about the Cleveland area population. They did, however, have this information on the more than 2,000 families on their referral list. Therefore, they had to first take those families and identify each according to its geographic area of residence, race, and generational configuration. They then randomly selected a sample of families so that the proportions of the sample within each stratum (urban; rural; suburban; white; African American; one-, two-, and three-generational families) were similar to the proportions in the more than 2,000 families from which the sample was drawn. In this way, the researchers guaranteed that their sample of 614 families was similar to the referral list of more than 2,000 families on the stratified variables.

What did the researchers find? In the sample of 614 families, elderly care recipients averaged 78.2 years of age. Two thirds were female. They had been receiving care from their spouse or children for an average of 6 years.

This research also contributed to our understanding of the causes of stress for caregivers of the impaired elderly. It is often assumed that care recipients' cognitive incapacity (forgetfulness and confusion) is the cause of stress on caregivers. This study found that other factors—disruptive behavior and social functioning (the older care recipients' level of cooperation, withdrawal, and isolation)—were more important sources of stress for caregivers.

DISCUSSION QUESTIONS

1. What is wrong with the following conclusions?
   a. Engineering majors are nerds.
   b. Mothers on welfare choose to have additional children so that their benefits will increase.
   c. Older persons are forgetful.
   d. Many adults who recover memories of childhood sexual abuse later recant those memories.
2. What is the difference between a population, an element, and a sample?
3. Why do large random samples tend to be representative of the populations from which they are drawn?
4. What is the difference between random sampling from a population and random assignment to comparison groups?
5. Describe how you would identify the individuals in a simple random sample of all the students in your college (or all staff in your agency).
6. Match each item in the first column with the corresponding item in the second column:

Proportional stratified sampling	A research study that proposes to examine the differences between various income groups
Nonproportional stratified sampling	A research study that proposes to describe the population as a whole

7. Describe how you would use cluster sampling to study the attitudes of social workers in your city toward joining a union. How would you define your sampling clusters?

SHORT ASSIGNMENTS

1. Locate a journal article that describes a social work research study. (Refer to Box 5.2 in the preceding chapter for a list of social work journals that publish research articles.)

     a. Describe and name the type of sampling used in the study.

     b. Describe the population to which the researcher sought to generalize the findings. (Often the population is implied rather than described directly. Can you infer how the researcher defined the population?)

     c. What are the strengths and weaknesses of the sampling procedures used in this study?

     d. Are the researcher's generalizations from the sample to the population valid?

2. Staff members at the Morningside Community Center are interested in studying the social service needs of low-income families living in a large public housing project located near the center. The project consists of 10 buildings, each 10 floors high, with 5 apartments on each floor. (This makes a total of 500 apartments or families.) The housing authority will not release the names of tenants or any information about them.

Two persons are hired as interviewers for the study. Interviewer A is assigned five buildings on the north side of the project, and Interviewer B is assigned to the other five buildings on the south side. The interviewers are instructed to go from floor to floor until they have gathered 10 interviews in each building. They work from 9:00 a.m. to 5:00 p.m. over a period of 4 weekdays to complete their interviews.

     a. Discuss all the ways in which this sampling procedure might bias the results of the study.

     b. Describe a better (more representative) sampling procedure for obtaining 100 interviews using two interviewers.

FURTHER READING

Kish, L. (1965). *Survey sampling.* New York: John Wiley.

7 Group Research Designs

Suppose we have selected our sample: the individuals, groups, or other units of analysis that we wish to study. A plan is then needed to tell us how to carry out the study.

We need to know if the individuals in the sample will be divided into groups, and, if so, how that will be done. (In the discussion that follows, I refer to the individuals in a research study. Most commonly, it is individuals that are the unit of analysis. The unit of analysis, however, might also be the family, group, organization, agency, and so on.)

If the study is experimental, we need to know which group or groups will be exposed to the independent variable (say, a treatment program). If the study is nonexperimental, we need to understand how the independent variable (say, race, sex, or occupation) affects the various groups in the study. We need to know who will be measured and at what times. We need to specify time order: When will measurement of individuals and exposure to the independent variable occur? And which, if any, events will occur simultaneously in the various groups? Research designs are plans that provide answers to these questions.

NOTATION

Much of the material in this chapter is drawn from two books: *Experimental and Quasi-Experimental Designs for Research,* by Donald T. Campbell and

Julian C. Stanley (1963), and a later book, *Quasi-Experimentation: Design and Analysis Issues for Field Settings,* by Thomas D. Cook and Donald T. Campbell (1979). These books are a basic reference resource for understanding all aspects of group research design. Campbell and Stanley (1963) developed a shorthand notation to describe research designs. Because it would be cumbersome to give a verbal description every time we wanted to specify a research design, this shorthand will prove invaluable.

According to this notation, X represents the exposure of an individual or group to an independent variable. In an experimental study, the X is an event administered by the researcher to the study participants, such as exposure to a treatment program. In a nonexperimental study, the X represents some event or characteristic whose effect on participants is to be studied.

For instance, in a study of differences between blue-collar and white-collar workers, the X represents the exposure of participants to blue-collar or white-collar status. These could be symbolized as X_{BC} and X_{WC}, respectively.

O represents the measurement or observation of an individual or group. It is an event such as administering a test or questionnaire or conducting an interview. It is the means by which the dependent variable is measured: It is a measure of the effect of X. For instance, if X is a job training program, then O might be a measure of how many days the trainee has been employed, as determined by his or her responses to a questionnaire.

When Xs and Os appear in the same row, this means that they are applied to the same set of persons. Each row of symbols, then, represents a separate group. Time order is indicated by the position of the symbols, from left to right. Xs and Os vertical to one another occur at the same time. I have summarized these notation rules in Table 7.1.

As we saw in Chapter 6, comparison groups can be formed by random assignment. This is equivalent to writing each person's name on a slip of paper and randomly drawing names out of a hat. If there are two groups, the first half of all names will go into one group and the remaining names into the other. In Chapter 6, I described how this is done.

In many instances, comparison groups are not formed by random assignment. In the study comparing blue-collar and white-collar workers, the two groups of workers already existed in the real world. In practical terms this means that the researcher did not assign individuals to belong to one group or the other but merely asked respondents about their occupational status. This is a common research design and is referred to as an *intact groups* or *already formed groups* design.

TABLE 7.1 Summary of Notation Rules for Group Research Designs

---

X = Exposure of a group to the independent variable, treatment, or intervention

R = Random assignment to separate groups

O = Observation or measurement

Left to right dimension indicates time order.

Xs and Os vertical to one another occur at the same time.

Parallel rows preceded by R and unseparated by dashed lines represent comparison groups formed by random assignment of subjects.

Dashed lines separate comparison groups not formed by random assignment of subjects.

When groups are formed by random assignment, we indicate this by placing the letter R in front of each group. When groups are not formed by random assignment (having intact groups is one such situation), then no Rs are used, but a dashed line is drawn to separate the groups.

For example, suppose we want to evaluate the effects of a reading comprehension program on the reading scores of elementary school children. X represents exposure to the reading program. O represents the administration of a reading test. Our school principal has allowed us to work with two classrooms, so we decide to run the reading program in one classroom and to use the other classroom as a control group. Our design might look like this:

X	O	Mr. Stern's class

	O	Mr. Happy's class

In this design, we run the reading program in Mr. Stern's class, and when the program is finished, we administer a reading test to all students in both classes.

An alternative is to use comparison groups formed by random assignment. This, of course, presents many practical difficulties because the students will have to be placed into newly formed groups, different from their classroom groups. We would need to assign each student a number and then use the random number table to assign half the students to one group and half to the other group. Each group, then, will have some students from each of the classrooms, and the design will look like this:

R	X	O
R		O

In these examples, tests (*Os*) were given after exposure to *X*—in this case, the reading program. Tests or measurements given after exposure to the independent variable are called *posttests*. Tests or measurements given before exposure to the independent variable are called *pretests*. In the following examples, two groups experience simultaneous pretests and posttests:

Comparison groups formed by random assignment, then pretested and posttested:

R   *O* *X* *O*

R   *O*   *O*

Intact (already formed) groups, pretested and posttested:

In what follows, I have used notation to describe three additional designs. See if you can give a verbal description of each of these designs and then refer to the verbal descriptions I have given, to see if you were correct.

a.   R *O* *X* *O*
      R *O*   *O*

b.   *O* *X* *O*
     - - - - - - - - - - -
      O   *O*

c.   R *O* *X* *O*
      R *O*   *O*
     - - - - - - - - - - - - - - - - -
      R *O* *X* *O*
      R *O*   *O*

a. In this design, individuals are randomly assigned to two groups. Both groups are pretested simultaneously and then one group is exposed to an independent variable or treatment. Sometime after this exposure, both groups are posttested simultaneously.

b. In this design, we have two groups not formed by random assignment. (They might be two classrooms, for instance.) Both are pretested simultaneously, and then one group is exposed to an independent variable or treatment. Sometime after this exposure, both groups are posttested simultaneously.

c. In this design, we have four groups of individuals. One group is randomly divided into two groups. Another, separate, group of individuals is also randomly divided into two groups. All four groups are pretested simultaneously. Then one of the two randomly formed groups within each of the two original groups is exposed to an independent variable or treatment. The groups to receive the treatment are themselves, randomly selected. Sometime after this exposure all four groups are posttested simultaneously.

These descriptions illustrate the usefulness of design notation: Notation allows us to describe designs clearly and efficiently. They prove the maxim that "a picture is worth a thousand words."

WHY IS RESEARCH DESIGN IMPORTANT?

Before getting into the specifics of research design, I will present two examples that illustrate how important it is to understand basic principles of good design. In both examples, the researchers came up with wrong conclusions because they used inappropriate designs.

The first example comes from the research literature on aging. For many years, gerontological researchers thought they had confirmed what many people believe: that intelligence declines with advanced age. They proposed a relationship between age and intelligence as shown in Figure 7.1.

This finding proved to be untrue. Later research indicated that there is little, if any, decline of verbal intelligence as people grow older (Edinberg, 1985, p. 16). (There is, however, a decline in psychomotor skills with increasing age.)

What happened? The original researchers had used an inappropriate design: a *cross-sectional design.* In this type of design, the researchers measured the intelligence of different age cohorts (people of similar age) at the same point in time—for example, all 20-year-olds, all 30-year-olds, and so on, as shown here:

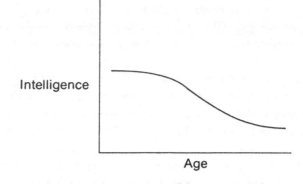

Figure 7.1. Graph Illustrating a Decline in Intelligence With Age

$$X_{20} \quad O$$

$$X_{30} \quad O$$

$$X_{40} \quad O$$

. . . and so on

So each point on the graph in Figure 7.1 represents the average intelligence score of a *different* group of people.

The problem was this. The different age cohorts differed not only in age (the independent variable) but also in number of years of schooling. Older cohorts had fewer years of schooling than younger cohorts, because less education was available when these older folks were of school age. Persons with more years of schooling do better on all types of paper-and-pencil tests: They have more experience. In addition, for the younger cohorts the test-taking experience was more recent. Apparently, it was this difference in the amount of schooling and its effect on taking tests (rather than the difference in age) that led to a difference in intelligence test scores.[1] (Later in this chapter, I will refer to factors such as the differences in amount of education between groups as a bias due to selection.)

This was illustrated when researchers used a more appropriate research design: a *longitudinal design.* In this design, the *same* group of individuals is followed over time and measured repeatedly to detect any changes in intelligence with age, as shown here:

$$X \quad O_{20} \ O_{30} \ O_{40} \ O_{50} \ \ldots \text{and so on.}$$

It is easy to see why early researchers opted for the cross-sectional design. The longitudinal design requires much more effort because the researcher must keep track of individuals over a long period of time, and results are not available until after many years. The longitudinal design, however, leads to a more accurate conclusion because differences between the "age groups" are due solely to age and not to other factors, such as differences in the amount of schooling. Therefore, these other factors are not around to "contaminate" the results.

The second study to illustrate the importance of research design is hypothetical. In this example, a family planning agency wishes to determine the most effective way to get couples to use birth control. A review of the literature and a look at programs used by other agencies suggest two strategies: television advertisements and a door-to-door educational campaign conducted by trained personnel. The literature suggests that personal contact, which is part of the door-to-door method, is the most powerful way to change public attitudes. The advantages of the door-to-door method, however, must be weighed against its cost. It is expensive and time-consuming. Television messages, although less powerful, reach a much larger audience. Given all these factors, the research question is, Which method will have the most influence on a community?

The family planning researchers decide to test the two methods in two cities that they believe to be very similar. If this is true, then any differences in birth control practices or attitudes will be due to the different educational campaigns. For a period of 6 months, television advertisements are played on local stations in City A, and door-to-door visits are used in City B. The cities are in different parts of the country to ensure that couples in each city are exposed only to the campaign that is directed at that city. At the end of 2 years, the birthrates are determined from records at the county clerk's office in both cities. The design is as follows:

City A—TV Campaign $\qquad X_a \qquad O_1$

- - - - - - - - - - -

City B—Door-to-Door Campaign $\qquad X_b \qquad O_2$

Suppose that the researchers find that the birthrate is lower in City B at the conclusion of the study. Can they say with confidence that the door-to-door campaign was more effective in lowering the birthrate? The answer is no. A number of weaknesses in the research design make this conclusion suspect. Specifically, many factors *other than* the type of campaign (the independent variable) could account for the lower birthrate in City B. Consider just a couple of examples.

We know that economic conditions are an important factor in couples' decisions to use birth control, but we don't know if economic conditions are similar in the two cities. What if a large factory closed in City B during the course of the study? The resulting unemployment and concern about economic conditions could be responsible for a lower birthrate in City B, even if there was no difference in the effectiveness of the two campaigns.

Here's another problem in interpreting the results. The researchers selected two cities that were similar. But it is never possible to select two areas that are exactly alike. Any differences in the type of people in the two towns could be responsible for the different birthrates, even if the two campaigns did not differ.

For instance, perhaps the lower birthrate in City B was due to the fact that residents of that city are older than those of City A and had a lower birthrate to begin with, or perhaps City B has more upwardly mobile families who want to limit family size. Countless such variables may have led to the difference in birthrates between the two cities. Therefore, we cannot have much confidence that the difference was in fact due to the different campaigns.

This example illustrates the logic of research design. All research designs follow this logic, which can be described as follows: The goal of any research design is to show that the *experimental hypothesis* is correct. The experimental hypothesis is that X is responsible for the observed effect. To show that this is true, we have to rule out all *plausible alternative hypotheses.* These are a series of hypotheses that state that factors *other than X* are responsible for the observed effect.

In the family planning example, the experimental hypothesis is that the different educational campaigns are responsible for the different birthrates in the two cities. There are a series of plausible alternative hypotheses: that the closing of a factory in City B, that the older ages of City B residents, and so on—that these factors are responsible for the difference in birthrates between the cities.

The purpose of research design is to set up a situation so that we can rule out plausible alternative hypotheses. If we can rule out all hypotheses that are plausible alternatives to the experimental hypothesis, then the experimental hypothesis must be true. Another way to say this is that if we have comparison groups that are equal in every way except for the independent variable, then any resulting differences between the groups must be due to the independent variable. (So, for example, if City A and City B are exactly equal on all factors other than the presence of two types of educational campaigns, then any subsequent differences that we find must be due to the difference in educational campaigns.)

To the extent that we have ruled out plausible alternative hypotheses, we can say with confidence that we have shown that X was responsible for subsequent differences that we observe. When we have done this, we have established that the study has *internal validity.*

Definition: *Internal validity* asks the question, Did the experimental treatment make a difference in this specific instance, with these study participants, in this setting, at this time?

When we conduct a research study, we are teasing out the effect of an independent variable or variables on a dependent variable or variables. In other words, we are looking for an effect, such as the effect of an educational birth control campaign on subsequent birthrates. The first order of business, of course, is to show that effect in the particular sample we are studying. In this case, we want to show a difference in birthrates between City A and City B.

In most studies, however, we would like to make statements about effects that apply beyond the particular sample we have studied. In the family planning study, for instance, we are almost certainly interested in finding the most effective educational medium so that it can be applied in other areas of the country, administered by different local groups and using different personnel. We might also want the program to show an effect when its outcome is measured in different ways—say, by measuring respondents' reported use of birth control rather than the birthrate.

Definition: *External validity* asks these questions: To what other groups of people, families, organizations, and the like can the observed effect be generalized? In what other settings and with what other treatment variables and outcome variables will this effect hold true?

The goal of every research design is to establish both internal and external validity. Internal validity is the first requirement of a research design because we must first establish that a particular effect occurs (such as the lowering of the birthrate due to an educational campaign). Generally, it is also desirable for the finding to have high external validity—that is, for the finding to be valid among other groups, in different settings, with other ways of implementing the treatment, and with other ways of measuring its effect.

Ideally, a good research design will be high in both internal and external validity. In this chapter, I will evaluate a number of designs in terms of their internal and external validity. But first, I must note a number of factors or threats to internal validity. Each of these factors represents a plausible alternative hypothesis—that is, a hypothesis that some factor other than X is responsible for an observed effect.

FACTORS OF INTERNAL VALIDITY

History. This refers to specific events other than the experimental variable that occur during the course of the study and that may affect the outcome. In the family planning study, the closing of a factory in one of the cities was a factor of history. This event represents a plausible alternative hypothesis to the hypothesis that the difference in educational campaigns was responsible for the difference in birthrates between the cities. It is easy to understand that a factory closing will lead to economic problems that, in turn, might plausibly affect young families' desire to have children and thus affect the birthrate.

We must always be attuned to events in the environment that may affect our studies, because the environment is constantly changing and because research, especially social work research, is not conducted in a vacuum. Here is another example of a factor of history. Suppose we have developed a program of intensive services for the frail elderly with the goal of delaying or preventing placement in a nursing home. That is our X. The dependent variable is the length of time the older individual continues to live at home.

Now suppose that during the course of the study the federal government implements Title XX, a law that provides money for services to keep people out of institutions for as long as possible. We cannot prevent our frail elderly clients from receiving other services, and to do so would be unethical. But this does present a problem for the research design. If the program "works"— that is, if it is successful in keeping clients out of institutions—was it due to our program or to newly available Title XX services? Or was it due to the combination of the two? The implementation of Title XX, then, may be a plausible alternative hypothesis.

Maturation. According to Campbell and Stanley (1963), maturation refers to "processes within the respondents operating as a function of the passage of time per se (not specific to the particular events), including growing older, growing hungrier, growing more tired and the like" (p. 5). For example, whenever we study the performance of young persons who are still growing and developing physically and mentally, we must take account of the fact that they are going to show performance changes (generally improvements) over time. This is due to maturation and would have occurred even without the experimental treatment.

For example, if I measure the reading achievement of a group of students in the fourth grade and again when these students are in the sixth grade, there will probably be an increase in performance due solely to maturation. If we want to show that a reading improvement program increased achievement, we need to show an increase in scores above what would be expected from maturation alone.

Maturation also refers to decreases in ability over time. For example, suppose we used the following design to evaluate an activity program designed to increase the alertness and orientation of a group of frail elderly persons:

$$O_1 \qquad X \qquad O_2$$

At O_1 and O_2 we administer the Mental Status Quiz (Goldfarb, 1962), a short questionnaire that measures orientation. (It asks questions such as, "Can you name the two streets that form the nearest intersection?") We may find, to our disappointment, that there is no change in mental status between O_1 and O_2. We need to take into account, however, an important factor of maturation: The mental alertness of the participants may be declining over time. In the absence of the activity program, there may have been a decrease in orientation at O_2. When we take maturation into account, we may actually be able to say that the program was a success, despite a lack of change: The program was successful in preventing or slowing deterioration.

Another situation in which maturational effects are likely is when the experimental treatment or testing process is long enough for research participants to tire. For example, if we test participants at the beginning and then again at the end of a long day of training, we have to consider that they will probably be slowed down by fatigue.

Testing. Testing occurs whenever performance on a test is affected by having taken a previous test. The second test may or may not be the same as the first test. It is very common, for example, for participants to do better the second time they take a test that was the same as or similar to an earlier test.

Think about the first time you took an academic aptitude test. It probably took some time to learn the ropes: to learn how to pace yourself, how to guess when you didn't know the answer, and how to fill in the bubbles on the computer answer sheet. Chances are that you will do better the second time around simply because you are familiar with the process. You may also be more self-confident the second time around, and that will help your performance. Or if you had a bad first experience, you may actually be less confident the second time, and that will lower your performance. That, too, is an effect of testing.

Instrumentation. In some situations, there may be unintended changes over time in the way an effect is measured. This is a problem of instrumentation. A good analogy from the physical sciences is the change in calibration of a spring scale as it is used repeatedly. After weighing a number of heavy objects, the spring loosens enough to give inaccurate readings in subsequent weighings. That is why most spring scales have calibration adjustments, which allow the user to tighten the spring so that it is once again accurate. (Check your bathroom scale and you'll probably find one.)

Instrumentation problems in social work research are often more subtle and a bit harder to correct. An example of instrumentation comes from a study of the effectiveness of marital communication counseling in improving family interaction. Suppose that we measure the dependent variable, quality of communication, by placing each family in a room with a one-way mirror and asking them to hold a discussion to make a family decision, say, where to spend the next vacation. In an adjoining room behind the one-way mirror, we have placed an observer who has been trained to record one aspect of the quality of communication. The observer records the frequency of positive statements ("I really like how you did that, Sweetheart") and negative statements ("That was dumb!").

When Mr. and Mrs. Grumpy and their children Nasty and Hardly are given this assignment, they seem to take forever to come to a decision. Meanwhile, time is passing and behind the mirror, our trusty observer is growing bored. Despite the best of intentions, the observer unwittingly changes the standard by which she or he judges whether a comment is positive. Perhaps the observer loosens up and judges a comment as positive, which she or he would previously have judged as neutral. This is an instrumentation problem. It is a problem because we would like to be certain that any changes in the quality of communication are due to the program and not to an inconsistent (if well-meaning) observer. (The solution to this problem, by the way, is to have clear and specific operational definitions for the dependent variables—in this case, positive and negative communications—and to thoroughly train the observers.)

Statistical Regression. This phenomenon occurs with retesting of groups that have been selected because they have extreme scores—scores that are either higher than average or lower than average. This is not an uncommon situation. For instance, in school settings we often select those children with the lowest performance scores to participate in remedial programs.

Regression refers to the fact that when such a group is retested, the average score at the second testing is likely to be closer to the mean score for the entire group. In other words, if we selected a group of low-scoring students and retested them, at the retest their average score would be somewhat higher than the average at the first testing. Two important things to keep in mind are that (a) regression occurs only when groups are selected because they have extreme scores and (b) regression is apparent for the group. It will not necessarily happen to an individual score.

An example of a situation in which regression is an important factor is the evaluation of the Head Start program. Head Start is a learning enrichment program for preschoolers. Head Start programs select children from families in areas where children have shown poor school performance in the past. In that sense, participants in Head Start are chosen precisely because they are from groups that tend to have low scores on tests of academic achievement. Consider the following design:

$$O_1 \qquad X \qquad O_2$$

X is participation in the Head Start program and O_1 and O_2 are pre- and posttests of academic performance. Because a regression effect is very likely in this situation, this is a poor design. If there is an increase in academic achievement at O_2, it may be due to regression, even if the Head Start program had no effect. It is also possible that regression and the program each contributed to a part of the increase at O_2, but there is no way in this design to separate the effect of these two factors.

Regression effects may also occur when participants are retested on a test different from the original test. Campbell and Stanley (1963) give the following example:

> The principal who observes that his highest-IQ students tend to have less than the highest achievement-test scores (though quite high) and that his lowest-IQ students are usually not right at the bottom of the achievement-test heap (though quite low) would be guilty of the regression fallacy if he declared that his school is understimulating the brightest pupils and overworking the dullest. (p. 11)

This hypothetical situation can be diagrammed as follows:

Highest IQ scorers   have   somewhat below highest achievement scores
Lowest IQ scorers   have   somewhat above lowest achievement scores

A statistical explanation for why regression occurs is beyond the scope of this text. But we can get an intuitive idea of what happens. Unlike the physical sciences, in social work research most of the measurements are imprecise. In other words, every measurement or observed score is composed of a theoretical "true" component and an "error" component, which is usually a relatively small positive or negative number. In other words, we assume that most of the time we are able to measure concepts and variables accurately within a small margin of error—we may be a bit high or a bit low at each measurement. This can be expressed by the following equation:

$$X_{observed} = X_{true} + X_{error}$$

When we choose only study participants with extreme scores, we are choosing those scores that are most likely to have large error components. When that extreme scorer was measured, there happened to have been a large error component in the score. But because these errors are random, chances are that next time the score is measured, its error component won't be as large. In other words, the retest score will be closer to the mean. When this happens to a set of retest scores, the average score will be closer to the mean.

Selection. This is another factor of internal validity. Selection problems occur when there are comparison groups and when the participants in the groups differ on characteristics related to the dependent variable. When comparison groups are formed by random assignment of participants to groups and when they are large enough (as was illustrated in Chapter 6), the groups will probably not differ on such characteristics. But when comparison groups are formed in any other way, such differences are common. It is often hard to know exactly how the groups differ and whether these differences might affect the outcome of the study.

For example, the family planning study described earlier presented selection problems. Some selection factors (such as a higher proportion of older residents in City B) might certainly affect birthrates. Other ways in which the cities differed (say, differences in weather) may not. But it is always hard to tell. For instance, one of my more impertinent students suggested that in cold weather people spend more time indoors and are thus more likely to engage in reproductive activities. Thus a selection factor that at first may not appear to be a plausible alternative hypothesis may in fact be a plausible alternative to the experimental hypothesis (in this case, that differences in birthrates between the two cities were due to the different educational campaigns).

Here is another common selection problem. Let's say that we believe that much of current unemployment is due to the lack of skills of unemployed workers. We develop a 6-week job training program and hypothesize that the program will result in higher employment levels for participants. These participants are recruited by placing a big sign in the job service office advertising the program. All workers who telephone us requesting the program are run through the 1-month training. For a comparison group, we randomly select an equal number of unemployed persons from the state's unemployment files. The design looks like this:

Workers who request training	X	O

Workers drawn from files		O

To measure the effect of the program, we record the number of days of employment for workers in both groups for a period of 6 months after conclusion of the training. That is what the Os in the design represent. Suppose that at the end of the 6-month follow-up we find that employment rates are higher for the trained group. Do we have cause for celebration? Did the training program work?

By now, you have probably learned to be more cautious. We cannot tell if the program was effective in increasing employment of trained workers. The problem is that a factor of selection may be responsible for the difference in employment rates, even if the program had no effect. Remember how we recruited workers for the training group? Workers in the training group were volunteers: Among all unemployed workers, they were the only ones to take the initiative to respond to the ad. In this situation, and in many others, volunteers are very different from nonvolunteers. They are usually more motivated, better educated, and more skilled, and they are the most likely to succeed even if they receive no help. In our study, we were comparing these types of people with others who did not volunteer. Therefore, the trained group may have been more successful because of their personal characteristics, even if the training program was completely useless.

Mortality. This is the final factor of internal validity that must concern us. Mortality results when we have comparison groups and when participants drop out of these groups. Even if the groups were comparable before the dropout, once dropout occurs we can no longer be certain that the groups are comparable. If only a very few participants drop out of the study relative to the size of the groups, this is probably not a serious problem. Some researchers have argued that if equal numbers of participants drop out of comparison groups that mortality is not a problem, because equal dropout rates equalize the groups. This is not good thinking. For example, consider the following example.

Suppose that we again want to evaluate the effectiveness of job training on subsequent employment rates. But this time, we select a number of unemployed workers and randomly assign equal numbers to two comparison groups. Given the random assignment, we can feel comfortable in assuming that the groups are indeed comparable. (We'll assume that everyone we have selected agrees to participate.)

In the first group, we run the standard 1-month job training program. Now, it turns out that this is a very difficult program: It requires many hours of classroom contact, numerous take-home assignments, and so on. We wonder whether we would not be just as successful if the program was less difficult. So we design an "easy" job training program, with fewer classroom hours and more fun assignments. We run this program with the second group of unemployed workers:

$$R \quad X_{hard} \quad O$$
$$R \quad X_{easy} \quad O$$

TABLE 7.2 An Illustration of the Effects of Dropout on Comparison Groups

Hard program	→	Least-motivated workers drop out	→	A more motivated group remains
Easy program	→	Most-motivated workers drop out	→	A less motivated group remains

Alas, this time we find that a sizable (but equal) number of workers have dropped out of both groups. Because the number of dropouts was equal, can we still assume that the groups are comparable? If the remaining workers in the hard training group had higher employment rates, can we conclude that the hard program was more effective than the easy program?

Because equal numbers dropped out of both groups, it would be tempting to conclude that the dropout affected the groups equally and that we can confidently conclude that the hard program was better. But this may not be an accurate conclusion. The reason is that workers in the two groups may have dropped out for *different* reasons, leaving behind two groups that are no longer comparable.

Consider this: What if the *least-motivated* workers dropped out of the hard program (they felt it was too much work)? But the *most-motivated* dropped out of the easy program (they felt unstimulated). (Table 7.2 summarizes these events.) The end result would be that the workers left in the hard group were the most motivated, and the workers left in the easy group were the least motivated. If this were true, then the workers who received the hard program would have been more successful than those in the easy program, even if the two programs did not differ in effectiveness.

In any design in which there are comparison groups and in which one of the groups is asked to participate to a greater degree, participants may drop out of that group in response to the demands placed on them. This is a serious mortality problem because remaining participants are likely to be more motivated and therefore more successful, on the average, than participants in the other groups, where there has been less dropout. This situation is not uncommon in studies that attempt to show that some treatment or training program is successful.

One solution is to ensure that control groups (those that are used as a comparison so that we can show that the treated group did better) are as similar as possible to the treated group in terms of the time and effort required. For example, in the job training study mentioned earlier, workers in the control group may also be required to come to class. They may be asked to spend the same number of hours in class and to expend an effort similar to those in the treatment group. The only difference between the two groups would then be in the *content* of the training. Then, any subsequent difference in employment rates between the two groups will be due to the specific content of the training.

FACTORS OF EXTERNAL VALIDITY

As I said earlier, internal validity factors represent plausible alternative hypotheses that the observed effect was due to some factor other than the experimental treatment or independent variable. To the extent that we can rule out these factors, we can say that the study has internal validity: In this particular instance, with these participants, the observed effect was due to the experimental treatment.

When we begin to talk about the generalizability of the findings to other settings, individuals, independent variables, and dependent variables, we are talking about external validity. Just as it was the goal to rule out factors of internal validity as alternative hypotheses, it is also the goal to rule out factors of external validity in order that we may be able to generalize the findings. There are four such factors of external validity.

Interaction of Testing and X. This is the first factor of external validity. (It is also called the reactive effect of testing.) This factor is a problem when taking a pretest *changes* the way a participant responds to the independent variable. Sometimes this is referred to as the "sensitizing effect" of a test. An example of a sensitizing test might be a questionnaire to measure prejudice, administered before and after a human relations training course. The items on the questionnaire may stimulate study participants to think about issues that they have not considered before: What are their attitudes toward minorities? Do they feel that minorities are different from nonminorities and in what ways? Are their feelings and attitudes appropriate? Are they racist?

Given the provocative nature of a questionnaire on prejudice, it is not surprising that a pretested participant's response to human relations training may be different from that of a participant who has not been tested. If there is a decrease in prejudice after the training, we cannot be sure it was the training alone that was responsible for this change. If the pretest is in fact reactive, this may mean that only the combination of a sensitizing pretest followed by the training resulted in decreased prejudice. In other words, it may be that the training "works" only when preceded by a pretest.

The interaction of testing and X is a concern only when the testing is unexpected, is unusual, or causes participants to change their behavior or thinking in some way. In some settings, such as school systems, tests are so common that they are an expected part of the environment and are not likely to be sensitizing. In other words, there is usually little problem in using pretests in school settings. All other things being equal, the reactions of pretested students in one school system are likely to be indicative of the responses of students in other school systems, because testing is a common feature in all school settings. This supposes, of course, that the testing is of the type normally done in the schools. A highly unusual test may in fact sensitize a student so that his or her reaction to a subsequent treatment or program is changed.

The interaction of testing and X can also be illustrated by looking at a study to evaluate the effectiveness of a weight loss program. The study used the following design:

Group A:	R	O	X_1	O
Group B:	R	O	X_0	O
Group C:	R		X_1	O
Group D:	R		X_0	O

To evaluate the effectiveness of the program in helping clients to lose weight, individuals were randomly assigned to four comparison groups. Two of the groups participated in the weight loss program that taught skills such as monitoring, stimulus control, shaping, and breaking chains of behavior. Exposure to this program is indicated by X_1. The other two groups participated in group sessions of equal duration, but they did not receive training in any specific weight reduction procedures. These groups served as a control. Exposure to the control condition is indicated by X_0.

In this design, two of the groups were pretested and two were not. This design illustrates the effects of a sensitizing pretest. What might a sensitizing pretest look like?

Let's suppose that a highly sensitizing pretest was used in this study: At the start of the first class session each participant was asked to come to the front of the room and to step on a scale. The participant's weight was then

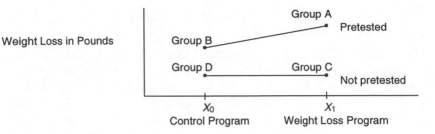

Figure 7.2. Illustration of a Reactive Pretest in a Study to Evaluate the Effectiveness of a Weight Reduction Training Program

called off in front of the group and recorded on the researcher's data sheet. Given the embarrassment that most overweight people feel about their condition, it is not surprising that this pretest would change the way participants respond to a weight loss program! In fact, peer pressure may be a strong motivator to work on weight reduction.

Figure 7.2 illustrates the outcome of the study, assuming that the weight loss program worked only for those participants who were subjected to the embarrassing pretest. Note that the only one of the four groups to show a weight loss was the group that received the weight loss program *and* was pretested.

Interaction of Selection and X. This is another factor of external validity. We say that there is an interaction of selection and *X* when the results are applicable only to the particular persons and the particular situation that we have studied. If we cannot generalize the findings to different persons, locations, and independent and dependent variables, then we have an interaction of selection and *X*. It should be obvious that we can almost never say that this factor is completely controlled. The extent to which we can generalize beyond the particulars of the study is partly a matter of judgment and partly a matter of collecting additional data from other settings, persons, and so on. A reasonable goal, however, might be to conduct the study so that the findings are generalizable to the greatest extent possible.

The interaction of selection and *X* is often a problem in demonstration studies. In this type of study, a group of researchers or planners receives a grant from a governmental or private source to set up a program that will "demonstrate" the effectiveness of a particular idea or service. For instance, a county public health department might set up a program of decentralized well-baby clinics as a demonstration of the effectiveness of accessible low-cost health services in reducing infant mortality in a particular area.

A problem often arises in that the researchers or planners have a vested interest in showing that their program works. So it is not uncommon for them to select demonstration sites that offer the best conditions for their program. For example, a county health department may set up its demonstration program in an area that has good public transportation, maximizing the likelihood that the well-baby clinics will be used. The limitation of this approach is that although funding agencies may be impressed with the results of the demonstration project, when the program is later applied to other areas or situations it does not work as well. If that is true, then what we have is clearly an interaction of selection and X: The result obtained in the demonstration project cannot necessarily be generalized to other settings.

Let's look at another example where we can again graphically illustrate the interaction of selection and X. Suppose that Dr. Feelgood, an internationally renowned therapist, has developed a goal-setting form (GSF). With the help of the GSF, the worker and client mutually agree on goals to be worked on in therapy. Dr. Feelgood claims that use of this form with clients will result in higher client satisfaction. Because Dr. Feelgood holds an exclusive distributorship and copyright for the GSF, he is understandably eager to get mental health centers across the country to use the GSF. But to do that, he must conduct research to substantiate his hypothesis. He decides to use the following research design:

$$R \quad X_{GSF} \quad O$$
$$R \qquad\qquad O$$

In this design, one group of therapists uses the GSF with clients, and another group does not. At the conclusion of therapy, all clients complete a questionnaire indicating their level of satisfaction with the services received. Dr. Feelgood predicts with great confidence that the clients who received the GSF will report higher levels of satisfaction.

Dr. Feelgood runs into a bit of a hitch. It seems that some of the agencies in town are not as excited as Dr. F. about the potential benefits of the GSF. (It also turns out that the directors of some of the older agencies remember that unfortunate scandal some years back in which Dr. Feelgood was charged with running bogus sex therapy-assertiveness training groups.) At any rate, as luck would have it, the first five agencies approached by Dr. F. as sites for his research project turn him down. "We've already got enough paperwork!" they say. Dr. F. dismisses these agencies as organizations that are not open to innovation. Finally, he finds an agency that is eager to cooperate. He carries out the study diagrammed earlier and confirms his hypothesis: Clients who receive the GSF are in fact more satisfied.

At this point, we should be suspicious of Dr. Feelgood's claims. He did show that the GSF increased client satisfaction, but that was true in only one agency. We know that agencies that cooperate with researchers are different from those that do not: They are likely to have staff who are more open to new ideas and more concerned about quality of service. We know furthermore that an interaction of selection and X is likely here. The GSF might not work in agencies that do not share these characteristics.

To illustrate the effect of an interaction of selection and X, we will have to imagine that we are able to replicate—that is, to repeat—the study in one of the uncooperative agencies. The design would look like this:

Cooperative agency:	R	X_{GSF}	O_1
	R		O_2
		- - - - - - - - - - - - - - - -	
Uncooperative agency:	R	X_{GSF}	O_3
	R		O_4

Figure 7.3 is a graph in which the four groups' average posttest satisfaction scores are plotted. This illustrates an interaction of selection and X because it shows that the GSF results in high client satisfaction only when used in a cooperative agency. In an uncooperative agency, where workers are perhaps less open to innovation and less concerned with the quality of service, the GSF appears to have no effect at all. In this case, as in other situations in which there is an interaction of selection and X, we cannot necessarily generalize the findings to other settings.

Reactive Arrangements. This is a third threat to external validity. Reactive arrangements become a concern when the setting of the study is artificial or different in some way from what would routinely be expected in that setting. Reactive arrangements limit generalizability of findings to the extent that the effects observed in the study would not occur in the real world, outside of the experimental situation.

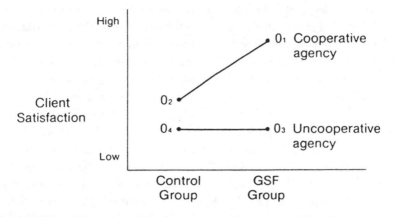

Figure 7.3. An Illustration of the Interaction of Selection and *X*: A Program Works Only in a Cooperative Agency

In the 1930s, a group of industrial researchers conducted a series of studies directed at improving the productivity of workers in the General Electric plant in a town called Hawthorne. The unexpected findings of these studies have been classic examples of effects due to reactive arrangements. In fact, this phenomenon is sometimes referred to as the "Hawthorne effect" (Homans, 1965).

In the Hawthorne studies, a group of researchers in their white lab coats descended on the plant and proceeded to carry out a number of experiments that were highly visible to the workers in the plant. In one of these studies, the researchers examined the effect of various changes in work conditions on the speed with which workers produced wire relay boards. They tried altering the size of the work group, lowering and raising the level of illumination in the work area, changing the size of the room, and so on.

To their surprise the Hawthorne researchers found that *any* change resulted in an increased output of relay boards. Even when the room lighting was lowered to a level that made it difficult to see how to solder the wires, output still went up. What had happened?

The researchers in this study failed to realize that they had created an artificial situation. The workers who were selected for study were aware of the study and of the fact that they were being closely monitored. They were probably flattered by the attention they received. The most likely explanation for their curious behavior is that the artificial nature of the situation prompted the workers to try to play the role of good participants. They tried to figure out what the researchers expected of them—in this case, it was increased productivity—and they acted accordingly. The problem, of course, was that the responses of these workers to the various changes in work conditions were not typical: They could not be generalized to other plants that were not being studied.

Reactive arrangements are likely to threaten the external validity of any study in which the study participants are placed in new or unusual situations—that is, situations that are not typical of the real world to which we would like to generalize the results. That sometimes happens in schools when a new program is introduced and creates an unusual situation, such as a lot of excitement on the part of teachers, a change in routine, or a new way to group students. In the laboratory experiments that are so often obligatory for undergraduate psychology students, reactive arrangements should always be taken into account. They are less likely to limit the generalizability of studies of motor reaction time or color perception. But the laboratory behavior of a student who is asked to problem solve, cooperate with others, or state an opinion may be very different from the behavior of that student in the real world.

Multiple-Treatment Interference. A final threat to external validity occurs when several treatments or interventions are administered in sequence to the same persons. The researcher's concern here is that the effects of prior interventions cannot be erased. Consider, for instance, a study to determine whether punishment or praise is more effective in getting emotionally disturbed children to comply with requests from a teacher. During an initial period, the child is punished for lack of compliance; during a later period, the punishment is dropped but the teacher provides praise whenever the child complies. The level of compliance is monitored throughout—perhaps by recording the proportion of teacher requests that are obeyed. The design looks like this:

$$O_1 \quad X_{\text{punish}} \quad O_2 \quad X_{\text{praise}} \quad O_3 \quad O_4$$

If the children's compliance increases at O_3 and O_4, we cannot say with confidence that this change was the result of praise. It may have been the result of the punishment: Perhaps it just took a while for the punishment to set in, a delayed effect. Or it may be that praise alone is not effective. Only when praise follows punishment is the contrast and relief great enough to make that praise effective in increasing compliance.

When there are more than two treatments—such as in a study to evaluate the effectiveness of five different drugs—it is even more difficult to determine which single intervention or combination or sequence of interventions is responsible for any observed changes. (In Chapter 9, we will learn how to use a different type of research design to evaluate the effects of multiple treatments.)

GROUP RESEARCH DESIGNS

Now that we understand the factors that pose threats to the internal and external validity of research designs, let us look at some common group designs.

1. THE ONE-SHOT CASE STUDY

$$X \quad O$$

This is the most rudimentary of the designs. In this design, a single individual, family, group, community, or other unit is studied at one point in time to determine the effect of a treatment or other independent variable. Campbell and Stanley (1963) argue that use of this design is hardly ever justified because it provides a total lack of control for all of the threats to internal and external validity that we have discussed.

For example, this design has been used to study the behavior of an autistic child. The purpose was to discover the effects of autism on the full range of child behaviors. But in this study, it would be impossible to determine if any observed behavior was a result of autism or whether it was specific to this particular child. For example, some aspects of the child's current behavior may be due to history, say, a medical emergency that occurred during the course of the child's development. We have no way of knowing if this child's behavior is typical of autistic behavior in other children, and hence there is no control for the interaction of selection and X.

The situation may be improved somewhat by studying several children rather than one child. We might even counter the effects of an interaction of selection and X by randomly choosing autistic children from a defined population of such children. But even so, this design leaves most factors of internal validity uncontrolled.

Campbell and Stanley (1963) note that the weakness of this design is that it fails to provide comparison. We have no point of reference. Because we study the unit or sample at only one point in time, we cannot compare an observation or test with subsequent tests. And there is no comparison group to serve as a benchmark. In this example, it would be impossible to identify the effects of autism unless we could compare the behavior of the study participant or participants to the behavior of normal children.

Campbell and Stanley note further that in one-shot case studies, a great deal of effort is often put into studying the single case intensively. Because this design provides virtually no conclusive evidence about the effects of X, they suggest that this effort would be better used in studying fewer details and in putting the effort saved into formation of a comparison group.

2. THE ONE-GROUP PRETEST-POSTTEST DESIGN

$$O_1 \quad X \quad O_2$$

This design represents an improvement over Design 1 because it provides at least a minimal point of comparison: The researcher can look at the difference in performance between the pretest and the posttest. Because this design is easy to implement—it does not require the recruitment and testing of a control group—it is used often. But it is a weak design because, like Design 1, it fails to rule out most of the threats to internal and external validity.

For example, assume that we used Design 2 to evaluate the job training program discussed earlier in this chapter. (That is, X represents a job training program, and the Os represent measures of the number of days of employment during specific time periods.) From that discussion, it should be easy to see that any change in employment rates between O_1 and O_2 may be due to a number of factors other than the training program itself. For example, they may be due to an improvement in the economy during the course of the study (history) or to the particular individuals selected for the program, who may not be typical of unemployed workers (interaction of selection and X).

There is another type of history (a factor of internal validity) that we have not discussed but that is likely, in some situations, to affect the results in a study using this design. These are effects of history due to *season* and *institutional event schedules.*

For example, imagine that you are director of the Student Counseling Center at Big Shot University. Big Shot University is a great place to be, but it is very competitive—so competitive, in fact, that many students are becoming ill due to stress. You decide it's time to do something about the problem.

You select a group of students to participate in a series of stress management workshops over a period of several weeks. A stress questionnaire is used to assess their level of stress before and after the program. To your dismay, you find that the level of stress has actually increased after the workshops.

Your program may have been a victim of institutional event schedule. Because the stress workshops took several weeks to carry out, it was necessary to pretest the students at the beginning of the semester. The posttest took place toward the end of the semester. As luck would have it, that happened to be the period immediately before final exams! The increase in stress may have been due to this factor, so it is impossible to come to any conclusion about the effectiveness of the stress management workshops on the level of student stress.

Seasonal events can also wreak havoc with Design 2. For instance, a study to evaluate the effectiveness of a program to treat depression will have to take account of anticipated variations in mood that are associated with the weather: In northern climates, people tend to be more depressed during the long, gray winter months.

Maturation, instrumentation, and regression may also present problems in interpreting the results of Design 2: There may be changes over time independent of X that affect the dependent variable, the calibration of the measuring instrument may change, or the participants in the study may have been selected because of their extreme scores. The fact that participants were pretested may also affect their performance on the posttest even if X had no effect. As we will see later, these weaknesses are inherent in any design that does not use a comparison group. When we include a comparison group in the design, we can distribute many of these internal validity factors equally among the groups. Then, any difference between the groups must be due to X rather than to these factors.

One way in which this design differs from the one-shot case study is that this design employs a pretest. Therefore, the two factors of testing (internal validity) and the interaction of testing and X (external validity) may be of concern. For example, if X is a reading improvement program and the Os represent administration of reading tests, we would expect some improvement on the posttest even if the program had no effect. That improvement would be the result of having had some practice in taking the test earlier. This design does not allow us to separate any improvement due to the program from the effects of testing. This makes it difficult to interpret the findings.

An interaction of testing and X is of concern if the testing is novel or unusual. Suppose that we used Design 2 to evaluate the effect of a teacher training program on the classroom performance of high school teachers. A common method for judging teacher performance is to have the school principal or some other important person observe a class session. The Os in the design may represent such an observation. But as any high school student who has seen his teacher develop a sudden burst of motivation on teacher evaluation day knows, classroom observation is a reactive measurement. The teacher's performance under observation may not be typical of that teacher's day-to-day classroom performance. Therefore, any effects of a training program may not apply beyond the observation days.

3. THE STATIC GROUP COMPARISON

$$X \qquad O_1$$
$$\text{-----------}$$
$$O_2$$

In this design, a group that has experienced X is compared with one that has not. The two groups may be already formed (such as two classrooms), or they may be self-selected groups (such as voters and nonvoters). The static group comparison represents a substantial improvement over the first two designs because of the introduction of a comparison group. There is now a benchmark (control group) against which to compare the performance of the experimental group.

The factor of internal validity that is of greatest concern in this design is selection. Remember, the groups in this design are not formed by random assignment, a procedure that tends to distribute all participant characteristics equally among comparison groups. Where we have groups that were not formed by random assignment, we cannot be sure that the groups were truly equivalent. This is a problem because any difference between O_1 and O_2 cannot be attributed solely to X; the two groups differed in ways that affected the dependent variable.

Imagine that X is a program to improve the math skills of third graders. In this design, the program is run in Classroom A, and Classroom B serves as a control. The problem is that a difference in math performance between the two classes may be due to differences between the classes—for example, the children in Classroom A may be brighter, or the teacher may be more enthusiastic about the program. Any difference in math performance between the two groups may be due to these selection differences, to the program, or to a combination of the two.

Mortality can be another serious limitation of this design. In many studies, participants who receive the *X* are called on to make a greater effort than those in the control group—for example, they may have to participate in a training program that requires a lot of work. In such situations, the least-motivated participants will tend to drop out of the experimental group, leaving behind an experimental group that is more highly motivated, on average, than the control group. In the earlier discussion of the job training program, we saw how this causes a bias in favor of finding that the program was successful, even if it was not.

The absence of pretests in this design has advantages and disadvantages. A disadvantage is that without pretests we have no check as to whether the groups are really similar on the dependent variable. If we measure IQ level after some intervention, it would be nice to know that the pretest IQ levels of the two groups were not significantly different. If they were, we could have more confidence in the findings. It is not always possible, however, to include a pretest. The data may not be available, or we may not have the time or money to do more than one testing. In some situations, it makes no sense to do a pretest. This was true in Dr. Feelgood's study on client satisfaction with services (see Figure 7.3). The client satisfaction measure could be given only after the client received the service that was being evaluated.

An advantage of not pretesting is that the interaction of testing and *X* is ruled out as a source of bias in the design. If the testing process is reactive (such as with classroom observations), then the absence of pretests allows us to generalize the findings to groups that are not normally pretested.

4. THE NONEQUIVALENT CONTROL GROUP DESIGN

$$O \quad X \quad O$$
$$\text{-----------}$$
$$O \qquad\quad O$$

This design is equivalent to the static group comparison, with the addition of pretests. The inclusion of a comparison group that is evaluated at the same time as the experimental group adds to the strength of the design. The two groups in Design 4 may be already formed groups, such as two school classrooms. Or the groups may be self-selected. For example, the experimental group may be composed of participants who sought the services of an agency, and the control group may be selected from among those who did not seek services.

It is important to remember that the groups in this design are not formed by random assignment. This means that we still cannot rule out the possibility that important differences exist between the groups that might affect the results. In this design, however, we have at least a rough estimate of comparability in that we are able to compare pretest performance of the two groups.

In group designs in which we use pretests, it is customary to run statistical tests between the groups to see if they differ on the dependent variable (say, some measure of performance) and on other variables that might affect the dependent variable (say, sex, race, or income). As long as these tests indicate no significant differences, we have some assurance that the groups are equivalent. Nevertheless, it is important to be vigilant for differences between the groups that may influence the results. For example, as we saw earlier, if volunteers are recruited for the experimental group and nonvolunteers for the control group, this selection factor may invalidate the results.

A better method for achieving equivalent comparison groups is to form these groups through random assignment. But this is often impossible. For example, if we want to study differences between men and women or between blue-collar and white-collar workers, we are not able to assign individuals to one or the other of these groups. (For this reason, Design 4 is a nonexperimental design.) In such situations, Design 4 is an excellent alternative to an experimental design using groups formed by random assignment.

Because we have a simultaneous comparison in this design, most of the sources of internal validity are ruled out as possible explanations for the findings. It is possible, but unlikely, that effects of maturation, history, testing, or instrumentation would be a problem. This is because any effect of these factors in one group is likely to be equivalent in the other group. For example, if pretesting leads participants to do a bit better on the posttest, this will be equally true for participants in both groups. Any difference between the groups, then, cannot be attributed to having taken a pretest. In other words, control group designs *control* for factors of internal validity.

We should, however, note one type of history that may not be controlled, even when we have a comparison group. This factor is called *intrasession history*. It refers to any event that occurs in one group but not in the other. For example, in the stress management training study at Big Shot University, one of the groups could have been exposed (inadvertently) to a fire drill during the training or the testing. This factor of intrasession history represents a way in which the comparison groups differed (assuming that the control participants were in another building and did not experience the fire drill). In general, it should be possible to at least monitor such instances. It is also important to make every effort to expose comparison groups to conditions that are as similar as possible, with the exception of the treatment or independent variable.

Regression may be a problem in a design with two comparison groups but only if one group is selected because of its extreme scores. For example, if we study the effect of a training program on low-achievement children compared with average achievers, we should expect that at least part of the improvement of the low achievers on the posttest will be due to regression. To avoid this problem, it is best to use one of the experimental designs described next. In these designs, comparison groups are formed by random assignment so that extreme scorers, and hence regression effects, are distributed equally among the groups. Any difference between the groups, then, could not be due to regression.

The following designs—5, 6, and 7—are true experimental designs.

5. PRETEST-POSTTEST CONTROL GROUP DESIGN

$$R \quad O \quad X \quad O$$
$$R \quad O \quad \quad O$$

6. SOLOMON FOUR-GROUP DESIGN

$$R \quad O \quad X \quad O$$
$$R \quad O \quad \quad O$$
$$R \quad \quad X \quad O$$
$$R \quad \quad \quad O$$

7. POSTTEST-ONLY CONTROL GROUP DESIGN

$$R \quad X \quad O$$
$$R \quad \quad O$$

The defining characteristic of Designs 5 through 7 is that they all use groups formed by random assignment. As we have said before, this is the best way to ensure that comparison groups are equivalent, although it is not a guarantee. When using Design 5, we should compare the pretest scores of the groups as an additional check. In any situation in which comparison groups are used, we can also compare the groups on demographic variables for which we have data: sex, age, race, and so on. The results of the study must be tempered by any differences found between the groups.

All three of these designs generally control for all factors of internal validity. This is a result of using groups formed by random assignment and of ensuring that the groups are equivalent in all ways except for exposure to the independent variable in the experimental groups. In this situation, any factor of internal validity that is operative affects the comparison groups equally. Therefore, any difference between the groups cannot be due to these factors.

We should pause for a moment to consider the meaning of the statement, "Experimental designs control for factors of internal validity." By this, we do not mean that these factors are magically erased. For example, in the study of birth control, we have no way to eliminate events of history, such as an economic depression or a new law that makes it difficult to obtain contraceptives over the counter. What we *can* do is to use an experimental design that distributes the impact of these factors equally among the comparison groups. Then any observed difference between groups cannot be due to these factors. We say they are controlled. What we have done is to rule out plausible alternative hypotheses—hypotheses alternative to the experimental hypothesis. (The experimental hypothesis, you will remember, is that the treatment or independent variable is responsible for the observed difference.)

Despite the excellent control these designs provide for internal validity, we cannot blindly assume that all factors are controlled each time we use one of these designs. For example, intrasession history may not be controlled if one, but not another, group is exposed to an event such as a fire drill or an accident.

If participants drop out of the study, we may also have a mortality problem. As mentioned earlier, this may be a problem even if equal numbers of persons drop out of each group, because dropout may occur for different reasons in different groups. Then, the groups that remain may be different in important ways. Because dropout is a common problem in research studies, it is useful to suggest solutions to this problem.

Campbell and Stanley (1963) suggest that if participants drop out of the treatment, the researcher should still use the data of all participants (including the dropouts) on both the pretest and the posttest. This will bias the results in a conservative direction: That is, by "weakening" the effect of the treatment, we will make it less likely that the results will show that the treatment had its intended effect. If, despite this conservative bias, the data show that the treatment worked, we can be confident of the validity of that finding.

This is certainly a valid solution. In my experience, however, when participants drop out of a treatment or intervention, they are rarely available to take the posttest. We are left with the problem of missing data. There are statistical procedures available to handle missing data problems. Perhaps the most common is the "replacement with means" method. In this method, each missing score is replaced by the average score on that variable for all available scores. In other words, the researcher makes the assumption that participants who were not measured would have gotten average scores had they been around to be measured.

This is not a good solution, however, because we may not be justified in assuming that the dropouts were "average." There are also statistical problems that are beyond the scope of this book. There really is no good after-the-fact solution to the problem of missing data. There are, however, ways to *prevent* the problem. As in so many other endeavors, prevention is the best solution.

If the study requires attendance at treatment and testing sessions, we can provide incentives for participants to show up. I was part of a research and training team involved in evaluating interpersonal skill development groups. We required a cash deposit from each person who signed up to participate in the 6-week group sessions. A portion was refunded if the participant attended the treatment sessions, with a larger amount refunded if all sessions were attended. Additional portions of the deposit were refunded for participating in the posttest assessment (immediately following treatment) and in the follow-up assessment (3 to 6 months after training). The participant could regain the entire deposit by attending all treatment and evaluation sessions. In addition, we made each session attractive to participants by providing comfortable furnishings and refreshments.

In longitudinal studies, in which participants must be followed and measured over a long period of time, mortality is a particularly crucial issue. Marriage and change of name, change of phone numbers, and moving often make it difficult to locate participants. A common procedure to help in locating participants is to ask them at the beginning of the study to provide the names, addresses, and phone numbers of two adults who are likely to know where they can be reached.

Another important issue in designs involving more than one group concerns the events occurring in the control group. In the notation, a blank space appears in the control groups during the time when the experimental groups are experiencing the X. This is a bit misleading. As we have seen, it is important that comparison groups be as similar as possible with the exception of the treatment or independent variable. So if we want to know if the specific content of the experimental treatment leads to the desired change, we must make sure that the control participants receive a control "treatment" that takes as much effort and arouses as much expectation of improvement as the experimental treatment. Then, any difference between groups must be due to the specific treatment and not to the fact that experimental participants worked hard, that they expected to change, or that they merely had contact with a helper.

This is why medical researchers use a sugar placebo when evaluating the effectiveness of a drug. The effectiveness of any drug may be because the patient receiving it believed that it worked. When we give a placebo drug to participants in the control group, we are controlling for the expectancy effect. We compare the result in the experimental group (patients who received the real drug) with the result in the control group (patients who received the sugar pill). Assuming that the drug worked, the difference represents the effectiveness of the drug above and beyond that due to the mere fact of expecting to benefit or getting attention from a doctor.

The point of all this is to serve as a reminder that although the notation makes it appear that nothing is happening to control group participants during the treatment period, that is never the case. In the experiments, it is important to control for attention and effort by providing control participants with an experience comparable to experimental participants—with the exception of the treatment itself.

For example, suppose we wanted to study the effectiveness of a film in reducing prejudice. We could use Design 5. Employing a questionnaire, we would measure level of prejudice before and after the film. The experimental participants would, of course, see the antiprejudice film. The control participants should be exposed to a similar experience without the specific antiprejudice content. We need to control for the effect that seeing a film—any film—might have on responses to the questionnaire. So although the experimental participants are seeing the antiprejudice film, control participants would be viewing a film of approximately equal length, on a neutral topic, not related to prejudice.

Another example of the use of an appropriate control group comes from a study conducted by the Benjamin Rose Institute in Cleveland in the mid-1960s. These researchers developed an intensive casework program designed to improve or maintain the functioning of frail elderly people who were no longer competent to care for themselves (Blenkner et al., 1971).

Using Design 5, the researchers randomly assigned clients to two groups: The experimental group received the intensive casework program that included counseling, financial assistance, guardianship, and a number of other interventions. In deciding how to deal with the control group, the researchers realized that it would be unfair to compare their program with one in which clients received no services at all. Many of the frail elderly receive at least some services—perhaps a visiting nurse or some financial assistance. So to show that their program worked, they knew they had to compare it with what was normally available to the frail elderly in that community. Therefore, in the control group, clients continued to receive the services that they normally would have received had they not been selected for study.

(As it turned out, the intensive casework program did not lead to much improvement over and beyond what clients could expect as the result of receiving regular services. Had the researchers used an artificially constructed control group in which no services were provided, we might have been led to conclude incorrectly that the intensive program had an effect when it did not. See the case study at the end of this chapter.)

So far we have discussed the internal validity of the three true experimental designs. What about their external validity? To the extent that the participants in any of these designs are not typical of the population to which we want to generalize the findings, the interaction of selection and X is not controlled. Controlling for this factor depends on obtaining a representative sample. To the extent that a study using one of these designs creates an atypical situation that makes participants respond to the treatment in a way that they would not if they were not being studied, reactive arrangements are not controlled. The solution is to study the effect of the treatment in as naturalistic a setting as possible.

Design 5 is the only one of the three designs that will fail to control for the interaction of testing and X when the pretest is sensitizing—that is, when it changes the way participants respond to the treatment or independent variable. If the testing procedure is sensitizing and we would like to generalize the findings to the world at large (where pretests are not used), then Designs 6 and 7 are preferable.

Let us return, for example, to the evaluation of the teacher training program in which we measure the teacher's classroom performance by sending the principal in to observe the teacher's instruction. We want to evaluate how effective the program is in producing better teachers without having to limit our conclusions to situations in which teachers are evaluated in this manner.

Does the training program work even if we don't send the principal in to observe?

Although Design 7 looks sparse, it is actually a powerful design. It uses comparison groups formed by random assignment, and it resolves the problem of sensitizing pretests by avoiding them. This design, however, should be used only where there can be some assurance that the comparison groups are equivalent. If the experimental and control groups of teachers differ in level of competence, enthusiasm, or years of experience, it will not be clear whether the results are due to these factors, to the program, or to their combination.

Design 6, the Solomon four-group design, might be used in its place. Not only does this design control for the interaction of testing and X, it actually allows us to measure the influence, if any, of the pretest on the results. We do this by comparing the results for the pretested (first two) groups with the results for the unpretested (second two) groups. This design is actually a combination of Designs 5 and 7, so it enables us to repeat or replicate our finding: Any difference in performance as a result of treatment should be evident in the difference between the first two groups and in the difference between the second two groups.

A disadvantage of this design is that because it uses four groups, it requires a greater number of participants. If a limited number of participants is available, we may want to devise a less sensitizing test so that we can use Design 5, the pretest-posttest control group design. For example, where student evaluations are routinely used, we may want to measure teacher performance in this way rather than by sending the school principal in for a classroom observation. Of course, when the testing procedure is not likely to be sensitizing, Design 5 is the design of choice.

SUMMARY

Research designs are plans. They specify the sequencing and arrangement of independent and dependent variables in research studies. The purpose of research design is to help establish that an independent variable or variables or a treatment is responsible for some observed effect, such as client improvement. This is the experimental hypothesis.

Research designs are helpful in that they assist in eliminating plausible alternative hypotheses—that is, hypotheses that factors other than the independent variable or treatment are responsible for the observed effect. These factors fall into two categories: those associated with internal validity and those associated with external validity.

Internal validity issues concern the extent to which we can conclude that the treatment or independent variable was indeed responsible for the observed effect in the study: for the participants, settings, and independent variables employed in this particular instance. External validity concerns the extent to which the observed findings can be generalized to other participants, settings, treatments, and measures. A number of research designs, varying in their ability to control for factors of internal and external validity, are available for the researcher's use.

CASE STUDY

This was one of the earliest social work research studies to use an experimental design (Blenkner et al., 1971). Even today, more than two decades later, it stands as an example of a carefully designed and well-controlled research study. It became somewhat infamous because of a surprising and disturbing finding that will be presented at the end of this case study.

The research was conducted in the mid-1960s in Cleveland, Ohio. It was sponsored by the Benjamin Rose Institute, a large and well-known agency that serves the elderly. Margaret Blenkner and her colleagues had become aware of a critical problem among the elderly living in the community. Social workers had been finding an increasing number of very old persons who were no longer able to care for themselves but who had no one else to help. Some of these older people suffered from physical disabilities that hampered their ability to prepare food, to groom, and to do other tasks of daily living. Others were mentally incompetent. Their disorientation or confusion made them a danger to themselves and sometimes to others.

The Benjamin Rose Institute believed that a program of intensive casework services could benefit these older persons, whom they called "elderly protectives." So they designed such a program and set out to demonstrate its usefulness. To do that, they chose to use a variation of Design 5, the pretest-posttest control group design. By comparing elderly protectives who received the intensive service with those who did not, they hoped to show that their program was helpful to the elderly.

The researchers decided to include in their sample elderly protectives who were referred to the Benjamin Rose Institute by one of 13 community agencies. In a typical case, an elderly protective would come to the attention of the Visiting Nurse Association or the public aid department, and these agencies contacted the Institute for help. Over a 12-month period from June 1964 to May 1965, 164 elderly protectives were recruited. As each case folder came into the Institute, it was randomly assigned to one of two groups.

Protectives in the service (experimental) group received a specially designed program of intensive services for a period of 1 year from their referral. Those assigned to the control group continued to receive only those services normally available in the community.

Both groups were carefully evaluated at the time of referral and again 1 year later. The researchers conducted intensive interviews with protectives and their collaterals. (A *collateral* was defined as the person most closely involved with the protective, usually a friend, relative, or neighbor.) They interviewed staff members of the agencies that had referred the protective. They observed and rated the quality of the protective's physical environment, such as the adequacy of housing. They administered mental status tests to protectives to determine their orientation and judgment. Finally, they kept track of how long each protective lived (this variable was called *survival*) and whether the protective was placed in an institution (*institutionalization*). On these last two variables, the researchers followed up for 7 years to see which protectives had survived and which ones had been institutionalized.

The design can be summarized as follows:

$$R \quad O \quad X \quad O \quad O \quad O \quad O \quad O \quad O \quad O$$
$$R \quad O \qquad \quad O \quad O \quad O \quad O \quad O \quad O \quad O$$

This design illustrates an issue discussed earlier in this chapter. Although the notation makes it appear that nothing was happening to protectives in the control group during the demonstration year, that was clearly not the case. As we said, control participants continued to receive the services that were normally available to them. And after the demonstration year, the service protectives no longer received the intensive casework program. In other words, after the first year, both groups continued to receive some services. Didn't this make it difficult to show that the service program worked?

The answer is yes. But that wasn't necessarily a bad thing. It certainly would have been easier to show that the intensive service program worked if we compared it with a control group of elderly protectives who received no services whatsoever. But that really would not have been possible for ethical reasons. All of the protectives were in critical, life-threatening situations and had to be helped. It would not have been possible or ethical to ask the referring agencies to withdraw their services.

But there is another reason why using a control group that received some services is a good idea. It decreases the likelihood that the design will be limited by the interaction of selection and X. Remember, interaction of selection and X is a problem in which the results cannot be generalized beyond the particular events in the study. If we want to know if the program works in the real world, we need to use a real-world comparison in the design. It was more realistic to compare an intensive service program to a control program of limited services because in the real world, many frail elderly do receive at least limited services. Comparison with a totally unserved control group would have stacked the cards in the researchers' favor. It would leave open the possibility that even if the study found that the program worked, it might not be an improvement over what was already available in the community.

As it turned out, the service program did not work as well as the Benjamin Rose Institute had hoped. Although protectives in the service group did better in a couple of ways (for instance, their collaterals reported significantly less stress as a result of the program), for the most part the two groups did not differ. There were two very troubling differences, however. At every point over the 7-year follow-up, protectives in the service group were more likely to find themselves in a nursing home. More troubling still, they had a consistent pattern of early death. Those who received the intensive services died sooner than those who did not.

Because it includes a pretest, one of the advantages of the pretest-posttest control group design is that it allows the researcher to see if the comparison groups were similar at the start of the study (at least on the variables for which data are available). As we said in Chapter 6, groups formed by random assignment, as they were in this study, tend to be very similar.

But this study illustrated that this is not always the case. In an attempt to understand the troubling finding of early death, Berger and Piliavin (1976a, 1976b) reanalyzed the Benjamin Rose data. They found that, on the average, service participants were somewhat older than control participants. It *is* possible that this difference contributed to the earlier death of service participants.

It also appeared that the service participants were more debilitated: They had lower physical functioning and mental status scores on the pretest. It was not clear, however, if these two differences were real because a great deal of the pretest data on these variables were missing. Either they had not been collected or they were never recorded. As a result, the unhappy findings of this study remain clouded in mystery to this day.

DISCUSSION QUESTIONS

1. Group research designs are best presented using notation. In group research design notation, what do the following symbols represent?

    a. R
    b. *X*
    c. *O*
    d. A dashed line between groups

2. Provide a verbal description for each of the following designs:

    a.   *X   O*

    b.   *X   O*
            - - - - - - -
               O

    c.   *X   O   O   O   O*

    d.   R   *O*   *X*   *O*
            R   *O*   *O*
            - - - - - - - - - - - - - - -
            R   *O*   *X*   *O*
            R   *O*   *O*

3. For each of the designs in Question 2, provide an example of a study using that design. Describe the nature of the assessments and independent variables. Describe how the groups were formed or identified.

4. Define and give an example of each type of *internal validity* described in this chapter:

    a. History
    b. Maturation
    c. Testing
    d. Instrumentation
    e. Statistical regression
    f. Selection
    g. Mortality

5. Define and give an example of each type of *external validity* described in this chapter:

    a. Interaction of testing and *X*
    b. Interaction of selection and *X*
    c. Reactive arrangements
    d. Multiple treatment interference

6. Explain how experimental research designs "control for internal validity."

7. The one-shot case study is diagrammed as follows:

$$X \quad O$$

Why is this a poor design?

8. The static group comparison is diagrammed as follows:

$$X \quad O$$

$$O$$

Which of the following factors of *internal validity* is *not* of concern in this design? Explain why.

a. History
b. Maturation
c. Testing
d. Instrumentation
e. Statistical regression
f. Selection
g. Mortality

Which of the following factors of *external validity* is *not* of concern in this design? Explain why.

a. Interaction of testing and *X*
b. Interaction of selection and *X*
c. Reactive arrangements

9. The pretest-posttest control group design is diagrammed as follows:

$$R \quad O \quad X \quad O$$
$$R \quad O \quad \quad O$$

Which factors of internal and external validity *may not* be controlled in this design? Explain why.

SHORT ASSIGNMENT

1. Select a social problem area that is of interest to you. This might be child abuse, gang violence, the frail elderly, divorce, family discord, workplace stress, or any other problem area.

Choose one of the research designs discussed in this chapter. Design an intervention appropriate to your problem area. This might be a child abuse identification program, an early intervention program to curb gang violence, a homemaker program to prevent nursing home placement of the elderly, and so on.

For this study, answer the following questions:

a. What is (are) your X(s)?
b. How will you measure the dependent variable or variables (for example, by questionnaire, interview, or observation)?
c. For each factor of internal and external validity, state whether that factor is controlled, not controlled, or uncertain. Explain *why* and give an example of how that factor might affect the conclusions of the study.

NOTE

1. There is some disagreement in the literature as to whether longitudinal studies do indeed fail to show a decline in intelligence with age, which is apparent in cross-sectional studies. Botwinick (1978) argues that both types of research show a decline in intellectual abilities with age, although "longitudinal research tends to reflect lesser decline, starting later in life" (p. 225). Nevertheless, this example illustrates the importance of understanding research design.

FURTHER READING

Campbell, D. T., & Stanley, J. C. (1963). *Experimental and quasi-experimental designs for research*. Chicago: Rand McNally.

Rosenthal, R., & Rosnow, R. L. (1991). *Essentials of behavioral research: Methods and data analysis* (2nd ed.). New York: McGraw-Hill.

8 An Alternative to Group Research Designs

The Logic of Elaboration

A s we saw in the previous chapter, researchers use group research designs to determine if certain independent variables are related to certain dependent variables. (For example, a researcher might want to determine if clients who participated in a treatment group improved more than those who did not. The independent variable is the treatment; the dependent variable is a measure of improvement.)

EX POST FACTO RESEARCH

In an ideal situation, the researcher will be able to assign individuals or cases to comparison groups. This allows the researcher to rule out "competing" explanations for the results (see Chapter 7). Ideally, social scientists use group research designs for situations that involve relatively small samples, in which the design can be specified before the occurrence of the events under study. This practice is most common in psychology and in clinical social work.

It is not always possible, however, to specify a research design *before* individuals are exposed to the effects of various independent variables or life events. In many research situations, we have data on a large number of individuals (or cases)—but the research takes place long after the events under study. This type of research is called *ex post facto*. (Ex post facto means "done or made after something.")

For example, social work researchers may want to study how divorce affects men and women differently; or they may want to compare older persons currently living in their own homes with those living in residential care communities; or they may want to know how child-rearing practices differ among various ethnic groups. This type of ex post facto research is common among sociologists and those social workers who are interested in broad social questions. It is often associated with surveys.

Definition: A *survey* is a research study in which a large number of persons or other units respond to an interview or questionnaire. This may involve hundreds or thousands of individuals. Typically, researchers use surveys to study broad social phenomena, such as public opinion; differences between men and women; and differences among large groups of people.

Let's say that we want to study the relationship between education and attitudes toward social welfare programs, such as job training and well-baby clinics for low-income families. We might hypothesize that those who are better educated are more likely to hold favorable attitudes toward funding social welfare programs.

To test this hypothesis, we must use ex post facto research. That is, we enter this research situation after the fact, after levels of education are already determined in the real world. The task is to find people with various levels of education, representative of the educational levels in the population.

Because attitudes toward social welfare programs are a characteristic of a broad segment of the public, we will probably want to generalize the findings to a large group of people—perhaps all adults in one county, state, or region or in the entire country. We will therefore want to conduct a survey of at least several hundred people so that we obtain a representative sampling of differing educational levels and attitudes. This is an example of survey research using an ex post facto design.

In group research designs, we use a comparison group to determine if the observed relationship between the independent and dependent variable is real—that is, not caused by factors other than the independent variable. Ex post facto research does not provide us with such a simple device to determine if the observed relationship is real. Rather, in ex post facto studies, we can gather evidence to support this conclusion or to reject it. We do this by introducing additional variables into the data analysis to see how they affect the observed relationship between the independent and dependent variables of interest. The way in which these introduced variables or "test factors" affect the original relationship can then tell us if the observed relationship is real.

For example, suppose that we observe that frail older persons who are involved with their adult children (independent variable) enjoy greater life satisfaction (dependent variable). If this is a true relationship—that is, if being involved with adult children directly leads to greater life satisfaction—then we would expect this relationship to be strongest among those older persons who hold traditional family values, which stress the importance of ties to adult children. Those older persons who hold traditional values but who are not involved with children would be expected to have the lowest life satisfaction. This can be diagrammed as follows:

Among older persons with traditional family values	Involvement with children	→	Life satisfaction	(Stronger relationship)

In this group, those who are involved with children will have the highest life satisfaction, and those who are not will have the lowest.

Among older persons with weak family values	Involvement with children	→	Life satisfaction	(Weaker relationship)

In this group, involvement with children will not have as great an impact on life satisfaction.

In other words, we can confirm the original relationship (indicating that older persons involved with their adult children have higher life satisfaction) by introducing a third variable (type of family values) into the analysis. That third variable is called a *test factor*. The process of analyzing the relationship between two variables by introducing a test factor is called *elaboration*. In the rest of this chapter I will describe more specific elaboration analyses that are used to confirm, modify, or reject the conclusion that the relationship between two variables is real.

TYPES OF TWO-VARIABLE RELATIONSHIPS

Some social work research studies aim only to describe phenomena. For example, one social work researcher interviewed African American ministers to find out what they believed about the AIDS epidemic. Her purpose was merely to describe a set of beliefs and attitudes. She did not test hypotheses and did not look for relationships between variables. This is an example of *descriptive research.* This type of study is often used to explore a new area of inquiry where there is little theory or experience to predict how variables will affect one another. In descriptive research studies, there is no need to examine relationships between variables and hence no need for elaboration. (Descriptive research is discussed in more detail in Chapter 2.)

The goal of much social work research, however, goes beyond description. It aims to understand the "how" and "why" of social phenomena, to understand the laws or rules that govern human behavior. This is just another way of saying that social work research often aims to understand how different variables—such as age, race, income, and participation in a program—are *related* to one another.

Some variables are completely unrelated—that is, having information about one variable tells the researcher nothing about the other. For example, knowing a student's hair color is completely unrelated to the student's IQ score. The student's IQ score, however, is certainly related to school performance: Students with above-average IQs tend to show above-average school performance (as measured by achievement tests).

In a book on survey analysis, Rosenberg (1968) argues that there are three ways in which two variables may be related. In *symmetrical* relationships, neither variable influences the other. Neither variable causes the other. In *reciprocal* relationships, the two variables influence one another. It is impossible, however, to determine which came first. Finally, when one variable influences the other but not vice versa, the relationship is said to be *asymmetrical.* In asymmetrical relationships, it is possible to identify which variable came first—that is, to state that A influences B and not the other way around. The following discussion illustrates these three types of relationships.

Symmetrical Relationships. Psychologists have known for a long time that there is a positive relationship between palmar perspiration ("sweaty palms") and heart rate. A client with sweaty palms is likely to have an increased heart rate and vice versa. Sweaty palms do not cause an increase in heart rate nor do they trigger any physical events that would cause the heart rate to increase. Conversely, a rapid heart rate does not cause sweaty palms. The relationship between these variables is symmetrical because neither variable influences the other. Rather, they are both the result of an individual's level of anxiety. They are both indicators of anxiety.

There are many examples of symmetrical relationships in social work. For example, in countries with high rates of literacy, women have fewer children. Literacy does not cause lower fertility; it does not even lead women to use birth control. Rather, both literacy and small family size are characteristics of advanced development in a country. Both are influenced by common factors, such as rising economic expectations and adoption of modern attitudes.

Reciprocal Relationships. Rosenberg (1968) describes these relationships as having "alternating symmetry." That is, two variables alternately affect one another. A good example of this is the relationship between the temperature of a home's living room and its furnace thermostat. As the temperature drops below the thermostat setting, the furnace turns on, increasing the temperature. This in turn affects the thermostat, which instructs the furnace to turn off. This lowers the room temperature, which affects the thermostat, and so on. The relationship between Variable A (room temperature) and Variable B (the thermostat position—"on" or "off") is reciprocal.

Sociologists have shown that people who interact a great deal with one another also tend to like each other. This is another example of a reciprocal relationship. It would be impossible to determine the time order of these two variables. When people like each other, does that lead them to spend more time together? Or does spending time together lead people to like each other more? We can never say. Rather, liking another person and interacting with that person influence each other. The same can be said for the relationship between level of self-disclosure and the degree to which people report that they feel intimate with the other person. Self-disclosure begets intimacy and vice versa.

Asymmetrical Relationships. In these relationships, it is possible to tell which variable came first. As we saw in Chapter 2, the variable that is assumed to have occurred first is called the independent variable. In this sense, the first variable is responsible for the second (although we cannot always say that the first variable caused the second). In social work research, demographic variables or characteristics that are permanent or fixed—such as age, gender, race, and social class—are often the first variable in asymmetrical two-variable relationships. For example, age (first variable) is related to intelligence level (second variable)—intelligence increases with age and then levels off in young adulthood. Logically, the age variable had to come first, so this is clearly an example of an asymmetrical relationship. Other examples include the relationship between gender and family role (women are more likely to be caretakers) and the relationship between race and income (ethnic minorities tend to have lower incomes than Caucasians).

ELABORATION

As indicated earlier, elaboration is a way of analyzing survey data that helps us to determine the type of relationship between two variables that are related. We always begin by looking at the relationship between two variables—let us call this the "original relationship." Then we introduce a third variable that we think might tell us something about the original relationship. We call this third variable a test factor.

The process of elaboration can be illustrated by a recent social work study of older persons caring for a disabled spouse. In this study, the researcher examined the relationship between the level of caregiver burden (how difficult the caregiving was for the caregiver) and the caregivers' self-perceived health (poor or good).

The researcher began by looking at the original relationship between level of caregiver burden and the caregivers' self-perceived health:

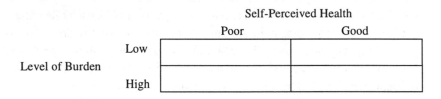

This relationship turned out to be asymmetrical: Caregivers who reported feeling high levels of burden were more likely to also report poor health.

The researcher then used elaboration to provide more information about this relationship—in other words, the researcher used elaboration to help understand the why and how of this relationship. In the literature on caregiving, the caregiver's gender—male or female—is one of the most important variables in understanding how people cope with the caregiver role. For example, families may expect more caregiving from women, and women may be more subject to stress than men because of competing demands from other family members. Therefore, the researcher used gender as a test factor to understand the original relationship between caregiver burden and perceived health of the caregiver. How was this done?

The original relationship was elaborated by examining the original relationship between the two variables *under each level* of the test factor. In other words, the researcher looked at the relationship between caregiver burden and perceived health separately for men and for women:

For Male Caregivers Only

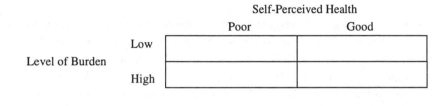

For Female Caregivers Only

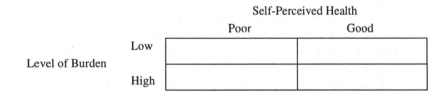

In this analysis, we say that the researcher "controlled" for the test factor (gender) or that the researcher "held the test factor constant." By doing so, the researcher could see if the original relationship between burden and health held true for both male and female caregivers, if it was affected differently for male and female caregivers, or if it disappeared entirely—in which case, the original relationship was due to some other variable.[1]

In a nutshell, this is the elaboration process used to understand the nature of two-variable relationships. To summarize, in elaboration, the researcher must do the following:

1. Observe an original relationship between two variables.

2. Select a test factor—a third variable that is likely to tell us more about the original relationship.
3. Repeat the analysis by looking at the original relationship separately for each level of the test factor. That is, the researcher controls for the test factor.

Rosenberg (1968) identified several types of test factors (third variables) that affect the original relationship in a different way. The following discussion presents procedures for identifying three types of test factors: extraneous, intervening, and antecedent.

EXTRANEOUS VARIABLES

During the War on Poverty in the 1960s, many policymakers and social workers believed that welfare clients could benefit from individual counseling. It was believed that regular counseling with a social worker would help those on public assistance to overcome their social and personal problems so that they would become better parents and be less dependent on assistance. With the help of federal funding, agencies across the nation offered individual casework or counseling to welfare recipients. These clients tended to have a great deal of contact with their public assistance agencies. Those clients who continued to receive only income maintenance services tended to have limited contact with agency social workers.

Imagine that a hypothetical group of researchers decided to survey public assistance agencies across the country to determine if counseling services had a beneficial effect on clients. There are many ways in which the researchers might have measured the "success" of the counseling intervention. In this example, the researchers chose to ask clients to respond to the question, "How would you rate the effectiveness of your social worker?" Table 8.1 illustrates the initial finding: Clients who received counseling were more likely than clients who received only income maintenance services to rate their social worker as effective.

In this example, the independent variable (type of service) seems to be related to the dependent variable (clients' rating of worker effectiveness). This is the original relationship tested in this study. Clients who receive counseling are more likely than those who receive income maintenance services only to rate their welfare worker as effective.

It would be tempting to conclude that the type of service is related to clients' perceptions about their workers' effectiveness. But is this relationship real? Or might it be due to another factor?

TABLE 8.1 Percentage of Workers Rated by Clients as Effective[a]

	Type of Service	
	Counseling	*Income Maintenance*
Percentage of workers rated effective	44 (390)	32 (282)
Total N	(885)	(869)

NOTE: This table shows the original relationship between the type of service received (independent variable) and clients' ratings of worker effectiveness (dependent variable).
a. Number of clients in parentheses.

Remember that clients who received counseling generally had a greater number of contacts with the public assistance agency than did those who received income maintenance services only. Was it possible that the number of contacts with the agency affected clients' ratings of the effectiveness of their social workers? The researchers decided to test this notion using the process of elaboration, described earlier.

The researchers had already carried out the first two steps: (a) They examined the original relationship between the type of service clients received and their ratings of worker effectiveness. They found a strong relationship: Clients who received counseling were more likely to rate their social workers as effective. (b) To see if the original relationship was real, they selected a test factor—a third variable that might affect the original relationship. That variable was the number of contacts that the client had with the agency.

In the third step, the researchers examined the original relationship separately for each level of the test factor. That is, they examined the relationship between type of service and client rating of workers separately for those clients who had a lot of contact with the agency and for those who had only minimal contact. This analysis is summarized in Table 8.2.

This elaboration of the original relationship between type of service and client ratings was very revealing. From the results in Table 8.2, the researchers concluded that the original relationship was not real—it was *spurious*. There is no inherent connection between the type of service that clients received and how they perceived their workers. It only appeared that counseling clients rated their workers as more effective because these clients had a lot of contact with the agency. That is, the original relationship appeared to be asymmetrical, but it was in fact symmetrical—type of service and client ratings did not influence one another.

TABLE 8.2 Percentage of Workers Rated by Counseling Versus Income Maintenance Clients as Effective, Controlling for Number of Contacts With the Agency[a]

	Type of Service			
	Counseling		Income Maintenance	
	Over 5 Contacts	*5 or Fewer Contacts*	*Over 5 Contacts*	*5 or Fewer Contacts*
Percentage of workers rated effective	52 (326)	25 (65)	52 (125)	25 (157)
Total *N*	(627)	(260)	(240)	(628)

NOTE: This table shows that the original relationship between type of service (independent variable) and clients' ratings of worker effectiveness (dependent variable) *disappears* when controlling for number of contacts with the agency (extraneous variable).
a. Number of clients in parenthesis.

We can see in Table 8.2 that if we look at clients with equal amounts of agency contact, *there is no difference* in client ratings between those who received counseling and those who did not. (When we compare clients who received the two types of service and those who have similar amounts of contact with the agency, the difference between ratings of clients who received the two types of service disappears. For example, among clients with over five agency contacts, a little over half in *both* service groups rated their social worker as effective.)

In the preceding example, the test factor—number of agency contacts—is said to be an *extraneous variable.*

Definitions: In an *elaboration* of the original relationship between an independent variable (IV) and a dependent variable (DV), we hold the test factor constant—that is, we control for the test factor. If the relationship between the IV and DV disappears, we conclude that the test factor was an extraneous variable, and we say that the original relationship was spurious.

This type of elaboration analysis is common in survey studies. Often, many apparent relationships between two variables are due to the effect of a third or extraneous variable. In the preceding example, it appeared that clients who received counseling were more likely to rate their workers as effective. In fact, it only appeared that way because clients who received counseling had greater contact with their agencies. Apparently, it was the effect of greater agency contact—rather than counseling—that led to clients' perceptions of their workers as effective. This finding is important. It suggests that rather than invest in expensive counseling services, public assistance agencies should attend to the amount of time and attention devoted to clients.

Rosenberg (1968) summarized the procedure for testing to determine if an original relationship between two variables is real or if it is due to extraneous variables:

1. Examine the original relationship between an IV and a DV.
2. Introduce a test factor only if there is a theoretical or empirical reason to believe that it may account for the original relationship.
3. For the test factor to be an extraneous variable, it must be related to both the IV and DV.
4. When the extraneous variable is controlled, the original relationship between the IV and DV disappears.
5. The researcher can introduce several test factors. Each time the researcher controls for a test factor and the original relationship remains, she or he can be more confident that the original relationship is real. Conversely, each time a test factor diminishes or eliminates the original relationship, the researcher must look to other variables to explain the original relationship. (pp. 27-40)

INTERVENING VARIABLES

In the preceding example, the test factor was found to be an extraneous variable. The association between the independent variable and the dependent variable was due entirely to the fact that they were both related to the extraneous variable:

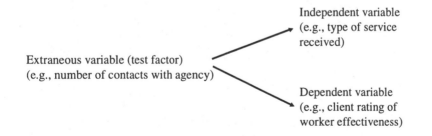

In some cases, when the original relationship between the independent variable and the dependent variable is controlled for by a test factor, that test factor turns out to be an *intervening variable.*

Definition: An *intervening variable* is a test factor that intervenes between the independent variable and the dependent variable:

Independent Variable   →   Intervening Variable   →   Dependent Variable

For example, a child welfare worker observed that some children in a group home seemed to have good social skills. They were better able than their peers to initiate interactions with other children, handle conflicts, and respond appropriately to authority figures, such as the group home managers. After further observation, the worker learned that these "high-skill" children grew up in large families. Presumably, the experience they gained in learning to get along with others in their large families of origin helped them to develop good social skills, which they later put to use in their group home. This three-variable relationship can be diagrammed as follows:

Independent Variable   →   *Intervening Variable*   →   *Dependent Variable*
Size of family of origin   Level of experience in   Level of social skills
                                  interacting with others   in group home

How does an intervening variable differ from an extraneous variable? For extraneous variables, the independent and dependent variables do not influence one another—they are symmetrical. For intervening variables, the independent variable does influence the dependent variable by influencing the intervening variable, which then influences the dependent variable. In other words, an intervening variable requires the presence of three asymmetrical relationships:

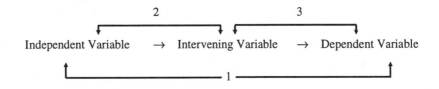

The procedure for intervening variable analysis is the same as that for extraneous variables:

1. The intervening variable is related to both the IV and DV.
2. The researcher begins by examining the original relationship between the IV and the DV.

   3. When the researcher examines the original relationship between the IV and DV, controlling for the intervening variable, the original relationship vanishes.

This procedure is illustrated in the following example. In the 1970s, many states began to release large numbers of hospitalized psychiatric patients into the community. As a result, there were a number of research studies concerned with the results of deinstitutionalization. Many younger psychiatric patients simply returned to live with parents, others were placed in group homes, and still others found themselves living on the streets or in single-room occupancy hotels.

One of the more interesting findings of these studies had to do with the effect on patients of returning to live with parents. Although one might think that living with parents would be beneficial to patients, the opposite often proved to be the case. Many of these patients had found their way into hospitals because the stress they experienced in their homes was very high and resulted in a worsening of their mental health problems. This is not to say that families caused mental illness in their children but, rather, that for a young, chronically mentally ill adult, living with family can lead to stress, which can, in turn, worsen the psychiatric illness. This is an example of an intervening variable relationship. It can be diagrammed as follows:

Independent Variable	→	*Intervening Variable*	→	*Dependent Variable*
Living arrangement		Level of stress		Rehospitalization
(with or without				(percentage
parents)				rehospitalized)

If this model is accurate, living with parents leads to stress, which leads in turn to rehospitalization. Stress is related to both the independent and dependent variables, and it intervenes between them.

Applying the elaboration process, researchers began by looking at the original relationship, that between the independent variable and the dependent variable. This is summarized in Table 8.3.

Table 8.3 indicates that patients who were living with parents were almost three times as likely to be rehospitalized, compared with patients who were not living with parents. This represents a strong relationship between the independent variable (living arrangements) and the dependent variable (rehospitalization).

In the next step of the elaboration process, the researchers test the hypothesis that the level of stress while living in the community was an intervening

TABLE 8.3 Effect of Living Arrangement on Rehospitalization[a]

	Living Arrangement	
	Living With Parents	Living Without Parents
Percentage rehospitalized	3.2 (141)	1.2 (89)
Total N	(4,417)	(7,180)

NOTE: This table shows the original relationship between living arrangement (independent variable) and rehospitalization (dependent variable).
a. Number of clients in parentheses.

TABLE 8.4 Effect of Living Arrangements on Rehospitalization, Controlling for Stress Level[a]

	High Stress		Low Stress	
	Living With Parents	Living Without Parents	Living With Parents	Living Without Parents
Percentage rehospitalized	3.5 (135)	2.8 (27)	1.1 (6)	1.0 (62)
Total N	(3,862)	(974)	(555)	(6,206)

NOTE: This table shows that the original relationship between living arrangements (independent variable) and rehospitalization (dependent variable) *disappears* when controlling for level of stress (intervening variable).
a. Number of clients in parentheses.

variable that was responsible for the original relationship. This analysis is summarized in Table 8.4.

Table 8.4 reveals that when stress is controlled for, the original relationship between living arrangements and rehospitalization disappears. That is, when we look only at patients whose stress levels are similar, there is little difference in rehospitalization rates between those who live with parents and those who live elsewhere. This finding supports the notion that stress is an intervening variable. That is, deinstitutionalized patients placed with their parents (IV) experience stress (intervening variable) as a result of renewed family conflict. This in turn leads to rehospitalization (DV).

This is an important finding. Future community adjustment programs, then, should look not only at patients' living arrangements but also at the levels of stress they experience in those settings. This illustrates the usefulness of an intervening variable analysis.

ANTECEDENT VARIABLES

An extraneous variable affects both the IV and the DV. An intervening variable intervenes between the IV and DV.

Definition: An *antecedent variable* occurs before the independent variable. It does not explain away the relationship between the independent variable and the dependent variable. Rather, it tells the researcher about an influence that came before the independent variable.

The procedure for *antecedent variable* analysis is similar to that for extraneous and intervening variables:

1. The antecedent variable is related to both the IV and DV.
2. The researcher begins by examining the original relationship between the IV and DV.
3. When the researcher examines the original relationship between the IV and DV, controlling for the antecedent variable, the original relationship *remains the same*. This is because the antecedent variable does not cause the original relationship; it merely precedes it in time.
4. When the independent variable is controlled, the relationship between the antecedent variable and the dependent variable disappears.

This procedure is illustrated by the following example. A group of social work researchers is interested in finding out why some people donate to local charities and others do not. On the basis of earlier research and their own knowledge of the community, they hypothesize that people who are knowledgeable about local charities (IV) are most likely to donate to them (DV). They also believe that having a higher level of education (antecedent variable) is associated with being more knowledgeable about local charities. This can be diagrammed as follows:

Level of education	$\rightarrow$	Level of knowledge about community charities	$\rightarrow$	Donating to charities
(Antecedent Variable)		(Independent Variable)		(Dependent Variable)

Following the steps of the antecedent variable analysis, they determine that level of education (antecedent variable) is related to both knowledge about charities (IV) and donating to them (DV).

TABLE 8.5 Knowledge About Community Charities, by Percentage Who Donated[a]

| | Knowledge of Community Charities | |
	Knowledgeable	Not Knowledgeable
Percentage who donated	18 (153)	3 (33)
Total *N*	(851)	(1,114)

NOTE: This table shows the original relationship between knowledge about community charities (independent variable) and donating (dependent variable).
a. Number of clients in parentheses.

TABLE 8.6 Knowledge About Community Charities, by Percentage Who Donated, Controlling for Level of Education[a]

| | High Education | | Low Education | |
	Knowledgeable	Not Knowledgeable	Knowledgeable	Not Knowledgeable
Percentage who donated	18 (77)	3 (11)	18 (77)	3 (22)
Total *N*	(426)	(372)	(425)	(742)

NOTE: This table shows that the original relationship between knowledge about community charities (independent variable) and donating (dependent variable) *remains* when controlling for level of education (antecedent variable).
a. Number of clients in parentheses.

Next, they examine the original relationship between knowledge about charities (IV) and donating (DV). This analysis is summarized in Table 8.5.

Table 8.5 reveals a strong relationship between IV and DV: Those community members who are knowledgeable about local charities are six times more likely to donate than are those who are not knowledgeable.

Next, the researchers examine this original relationship between knowledge (IV) and donating (DV), controlling for the test factor, level of education (antecedent variable). This analysis is summarized in Table 8.6.

Table 8.6 illustrates that the original relationship between knowledge about community charities (IV) and donating to them (DV) remains the same when controlling for level of education (antecedent variable). This is consistent with the conclusion that level of education is an antecedent variable.

The final step is to examine the relationship between level of education (antecedent variable) and donating (DV), controlling for knowledge about community charities (IV). This analysis is summarized in Table 8.7.

TABLE 8.7 Level of Education, by Percentage Who Donated, Controlling for Knowledge About Community Charities[a]

	Knowledgeable		Not Knowledgeable	
	High Education	Low Education	High Education	Low Education
Percentage who donated	18 (77)	18 (77)	3 (11)	3 (22)
Total N	(426)	(425)	(372)	(742)

NOTE: This table shows that the relationship between level of education (antecedent variable) and donating (dependent variable) *disappears* when controlling for knowledge about community charities (independent variable).
a. Number of clients in parentheses.

The results of Table 8.7 indicate that the relationship between level of education (antecedent variable) and donating (DV) disappears when controlling for knowledge about community charities (IV). Therefore, level of education is indeed an antecedent variable.

As a result of this antecedent variable analysis, we know a little more about the factors that underlie donations to local charities. The relationship between knowledge of community charities and the likelihood of donating to them is real—those who are well informed about these charities are more likely to donate. Level of education is another factor that predicts donations. People who are better educated are also more likely to donate, and it is probable that more education facilitates knowing about local charities and that, in turn, makes donating to them more likely. Although we cannot prove that getting a good education and learning about local charities will increase donations, we can infer that increasing education and informing the public about the services of local charities will enhance donations to them.

Rosenberg (1968) summarized procedures for testing for extraneous, intervening, and antecedent variables. All three types of analyses require that the researcher show that there is an original relationship between the IV and DV. The third variable selected as a test factor must be related to both the IV and DV, and there must be some empirical or theoretical reason to believe that it will affect the original relationship. If the test factor is an extraneous or intervening variable, when it is controlled, the original relationship disappears. If the test factor is an antecedent variable, the original relationship is unaffected. In an antecedent variable relationship, when the IV is controlled, the relationship between the antecedent variable and DV disappears.

SUMMARY

In many social work research situations, we cannot use designs that require us to assign individuals or cases to comparison groups or that require us to expose people to various experiences. Instead, we must study social phenomena by entering the scene "after the fact"—that is, after individuals have been exposed to various influences or experiences. This is ex post facto research. Ex post facto research is associated with the use of surveys in which researchers collect interview or questionnaire data from large numbers of persons. Surveys are often used to study broad social questions that involve public opinion; differences among large groups of people; or differences based on fixed characteristics, such as gender, race, education, and geographic location.

To understand the influence of various variables on the phenomenon under study, researchers begin by examining an original relationship between an independent variable and a dependent variable. Researchers then introduce a third variable—called a test factor—to see if the original relationship is real and how it is affected by this third variable. This process is called elaboration. The end result is a better understanding of which variables are related and the process by which they affect one another.

DISCUSSION QUESTIONS

1. What is a survey and how is it different from a group research design?
2. There are three types of two-variable relationships: *symmetrical, reciprocal*, and *asymmetrical*. Give one example of each type of relationship.
3. The following diagram summarizes the three types of analysis discussed in this chapter:
   a. extraneous variable → independent variable → dependent variable
   b. independent variable → intervening variable → dependent variable
   c. antecedent variable → independent variable → dependent variable
      1. Give an example of each of the three types of relationships just diagrammed. (For example, neighborhoods with many tenements [IV] have high crime rates [DV]. This association is because neighborhoods with many tenements are poor [extraneous variable]. The extraneous variable of poverty leads to high crime rates.)

2. For each example, describe what happens to the original relationship between the independent variable and the dependent variable, when controlling for the test factor (extraneous, intervening, or antecedent variable).

4. When the researcher controls for an *extraneous variable,* the original relationship between the IV and DV

a. Disappears

b. Remains the same

5. When the researcher controls for an *intervening variable,* the original relationship between the IV and DV

a. Disappears

b. Remains the same

6. When the researcher controls for an *antecedent variable,* the original relationship between the IV and DV

a. Disappears

b. Remains the same

SHORT ASSIGNMENT

A researcher has collected interview data on adult attitudes toward teenage birth control, as well as data on the age and marital status of the adult respondents. The data are as follows:

Attitudes Toward Teen Birth Control, by Marital Status and Age

Attitude Toward Teen Birth Control	Younger Than 25		25 and Older	
	Single	*Married*	*Single*	*Married*
Favor	631	407	120	874
Oppose	168	96	80	633
Totals	799	503	200	1,507

Respond to the following questions by creating tables similar to those presented in this chapter:

1. Assume that the researcher's hypothesis is that married respondents are less likely to favor teenage birth control. Create a table to test this hypothesis. Does this table confirm the researcher's hypothesis?

2. It may be that attitudes toward birth control are determined primarily by the respondent's age. Create a table to show the relationship between age and attitude toward teenage birth control. What do you conclude from this table?

3. Create a table that examines the original relationship between marital status and attitude toward teenage birth control, controlling for the test factor of age. What do you conclude?

4. What type of test factor is age? What do researchers call the type of relationship that exists between marital status and attitude toward teenage birth control?

NOTE

1. By the way, in this study, the researcher found that for both men and women caregivers, those who experienced a high level of burden reported lower levels of health. In other words, the original relationship between level of burden and self-perceived health was real and applied regardless of the gender of the caregiver.

FURTHER READING

Rosenberg, M. (1968). *The logic of survey analysis.* New York: Basic Books.

9 An Alternative to Group Research Designs

Single-Subject Designs

In Chapters 7 and 8, I discussed research involving groups of people. In this chapter, I discuss research that focuses primarily on one person, one group, or one unit. This type of research is often referred to as single-subject research, single-case research, "*N* of one" research, and research using time series designs.

Single-subject research can be used to study direct services, planning, and administration, and it provides immediate and practical feedback. It allows professionals to improve their practice and develop theories for intervention.

In single-subject research designs, we are concerned about two important questions:

1. Was there a change in behavior?
2. Was our intervention responsible for the change?

To answer these questions, we must first be able to collect data about the behavior so that we can tell if it did in fact change. In social work research, the methods available for data collection include interviews; questionnaires; standardized measures, such as personality and intelligence tests; records or archives, such as agency records or government documents; and direct observation.

Direct observation is a primary method of data collection in single-subject research. Observations can be made by independent observers or, in some cases, by clients who may monitor their own behavior.

STRATEGIES FOR OBSERVATIONAL RECORDING

When observations of behavior are made, they must be recorded. Social scientists working in the area of social learning theory (i.e., behavior modification) have developed methods for recording observations, although these methods can be used by researchers in any discipline. These methods are *frequency measures, interval recording,* and *duration measures* (Kazdin, 1982).

Frequency Measures. Observers using frequency measures record the number of times a behavior occurs in a given period of time. Frequency measures are the most common way to measure behavior. The number of cigarettes smoked, the number of swear words used by an adolescent, the number of times one is late for work, and the number of classes missed are all frequency measures.

This method is especially appropriate when the observed behaviors are discrete and can thus be counted with ease. In addition, the behavior should take place for a relatively constant length of time each time it occurs. Continuous behaviors generally are not suitable for frequency recording. These include ongoing behaviors, such as smiling, sitting in one's seat, talking, lying down, and reading a book.

Duration Measures. With duration measures, the length of time that a behavior occurs during an observation period is recorded. For example, the researcher can record the amount of time that a junior high school student spends sitting in his or her seat during a study period. The researcher records the total amount of time that the student is seated regardless of the number of times he or she leaves the seat.

When recording the duration of a behavior, the observer can measure time in seconds or minutes by using a stopwatch or by recording the time that the behavior begins and ends at each occurrence. Duration measures are particularly useful when the goal is to increase or decrease the length of time that a response is performed. Duration measures, however, can be used only when the onset and termination of the behavior are clearly defined.

Interval Recording. Interval recording measures the behavior in terms of units of time rather than discrete occurrences. Usually, we take a single block of time, such as a 30- or 60-minute time period each day. The block of time is divided into short intervals of 10, 20, 30, or more seconds. During each interval, we observe a client's behavior. If the behavior occurs during that interval, a response is scored. This is true if the behavior occurs only once or many times during the interval.

Interval recording is the most flexible way to measure behavior. All we record is the presence or absence of a behavior in each interval. Thus interval recording is suitable for discrete behavior as well as for ongoing behavior, such as sitting in one's seat.

Interval recording can also be used to record duration. If a behavior occurs during the entire interval, it is recorded. If the behavior occurs during only a portion of the interval, however, it is recorded as though it never occurred. For example, suppose we were interested in increasing the attention span of Sean, a preschooler who pays little attention to class activities. During nursery school, when it is time to color, work on stacking blocks, put puzzles together, or perform any other age-appropriate activities, Sean does not watch what he is doing but, rather, looks away.

We could divide the time spent on coloring, stacking blocks, and assembling puzzles into 10-second intervals. During these intervals, we would record if Sean's eyes were focused on the activity during the entire interval. On a recording sheet we could note whether Sean was paying attention (eyes focused on the activity) or not paying attention (eyes not focused on the activity) for each 10-second interval. If he was focused on the activity for less than the entire 10 seconds, it would be recorded that he was not paying attention. This method gives us a good approximation of the total amount of time that Sean attended to class activities.

ISSUES AND PROBLEMS IN SAMPLING BEHAVIOR

The purpose of monitoring is to get a representative sample or accurate picture of how often or how long a behavior occurs. Often, behavior fluctuates widely over a given day, week, or month. Therefore, we must be careful not to allow these fluctuations to misrepresent the overall rate of occurrence. For instance, if a child's temper tantrums occur only in the presence of the child's mother, we would monitor the behavior at times when the mother is present.

Otherwise, we would get a distorted picture of the child's behavior. To accurately assess the occurrence of behavior, we must make the following decisions about monitoring:

1. We must decide on the number of times that data will be collected per day, week, or month. Our decision depends on how much the behavior varies. If the behavior is very stable from one day to the next, daily assessment is less essential.

2. The length of time to be set aside for the observation period must be determined. Behavior should be observed for a period of time that will yield data that are representative of typical performance.

3. We must decide when the observations should be made. Do we conduct the observations in the morning, afternoon, or evening; during school hours; or on weekends? We can record behavior in a single block of time in a single day or at different times throughout the day. For instance, if a behavior occurs only during a specific time of day (e.g., lunchtime), this time of the day should be monitored. An advantage of observing behavior at various times through-out the day is that the observed behavior is more likely to be representative of the true occurrence.

4. If interval recording is used, we must decide on the length of the interval. If the behavior occurs frequently, short intervals should be used (e.g., 10-15 seconds). If long intervals are used with high-frequency behaviors, many behaviors will be counted as one occurrence, and a change in the frequency of behavior might go undetected. If we use very short intervals (5 seconds or less), however, it will be difficult for observers to score because the pace is too fast. If the behavior being measured is continuous (e.g., watching TV, reading) the length of the interval may not be as important as when the behavior is discrete because longer or shorter intervals are not as likely to exclude "instances" of continuous behavior.

ESTIMATING RELIABILITY

Behavior must be defined and measured carefully if an observer is going to be confident that the observations are accurate. To ensure that we are recording *consistently,* at some point, we need to ask two independent observers to record the *same* behavior at the *same* time using the *same* type of recording methods.

We then compare their observations and hope they are similar. Specifically, we can compute the percentage of agreement between two observers.

To ensure that our recorded observations are reliable, we must demonstrate that two or more observers agree more frequently than we would expect by chance alone. For example, if two observers are recording the results of a coin toss (at each toss, they record either "heads" or "tails"), we would expect the observers to agree 50% of the time, even if they were recording "heads" and "tails" randomly. Obviously, these recordings are not reliable. Therefore, when observers record events that can turn out in one of two ways—sitting still versus moving about, eating or not eating, paying attention or not paying attention—our observers must achieve agreement much more than 50% of the time. In practice, if the percentage of agreement is high (90% or higher), there is high reliability (i.e., both observers agree most of the time).

For frequency measures we use the following formula to calculate the reliability:

$$\text{Percentage of Agreement} = \frac{\text{Lowest Frequency Observed}}{\text{Highest Frequency Observed}} \times 100\%$$

Let's look at an example to see how this formula works. In a preschool program, there is a child named Jamie. Jamie is aggressive and will hit other children in his class. The teacher and the teacher's aide decide that they will record the frequency of Jamie's hitting other children during the next week of classes. They determine operational definitions of "hitting" and decide to record the frequencies. At the end of the week, the teacher and the aide compare the data that they have recorded. The teacher recorded 15 instances of Jamie's hitting, and the teacher's aide recorded 12 instances. The reliability of their observations is 80%. This was calculated using the preceding formula:

$$\text{Percentage of Agreement} = \frac{12}{15} \times 100\% = 80\%$$

The number 80% is a relatively high percentage agreement, so we have some confidence that our recording is reliable.

For duration measures, the reliability is calculated by a similar formula:

$$\text{Percentage of Agreement} = \frac{\text{Lowest Duration Observed}}{\text{Highest Duration Observed}} \times 100\%$$

To calculate the reliability of interval recording, we first have to define what we mean by an "agreement" and a "disagreement." If both observers record an occurrence of the behavior in the same interval, we have an agreement. If one observer does and the other does not, we have a disagreement. Now, knowing the difference between agreements and disagreements, we can compute the reliability using the following formula:

$$\text{Percentage of Agreement} = \frac{\text{Number of Agreements}}{\begin{array}{c}\text{Number of Agreements} + \\ \text{Number of Disagreements}\end{array}} \times 100\%$$

Note that intervals in which neither observer recorded a behavior are not included in the denominator of this formula (the bottom of the ratio).

Let's use this formula to calculate the reliability of interval recording. Assume that two observers record a behavior for fifty 10-second intervals. Both observers agree on the occurrence of behavior in 20 intervals, disagree in 5 intervals, and neither records any occurrence of behavior in the remaining 25 intervals. The reliability would be 80%, calculated by the following:

$$\text{Percentage of Agreement} = \frac{20}{20+5} \times 100\% = 80\%$$

Those 25 intervals in which neither observer recorded an occurrence of the behavior are not used in the computation.

GRAPHING OBSERVATIONAL DATA

After observers have gathered data, they usually incorporate the data into a graph. The old adage "A picture is worth a thousand words" holds true here. By converting the data into a graph, we can see the changes that occur over time.

A line graph, which shows the relationship between two or more variables, is used to "picture" the data. Time, which may be represented in seconds, minutes, days, weeks, and so on, is placed along the horizontal axis of the graph. Frequency, duration, or percentage is represented along the vertical axis. Then, each point on the graph represents the occurrence of the behavior for the given time period. The usual convention for graphing the data is illustrated in Figure 9.1.

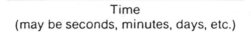
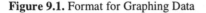

Figure 9.1. Format for Graphing Data

Once we plot the data, it is important for us to look at the graph to examine the trend. The trend can be stable, increasing, decreasing, or variable. A stable trend is one in which the frequency, duration, or percentage remains relatively constant for three to five time periods. An increasing trend is one in which the frequency, duration, or percentage ascends with time, whereas a decreasing trend is one in which the trend moves downward. A variable trend is one in which the frequency, duration, or percentage fluctuates within upper and lower bounds. Examples of these trends are shown in Figure 9.2.

DESIGNS

In the beginning of this chapter, I said that the purpose of single-subject research is to see if there is a change in behavior and to determine if our intervention is responsible for that change. Graphing the data allows us to see if there has been a change in behavior. To determine if our intervention was responsible for that change, we must employ a research design (Barlow & Hersen, 1984; Bloom & Fischer, 1982; Hersen & Barlow, 1976).

The discussion will be limited to simple single-case research designs. In these designs, the dependent variable or behavior is monitored continuously before, during, and after intervention. The periods of monitoring before and after intervention are called baseline or "A" phases. The "B" phase is the period of monitoring during the intervention.

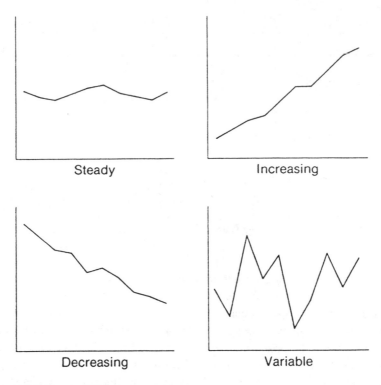

Figure 9.2. Types of Trends

By using combinations of baseline (A) and intervention (B) phases, we can construct a number of designs. The three most common designs are the AB design, the reversal and withdrawal designs (ABAB), and the multiple-baseline design.

AB DESIGN

The AB design is the most basic of the single-subject designs. This design consists of a baseline (A) followed by a period of intervention (B). Baseline information is gathered until there is a satisfactory estimate of the frequency, duration, or percentage of occurrence of the behavior. Once the baseline information is collected, then the treatment is introduced. Information about

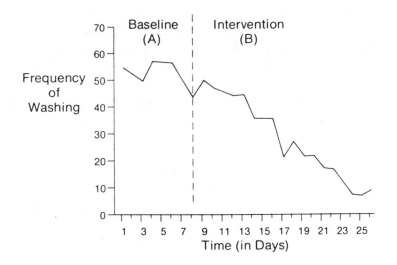

Figure 9.3. Example of the AB Design

the behavior continues to be gathered throughout the intervention phase. All of the information is plotted on a graph that shows the occurrence of the behavior during the baseline and the treatment phases.

As an example, assume that a social worker used an AB design to evaluate the effectiveness of a clinical program to reduce compulsive hand washing by a client named Janet. The worker asked Janet to record the number of times she washed her hands each day for 7 days. These recordings served as the baseline or A phase of the research design. After therapy began, Janet continued to record the number of times she washed her hands each day. This represented the B or intervention phase. The data were then graphed to see if hand washing had decreased (see Figure 9.3).

The AB design is useful because it can be applied in most treatment situations and settings. It provides for a data-based comparison of the behavior before and after treatment. There is, however, a basic problem with the design. Even though there is a clear increase or decrease in the behavior during the intervention phase, we cannot say for certain that the change was caused by the treatment.

For example, in Janet's case, she could have reduced the frequency of washing her hands because they became so sore that it was too painful for her to be constantly washing them. Perhaps Janet found another job in which she kept so busy that she did not have time to wash her hands. Also, Janet could have become so embarrassed by the way her hands looked that she stopped washing them so often. The point is that many things could have accounted for the decline in her hand-washing behavior, and the AB design does not allow us to conclude with confidence that the decline was due to the therapy or treatment. For this reason, the AB design is considered to be a relatively weak design. Nevertheless, it is useful when no other designs are feasible.

The strength of this design can be increased by repeating or *replicating* the A and B phases with additional clients. For example, if the worker's treatment was successful in reducing compulsive hand washing in a number of clients in addition to Janet, our confidence would be increased that it was in fact the treatment (and not some other factor) that caused the reduction in hand washing.

REVERSAL AND WITHDRAWAL DESIGNS (ABAB)

The reversal and withdrawal designs consist of a baseline (A), followed by intervention (B), a return to baseline (A), and a reapplication of the intervention (B). The logic behind these designs is that if the treatment is responsible for the change in behavior, then the behavior should return to pretreatment levels when the treatment is withdrawn or reversed. If this does happen, then other possible causes for the change in behavior can be ruled out. Thus ABAB designs overcome the major weakness of the AB design.

Although some researchers do not distinguish between reversal and withdrawal designs, Leitenberg (1973) points out an important difference. In the withdrawal design, a treatment is *withdrawn* in the third phase (A). In the reversal design, during the third phase, the same treatment is applied to an alternative but incompatible behavior. In both cases, however, the target behavior is expected to return to baseline levels in the third phase.

An example of a reversal design can be seen in the case of Mort, a caseworker at a shelter for the homeless. The workers at the shelter noticed that Mort interacted a great deal with other staff and spent little time with clients. The workers felt that they contributed to Mort's behavior by giving him attention and engaging in conversations with him. They decided on a plan to increase Mort's interaction with clients. The treatment consisted of shortening their conversations with him or, if possible, ignoring him when he approached them. They also decided to praise him verbally when he interacted with clients.

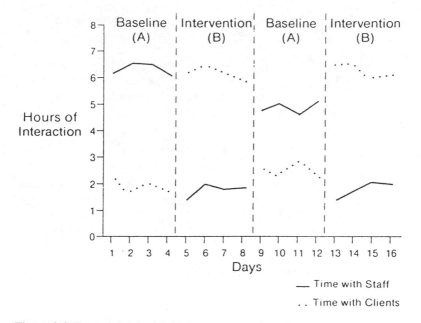

Figure 9.4. Example of the ABAB Reversal Design

Baseline was established, and the number of hours of Mort's interactions with staff and the number of hours of his interactions with clients were recorded for 4 days (first A or baseline phase). On the 5th day, the treatment (first B phase) was introduced—ignoring him when he approached staff and praising him when he interacted with clients. On the 9th day, conditions were *reversed*—staff again interacted with Mort when he approached them, and they did not praise him when he interacted with clients (the second A phase). Then, treatment was reintroduced in the second B phase on the 13th day. Throughout the study, staff recorded the amount of time Mort spent interacting with clients and the time he spent interacting with staff. These data are presented in Figure 9.4. They reveal that during the treatment phases, Mort's behavior changed in the desired direction: He increased his interactions with clients and decreased his interactions with other staff.

The situation of Rachel, a social worker, illustrates the withdrawal design. Rachel always arrived late for meetings and appointments. She wanted to change this behavior, so she decided to use herself as a subject in her own study. She monitored her behavior for 1 week by recording the number of

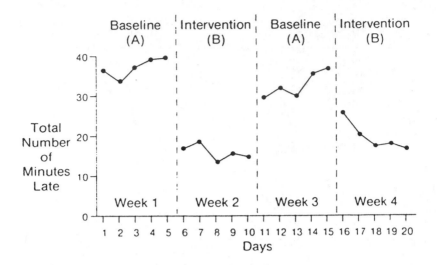

Figure 9.5. Example of the ABAB Withdrawal Design

minutes she was late for meetings and appointments (baseline). During the next week, she rewarded herself at the end of each day in which her tardiness had decreased (intervention). Her reward consisted of engaging in an enjoyable activity at the end of the day, such as eating dinner at a restaurant, playing tennis, or going to a movie. During the 3rd week, she did not reward herself (baseline), whereas during the 4th week, she once again engaged in enjoyable activities when she had reduced the amount of time she was late (intervention). As shown in Figure 9.5, her intervention (rewards for on-time behavior) was associated with a decrease in tardiness.

Numerous variations of the ABAB design can be employed depending on the particular research situation. Hersen and Barlow (1976) provide the following examples:

A-B-A-B-A-B

A-B-A-C-A-C-A   where B = Treatment 1 (e.g., feedback), and C = Treatment 2
                 (e.g., token reinforcement)

A-B-A-B-B'-B''-B'''   where B, B', B'', and B''' = varying amounts of something
                 (e.g., free playtime allowed)

A-B-A-B-BC   where B = Treatment 1, C = Treatment 2, and BC = a combi-
                 nation of Treatment 1 and Treatment 2 given simultaneously

A-B-BC-BCD   where B = Treatment 1, C = Treatment 2, D = Treatment 3,
                    BC = Treatment 1 and Treatment 2 given simultaneously,
                    and BCD = Treatment 1, Treatment 2, and Treatment 3
                    given simultaneously

A major limitation to using reversal and withdrawal designs is that it is not always possible to stop treatment to see if the behavior returns to baseline levels. In many cases, it would be unethical to withdraw the treatment. This would be the case, for instance, if the behavior under treatment was self-injury by an autistic child. If the injurious behavior was successfully reduced in the first treatment phase, it would be unethical to allow it to return to its original level during the second baseline.

Another limitation of withdrawal and reversal designs is that they are not suitable for evaluating the effect of a treatment on behaviors that cannot be reversed. For example, assume that a treatment program increases the level of reading comprehension in the first treatment phase. Because reading comprehension cannot be unlearned, it will not be possible to reestablish baseline in this study. This makes it impossible to evaluate the effectiveness of the treatment in this instance. A more appropriate design, such as the multiple-baseline design (described next), should be used to evaluate the effect of treatment on behaviors that cannot be reversed.

MULTIPLE-BASELINE DESIGN

A multiple-baseline design uses the AB format—baseline followed by intervention. The AB design, however, is repeated by applying the intervention to two or more behaviors, subjects, or settings. In this design, baseline is established for a number of behaviors, subjects, or settings, and the treatment is systematically applied to one behavior, subject, or setting at a time.

The logic of the multiple-baseline design is that if the treatment is effective, each behavior (subject or setting) should respond only when the treatment is applied to that specific behavior (subject or setting). All other behaviors (subjects or settings) should remain at baseline levels until the treatment is applied.

Multiple-baseline designs are used in place of reversal and withdrawal designs where treatment is irreversible, as in the case in which a client has learned a new behavior that cannot be unlearned. (This was the case in the reading comprehension example discussed earlier.) Multiple-baseline designs are also used when it is ethically impossible to stop treatment to return to baseline—for example, when treatment has reduced a client's self-destructive behavior.

A limitation of the multiple-baseline design is that the treated behaviors must be independent. Otherwise, the specific effect of treatment on each behavior cannot be demonstrated. This is also true of multiple-baseline designs across settings and subjects. The settings must be independent, with no carryover from one setting to the other, and each subject's behavior must be unaffected by other subjects. In addition, it must be assumed that the subjects are being exposed to similar environmental conditions.

The use of a multiple-baseline design across settings is illustrated by the treatment of Alicia, an unassertive high school student who rarely spoke to students or teachers. Alicia was also nearly silent with the school social worker.

The worker designed an assertiveness training program that used guided instruction, role-playing, and praise to help Alicia increase the number of times she spoke to others. With careful instruction from the worker, Alicia learned to record the frequency of her verbalizations. Because the worker was least threatening to Alicia, the treatment program began with praise and directions to speak to the social worker. Later, the treatment program was applied to "speaking with teachers" and, finally, to "speaking to other students." Alicia monitored her talking with the worker, teachers, and students throughout the program. The data are graphed in Figure 9.6.

An example of a multiple-baseline across behaviors can be seen in the case of a 14-year-old girl named Eve. Eve's negative behaviors included hitting her siblings, cursing, and coming home late after school. After a stable baseline was established for each behavior, an intervention was introduced to address the hitting behavior. One week later the intervention was introduced to address her cursing, and after another week, the intervention addressed the third behavior, coming home late after school.

The intervention consisted of applying techniques that the parents had learned in a course on Parent Effectiveness Training that they had just completed. The parents monitored each of these behaviors and recorded the number of times Eve hit her siblings, the number of times she cursed, and the number of minutes that she came home late from school. The multiple-baseline design across behaviors showed that the frequency of each of these behaviors decreased as the intervention was applied.

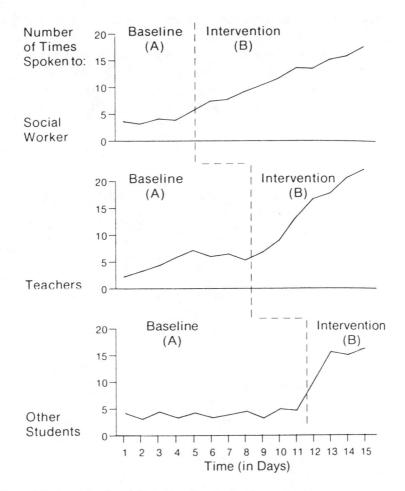

Figure 9.6. Example of a Multiple-Baseline Design Across Settings

A multiple-baseline design across subjects was used to determine the effectiveness of a special program of mother-child interaction on the attention span of preschoolers in a nursery school. Paul's mother was taught special techniques to increase Paul's attention span. Several days later, these techniques were taught to Jennifer's mother, who began to implement them. The techniques were then implemented sequentially with the other mothers in the program. Trained observers monitored all the children's attention spans in the classroom before the program and continuously as each mother-child pair began the program.

The multiple-baseline design across subjects (children) showed that each child's classroom attention span increased only after the in-home training program began for that child. This was evidence that the training program was responsible for the increased classroom attention span of the children.

SUMMARY

Single-subject designs offer social work researchers a practical methodology to test the effectiveness of an intervention. They allow us to determine if there was a change in behavior and if our intervention was responsible for the change.

To answer these questions, we must be able to monitor behavior. Monitoring includes measuring the frequency, duration, or percentage of occurrence of the behavior. We must also test the consistency of our observations. To do this, another observer makes independent observations, and the reliability of the observations is calculated by computing the percentage of agreement between the two observers.

Single-subject designs for research begin with a baseline phase (A) followed by an intervention phase (B). Depending on the nature of the study, a variety of baseline and intervention phases may be employed. The most common single-subject designs are the AB, the reversal and withdrawal, and the multiple-baseline designs. Data about the behavior are graphed to demonstrate if any change occurred and, if so, to determine whether our intervention was responsible for that change.

CASE STUDY

This study (Carstensen & Erickson, 1986) used a withdrawal design to validate a commonly held belief that serving food during an activity at a nursing home would facilitate interaction among residents. The researchers believed that serving refreshments consisting of unsweetened apple juice and plain butter cookies during a social hour at a nursing home would result in increased rates of social interaction among the residents. It was expected that the quality of social interaction would improve as well. This would be indicated by an increase in the number of positive statements made by the residents during the social hour and the number of the positive statements reciprocated by their peers.

The nursing home had 32 residents. Of these, 30 participated in the study. (One was out of the facility during the social hour, and another was too ill to participate.) There were 5 male and 25 female residents, and their ages ranged from 55 to 97 years.

Carstensen and Erickson (1986) considered interaction to have occurred when any of a group of operationally defined behaviors was directed to another resident. These included speech or other audible sounds, eye contact, facial expressions, and gestures.

It was not necessary for the resident to whom the interaction was directed to respond for the behavior to be considered an interaction. Interactions were distinguished from one another when there was a period of noninteraction lasting for 10 seconds or longer. Only resident-to-resident interactions were included in the analysis of this study.

Observations were made by two trained observers during each social hour. They collected data 5 days a week over a period of 5 weeks for 20 minutes a day during the social hour, which occurred between 3:30 and 4:30 p.m. For purposes of monitoring, the two observers divided the subjects into two equal groups before entering the activity area and then situated themselves closest to the residents they were to observe. The observers recorded each interaction that had occurred by repeating verbatim what they had heard into a tape recorder. If the interaction was not heard or understandable, then the observers said "inaudible interaction" into the recorder. When a resident would speak to an observer, the observer would say, "I cannot talk to you now; I will talk to you later." This minimized interactions with the observers.

To check the reliability of the observations, an independent observer recorded all interactions during 5-minute periods twice a week. This observer stood behind a wooden partition and was not visible to the principal observers. She recorded her observations in writing so that the principal observers would not hear her and be alerted that an observation was being recorded. The interobserver reliability was 100% for the recordings of the number of residents in attendance during each observational period. Consistency of the tape-recorded observations with those made in writing by the independent observer was 99% using a percentage agreement statistic (i.e., the number of agreements between observers divided by the total number of observations made by either observer, multiplied by 100).

For each day of the study, the researchers computed two dependent variables: the number of patients in attendance at the activity and the number of patient interactions. The study followed an ABAB withdrawal design. It consisted of a baseline phase with no refreshments (Baseline 1), serving

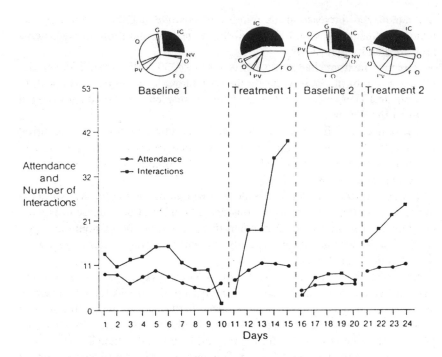

Figure 9.7. Frequency of Attendance and Number of Social Interactions During
Baseline 1, Treatment 1, Baseline 2, and Treatment 2

SOURCE: From Cartensen and Erickson (1986).
NOTE: Pie charts illustrate the breakdown by percentage of vocal content during each phase: IC = ineffective
communication; NV = negative vocals; O = other; F/O = facts/opinions; PV = positive vocals; I = instructions;
Q = questions; and G = greetings.

refreshments to the residents (Treatment 1), a withdrawal condition with no
refreshments (Baseline 2), and refreshments once again being served (Treatment 2). The duration of each phase varied, with Baseline 1 lasting for 10
days, Treatment 1 for 5 days, Baseline 2 for 5 days, and Treatment 2 for 4
days (see Figure 9.7).

The procedure for serving the refreshments consisted of an attendant's
passing juice and cookies to the residents at the beginning of the observational
period and once again 15 minutes later. All residents were asked if they would
like to have some juice and a cookie. After serving the refreshments, the
attendant left the activity area and returned only at the time of the second
serving. Because the purpose of the intervention was to facilitate interaction
among residents, if a resident spoke to the attendant while refreshments were
being served, to minimize interaction the attendant would respond by saying,
"I cannot talk to you now; I have to get some more juice."

All of the tape recordings were transcribed verbatim. Two independent raters, who were blind to the purpose of the study, classified the transcriptions. The raters categorized the vocal behavior according to its content. With 20 possible codes available for classification, the vocal behaviors fell into eight categories—positive vocal (e.g., praise, compliments), negative vocal (e.g., reprimands, discouragement, derogatory remarks), facts/opinions, questions, greetings, instructions, ineffective communication (i.e., communication that was incoherent or nonsensical in content and directed toward another resident who did not respond to it), and other (e.g., singing). If there was a discrepancy between the classifications of the two raters, a third rater was asked to evaluate the content.

This study used a single-case design to modify conclusions that had been drawn from earlier studies of social interactions in nursing homes. Earlier studies showed that when refreshments were served during a social hour, residents interacted with each other more frequently. These studies were interpreted to mean that serving refreshments led to an increased quality of life for nursing home residents.

Carstensen and Erickson decided to look at this interpretation more closely. They replicated earlier studies by applying a withdrawal design to study the effects of refreshments on social interaction of nursing home residents. But they added an element to their design: In addition to monitoring frequency of interactions, they also recorded the *types* of interactions exhibited by residents. Their results were surprising (see Figure 9.7).

As in the earlier studies, there was an increase in interactions when refreshments were served. But most of the increase was in *ineffective* communication: nonsensical or inappropriate statements or mumbling. In addition, during the refreshment-high-interaction phases (Treatments 1 and 2 in Figure 9.7), more appropriate interactions, such as questions, praise, and positive feedback, actually decreased.

The implication is clear: Simply increasing the frequency of interactions among nursing home residents does not ensure that those interactions will be meaningful. If we are to increase the quality of life in nursing homes, we need to attend to *how* residents interact with one another. Single-case designs are useful ways to study social interactions if we use them to study both the quantity and the quality of human interaction.

DISCUSSION QUESTIONS

1. Single-subject research designs are used to answer two questions. What are they?

2. Match the behavior in the left column with the most appropriate procedure(s) for observing and recording that behavior in the right column:

Behavior	*Recording procedure*
Smoking cigarettes	Frequency measure
Watching television	Duration measure
Fighting in class	Interval recording
Nail biting	
Praising spouse	
Participating in class	
Asking a question in the group	
Working in the garden	

3. What is the most common procedure to evaluate the reliability of observational recording measures?

4. How is "percentage of agreement" computed for the following?

   a. Frequency measures
   b. Duration measures
   c. Interval measures

5. What are four types of trends that may occur in graphs of observational data?

6. Give an example of how each of the following designs would be used to evaluate the effectiveness of a treatment program:

   a. AB design
   b. ABAB design
   c. Multiple-baseline design across behaviors

SHORT ASSIGNMENT

Imagine that you are a social worker who specializes in teaching living skills to severely autistic children. (Autistic children are greatly impaired in their ability to communicate with others; they are withdrawn and often avoid most types of interactions with others.)

Recently, you have begun to use a controversial technique called *facilitated communication*. This technique consists of supporting the autistic child's hand while he or she types responses to questions on a computer keyboard.

You have noticed that several of the autistic children in your group are able to use the keyboard for only a few seconds at a time. Your goal is to increase the amount of time these children spend communicating by sitting at a work station and typing on the keyboard. The intervention consists of praising the child each time he or she uses the keyboard in an appropriate manner. (At this point, you are not concerned with the content of the children's communication or whether they are truly communicating their own beliefs and feelings. You are concerned solely with increasing the amount of time they spend typing appropriately on the keyboard.)

To evaluate whether this intervention "works," you decide to monitor the amount of time they spend using the keyboard appropriately during two 1-hour periods every day when the children have access to the computer. You consider using the following designs:

AB

ABAB (reversal or withdrawal design)

Multiple-baseline design across children

    a. State the advantages and disadvantages of each of the preceding designs to evaluate the effectiveness of your intervention.

    b. Which design is most appropriate to answer the research question? Why?

(Hint: There is no one correct answer. You should be able to identify the strengths and drawbacks of each design.)

FURTHER READING

Barlow, D. H., & Hersen, M. (1984). *Single-case experimental designs: Strategies for studying behavioral change.* New York: Pergamon.

Bloom, M., & Fischer, J. (1982). *Evaluating practice: Guidelines for the accountable professional.* Englewood Cliffs, NJ: Prentice Hall.

10   Qualitative Research

In Chapter 1, I said that social work research is based on a view of the world called the scientific method. For the most part that is true. Since the 1970s, however, an increasing number of social work researchers have turned to a different type of research that departs from the traditional scientific method. To understand the relationship between how researchers think about the world and how they conduct research, it is necessary to define the concept of the *paradigm.*

THE PARADIGM AS A WAY OF VIEWING THE WORLD

Definition: According to Guba and Lincoln (1994), a *paradigm* is "a set of basic beliefs. . . . It represents a world view that defines for its holder, the nature of the 'world,' the individual's place in it, and the range of possible relationships to that world" (p. 107).

For example, during the Middle Ages in Europe, the predominant paradigm was that established by the Church. People believed that the earth was the center of the universe, that it had been created by God, that everything that happened was a result of God's will, and that common people could not hope to understand why or how events occurred.

In the 17th century, this paradigm was challenged by Sir Francis Bacon and by discoveries that led to the conclusion that, far from being at the center of the universe, the earth was a very small part of an enormous cosmos. As this new paradigm took hold, people believed that the world operated according to a set of laws or rules that were systematic and predictable and that applied at all times and in all places. It was no longer necessary to turn to religious ideas and religious leaders to understand everything about the world. Rather, by careful observation and study, people could uncover the laws that governed events, explaining how and why they happened. This paradigm had a profound influence on civilization. It led to the development of the physical sciences—based on the scientific method—and to the rapid advance of technologies that determine how we live today. The social sciences developed much later, in the latter part of the 19th century, and social work developed in the early part of the 20th century. By then, the new paradigm was firmly established. It is not surprising, then, that social work research adopted this scientific paradigm (although some early forms of social work were based on a charitable and religious paradigm).

The new paradigm that began to develop in the 17th century took shape in the form of several schools of philosophy. The school of philosophy that is most closely associated with the scientific method of social work research is called *positivism.* This is a term first used by Auguste Comte, a French philosopher, in the 1820s. Comte's positivism promoted the idea that we should attempt to study the world using scientific methods.

POSITIVISM AND POSITIVISTIC RESEARCH

Positivism can be thought of as a paradigm—a series of beliefs about the nature of things—that underlies the scientific method. Positivism holds to the following ideas:

1. There is an "objective" world that exists independently of our existence or our perception of it.
2. Events in the world are determined by the operation of natural laws and mechanisms. Researchers can gain an understanding of the world by discovering these laws and mechanisms.
3. The observer-researcher and the phenomena being studied are completely independent. Therefore, the researcher can study phenomena without affecting them in any way.

4. Although it is possible for bias to enter into the researcher's observations or methods, this can be avoided by strictly adhering to scientific procedures—for example, by using independent observers or by being systematic about selecting observations.

5. As long as the researcher adheres to these scientific procedures, the researcher's own biases and values will not affect the outcome of the research. In other words, research is "value-free."

6. To understand the world, standard scientific procedures must be used. (These were also discussed in Chapter 1.) These procedures include the following:

Researchers must use a theory to state propositions or hypotheses.

These must be tested by objective observation or study of phenomena.

Before testing, all operations must be reduced to things that can be observed or objectively measured.

"Confounding" conditions, such as the researcher's own bias or the effect of other variables, must be controlled or manipulated to prevent errors. (This is the rationale for careful statement of hypotheses, for sampling procedures, for group and single-case research designs, and for elaboration procedures—all discussed in earlier chapters.)

The researcher's conclusions are based on deduction from the general level to the specific level: The research moves from the formulation of a general theory to specific observations and propositions that state how individual variables or concepts are related to one another.

DRAWBACKS OF POSITIVISTIC RESEARCH

Guba and Lincoln (1994) note that persons who hold to a particular paradigm do so on faith. Even though they may provide good arguments to support their belief system, ultimately, there is no way to prove that their belief system is any more "true" than others. Ironically, this applies to those who adopt the scientific method: Even though the scientific method is based on the notion of proving hypotheses and theories, the paradigm that underlies this method (and all others) must be accepted on faith.

One characteristic of paradigms is that they are so ingrained into our thinking that we may not be aware that we have adopted a set of beliefs that are arbitrary. For example, until recently it was so well accepted among social scientists that the proper way to do research was to follow the standard scientific method—create a theory, derive hypotheses from it, test those hypotheses using means that can be verified objectively, and so on—that few researchers questioned the paradigm that supported their way of doing research.

It is also true that paradigms do not last forever. There are always elements and features of every paradigm that lead to problems or dissatisfactions. As these dissatisfactions grow, a new paradigm, a new way of thinking about the world, replaces the old. In recent years, social scientists and social work researchers have become dissatisfied with what they saw as limitations of this method. I can summarize these dissatisfactions as follows:

1. Positivistic research does not provide an accurate view of reality. This type of research reduces all social phenomena to specific propositions, and it studies only a limited set of variables. This produces knowledge that may be useful but that is very limited. It does not explain the truly complex patterns and reciprocal influences that operate in human interactions. For example, operant theory (a positivistic approach) may help us to understand that a child's acting out at home increases when the parents pay attention to the misbehavior. A positivistic approach, however, tells us nothing about the ways in which the family's history and its complex relationships between parents, children, siblings, and outsiders affect the functioning of the family.

2. The knowledge that is derived from positivistic research is often so limited that it provides few practical applications in the real world. Much of positivistic research is motivated by a desire to discover how variables influence one another. But this often occurs under such carefully controlled conditions that it has little relevance to the real world. For example, social psychologist Stanley Milgram (1963, 1965) showed that study participants recruited to a laboratory setting were willing to administer what they thought were painful electric shocks to other participants. But because the studies occurred in laboratory settings, it is not clear what relevance they have to ethical conduct in more realistic settings.

3. The worldviews and perspectives of oppressed groups are often not reflected in the research questions or in the results. Although positivistic research claims to be value-free, researchers often fail to recognize that they impose their own values (and fail to represent the values of those they study) simply by selecting particular research questions over others. (As I explained in Chapter 4, I believe that qualitative methods may be no better than quantitative methods in reflecting the perceptions and values of oppressed groups. I showed how some qualitative methods may actually make it easier for the researcher's bias to affect the study [p. 62]. Thus the criticism that quantitative research is insensitive to oppressed groups may apply as well to

qualitative research. The critical element in conducting a valid study may not be the particular method used but, rather, the researcher's ability to incorporate the views of those studied.)

4. Social workers should be motivated by their passion for social justice. When social work researchers insist that we be neutral and objective observers, they reduce our passion for helping the people we study. They make it impossible to be advocates.

5. Social workers are concerned with how humans interact with one another and with their institutions, such as families, schools, neighborhoods, and social welfare agencies. Positivistic research methods were first developed in the physical sciences and are appropriate for the study of physical phenomena. They are not appropriate for the study of human interactions, which are qualitatively different from physical phenomena. Human interactions cannot be quantified.

6. Positivistic methods assume that observing or measuring a phenomenon does not change it. In reality, any time we observe or measure something, we change it. For example, when we interview mothers to ask about their child-rearing practices, it is impossible for our questions about child care not to influence the mothers' knowledge, beliefs, or attitudes about that topic.

QUALITATIVE RESEARCH

In response to the concerns discussed earlier, researchers in social work, sociology, psychology, education, nursing, and other disciplines have developed alternative research approaches and methods. For example, the qualitative approach began in sociology in the 1920s and 1930s with the "Chicago school" of sociologists who felt that descriptive, qualitative methods were best for the study of how people interact in groups. During the same time, in anthropology, pioneering field researchers such as Margaret Mead developed qualitative methods for the intensive study of the customs and cultures of primitive societies (Denzin & Lincoln, 1994). These approaches are usually called *qualitative* research, to distinguish them from the more traditional *quantitative* research.

Definition: *Quantitative* approaches study phenomena using numerical means. In these approaches, there is an emphasis on counting, describing, and using standard statistics, such as means and standard deviations. Quantitative researchers are likely to use complex analysis procedures, such as multiple regression and factor analysis.

Definition: *Qualitative* approaches study phenomena using general description to describe or explain. Qualitative researchers tend to use narrative descriptions of persons, events, and relationships. Their findings may be presented in the form of categories or general statements about the complex nature of persons, groups, or events.

This terminology is somewhat misleading. Strictly speaking, the terms *qualitative* and *quantitative* refer to types of measurement (see Chapter 13) rather than to research paradigms. The term *qualitative research,* however, is now widely used to describe a research paradigm that is an alternative to positivistic research and that has gained in popularity in the past two decades. Therefore, in the following discussion of this new approach, I will use the term *qualitative research.* In reality, we should be aware that both quantitative (numerical) procedures and qualitative (narrative) procedures can be used in both research paradigms. It is true, however, that positivistic researchers favor quantitative results, whereas qualitative researchers favor qualitative or narrative results.

In the positivistic paradigm, social science researchers tended to follow a standard method based on problem identification, theorizing, hypothesis formulation, sampling, testing, analyzing data, and stating conclusions. The rest of this book reflects those steps in the positivistic research process.

Qualitative researchers have been more creative in devising procedures and methods. In a sense, they have been more concerned with a deep understanding of their study participants than with a standard method.

Unlike positivistic research, in qualitative research, the choice of research procedures is not set in advance. The qualitative researcher uses whatever research tools are best for the situation, often with reliance on a variety of methods (Denzin & Lincoln, 1994). As a result, there are actually a number of qualitative research methods: *grounded theory, ethnography, participant observation, naturalistic observation, field research, phenomenology, the case study, the historical method,* and *action research.* I will briefly describe each of these. First, however, it will be useful to discuss the characteristics of qualitative research and the ways in which this research differs from positivistic research.

Positivistic Research

Qualitative Research

Data collection   ⟷   Theory

↕

Conclusions

Figure 10.1. Sequence of Steps in the Research Process

CHARACTERISTICS OF QUALITATIVE RESEARCH

1. The positivistic researcher moves from theory to hypothesis formulation to verification of hypotheses by examining data. The researcher then uses the knowledge gained to modify or refine the theory. In qualitative research, the researcher moves freely back and forth between data collection and theoretical analysis (see Figure 10.1). Qualitative researchers generally enter into a research study without any formal theory. They begin by immersing themselves in the social situation or culture under study. They observe or interact intensively with the research participants, often taking copious notes. Eventually, they develop organizing principles, categories, or other concepts to explain what they are observing. But these explanatory concepts are not fixed. Rather, the researcher continues to collect information based on these explanatory concepts. As more data are collected, it is almost always necessary to change, modify, or extend these explanatory concepts based on the new information. This back-and-forth process may continue for a long time, until the researchers are satisfied that they have examined enough data to determine that the theory is accurate.

2. Qualitative methods proceed from the specific to the general level. They begin at a specific level: collecting data about a specific social phenomenon, usually by interviews and observations. The qualitative researcher then moves to a general level: making guesses about what variables are relevant and how they relate to each other and from this creating theory to explain the data. As I noted earlier, positivistic methods take the opposite approach, moving from the general to the specific. This difference in approaches is summarized in Figure 10.2.

3. In qualitative research, the results are complex and "rich." They usually take the form of narrative descriptions or lengthy explanations. Thus more

Positivistic Research

General level → Specific level

Theory → Collect data to test specific hypotheses
derived from general theory

Qualitative Research[a]

Specific level → General level

Data collection → Theory
Observations
Interviews
Analysis of materials

Figure 10.2. Comparison of Positivistic and Qualitative Approaches

NOTE: a. The process of moving from data collection (through observations, interviews, and analysis) to theory is usually repeated several times.

than quantitative research, the results of qualitative research closely fit the reality of the persons or cases studied.

4. Generally, quantitative researchers are interested in outcomes. For example, does a particular type of family therapy prevent spouse abuse? Qualitative researchers are more interested in process. In this example, they would be interested less in learning the eventual outcome of family therapy and more interested in the patterns and processes that take place in therapy and in the home situation. They would try to find out how abuse-prone couples interact, what motivates them, and how contact with a therapy program affects these patterns.

5. Qualitative research is flexible and intuitive. Compared with the positivistic approach, qualitative research does not adhere to a predetermined set of research steps. Qualitative researchers use their experience and "hunches" to select steps, procedures, and new explanatory concepts.

6. Theories generated by qualitative research are less generalizable beyond the particular persons or units studied. Although positivistic researchers attempt to discover theories that are "true" in a wide range of situations and across different places and times, the theories generated by qualitative researchers are more tentative. Because qualitative theories are so closely tied to the intensive study of a particular group, they may or may not apply more

widely. Thus the generalizability of the results is sacrificed in favor of obtaining a rich and complex understanding about the particular situation under study.

7. Qualitative researchers do not assume that there is an objective world that exists independently of their observations. They recognize that the very act of observation affects the phenomenon being studied. The researcher's subjective perceptions, feelings, and interpretations, and those of the study participants, are all considered legitimate data.

8. Qualitative researchers may use any method of data collection, including questionnaires and structured interviews. They tend, however, to favor data collection methods that allow for complex responses and for individual perspectives: unstructured in-depth interviews, observation, and participant observation. They may also use "subjective" sources of data, such as personal diaries, historical accounts, and autobiographies. Much more than quantitative research, qualitative research gets "close" to the perspectives of the persons studied (Denzin & Lincoln, 1994).

9. The goal of qualitative research is to enhance our general knowledge about complex events and processes.

These characteristics describe the common features of all qualitative research methods. There are, however, many different schools or approaches to qualitative methods, developed in different disciplines and with the goal of studying different phenomena. The following discussion summarizes the features of several qualitative research methods.

GROUNDED THEORY

Grounded theory is a method for studying complex social phenomena that was developed and first presented in 1967 by two sociologists, Barney Glaser and Anselm Strauss. For many of the reasons outlined earlier in this chapter, Glaser and Strauss were dissatisfied with traditional positivistic methods. Although their grounded theory method was first used in sociology, in the almost three decades that it has been in existence, it has been used in many other disciplines, including social work, nursing, psychology, anthropology, and education. It has been used to study diverse areas, such as terminal illness, chronic mental illness, drug addiction, the operation of a hospital, and public assistance. (Much of the following description of grounded theory is drawn from a discussion by Strauss & Corbin, 1994.)

When social work researchers use this approach, their goal is to develop a theory about the persons, events, or things under study. Rather than starting with a theory, generating hypotheses from that theory, and then testing them, in this approach, theory is generated from data. Grounded theorists usually study areas in which there is little or no theory to explain human behavior. Sometimes, the researcher may find an existing theory that seems applicable. In this case, it may be appropriate to start out with that theory, but it will later be elaborated and modified based on examination of data.

Grounded theory studies tend to use in-depth interviews and observations in real-life settings. Researchers using this approach, however, are encouraged to use all sources of data—the more varied the types of data obtained, the more accurate the final results are likely to be. Therefore, grounded theory researchers have used letters, life stories, introspective accounts, autobiographies, diaries, historical accounts, and newspaper reports. Several researchers have encouraged the use of quantitative data—such as census data and questionnaire results—to supplement qualitative data (Flick, 1992).

Researchers working with grounded theory use a number of analytic tools. These were first presented by Glaser and Strauss (1967) and later modified and elaborated by their followers.

Constant Comparison. Because grounded theory researchers use unstructured interviews and observations, they are usually faced with a large body of data in the form of extensive notes or recordings. Researchers begin by immersing themselves in these data and then creating concepts or categories to explain them. Using these categories the researchers then "reenter" the data to see if the newly developed categories seem to explain the data. That is, researchers *compare* their tentative concepts against the data. This may lead them to change or modify the concepts or categories.

This process is repeated until reexamination of the data yields no new insights. Researchers may then turn to a new set of individuals, perhaps in a different setting. They can then compare the adequacy of their concepts or explanations with a new group of persons. Or they may compare how well their concepts work when the same persons interact in somewhat different situations or when facing different tasks. The central feature of this method is the repetitive comparison of the researcher's explanations with new data until the researcher determines that the explanations or concepts seem to apply and do not have to be modified any further.

Theoretical Sampling. Positivistic researchers prefer random samples to enhance their ability to generalize their findings to large populations. Grounded theory researchers use purposive samples. That is, they pick particular individuals or cases based on their belief that these individuals are typical of the phenomenon they want to study. Researchers also apply the method of constant comparison to their selection of individuals for study. For example, if a set of concepts seems to explain the behavior of children in one classroom, the researcher may deliberately select children from another classroom for comparative study.

Systematic Coding. As noted earlier, grounded theory researchers develop categories or explanatory codes to make sense of their data. These codes should go beyond mere description of the events or behaviors. They should explain them. The researcher's goal is to refine and develop these concepts and then to use them to formulate hypotheses that will form the basis for a theory.

Multiple Perspectives. In a grounded theory approach, researchers do not just report observations and other data—they interpret them. These interpretations include the perspectives of the people being studied, but they must go beyond the mere reporting of the viewpoints of participants. No one person's perspective is any more true than that of another. Therefore, it is the task of the researcher to synthesize and interpret all information collected, including the perspectives of the various actors in a social situation. Because persons from different groups often have widely differing views of the same phenomena, researchers should be sensitive to perspectives based on gender, class, and race. Grounded theorists also recognize that their interpretation of the results is colored by their own perspective, and they openly acknowledge this.

Reciprocal Relationship Between Researcher and Participants. In the research situation, the researcher and the study participants interact and, inevitably, influence one another. For example, in a follow-up interview, the researcher may suggest an explanation or a concept that was developed in an earlier phase of observation. This suggestion may affect the participant's future behavior. When researchers conduct observations, their presence is usually obvious to participants, and they may even participate in activities along with the participants. This is also likely to affect the participants' behavior. Rather than attempt to minimize their influence on participants, grounded theory researchers recognize this influence as inevitable and attempt to use their own reflections and thoughts, as well as those of the participants, as additional sources of data.

Conditional Matrix. This concept is a recent development in grounded theory. It encourages the researcher to specify the consequences and conditions of behavior in a variety of situations. In this way, the researcher is able to build a theory that will be applicable in more than just the present situation.

The following example illustrates the use of grounded theory in a study of the work culture of intensive care nurses.

Intensive care nursing is a high-stress occupation, and the researcher wanted to find out how these nurses handled the many demands and pressures of their work. She began by sitting at a central nurse's station, where she could hear conversations between nurses, and she took extensive notes and tape-recorded a sampling of interactions.

This researcher's work proceeded in steps that went back and forth between theory (explanatory concepts) and observations. In Step 1, after a few days of initial observation, the researcher determined that the nurses' interactions could be categorized into two types of talk: "Work talk" involved procedures that were necessary for patient care. "Friendly talk," on the other hand, was used to relieve tension, avoid conflict, or strengthen relationships between the nurse and another person.

Using these categories developed in Step 1, the researcher continued her observations and also interviewed a number of nurses. The result was Step 2. In Step 2, the researcher theorized that nurses' interactions could be described along two dimensions. The first dimension was the type of talk. But a second dimension was equally important: the audience or person spoken to. In the intensive care unit, nurses interacted with other nurses, with their supervising nurse, with doctors, and with "outsiders"—family and friends of the patient. Nurses engaged in work talk and friendly talk with each of these audiences but for different purposes and in different ways. For example, they resisted efforts of outsiders to gain more information about the patient (work talk) and instead diffused the situation using friendly talk.

As the research proceeded, the researcher went back and forth again between her data collection and her emerging theory. For example, in a later step, the researcher determined that there were two types of work talk. Nurses used "instrumental work talk" to get their nurse colleagues to complete tasks that were necessary for patient care. But there was an entirely different type of work talk that nurses used when one of their colleagues failed to complete a necessary medical task. Because of the heavy demands of intensive care nursing, this was a common occurrence and at times jeopardized patient care. Nurses handled this problem by engaging in "protective work talk"—interactions that helped to alleviate nurses' anxiety and reassure them that the omission would not come to the attention of any of the other actors.

This example illustrates the way in which qualitative researchers engage in a circular process, going back and forth between data collection and theorizing. The end result is a theory or explanation, one that is based on intensive data collection and on the perspectives of a variety of persons.

CASE STUDIES

Stake (1994) argues that the case study is not a methodology but a choice of subject: When researchers decide to study a single case, they are conducting a case study. They may use any number of methods, both qualitative and quantitative. Case studies, however, are usually associated with research that is qualitative and holistic (includes the full complexities of people's lives). The case study is used in *naturalistic* studies (that describe people in their natural day-to-day settings) and in *fieldwork* research (a type of study in which the researcher collects data in the "field" or natural habitat of the persons being studied).

The defining characteristic of the case study is that it focuses on a single case. That case may be an individual. But it also might be a family, a small group, or even an organization or community. According to Stake (1994), for the phenomenon to be a case, we must be able to define its boundaries and say clearly which features are included within the case and which are not. The main emphasis is on understanding the single case by conducting an intensive study of it. The results of this study are called a *case report*.

Why do a case study? Case studies are valuable because they provide great detail that helps us to understand the complexities of human behavior. For example, a group study of why patients comply or fail to comply with their medication regimes may obscure individual factors such as personal history and unique events in the patients' lives. Researchers often use case studies when they begin to do research in areas where there is little knowledge or theory to guide them. The results of a case study may in fact suggest areas that should be examined, highlight critical issues, or suggest concepts that can serve as the basis for a theory. Case studies sometimes have been used to determine the causes of complex social behaviors, such as riots (Robertson, 1981, p. 42).

Case studies also have been used to study a wide range of phenomena. For example, they have been used to study (a) the social organization of a small town, (b) the culture of a religious school, (c) the training of medical students, (d) the "culture of poverty" among lower-class Puerto Ricans, and (e) the characteristics of a cult.

Stake (1994) identifies three types of case studies, all with different purposes. Researchers conduct *intrinsic case studies* solely to gain a better understanding of the individual case. The purpose is not to generate a theory or to understand a broad social issue, such as child abuse. The reader of the case report may draw generalizations from the study, but the researcher's purpose is only to describe the case under study.

The *instrumental case study* is used to elaborate a theory or to gain a better understanding of a social issue, such as drug addiction or help-seeking behavior. The researcher's primary interest is in learning about the social issue, and the case study merely serves to facilitate that learning.

Researchers may also use a *collective case study* to further their understanding about a social issue or a group of people. They do this by conducting case studies on a group of individuals or cases. These cases are chosen so that comparisons can be made between cases and concepts and so that theories can be extended and validated. The interest in the individual case is secondary to the researcher's interest in the social issue or population being studied.

When researchers use group research studies, they devote their effort to sampling and to following the dictates of the research design. (I discussed these in Chapters 6 and 7.) When researchers use case studies, they invest their time in obtaining very detailed and extensive information about the case. Stake (1994) argues that case study researchers should study what is unique to the individual case, as well as what the case has in common with other cases. He suggests that they collect data on the following:

1. The nature of the case
2. Its historical background
3. The physical setting
4. Other contexts, including economic, political, legal, and aesthetic

5. Other cases . . .

6. Those informants through whom the case can be known (p. 238)

Case studies employ several research strategies, including triangulation, comparisons, intensive involvement, and case selection. Stake (1994) defines *triangulation* as the "process of using multiple perceptions to clarify meaning, verifying the repeatability of an observation or interpretation" (p. 241). Triangulation is a method for verifying a concept or a conclusion put forth by the researcher by looking for multiple sources of confirmation. For example, in his study of lower-class Puerto Rican families, Lewis (1968) found that his case study families had a present-time orientation. That is, their behavior was motivated only by immediate concerns. This characteristic was true among study participants who were studied in Puerto Rico as well as participants in New York. It was also true among both men and women, older and younger. These case study observations validated Lewis's conclusion about the present-time orientation of his study participants.

Although not all case studies seek to make *comparisons,* some do use comparisons to form or test generalizations. The researcher must be careful about which variables are selected for comparison, for the very process of selecting some variables for comparison means that other potential similarities or differences will be obscured (Stake, 1994, p. 242). For example, a school social worker may conduct a case study of an after-school socialization group for adolescent boys. Some boys may benefit from the group (as indicated by variables such as improved interactional skills and reduced truancy), whereas others may not. The social work researcher may compare these boys in terms of their behavior in the group and their family backgrounds. These variables may or may not be relevant to understanding why the group helped some boys and did not help others.

Intensive involvement is a necessary part of the case study approach. Researchers spend a great deal of time "on site" and personally interact with the study participant or participants. They gather much of the data themselves, through observation, participation in activities with the participants, taking notes, and recording on tape. They can also interview informants and examine documents such as newspaper accounts and court records. Regardless of the methods used, researchers must develop a "feel" for the persons, group, or phenomenon being studied, and this can occur only when researchers immerse themselves in the research setting.

Unlike positivistic researchers, case study researchers do not use random or representative sampling. Such types of sampling are more appropriate when the study calls for a relatively large number of study participants and seeks to generalize its findings to a still larger population.

Stake (1994) argues that the sole criterion for *selecting cases* for a case study should be the "opportunity to learn" (p. 244). This may mean, for example, that the researcher should select the most atypical or most unusual case. The unusual case can help to challenge previously accepted generalizations. For example, children from low-income multiproblem families rarely become economically successful adults. By conducting a case study of the atypical successful adult from this background, however, the researcher can call into question the supposedly inevitable connection between childhood deprivation and poor adult adaptation. The researcher may be able to identify factors that explain atypical outcomes from multiproblem families. As Stake (1994) notes, "Often it is better to learn a lot from an atypical case than a little from a typical case" (p. 243).

The case study researcher's selection of cases may also reflect practical considerations. For example, in a study of the home lives of elementary school children, the researchers may have access to 30 families. Because their work is intensive, however, the researchers will be able to select only five families for study. Because the research results are dependent on these five families, it may be wise to select only families that are cooperative and will allow the researcher full access to their day-to-day activities. For the same reason, it will probably be impossible to study enough families to represent all the characteristics of such families, as would be the case in a positivistic group study—for example, urban versus suburban versus rural residence, large and small families, democratic and authoritarian families, and so on. Stake (1994) notes that although it is important to attempt a balance of study participant characteristics, in case study research the cases are usually hand picked by the researcher on the basis of practical needs and the likelihood of obtaining the most interesting and useful information.

ETHNOGRAPHY

According to Van Maanen (1988) "an *ethnography* is written representation of a culture (or selected aspects of a culture)" (p. 2). And "*Culture* refers to the knowledge members ('natives') of a given group are thought to more or less share; knowledge of the sort that is said to inform, embed, shape, and account for the routine and not-so-routine activities of the members of the culture" (p. 3).

Because culture is a set of abstract ideas—the patterns, values, expectations, and traditions by which a group of people order life—it is never seen. Rather, the culture of a group is described by an observer. That description takes the form of a narrative account called an ethnography.

Fieldwork is the method that is used to create an ethnography. The term *fieldwork* has its origins in the idea that the researcher goes "into the field" to study a group of people and events in their natural setting. This method was originated by anthropologists who, in the late 19th and early 20th centuries, visited and often lived in primitive societies. Early anthropologists believed that primitive cultures could be studied merely by visiting them and paying natives to serve as informants. By the late 1920s, however, anthropologist field-workers were spending extended amounts of time living with native people in their natural habitat (Van Maanen, 1988).

In sociology, the fieldwork method received its first impetus from the Chicago School, a group of sociologists who studied social problems in urban settings. They emphasized social reform: exposing the inequities of the day and documenting the plight of groups from the lower classes—hobos, gangs, opium addicts, and other groups.

In both disciplines—anthropology and sociology—fieldwork became a well-established qualitative method. The fieldwork researcher believed that the only way to gain true knowledge about something was to "go out and do it." This was the basis for *participant observation.*

Participant observation is the role played by ethnographers when they conduct fieldwork. The participant observer becomes part of "an ongoing social setting for the purpose of making a qualitative analysis of that setting" (Lofland, 1971, p. 93). This involves living with or having extensive contact with the people being studied for months or years at a time and participating in their lives, often as a friend, associate, or coworker. For example, in the case study at the end of this chapter, the sociologist Elliot Licbow spent a period of over a year "hanging out" with a group of lower-class African American men to understand their lives.

Participant observation is sometimes contrasted with *nonparticipant observation.* In this role, the researcher observes the persons being studied but does not actually participate in their activities. For example, the researcher may attend meetings of a neighborhood association without actually participating in their deliberations. In practice, it may be difficult to distinguish between the two roles. For example, in the Humphreys (1970) study discussed in Chapter 3 on ethics, the researcher observed men having sex with each other in public restrooms although he did not participate directly. To provide a rationale for remaining in this setting, however, he had to play a role: He served as a "lookout" to alert study participants of the approach of intruders. In this sense, he did participate in their activities.

Some researchers (e.g., Lofland, 1971) have raised ethical concerns about participant observation. To avoid changing the behavior of those observed, participant observers may not inform the persons being observed of their true identity as researchers. Even in situations in which researchers have informed their contacts, they may find themselves interacting with others who are not aware of their role. It may be difficult to avoid behavior that would otherwise be seen as ethically wrong—such as taking an illegal drug or concealing a crime. These concerns must be balanced against the research advantages of playing a hidden role. Taking on the identity of a natural participant may be the only way to study a group—for example, a street gang or a ring of white-collar criminals (Lofland, 1971, p. 94). The behaviors being observed are most likely to reflect real-life behavior when the actors do not know they are being observed.

Ethnographers write from a qualitative point of view. That is, the underlying assumption of ethnography is that "reality" is not a fixed characteristic of the world. Rather, it is "constructed" by the observer. Therefore, the writing of ethnography is an interpretive act, inevitably colored by the ethnographer's point of view, biases, methods, experiences, and selective attention. These are constraints that determine how the culture or social group will be presented. Van Maanen (1988) discusses several such constraints:

1. Ethnographies are based on what the ethnographer experienced in the fieldwork. What the ethnographer experienced may or may not reflect the natives' own view. For example, natives grant quick access to some aspects of their culture but are reticent to reveal other aspects—for example, sacred rituals. The gender of the researcher may determine how readily the ethnographer is allowed to observe certain events, such as male initiation rites or activities engaged in only by women. The setting and the person affect what is accessible to the ethnographer.

2. The nature of the ethnography is affected by politics. The ethnographer, rather than the natives, is the one who determines what is said about the culture. The ethnographer's choice of subject, group, or method may be determined by budgetary constraints, the politics of the academic department, and the preferences of the foundations funding the research.

3. Ethnographers are affected by the particular disciplines they are affiliated with and by the currently popular practices in those disciplines. Ethnographers will tend to see what they expect to see.

4. The way ethnography is done—particular procedures or areas of interest—changes over time.

Van Maanen (1988) also argues that ethnographers shape their ethnographic reports by the narrative style they use. He identifies three types of ethnographic reports, or "tales," that represent three different narrative styles:

1. The most common ethnographic report is the *realist tale.* In this type of ethnography, the researcher tries to present the material as "accurately" as possible. The researcher avoids the use of "I" statements and focuses exclusively on reporting what happened and exactly what the natives said and did. The style is that of a documentary. Rather than presenting their own analysis or opinion, researchers present extensive and minute details about the lives of natives—for example, describing eating patterns, living quarters, or rituals in great detail. There is an effort to present the natives' own points of view as they were expressed by the natives.

2. In the *confessional tale* researchers "confess" their own participation in and reaction to the fieldwork. These tales may describe how the researchers faced barriers and overcame them, how they gained access to the culture, how the fieldwork experience affected them, and how they gained rapport with natives. The ethnographic report is written in the first person ("I spoke to . . .") with an emphasis on the point of view of the field researcher. Rather than presenting a sanitized view of fieldwork, researchers report the full range of unplanned and unexpected developments—episodes that shocked the researchers, mistakes that were made, and so on.

3. The *impressionist tale* is an ethnography that is written to startle the reader. Rather than describing ordinary or usual events, the researcher describes rare or extraordinary events. The style is one of a series of events remembered by the author so that the final result is much like that of an impressionist painting—the reader gets a highly personal view rather than a photograph. As in the confessional tale, there are many references to the personal reactions of the author. The author uses dramatic recall—the purpose being to engage the reader with the story and to enable the reader to experience

the events in the same way as the writer who experienced them. The ethnography reads like a novel, but the plot—the meaning of all the events presented—is not clear. This is a story that maintains the reader's interest and seems true to life.

SUMMARY

Most social work research adheres to the scientific method. This method is based on a paradigm—or view of the world— called positivism. According to the positivistic paradigm, there is an "objective" world that exists independently of the observer and that is governed by universal laws that can be understood by scientists using positivistic methods. These methods rely on verifying relationships between variables by using scientific procedures, such as testing hypotheses derived from theory and verifying results by use of independent observers.

In recent years, social work researchers have criticized this positivistic research paradigm for distorting and trivializing reality. An alternative to the positivistic approach—qualitative research—has become increasingly popular among social work researchers.

Qualitative researchers recognize the subjective nature of reality so that the researcher's point of view becomes part of the research findings. Rather than follow a fixed series of steps from theory formulation to hypothesis testing, qualitative researchers use a back-and-forth process. Beginning with intensive examination of data, they devise explanatory concepts to explain the data and revise these concepts repeatedly based on further analysis.

Qualitative research favors intensive analysis of one or a few cases, in-depth unstructured interviews and observation, and narrative rather than numerical reporting. Common qualitative research methods include grounded theory, case studies, and ethnography. Grounded theory is a method for studying complex social phenomena, in which theories are developed from, or grounded in, data. In the case study, the researcher intensely examines a single case in its natural setting. Ethnography uses fieldwork—living in and with a group of people for an extended period of time—to study a particular culture. All qualitative research seeks to develop rich insights that have direct relevance to real-world behavior.

CASE STUDY

Elliot Liebow, a sociologist, collected data by participant observation of lower class African American men who spent time hanging out on a street corner in a blighted inner-city neighborhood of Washington, D.C. Most of the data were collected during 1962 and 1963.

Liebow's (1967) study was an important contribution to knowledge about lower-class urban African American men. Although most poor people in the United States are not African American, African Americans are much more likely than whites to be poor. African Americans tend to be among the very poorest, and they often tend to remain in poverty over several generations. As a result, researchers have been interested in discovering the conditions that create and maintain poverty among African Americans. With migration from rural areas to the cities after World War II, this poverty has been increasingly concentrated in minority inner-city neighborhoods.

This study grew out of a larger study of child-rearing practices of low-income families in the District of Columbia. Because the father was absent in many low-income families, most research on this group—including the larger study that spawned Liebow's research—focused on mothers and children. Elliot Liebow set out to study a segment of the low-income African American community that had been invisible to researchers and social workers: African American males. At that time, much of what was known about African American males came from the minority of African Americans who had come into contact with the law. Liebow wanted to find out what life was like for a more representative group of African American males.

Like most qualitative research, this study did not set out to test any hypotheses or theories. Its aim was to get a clear picture of the reality of day-to-day life for lower-class inner-city African American men. The conventional techniques of questionnaires and interviews were not appropriate to this task. Many of these men were illiterate. In any case, their reluctance to respond to research studies made them poor candidates for questionnaires and interviews, techniques that are generally inappropriate for marginal or disenfranchised groups. Instead, Liebow played the role of participant observer. He spent large amounts of time interacting with two dozen African American men who spent long hours on a street corner near a "carry-out" food store.

Liebow began simply by showing up at a street corner that was popular among these men. He began to interact with them, and over time, he gained their confidence. Some of the men knew that Liebow was a university researcher seeking to gain an understanding of their lives. It was obvious to all of them that he was white. Nevertheless, he became part of their day-to-day lives and integrated into their social networks. Over the 18 months of the study, he observed these men on the street corner and in alleys, hallways, poolrooms, private homes, and bars. As opportunities arose, he also followed these men into hospitals, dance parlors, courtrooms, and jails.

Liebow affected a style of dress and speech that fit with these men. He occasionally provided them with small amounts of money, accepted gifts, and participated in betting and buying "numbers." Unlike these men, however, he did not live in the neighborhood, and he avoided sexual relations with the women he encountered.

To record his observations, Liebow took copious notes on everything he observed and did. Presumably, he recorded these immediately after each observation. To bring some order to these notes, he divided all observations into five categories. These categories involved the various roles played by these men: breadwinner, father, husband, lover, and friend. Liebow argued that this framework fit the data well because it was consistent with the way these men viewed their own lives. Liebow also described physical settings in great detail.

The following is an example of Liebow's description of one of the men:

> Tally is a brown-skinned man, thirty-one years old. He is six feet tall and weighs just under two hundred pounds. His size and carriage lend credibility to the general belief that he was once a professional heavyweight fighter. When asked to affirm or deny this status, Tally merely grins, assumes the classic stance of the boxer, and invites the questioner to "come on." No one does.
>
> Tally moved into a room in the [neighborhood] in the winter of 1961. In the eight years he has been in Washington, Tally has lived in the Northeast, Southeast, and Northwest sections of the city. During this same period, he has married and separated and fathered eight children, three with his wife and five others with five different women. (Liebow, 1967, pp. 23-24)

Liebow's book—*Tally's Corner*—is a description of the findings from this qualitative study. His conclusions include the following:

- The structural and cultural features of the daily lives of these street corner men resembled those reported among urban poor in other large cities in other parts of the United States.
- Men, women, and children spent a great deal of time on the street, hanging out on street corners, sitting in front of buildings, or leaning out of windows. These settings were conducive to a great deal of social interaction.
- "Serial monogamy" appeared to be the norm. Men and women married in their 20s with the expectation, or at least the hope, of enduring partnerships.

Faced with numerous social and economic difficulties, the couple inevitably failed in this goal. Both men and women moved on to new partners. Men lived with women and fathered children as readily with or without marriage.

- Illiteracy, lack of skills, low expectations, and poor job opportunities combined to create a lifelong experience of intermittent and marginal employment. The longer these men worked, the longer they were unable to support a family. They had little vested interest in their menial jobs. Their work status was associated with poor self-esteem.

- The street corner man saw himself as a failure in the world of work and also in his family life. In reaction to the humiliation he felt, he often struck out physically at his children and his spouse.

- In response to these failures, he turned to street corner society, where an alternative view prevailed, one in which he was not seen as a failure. His failures were rationalized into successes. To his street corner buddies, he was not a failure as a husband but a success as an "exploiter of women," a manly individual with a taste for whiskey and women.

- On the street corner, friendships were an important source of physical and emotional security. Friends served as sources of money, goods, and services in a world where such resources were in short supply. As a result, friendships were often quick to form and quick to become intense. In reality, these friendships were fragile because they were short-lived. There was too much transience in these neighborhoods for long-term friendships to form. Unlike earlier charac-terizations of lower-class life, this lower-class urban neighborhood was not a tightly knit community whose members shared a sense of belonging.

- The world of lower-class urban African Americans did not constitute a separate subculture with values different from those of the larger commu-nity. Rather, these men had the same values regarding family, love, work, and achievement as did men in the rest of society. But having failed to achieve these values, street corner men attempted to conceal this failure from others and from themselves.

Employing qualitative research methods, Liebow was able to paint a detailed and accurate picture of the lives of lower-class African American men in an inner-city neighborhood. Liebow's research informed social scientists about the complex ways in which the men viewed their roles as husbands, lovers, fathers, friends, and employees. As a result, researchers and social workers were better informed about this largely ignored group.

DISCUSSION QUESTIONS

1. What is a paradigm? How is it relevant to social work research?

2. What are the basic assumptions of positivistic research?

3. What are the basic characteristics of qualitative research?

4. What is grounded theory? What are some of its methods?

5. What data should researchers collect when they conduct a case study?

6. What are some of the methods used by ethnographers?

SHORT ASSIGNMENTS

1. Review journals that publish social work research articles to find an article that reports on a qualitative research study. (See Chapter 5 for a list of journals.) On the basis of a careful reading of the article, answer the following questions:

a. What research questions were addressed?

b. Why did the researcher choose these particular research questions?

c. Why did the researcher choose qualitative methods?

d. What specific methods were used to collect the data (for example, in-depth interviews, observation)?

e. What were the findings?

f. Were the qualitative methods that were employed appropriate to answer the research questions? Could other qualitative or quantitative methods also have been used? If so, which ones?

2. Select a social problem area of interest to you. Think of a research question related to that area. Describe a qualitative study that can be used to answer the research question. Be sure to include a description of the events, persons, or phenomena to be studied; how data will be collected; who will collect them; and how the results will be presented.

FURTHER READING

Denzin, N. K., & Lincoln, Y. S. (Eds.). (1994). *Handbook of qualitative research.* Thousand Oaks, CA: Sage.

Patton, M. Q. (1990). *Qualitative evaluation and research methods* (2nd ed.). Newbury Park, CA: Sage.

Riessman, C. K. (Ed.). (1994). *Qualitative studies in social work research.* Thousand Oaks, CA: Sage.

11 Program Evaluation

Definition: Program evaluation is a type of research that uses established social science research methods (such as those discussed in this book) to evaluate the success or effect of a social service *program.*

It is useful to state what program evaluation is *not.* It is not "pure" or theoretical research, which has the goal of developing hypotheses and evaluating and creating theories. Although the aim of pure research is to create knowledge for its own sake, evaluation research is always concerned with a program that serves people. That program may be in operation, or it may be planned. But the results of program evaluation are always intended to be *applied* to a real-world program.

Program evaluation differs from clinical evaluation in the target or intended beneficiary of the research. Clinical evaluation is a type of research used to evaluate small-scale interventions applied to individuals, families, and small groups. Research into the effectiveness of psychotherapy is the most common type of clinical evaluation.

Program evaluation may be used to answer the following types of questions:

1. Does a job training program result in greater employment for trainees? Do trainees also obtain more skilled and higher-paying jobs as a result of participating in the program?

2. Does a program to provide in-home services (such as homemaking, chore and errand service, and telephone reassurance) to the noninstitutionalized frail elderly prevent or delay placement into a nursing home? If so, are in-home services less expensive than nursing home care?
3. Does establishment of a regional trauma center in a local hospital result in fewer deaths and better medical care for traumatically injured community residents?
4. Does a public education program about child sexual abuse reduce the incidence of this type of abuse?

As we saw in Chapters 7 and 9, research designs are used to direct the researcher's activities. Every design discussed in those chapters can be used with any of the types of research: pure research, clinical research, and program evaluation.

In practice, it is more often possible for the first two types of research to use rigorous designs—that is, designs that use control groups and randomization procedures. Pure research and clinical research are typically conducted in controlled settings, such as a psychology clinic or university lab, where the researcher is able to randomly select individuals and assign them to comparison groups. The researcher also has better control over the timing and circumstances of measurement—for example, the administration of intelligence tests or marital satisfaction surveys.

Program evaluators, on the other hand, are out in the real world where they often have little control over these factors. Program evaluators may be working with data that have been collected by others for other purposes (e.g., traffic fatality or birth data). Or they may be working within an agency, with staff who are more interested in providing services than in evaluating them.

For these reasons, program evaluations typically use "preexperimental" or "quasi-experimental" designs that are approximations to the experimental designs described in Chapter 7 of this book. Perhaps the most common research design in program evaluations is the one-group pretest-posttest design described in Chapter 7. In this design, a group is studied before and after an intervention. For example, a company may monitor the smoking of its employees before and after a campaign of incentives to stop smoking.

In recent years, with increasing public demands for accountability, government and agency researchers have been given the resources to evaluate programs with more rigorous designs.

For example, through the use of Medicaid waivers, the federal government has made it possible to study the effectiveness of in-home services in preventing or delaying the placement of frail older persons in nursing homes. In a number of such program evaluations, researchers were able to use experimental designs by randomly assigning older persons to receive in-home services or to receive only routine services. The status of all participants was then tracked over time to see if those who received in-home services were less likely to be placed in nursing homes.[1]

Although program evaluation often differs from other forms of research in the types of research designs used, all forms of research share a common purpose. They all seek to answer questions by using established social science research methodologies as described in this book. Use of these methodologies helps to ensure that answers to research questions are valid and reliable, whether they apply to individuals, families, groups, communities, or programs.

TYPES OF PROGRAM EVALUATION

Suchman (1967) suggests that program evaluation be classified into five types. Each type corresponds to a different criterion that can be used to evaluate a program: effort, performance, impact or adequacy of performance, efficiency, and process.

Effort. Effort evaluations ask, What did you do? and To what extent did you do it? Effort evaluations study the quantity and extent of the interventions that make up the program.

We might, for example, implement a program to increase public awareness of abuse of the elderly. At a very minimum, the funding source will expect us to provide data on our effort. An effort evaluation would record and present the following data: (a) dollars expended on print, radio, and television advertising; (b) number of educational workshops provided for professionals who come into contact with the elderly (this will include the numbers who attended); (c) the number of calls handled by a toll-free, abuse-reporting telephone service established as part of the program; (d) the number of leaflets and brochures distributed through the mail and at community meetings; and (e) the number of families who used senior day care services (a preventive measure).

It should be clear from this example, that effort evaluations tell us nothing about the *effectiveness* of the program. In the past, funding agencies were often satisfied with effort data alone. Today, most funding sources will also require researchers to document results as well as effort. This is done through the next type of evaluation.

Performance. Performance evaluations measure results rather than efforts. Although an effort evaluation is a useful first step, it is the performance evaluation that tells us if our goals were actually met.

In the preceding example, our long-term goal is to reduce elder abuse. Our performance evaluation would gather data on subgoals such as these:

How many additional cases (if any) of elder abuse were reported?

In how many of the reported cases was the abuse effectively stopped?

How many abusers were successfully prosecuted?

In how many instances of reported abuse was the older person required to relocate? What was the effect of this relocation on the well-being of the older person?

Ultimately, we want to assess, Has the actual incidence of elder abuse diminished in our community?

Obtaining performance data in addition to effort data is crucial to program evaluation, because successful effort does not ensure successful performance. In this example, the prevention program of advertising, workshops, and so on may not alter the actual incidence of elder abuse. Increased public awareness of the problem may in fact have a contrary effect in that it may cause family members to hide the abuse more effectively.

This does not mean that the program was useless. It may simply mean that other, more effective methods must be employed to address the problem.

Most comprehensive program evaluations involve more than one type of evaluation. Effort and performance evaluations are used to answer the questions, What did we do? and What results did it have? Often, these evaluations precede the next type of program evaluation.

Impact or Adequacy of Performance. This type of program evaluation asks, How effective is the program in meeting its goals, relative to the total amount of need?

This question is important, because an effective program (i.e., one that meets the performance criterion) may have little effect on a behavior or social problem unless the program is able to influence a sufficiently large number of people in the community. For example, this might happen in the following instance.

TABLE 11.1 Comparison of the Effect of Two Programs on Reducing Elder Abuse

	Number Exposed to Program	Performance (Rate of Effectiveness)	Impact (Number Influenced)
Intensive casework program	100	50%	50
Public education program	10,000	10%	1,000

Social workers have argued that disturbed family relationships are often the cause of elder abuse. The adult caretakers themselves may have been abused by the elderly parent whom they are now abusing, and family conflicts rooted in early family life can be reactivated by the stress of caring for a dependent older parent. Caretakers may feel that the family has unfairly forced them into that role, and the resulting resentment then expresses itself as abuse of the older person.

Given the importance of family dynamics in causing elder abuse, one agency designed an intensive family casework program to reduce the likelihood of abuse. The program was successful for the families that were served.

An impact evaluation, however, revealed that the program was not successful on the community level. The program was effective for the families it served. But because the agency was able to implement the program with only a limited number of families, the effect of the program on reducing elder abuse in the community was diminished. This is illustrated in Table 11.1.

Table 11.1 summarizes the results of the impact evaluation. Intensive casework is an effective intervention. But for the purpose of reducing elder abuse, a less potent campaign of public education is more adequate because it influences a larger number of people.

Efficiency. Efficiency evaluations assess the costs of implementing a program. Two types of questions are addressed by efficiency evaluations: (a) Do the benefits of implementing the program justify its costs? (b) Are there alternative, less costly methods that will achieve the same results?

Typically, a technique called *cost-benefit analysis* is used to answer the first question. This is a purely economic procedure in which dollar values are assigned to various costs and benefits. Then, total costs are divided into total benefits. If the ratio is greater than 1, this indicates that benefits outweigh costs.

Health economists have used cost-benefit analysis to evaluate the effect of universal national health insurance. The costs are primarily the dollar value of health insurance premiums to be paid by individuals, employers, and the government. The benefits include the dollar value of reduced number of sick days, savings from improved coordination of services, and so on.

Cost-benefit analysis is not as scientific as it appears at first. There is a great deal of subjectivity in deciding what will be included as costs and benefits. Nevertheless, it is a useful tool for evaluating the economic efficiency of a program and determining whether a program should be started or continued.

Because there is almost always more than one way—or one program—to achieve a single goal, the second efficiency question is also important: Are there alternative, less costly methods that will achieve the same results?

For example, federally funded school lunch programs have been widely used to improve nutrition among low-income children. Effort and performance evaluations, however, have revealed many problems with the program: (a) inefficient food purchasing that results in high costs relative to local supermarket prices, (b) disposal of large quantities of ordered food because of poor planning, and (c) unappetizing menus resulting in low student consumption (Lash & Sigal, 1976).

An efficiency evaluation of the school lunch program would compare the relative costs of more than one method to ensure adequate nutrition among low-income youth. Such an evaluation might find that expansion of the Food Stamp Program or increasing Aid to Families With Dependent Children (AFDC) grants results in the same level of nutrition at lower cost.

Process. The types of evaluation discussed so far tell us if the program was implemented as planned and if it was effective, adequate, and efficient. These criteria determine the success of the program.

But in addition to knowing whether the program was successful, it is often useful to know *why* it was or was not successful. That is the purpose of process evaluation.

A process evaluation assesses the components of a program to identify which ones contributed to its success and which did not. It traces the history of the program and the implementation of its various features to give us an understanding of what happened.

For example, imagine that the State Department on Aging implements a statewide elder abuse hotline. Staffed by local volunteers, the purpose of the hotline is to encourage citizens to report suspected abuse and to allow potential abusers to "let off steam" and find alternatives to abuse.

Assume that a program evaluation indicates that the program is successful (as measured perhaps by a reduced incidence of older persons appearing in emergency rooms with suspicious injuries, fewer complaints filed with the nursing home ombudsman, etc.). It is also useful to know how and why the hotline led to a decrease in abuse.

A process analysis might show that the program was associated with decreased abuse but only in urban and suburban areas. The incidence of abuse remained unchanged in rural areas of the state.

Further process analysis might reveal the reasons for this curious finding. Analysis of hotline records and interviews with rural service providers might reveal that rural citizens are less likely than their urban counterparts to use the hotline. Anonymity is the issue. Potential callers are dissuaded from calling because they may know the hotline volunteer or an acquaintance or relative of the volunteer. This kind of analysis is useful. In this case, it would lead the program directors to institute and publicize new procedures to ensure caller anonymity.

NEEDS ASSESSMENT

Another type of research that is often helpful to program designers and evaluators is *needs assessment.* A needs assessment is a research and planning activity designed to determine human service needs and service use patterns.

Needs assessments are often useful in providing data for the establishment of new programs or expansion of existing programs. For example, a needs assessment in a rural area found that many farmworker families experienced hunger before and after the harvest season. Although food surplus commodities were available, these were underused because of poor access to food distribution centers, shame associated with accepting in-kind assistance, and poor variety of available food. This needs assessment led to an outreach program to enlist more of these families in the Food Stamp Program. Food stamps are generally more acceptable to the poor; like cash, they can be used to supplement the family's food budget and therefore allow for greater choice and selection of food items.

The evaluation of existing programs can also be enhanced by a needs assessment. In the food stamp example, continuation of the needs assessment will tell us if the food stamp outreach program results in greater program participation and less hunger.

According to Warheit, Bell, and Schwab (1979), there are five approaches to conducting a needs assessment. These include (a) the key informant approach, (b) the community forum approach, (c) the rates-under-treatment approach, (d) the social indicators approach, and (e) the survey approach. These approaches can be used separately or in combination.

Key Informant. This approach relies on information obtained from persons who are in the position of knowing a community's needs and service use patterns. Key informants are the kinds of individuals who are familiar with a community, its residents and their needs, and available services. These persons normally include public officials, clergy, physicians, social workers, and other staff and board members of agencies and organizations. Usually, information is collected from key informants by interview or questionnaire.

Community Forum. This approach is based on individuals coming together at public meetings and expressing their opinions about the needs and services of a community. This approach, like the key informant approach, relies on the impressions of persons who know the community. Because the community forum approach uses public meetings, however, more of the general population can be involved, and even specific groups—such as the elderly or ethnic minorities—can be asked to provide testimony. To maximize the input and full participation of individuals, the public meetings are kept small in size. Large assemblies are usually avoided because they are not conducive to the open exchange that is needed. At these meetings, the researcher records the ideas, attitudes, and opinions of participants. Later, a summary of all suggestions made regarding the needs and services is prepared, and priority areas are noted.

Rates Under Treatment. This approach to needs assessment is based on descriptive characteristics gleaned from service use data. The underlying assumption is that the needs of a community can be determined by examining the needs of those who have received services. For example, if a home health agency finds that most of its cases consist of elderly individuals aged 75 and older who live alone, then the agency can infer that this group is more in need than those who are younger and living with others. Agency records can often provide descriptive characteristics of their clientele (e.g., age, sex, race, income); the presenting problems of their clients; the types, frequency, and duration of the services they received; and the outcome of the services provided. This information, when compiled, can be valuable in establishing the need for services.

Social Indicators. This approach relies on inferences made from descriptive information found in public records, documents, and reports. The assumption of this approach to needs assessment is that it is possible to estimate the needs of a community based on data that are known to be strong indicators of need. For example, if we used the social indicators approach to estimate the need for a drug and alcohol program in a specific community, we might examine arrests related to drug and alcohol violations, the number of driving-under-the-influence (DUI) offenses, the number of traffic accidents involving drugs or alcohol, coroner's reports that indicated the use of drugs or alcohol, the amount of beer and liquor sales within the community, hospital emergency room statistics, and so on. All these indicators, when taken together, give a good picture of the need for services.

Survey Approach. This is the most rigorous method for conducting a needs assessment. It uses questionnaires or interviews to collect data from a sample or an entire population. It relies on many of the principles and methods for social work research that are discussed throughout this text. With the survey approach, participants are asked to report on their problems, needs, and patterns of service use. For example, suppose an agency serving the elderly wants to find out if the needs of the elderly who reside in a new senior citizen high-rise are being met by the agency. The agency could conduct a needs assessment by interviewing all of the elderly residents in the building to examine their needs for, and use of, the services provided by the agency, including transportation, homemaker and chore services, Meals-on-Wheels, home health care, recreation and socialization programs, and case management. Using information gathered from the needs assessment, the agency could better tailor its services to clients.

SUMMARY

Program evaluation is like other types of social work research in that it uses established social science research methodology. It is distinguished by its focus on evaluating the performance and success of social service programs. Because of the constraints of doing research in the real world, program evaluators must often use modifications of the more rigorous experimental designs. Programs are evaluated on the basis of one or more of the following criteria: effort, performance, impact or adequacy of performance, efficiency, and process. Needs assessments, aimed at determining social service needs and use patterns, can also be used to evaluate the need for, or the effect of, social service programs. Five approaches exist for conducting a needs assessment: key informant, community forum, rates under treatment, social indicators, and the survey.

DISCUSSION QUESTIONS

1. How does program evaluation differ from the other types of research discussed in previous chapters? How is it similar?
2. Define and give an example of each of the following types of program evaluation:

   a. Effort
   b. Performance
   c. Impact or adequacy of performance
   d. Efficiency
   e. Process

3. In an intervention to increase the parenting skills of low-income teenage mothers in a community, would it be better to use a highly effective campaign that has a limited impact, or a less effective campaign that has widespread impact? Explain.
4. Your agency asks you to design an assessment of the need for low-cost housing in your community. Describe five ways in which you can obtain data on the need for such housing.

SHORT ASSIGNMENTS

1. Imagine that you are a school social worker. Your principal has asked you to design an intervention program to reduce truancy among students. You are also asked to design a plan to evaluate the program.

   a. What interventions will you recommend?
   b. Describe one way you will measure each of the following outcomes:

Program effort
Program performance
Impact of the program
The program process

2. Suppose you have been asked to evaluate a "targeting" program sponsored by the county sheriff's office. For the past 3 years, the sheriff's office has targeted youth with prior arrest records who are likely to commit new violent crimes: When these youth commit new crimes, they are immediately identified; their cases are processed in a special unit; and they receive stiffer sentences, including longer jail or prison terms that will keep them off the streets.

This program requires extra coordination among local police units, additional staff time, and related services. It is hoped, however, that the program will reduce the rate of violent offenses in the county against both persons and property.

As part of your evaluation, prepare a list of both costs and benefits of this program. Be sure to include costs and benefits to the county, to local police departments, and to community residents and business owners.

NOTE

1. By the way, the results of this research indicated that frail elderly who received in-home services used fewer days of hospital and nursing home care, but it is not clear if in-home maintenance is always less costly than nursing home care (Applebaum, Seidl, & Austin, 1980).

FURTHER READING

Posavac, E. J., & Carey, R. G. (1992). *Program evaluation: Methods and case studies* (4th ed.). Englewood Cliffs, NJ: Prentice Hall.

12 Sources of Data

Questionnaires, Interviews, Schedules,

and Available Materials

I n Chapter 6, I talked about how to select individuals or other elements for study (sampling), and in Chapters 7, 8, and 9, I discussed how to plan a study by specifying a research design. Once these steps have been completed, we are going to have to collect data. This chapter discusses three common methods for collecting data: the questionnaire, the interview, and available materials, such as census and registration data.

QUESTIONNAIRES AND INTERVIEWS

Definition: A *questionnaire* is a set of questions or items in written form that is self-administered.

Definition: An *interview* is a face-to-face situation in which an interviewer asks questions of one or more interviewees.

Interviews may be of two types. In the *unstandardized interview,* the general nature of the questions is specified in advance, but the specific questions are not. Keeping the research purpose in mind, the interviewer may determine the specific wording of the questions and their order. This allows for a naturalistic or informal interview in that the interviewer is free to ask questions in the order and manner that follow the natural flow of the interaction. A list of questions or question guidelines may be prepared, but a formal interview schedule is not generally used.

The *structured* or *standardized interview* is more common. Here, the interviewer is trained in using an interview schedule, which consists of a list of questions. In other words, the specific wording and order of questions are predetermined and standard for all interviewees. Often, there are precise instructions to the interviewer as to how and when the questions are to be asked; for example, certain questions may be skipped if the interviewee is female or if a previous question has been answered in a certain way.

A researcher used a standardized interview in a study of individuals who had experienced traumatic losses, such as massive accident injuries or death of a child (Berger, 1988). The purpose of this study was to discover how people coped with massive loss. On the interview schedule, questions were grouped under clear and easy-to-read subheadings, such as "Current Life," "The Loss," "Family," and "Social Network." These headings helped to orient the interviewers and allowed them easily to find the appropriate question at each point in the interview. As an example of the types of questions used, the following items appeared under the heading "Social Network": "Who are your closest friends?" "How have they reacted to your loss?" "How do you spend your leisure time?"

In some situations, researchers interview more than one person at a time. For example, a researcher interested in family functioning may interview a couple or even an entire family in one session. Or the researcher may select a number of individuals for a *group interview.* The group interview may be standardized with the use of predetermined questions in fixed order. Or it may be unstandardized, starting with a broad question and allowing respondents to discuss their experiences in a free-flowing manner.

One type of group interview is the *focus group interview.* This type of interview is commonly used by market researchers studying the opinion of consumers about a particular product or service. Focus group interviews are also used by political candidates and parties to determine voter reactions and preferences (Fontana & Frey, 1994). The researcher may use a focus group as an exploratory tool to identify preliminary research questions in a new area of inquiry. For example, Janesick (1994) used focus groups to study how deaf adults managed to cope with school and work despite their disability. Data collected from these groups allowed her to fashion more specific research questions for use in later interviews.

The focus group also can be used to test new research or clinical techniques, identify key informants (individuals who can supply information needed for a study), see if a particular way of defining a problem is accurate, see if the perspectives of research participants agree with the findings gathered from other sources of data, and pretest questionnaires or interview schedules.

The focus group interview provides a rich source of data and often leads to new and unexpected avenues for further research. It does, however, require a highly trained interviewer who can ensure that the discussion is not dominated by one or a few individuals, that individual views are represented, and that honest responses are forthcoming on sensitive topics (Fontana & Frey, 1994).

TYPES OF ITEMS

A variety of types of items are used in interviews and questionnaires. Some of the most common are *fixed-alternative (closed) items, scales,* and *open-end items.*

FIXED-ALTERNATIVE ITEMS

In a fixed-alternative or closed item, the respondent is presented with two or more alternatives provided by the interviewer or the questionnaire. The respondent is asked to choose one or more of these alternatives. For example, in a questionnaire study of attitudes toward welfare recipients, one item read as follows:

Public assistance discourages people from working. (Check one)

_____ Agree
_____ Disagree
_____ Not sure

The following fixed-alternative item was taken from an interview schedule designed to assess the level of functioning of frail elderly persons:

Can you get into or out of bed? (Ask respondent to choose one)

_____ Without any help or aids

_____ With occasional help or with assistive device

_____ Or are you totally dependent on someone else to lift you or to help with an assistive device?

_____ Or are you totally bedfast?

The Rathus Assertiveness Schedule, a questionnaire used to measure level of assertiveness, is described in the case study in Chapter 14 (Rathus, 1973). The instructions to respondents and the first three items appear as follows:

Directions: Indicate how characteristic or descriptive each of the following statements is of you by using the code given below.

+3 Very characteristic of me, extremely descriptive

+2 Rather characteristic of me, quite descriptive

+1 Somewhat characteristic of me, slightly descriptive

−1 Somewhat uncharacteristic of me, slightly nondescriptive

−2 Rather uncharacteristic of me, quite nondescriptive

−3 Very uncharacteristic of me, extremely nondescriptive

_____ 1. Most people seem to be more aggressive and assertive than I am.

_____ 2. I have hesitated to make or accept dates because of "shyness."

_____ 3. When the food served at a restaurant is not done to my satisfaction, I complain about it to the waiter or waitress.

This last illustration is also an example of a scale.

SCALES

Definition: A scale item is a special type of fixed-alternative item. A *scale* is a set of questionnaire or interview items to each of which an individual responds by expressing degrees of agreement or disagreement or some other type of response.

Definition: A *summated rating scale* is a set of scale items that are all weighted equally and to each of which the respondent responds with degrees of agreement or disagreement or some other response. An individual's score on a summated rating scale is the sum or average of scores across all items of the scale.

Scales commonly are used to measure attitudes and personality characteristics. Because these are complex variables, it is necessary to use a number of items to measure them. Self-acceptance, altruism, depression, liberalism, authoritarianism, religiosity, level of psychosomatic symptoms, life satisfaction, prejudice, and many other attitude and personality variables have been measured using summated rating scales.

The following items were adapted from a self-acceptance scale developed by Rosenberg (1965).

Instructions: Indicate the extent to which you agree that the statements below characterize you and your feelings.

After reading each statement, circle one code:

SA   Strongly agree
A   Agree
?   Are not sure
D   Disagree
SD   Strongly disagree

1. I am not as happy as others seem to be.	SA A ? D SD
2. I feel that I have a number of good qualities.	SA A ? D SD
3. All in all, I am inclined to think that I am a failure.	SA A ? D SD
4. On the whole, I am satisfied with myself.	SA A ? D SD

In a summated rating scale, there may be two to seven response alternatives for each question. In a two-response alternative, for example, the respondent may simply be asked to agree or disagree with each item or to indicate which items are characteristic of the respondent. Five-response alternatives from *strongly agree* to *strongly disagree* are common. More-than-seven-response alternatives tend to confuse the respondent. Most people are not able to make such fine distinctions reliably.

Some scale items merely provide a line representing a continuum, and respondents are asked to place a mark at any point along the line representing their attitude or feeling. Other scales, such as the semantic differential, provide a series of blanks or numbers that are not labeled. (An example of a semantic differential is contained in the case study in Chapter 14.) Labeling each response alternative, however, enhances reliability because it ensures that all respondents are interpreting each alternative in the same way. (Reliability of measurement is discussed further in Chapter 14.)

Notice that there are two types of items in the earlier excerpt from the self-acceptance scale. Items 1 and 3 are negative items: Agreement indicates low self-acceptance. Items 2 and 4 are positive items: Agreement indicates high self-acceptance. When researchers construct summated rating scales, they generally state half the items in a positive direction and half in a negative direction. This is done to correct for the tendency that many respondents have for always choosing one end of the scale (that is, always agreeing or disagreeing) regardless of their true attitude or feeling. Reverse wording forces the respondent to think about the answer to each item.

When we are computing a respondent's score on a summated rating scale, we must, of course, take the reverse wording of items into account. In this example, it makes sense to code the responses so that a high score indicates a high level of self-acceptance and vice versa. This will happen if we code responses as follows:

	SA	A	?	D	SD
Code for negatively worded items:	1	2	3	4	5
Code for positively worded items:	5	4	3	2	1

To obtain each respondent's total self-acceptance score, the individual item scores are summed or averaged.

As we can see from this example, an advantage of fixed-alternative items is that they are easy to code and tabulate. The researcher simply adds up or averages the scores corresponding to the alternatives selected by the respondent. Another advantage is that measurement is uniform across respondents and reliability is enhanced because each respondent's answers must fit into clearly defined categories.

Fixed-alternative items, however, are not always the best way to collect data. Perhaps the greatest weakness of the fixed-alternative item is its superficiality. Consider the following question, for example:

Do you favor a residential facility for developmentally disabled adults in your neighborhood? (Check one)

_____ Yes

_____ No

_____ Not sure

This question might be improved by adding additional response categories. For example, we could ask respondents to indicate their degree of support from "Yes, without reservations" to "Yes, with reservations" to "No, under any circumstances."

But no matter how ingenious our response alternatives, the fixed-alternative question imposes the researcher's frame of reference on the respondent. It does not allow the interviewer to probe for underlying attitudes, and it does not allow respondents to explain the "why" and "how" of their answers. For instance, respondents may approve of a residential facility in their neighborhood but only under certain circumstances, such as adequate staffing, and only if the facility is limited to a few residents. In fact, the absence of appropriate response alternatives may irritate respondents.

A fixed-alternative question also does not allow the researcher to explore reasons behind attitudes. For example, recent newspaper accounts or neighborhood events may play an important role in attitudes toward residential facilities, but a fixed-alternative question may not unearth these reasons.

When any of these reasons apply, we may find it best to use an open-end question.

OPEN-END ITEMS

An open-end item is one in which the respondent is free to respond in his or her own words. The question supplies a frame of reference but puts a minimum of restraint on the respondent's answer.

For example, in a study of the adaptation of older gay men, Berger (1984) used open-end interview questions to solicit information about discrimination:

Do you feel you have ever been discriminated against because of your homosexuality? For instance, have you lost or been denied a job, an apartment, a service, and so on?

If yes, when? What were the circumstances?
What did you do about it?

Do you feel you have ever been discriminated against because of your age? In the
  gay community or elsewhere?

If yes, when? What were the circumstances?
What did you do about it?

These types of open-end questions are sometimes called *funnel questions.*
They operate like a funnel because they begin with a broad question and work
their way down to more specific questions.

Often, an open-end question begins with a brief statement that sets the stage
for the question or provides background information:

As you know, a number of Vietnamese families have recently moved into this
  neighborhood. Do you feel that this will affect the neighborhood? If yes, in
  what ways?

The major advantages of open-end questions are their flexibility and depth.
In an interview, they allow the interviewer to probe into respondents' attitudes
and knowledge that may help to explain the response. Interviewers can find
out where the respondent has knowledge gaps. They can find ambiguities and
ask for clarification. The respondent has the opportunity to explain his or her
answer in detail. Open-end items are especially useful for measuring complex
attitudes for which standardized scales are not available. In an exploratory
study, respondents may give unexpected answers that can lead to new research
hypotheses or theoretical explanations.

The primary disadvantage of the open-end item is the difficulty in coding
responses. For example, in the preceding questions on Vietnamese families, the
researcher will have to devise some way of categorizing or summarizing responses. One way might be to come up with rules for categorizing responses into
"favorable," "neutral," and "unfavorable." This analysis, however, will be time-
consuming and difficult: The researcher will have to come up with the categories,
rules for identifying them, and judges who are trained to classify responses. In
addition, the judges' classifications will have to be checked to see if they are
reliable. (See Chapter 14 for a discussion of interrater reliability.)

Now that we have discussed closed and open-end items and scales, what
other factors should we consider in selecting or constructing a questionnaire
or interview schedule?

GUIDELINES FOR QUESTIONNAIRE
AND INTERVIEW ITEMS

1. Has another researcher developed a questionnaire or interview schedule that might serve the purpose? There is no point in reinventing the wheel. A hallmark of science is that researchers share their work through publication and that researchers build on the earlier work of others. So before we set out to do research, we must be thoroughly familiar with others' efforts in our area.

In many situations, we will find instruments that have been shown to be reliable and valid (for at least some populations) and that measure the dependent variables of interest to us. (Refer to Chapter 5 for ideas about how to conduct a library search, which should include a search for relevant instruments.) For example, in his study of the adaptation of older gay men, Berger (1984) included several scales that had been developed and validated by others. These scales measured self-acceptance, depression, psychosomatic symptoms, and life satisfaction. Berger (1984) developed his own items to measure only those variables for which validated instruments were not available or appropriate—for instance, perceived attitudes of younger gays toward older gays, and fear of aging.

Social scientists have developed a great many instruments to measure attitudes, feelings, and other characteristics. These include measures of anxiety, alienation, religious attitudes, morale, socioeconomic status, assertiveness, intelligence, tests of achievement in language usage, vocabulary, reading, arithmetic, social studies, personality, homophobia, sexism, authoritarianism, tolerance toward communists, ethnocentrism, and vocational and personal interests.

Walter Hudson, a social worker, has developed a series of brief summated rating scales that can be used to measure characteristics of clients in clinical or mental health settings. Each scale has 25 items and can be self-administered in just a few minutes. The scales measure level of contentment, self-esteem, marital satisfaction, sexual satisfaction, child's attitude toward mother, child's attitude toward father, parental attitudes toward child, quality of family relations, and quality of relations with peers (Hudson, 1981).

A practical resource for researchers seeking assessment measures is a two-volume book by Fischer and Corcoran (1994), *Measures for Clinical Practice.* In this book, the authors reproduce a large number of instruments for use with adults and children, along with detailed information on each test and scoring instructions. Fischer and Corcoran also provide a review of basic principles of measurement and guidelines for selecting the appropriate measures. *The Tenth Mental Measurements Yearbook* (Conoley & Kramer, 1989) also reproduces a variety of instruments to measure psychological characteristics.

2. Is there a purpose for every item on the questionnaire or interview schedule? When we devise our instrument we may have to fight the impulse to include too many questions. The feeling seems to be, "Well, since I have them answering my questions, why don't I just include these additional items?" The result may be a questionnaire or interview that is too long and therefore less likely to be completed.

In an exploratory study, it may be necessary to include a broad range of questions. But in a study in which we are testing specific hypotheses, we should carefully limit our questions. Every item should fall into one of two categories: The item should measure either (a) characteristics of respondents necessary for you to describe the sample, such as age and geographic location, or (b) a variable or concept in one or more of the study's hypotheses.

We should be able to describe the precise purpose of every item in our instrument. Is the purpose of the item to help us describe the sample? Is its purpose to measure a variable or concept and, if so, which one? Are items to be combined (for example, scale items) to produce a measure of a single variable? If so, how are they to be combined?

It is helpful to use one copy of the instrument as a key on which to indicate the purpose for each item and the variable for which it is to be a measure. This will help with the data analysis, which is described in Chapter 15.

3. Is the wording of the instrument appropriate to the level and sophistication of the intended respondents? It should be clear that the wording of a questionnaire designed for agency directors will be different from that of a questionnaire to be completed by teenage mothers receiving public assistance. Terms such as *mandated service, zero-based budgeting,* and *service accessibility* will be clear to the first group but not to the second.

Sometimes, the middle-class orientation of researchers leads them to miss the obvious. Selltiz et al. (1976) described such an instance:

> Survey researchers . . . interviewed southern sharecroppers shortly after World War II. On all but one . . . question designed to measure economic liberalism,

the respondents were extremely liberal. The exceptional item, on which respondents were extremely conservative, was "Do you think the government in Washington should regulate profits?" It turned out that the respondents, many of them illiterate, had thought the question referred to pro*phets,* whose regulation might best be left to God. (p. 330)

Social work, like all specialized endeavors, has a specialized vocabulary that may not be understood by laypersons. We should be careful to avoid specialized terms where possible or to define them for respondents. The following list illustrates some of these terms:

Means test
Casework
Eligibility
Corporal punishment
Change agent
Fair hearing
In-kind assistance
Specialization
Extinction

4. Is a closed or an open-end question most appropriate for the information we want? In eliciting certain types of information, it is possible for the researcher to specify all possible alternatives, and in such situations a closed question is most appropriate. For example,

At the present time what is your legal marital status? (Circle one letter)

   a. Never married
   b. Married
   c. Divorced
   d. Separated
   e. Widowed

It is neither necessary nor desirable to use an open-end question to elicit this kind of information, because open-end questions invite idiosyncratic responses that are not useful (such as "living together" in the preceding example, a response that would be difficult to interpret).

When you want to elicit information about complex attitudes or probe for reasons behind attitudes, values, or feelings, an open-end question is best. Consider the following questions:

> The federal government currently provides funds to Planned Parenthood, an agency that supplies birth control information to adults and teenagers.
>
>> Do you feel that the federal government should provide funds to agencies such as Planned Parenthood, which supply birth control information to teenagers?
>>
>> How do you feel about your own teenager receiving information about birth control?

In a delicate and complex situation such as this, open-end questions allow the interviewer to probe for feelings and attitudes and allow the respondent to answer in depth. Does the respondent favor giving birth control information to teenagers only under certain conditions? If yes, what are those conditions? Does the respondent feel differently about an agency supplying information to his or her own child?

The amount of detail that is required of a respondent's answer may also determine the most appropriate type of question. If we need to know the respondent's exact age, we should use one of these two open questions:

> What is your exact birth date? (Complete each of the blank spaces below)
>
>> Month _____
>> Day _____
>> Year _____

or

>> In the space below, write a whole number that indicates your age in years on your last birthday (e.g., 25, 53, etc.):
>>
>> _____

If we need to know only the respondent's approximate age, a closed question is best. There will be fewer idiosyncratic responses:

> How old are you, to the nearest year? (Circle one letter below)

a. Less than 25 years old
b. 25 to 34 years
c. 35 to 44 years
d. 45 to 54 years
e. 55 to 64 years
f. Over 64 years old

5. Does the question assume information or knowledge that a respondent may not have? For instance, if we are assessing public support for funding of the Department of Public Aid, it is not safe to assume that everyone knows what that department is. One approach is to ask respondents if they know what the Department of Public Aid is. But this may not be a useful approach because most people do not like to admit that they do not know something. They may not admit they don't have the knowledge or they may be insulted by the question.

A better approach is to provide a brief explanation prior to asking your question:

> The Department of Public Aid is an agency paid for and run by the state. It provides money and services to poor people, such as assistance to single mothers with small children, day care, food stamps, and transportation to a job.
>
> Do you believe the state should maintain its current level of funding to the Department of Public Aid?

6. Does the instrument use filter questions appropriately? Some questions may be appropriate for only a subgroup of respondents. Filter questions help to identify which questions are appropriate for which respondents. They instruct the questionnaire respondent or the interviewer to answer only the relevant questions and in the appropriate sequence. Here is an example:

1. Are you currently working part-time or full-time in an agency that provides home health services? (Check one)
   _____ Yes. Answer Question 2 below.
   _____ No. Skip to Question 3 below.
2. Indicate your agreement or disagreement with the following statement:
   In my home health agency, I feel that I am valued by my colleagues. (Check one)
   _____ Agree
   _____ I am not sure
   _____ Disagree

7. Have you provided the respondent with clear instructions about how to respond to each item? We have illustrated these instructions in the preceding examples, but it will be useful to summarize them. Don't assume that respondents know how you want them to answer. Phrases such as "circle one," "check one," or "check all items that apply" should be provided. Where a group of similar questions appear, such as the self-acceptance scale illustrated on page 245, the instructions should be given before the scale items—for example, "Circle SA if you strongly agree, A if you agree." If the instructions are at all complex it may be a good idea to provide a model—that is, a sample question in which an appropriate answer is checked or circled.

If certain respondents (for example, those who are not currently working for a home health agency) are to skip questions, make sure that the instructions are easy to follow. Allow plenty of room between questions, and number questions clearly so that they can be found easily. Finally, where similar response alternatives exist across different questions, use numbers and letters consistently. For example, use 0 to indicate "no" and 1 to indicate "yes," wherever these alternatives appear.

8. Have you avoided double-barreled questions? Double-barreled questions ask two questions simultaneously. They confuse the respondent and make interpretation of answers difficult. For example,

> Do you favor state licensing and more stringent continuing education requirements for social workers?

Respondents are likely to be confused by this question because they will not know which part to answer. They might favor state licensing but feel that continuing education requirements are already stringent enough or vice versa. Whenever we find a double-barreled question in our questionnaire or interview schedule, we should break it into two separate questions. We should ask only one question at a time.

9. Are there ambiguities in the questions? Because language is complex, we may find that a respondent's interpretation of a question will differ from our intention in asking that question. There is no foolproof method for ensuring that this does not happen. But it is possible to minimize this problem by avoiding ambiguous words, phrases, and expressions. For example, consider the following question:

How do you like your current job?

Although this might be a perfectly appropriate question to ask in a personal conversation, it is too ambiguous to serve any research purpose. Is the question asking about relationships with coworkers? Amount of workload? Satisfaction with pay? Opportunities for advancement? Once we have determined which aspects of job satisfaction we are interested in, we will need to ask specific questions about each aspect.

Some words are inherently ambiguous and should be avoided. The word *fair* is an example. "Do you feel that the workers in your agency receive fair treatment?" may be asking if you believe workers are treated "equitably" or, alternatively, if you believe they are "not treated too well."

The best way to ferret out these kinds of question ambiguities is to pretest the instrument: Distribute questionnaires or interview a number of persons who are as similar as possible to those who will be selected for the sample. Then ask for their feedback: "Which questions were unclear or difficult to follow?" These comments can then be useful in revising the items.

10. Have we avoided leading questions? A leading question is one in which the answer is implied in the question. These questions "lead the respondent on." Here is an example:

What can the government do to discourage teenagers from having sexual relations?

This question assumes that respondents are opposed to sexual relations between teenagers, which may not be the case. It is in essence telling respondents how the researcher *expects* them to answer questions on this topic. Because of this, respondents' answers may be biased in the direction they believe the researcher wants them to respond rather than being a valid measure of their own attitudes.

11. Have we avoided questions that are biased by social desirability? With this type of question, the respondent is led to answer in a socially desirable way, because to do otherwise would be embarrassing or socially unacceptable. For example,

Are you familiar with the governor's recent proposal to place a freeze on social welfare spending?

Because most people will not want to admit that they are unaware of this current event, many will answer "yes" even if they are not familiar with the event. (A better way to ask this particular question would be to preface it with explanatory information. See Guideline 5 above.)

Similar problems arise when we ask people if they voted, if they are prejudiced against minority groups, or if they contributed to charity. There is no simple way to get people to answer these questions accurately. If possible, we may have to observe their real-life behavior—for example, their actual voting behavior. But in general, questionnaires and interview schedules should avoid items that are loaded with social desirability.

12. Is the order of items appropriate? Care should be taken to order items in a way that will maximize the chances that respondents will complete all items appropriately. It is standard practice to ask sensitive questions—for instance, those that ask for age, income, family size, and other personal information—toward the end. If an interviewer or questionnaire asks this information at the very outset, many respondents will feel uncomfortable, and their cooperation will be less complete.

To make it easy for the respondent, there are two additional criteria for ordering items: ordering by content and ordering by question format. Questions should be grouped by content area so that the respondent is not forced to switch back and forth between topics. For instance, in Berger's (1984) study of the life adaptation of older gay men, interview questions were grouped into areas such as social life, involvement with the homosexual community, involvement with family, and exclusive relationships. Items on a questionnaire, which was also used in that study, were grouped in a similar way.

Ordering by question format is also important. Most questionnaires have items that ask respondents to indicate their answers in different ways. For example, some items may ask the respondent to circle one of five alternatives from *strongly agree* to *strongly disagree* (see earlier). Another set of items may ask respondents to circle how many times they engage in certain activities, with alternatives ranging from *never* to *very often*. Other items may ask the respondent merely to agree or disagree, to answer yes or no, to check one of several alternatives, or to write in information such as a birth date or address.

Whenever possible, all items that use a particular response format should appear together. Asking the respondent to switch back and forth between formats is confusing and usually results in many errors and missing responses.

Of course, it may not always be possible to simultaneously order items by content and by question format, but to the extent possible, this should be done. Also, within the guidelines presented here, we should place those questions that are most crucial to our study near the beginning. Particularly in a long instrument, sloppy or incomplete responding is most likely to occur toward the end.

13. If we are measuring a complex attitude, feeling, or belief have we used more than one item to measure it? When measuring an attitude, feeling, or belief, using multiple items to measure the same characteristic enhances the reliability and validity of the measurement (discussed further in Chapter 14). Using multiple items lessens the likelihood that the answer was a chance error or uncharacteristic response. Standardized scales, such as the self-acceptance scale, which was illustrated earlier, take advantage of this principle.

Some standardized tests deliberately include multiple items measuring the same characteristic to assess the reliability of the respondent's answer and to eliminate those who might be "faking." For instance, the Minnesota Multiphasic Personality Inventory (MMPI), a personality test, has a series of items that purportedly tells the researcher if the respondent is answering the questions honestly.

Berger and Anderson (1984) used multiple duplicated items in developing an inventory to assess the interpersonal skills of homemakers who served the frail elderly. The inventory asked respondents to rate how much of a problem they encountered with each of a number of difficult interpersonal situations. To ensure that homemakers were responding consistently, Berger and Anderson included a number of duplications: pairs of items that described the same situation but that were worded somewhat differently. One such pair of items reads as follows:

My client asks me to do a chore that is not on the chore list approved by my supervisor.
I am asked by my client to do a chore that has not been assigned to me.

Duplicated items were dispersed throughout the questionnaire so that their purpose was not obvious. Analysis of the data showed that respondents were reporting their experiences consistently.

14. Does the appearance of the instrument make it easy for the respondent or interviewer? This guideline concerns the spacing and formatting of items and the manner in which the instrument is reproduced, such as by photocopy, laser printer, or typesetting. The overall appearance of the instrument is a message to others about the importance and professionalism of the research project. With today's personal computers, laser printers, and desktop publishing software, it is easy to produce a questionnaire or interview schedule that has the "feel" of a typeset and printed copy. In my experience, the relatively small effort of producing a professional-looking instrument will result in a higher return rate and in more accurate and complete data.

As I said earlier, instructions for responding ought to be clear, and similarly formatted questions should be grouped. Sufficient space must be allowed between items to avoid confusion. The experience should be easy on the eyes. If elderly or visually handicapped persons are being asked to fill out a questionnaire, it makes sense to have it set in large type. Similar response alternatives should be aligned, as in the self-acceptance scale illustrated earlier.

One practice that enhances the appearance of an item is to place the response alternatives *below* the question rather than on the same line. For instance, compare the following two questions:

Do you find it difficult to get up in the morning? (Circle one letter) (a) nearly all the time, (b) pretty often, (c) not very much, or (d) never.

Do you find it difficult to get up in the morning? (Circle one letter)
   a. Nearly all the time
   b. Pretty often
   c. Not very much
   d. Never

When we include open-end questions on a questionnaire, we should allow enough room for the response. Some questionnaires ask respondents to continue a lengthy open-end response on the back side of the questionnaire. If this is done with more than one item it will be necessary to provide item numbers on the back or to ask respondents to number their responses.

One useful type of questionnaire is the mailer. Questions are printed on one side and on part of the reverse side of a single sheet of sturdy paper. One third of a side contains a return address and postage. After completing the questionnaire, the respondent simply folds it into thirds, seals it, and mails it. Return is encouraged by the brevity of the questionnaire and the ease with which it can be mailed. The number of questions that can be included is, of course, limited. If we use a desktop publishing program or have the copy typeset, however, we will be able to include a greater number of items and still have a readable instrument. The master copy can then be offset or photocopied. In either case, a good-quality heavy-weight paper should be used to prevent printing from the reverse side from showing through.

15. Have we introduced the respondent to the instrument? The manner in which the respondent is requested to complete the questionnaire or interview is crucial. The researcher or assistant should explain the general purpose of the study in lay terms. Most respondents are not interested in the technical aspects of research. The researcher should also explain how much time it will take to complete this task and perhaps something about the general nature of the questions that will be asked.

The respondent should be assured that all responses are to be held in confidence (if that is indeed the case). The researcher should provide the respondent with a piece of paper with a name, address, and phone number so that the respondent can ask further questions in the future. (Ethical requirements for research projects are described in more detail in Chapter 3.)

It is a nice idea to offer respondents a brief report of the results, to be mailed to the respondent after the data are analyzed. This is good public relations, and it tends to increase respondent cooperation.

For the interview, the researcher should prepare a written protocol with all this information. Interviewers should be required to read this statement or allow respondents to read the statement and ask questions. This ensures that all respondents are introduced to the research study in the same way. This is important because when we analyze the data we want to know that differences among respondents are real rather than due to different or inconsistent interviewers.

A cover letter is a good way to provide the required information for either an interview or a questionnaire. The cover letter may be attached to the questionnaire. Or the letter may indicate that an interviewer will be calling the respondent in the near future to request an appointment. This is generally a better way to recruit respondents than "cold calling," that is, calling without an introduction.

16. Is the instrument set up to facilitate coding of responses? This guideline is applicable to questionnaires and interview schedules, where responses are coded by assigning a number to each response and entering that number on a computer file. In Chapter 17, I will explain how the researcher uses these numbers to create a "data set" and how that data set is analyzed by computer.

At this point, it is necessary only to note that the work of "coding"—translating questionnaire responses into numbers and entering them into a computer data file—can be made easier with a bit of planning. The most common way to facilitate coding is to use "edge coding." A 1-inch column labeled DO NOT WRITE IN THIS SPACE appears at the edge of each page of the questionnaire. For each item, there appears a number indicating which column of the data set is reserved for that item. It is followed by a blank space where the respondent's answer is assigned a number. The following is an excerpt from a questionnaire that used edge coding:

DO NOT WRITE
IN THIS SPACE
col.

18 ____   12. What is your sex? (Circle one)
                       a. Male
                       b. Female
                   13. How old are you? (In the space below write a whole
                       number indicating your age in years at your last birthday.)
19-20 ____
21 ____   _____
                   14. What is your present religious preference? (Circle one)
                       a. No religious preference, atheist, or agnostic
                       b. Protestant
                       c. Roman Catholic
                       d. Jewish
                       e. Other (please specify) _____

The numbers on the left represent the appropriate columns for entering data from the questionnaire. For example, for Questionnaire Item 12, the coder will enter 0 in column 18 of the data set if the respondent is male and 1 if the respondent is female. Questionnaire Item 13 has two columns reserved for it, because two digits will be required to enter respondents' age into the data set (assuming that no respondent is over 99 years old). Responses to Question 14 will be coded in column 21 of the data set. The coder may be instructed to code 1 for response alternative "a," 2 for "b," and so on.

17. Have you pretested the instrument? If we have followed the guidelines reviewed above, the questionnaire or interview schedule should be ready for testing. There is no substitute for a pretest of the instrument. In a pretest, we recruit a number of respondents who are as similar as possible to those we will select for the final sample, and we ask them to complete the questionnaire or interview. It is also important to ask them for feedback on the instrument.

For example, Are any of the items ambiguous? How can they be reworded for clarity? Are any of the items inappropriate or even insulting to respondents? Is the order of items appropriate? Was the flow of questions clear and logical? For the closed items, were the response alternatives appropriate and complete? Are there additional alternatives that should be included?

Pretesting will also yield an estimate of how long it will take to complete the instrument. Except for certain categories of respondents, such as the frail elderly and small children, most adults can tolerate an hour-long interview. The interview should be even more brief if possible. Questionnaires should take much less time. Most respondents are unwilling to spend more than 15 to 20 minutes filling out a questionnaire on their own. Taking note of completion time on the pretesting should give you a good idea about whether you need to shorten the instrument.

Pretesting the instrument may also give you an idea of the expected response rate—that is, the proportion of people in the population who will complete and return a questionnaire or agree to an interview. For example, we might pretest a telephone interview by calling numbers from the phone directory of a city similar to the one in which the study will be conducted. An unusually small number of persons willing to complete the interview might be an indication that changes are needed. Perhaps the interview needs to be shortened, delicate questions may need to be reworded and moved to a point later in the interview, or a different introduction may be required.

If the instrument includes a summated rating scale, we will need to determine its internal consistency. (When summated rating scales are used, they are first tested for internal consistency. The scale is internally consistent if participants tend to respond consistently to each of the items—for example, indicating low self-esteem for all items rather than low self-esteem on some of the items and high self-esteem on others. Internal consistency of measures is discussed in greater detail in Chapter 14.)

Many standardized rating scales have been shown to be internally consistent for certain populations, but are they internally consistent for respondents in our sample? Pretesting the instrument on a similar sample can be a way of identifying potential problems with the internal consistency of scales. If the internal consistency of a pretested scale is low, this may mean that certain scale items will have to be revised or even dropped. If the pretest data indicate high internal consistency, then the scale can be used with some confidence in our study (assuming that the pretest sample was similar to the actual sample and that the size of the pretest sample was sufficient).

AVAILABLE MATERIALS

Available materials refer to data that have been collected by others, usually for purposes other than research. They include census data, registration data, newspapers and periodicals, institutional records, personal documents, archives, and physical traces. Often, these sources of data have been overlooked by social work researchers. If used properly, they can be a fascinating source of answers to important research questions.

CENSUS DATA

Every 10 years, the U.S. government undertakes a detailed census in which the demographic makeup of the population is studied. Less extensive data are collected at more frequent intervals. Census records contain information on variables such as the age, sex, family income, marital status, and geographic distribution of the population. These data are readily available and are broken down in a number of ways: by region, state, county, and census tract. The U.S. Government Printing Office publishes volumes summarizing census data. These volumes are available in the reference sections of most libraries.

REGISTRATION DATA

The local county clerk has names and addresses of individuals registered to vote. Public schools have information about school children and their families. (These data are protected by confidentiality laws, but researchers may gain access with permission from parents or school systems.)

Laud Humphreys (1970) used registration data to conduct a fascinating study of the lives of men who engaged in sex in public restrooms in a major city (see Chapter 3 on ethics). As an observer and quasi-participant (he served as a "lookout," warning participants about the approach of intruders), he recorded the ways in which men met in public restrooms and engaged each other in anonymous sex. Curious about their lives outside of this setting, he unobtrusively recorded license plate numbers of the cars in which they arrived and left. With the cooperation of the Motor Vehicle Department, he secured names and addresses corresponding to the license numbers. In this way, he was able to identify the men whom he had observed in the public restrooms.

A year later, interviewers were sent to interview these men in their homes as part of a large-scale survey of social health. The men were not aware of the connection between the interview and their earlier public sex activity. In this way, Humphreys was able to study a hidden segment of the gay community that would otherwise have remained inaccessible. He discovered that over half these men were heterosexually married and that they led heterosexual lives in every other respect.

NEWSPAPERS AND PERIODICALS

Newspapers and periodicals can be a rich source of information, particularly about community events and public opinion. Researchers may study the level of racial violence in a community by studying news reports. They can examine the ways in which the level or type of racial violence varies with events such as the assassination of a minority leader.

Newspaper editorials have been studied as a measure of public opinion. For example, after a highly publicized murder of a child by his foster parents, the researcher might study editorials to determine public attitudes toward the State Department of Children and Family Services. An often overlooked source of data are the files of newspaper offices, which contain back issues as well as additional historical material.

INSTITUTIONAL RECORDS

At some time, the name of every person finds its way into some institutional record. School systems, psychiatric and general hospitals, nursing homes, and social work agencies all keep extensive records. State statutes and federal laws control access to these data. But researchers can gain access if they obtain consent from respondents or if their research project is approved by the administrator or review board of an agency. In every case, researchers are bound to protect the anonymity of the individuals about whom they obtain information.

There are many ways in which institutional data can be used in social work research. For example, a gerontologist might study the medication records of elderly nursing home residents to determine if psychotropic medications are related to levels of patient participation in the home's activity program.

In an institution for developmentally disabled adults with which I am familiar, a social worker evaluated the effectiveness of a social skills training program in reducing the incidence of aggressive behavior by residents. One measure of the training program's effectiveness was a count of the number of aggressive acts committed by trained versus untrained residents. These counts were taken from daily logs entered by staff into residents' charts.

PERSONAL DOCUMENTS

Personal documents, such as wills, diaries, notes, correspondence, and suicide notes, are a particularly interesting source of data. Anne Frank's *Diary of a Young Girl* (1993), the moving account of a Jewish teenager's adolescence while in hiding from the Nazis, is one of the most well-known personal documents. It reveals a great deal about adolescent development and family relations under conditions of severe stress. A study of notes left by teenagers who have committed suicide may illuminate some of the causes of this increasing social problem.

ARCHIVES

Archives are public records or documents. They include records of births, deaths, marriages, and property transactions that are available in the offices of county clerks. They also include political records, such as the *Congressional Record* (a federal publication of proceedings of the U.S. Congress), and records and transcripts of legislative hearings. Judicial records, such as court transcripts and court decisions, and sales records are other examples.

Most archival data are accessible to the public. They can be an inexpensive way of answering research questions. Kastenbaum and Candy (1973) used archival data in their study of older persons. For years, it has been known that only about 4% of the elderly actually live in nursing homes at any given time. But Kastenbaum and Candy felt that this figure may have misrepresented the importance of nursing homes in housing the elderly. They analyzed local death certificates that, fortunately, indicated the place of death. Their analysis of these death certificates revealed that 20% to 25% of all persons died while a resident of a nursing home. Thus nursing homes play a much more important role in the lives of the elderly than we had previously believed.

PHYSICAL TRACES

Physical traces are an unusual source of data that have not been used widely in social work research. Physical traces can be used when the activity of interest leaves a marker or change in the environment that can be recorded. For instance, in one major urban museum, the popularity of exhibits is determined by recording the frequency with which floor tiles surrounding that exhibit need to be replaced. Popular exhibits receive heavy foot traffic that wears out the floor tile. This is a rough but relatively accurate and inexpensive measure of the popularity of museum exhibits. In another situation, the popularity of various radio stations was estimated by asking auto mechanics at service stations to record the position of radio dials on cars brought in for service.

USES FOR AVAILABLE MATERIALS

The greatest limitation of available materials is that the data were collected by others for their own purposes, which may not match the purpose of the researcher. The data may not be in a form that is useful for answering our research question, or they may simply not provide the kinds of information we need. Available materials are often useful in exploring new areas or suggesting hypotheses for further study. In some situations, available materials may allow us to test a hypothesis, as in the following example.

In recent years, the problem of physical and emotional abuse of the elderly has come to the attention of social workers. Social scientists believe that frail elderly persons who need high levels of care often place such a great physical and emotional burden on family members that these members respond with violence or neglect. Thus one researcher hypothesized that most physical abuse of the elderly is committed by family members (i.e., the elderly who live with family members are more likely than those who live alone or in institutions to be victims of physical abuse).

As an indirect test of this hypothesis, researchers studied hospital emergency room records. They identified those patients who were aged 65 or older who presented with "suspicious" injuries—that is, injuries not likely to have been caused by accident. The hypothesis that most elder abuse is committed by family members received support from the finding that 90% of elderly patients with suspicious injuries lived with family members (whereas only 40% of the elderly in that community lived with family members).

Census, registration, and institutional data can also be useful in drawing samples and checking their representativeness. (I discussed these issues in Chapter 6.) For example, in a study of voter preferences, we can draw a sample from a list of registered voters provided by the local voter registrar's office. To draw a quota sample or a stratified random sample from a population, we need to know the distribution of various characteristics (such as age, race, and sex) in that population. Census data, or data describing the demographic makeup of persons in other populations such as institutions, will be necessary for these types of sampling strategies. Once we have selected the sample, these available materials can also be useful in determining if the characteristics of the sample mirror those of the population. Census data often are used in this way.

SUMMARY

This chapter reviewed three sources of data for social work research: questionnaires, interview schedules, and available materials. Both question-naires and interviews ask respondents to provide answers to questions related to research questions or hypotheses, but questionnaires are self-administered, whereas interviews are conducted in a face-to-face format. Questionnaires and interviews make use of fixed-alternative and open-end items. Summated rating scales are a special type of fixed-alternative item that are often used to measure attitudes, feelings, and beliefs.

A number of guidelines were presented for constructing questionnaires and interviews, including suggestions for choosing the appropriate types of items, wording, appearance, ordering of items, and pretesting of the instrument. Available materials are an often overlooked source of data that include census data, registration data, newspapers, records, and physical traces.

DISCUSSION QUESTIONS

1. What is the difference between a questionnaire and an interview?
2. Provide an example of each of the following types of questionnaire or interview items. (You may create your own items.)

   a. Fixed-alternative item
   b. Open-end item
   c. Scale

3. What are the advantages and disadvantages of each of the following types of items?

   a. Fixed-alternative items
   b. Open-end items

4. Why are multiple questions used to assess characteristics such as attitudes?

5. Why is it important to search the literature to see if previous researchers have developed a questionnaire, interview schedule, or scale that might be useful in your research?

6. This chapter reviewed guidelines for writing good questionnaire and interview items. Name as many of these guidelines as you can.

7. What is social desirability? Give an example of a question that might elicit a social desirability response. How would you modify this question?

8. What is a double-barreled question? Give an example. How would you modify this question?

9. Questionnaires and interviews often are used to collect data. What are other sources of data for social work research studies?

SHORT ASSIGNMENT

Imagine that you are a research associate working for a public opinion research institute. Your task is to design a questionnaire to assess the public's attitudes about persons with AIDS (PWAs). The purpose of this study is to answer the following research questions:

a. How sympathetic are respondents to the needs of PWAs?

b. Does respondent sympathy vary with the "risk group" to which the PWA belongs? That is, are respondents more or less sympathetic to PWAs who are men who have sex with men, injection drug users, persons who contracted AIDS by heterosexual sex, hemophiliacs, men, or women?

c. Does respondent sympathy vary with the demographic characteristics of the respondent—that is, the respondent's age, gender, religious beliefs, political party affiliation, and socioeconomic status?

d. Does respondent sympathy vary with the level of experience the respondent has had with persons who belong to the various risk groups? For example, are respondents who have male friends or close relatives who are gay men more likely to be sympathetic to the needs of PWAs?

Hint: The questionnaire should include *only* items that measure demographic characteristics of the respondents and the variables in the research questions. You should prepare the questionnaire so that all items can be read and answered easily. The format and layout should be simple and attractive to the eye.

FURTHER READING

Bourque, L. B., & Fielder, E. P. (1995). *How to conduct self-administered and mail surveys.* Thousand Oaks, CA: Sage.

Fink, A. (1995). *How to ask survey questions.* Thousand Oaks, CA: Sage.

Fischer, J., & Corcoran, K. (1994). *Measures for clinical practice* (Vols. 1 & 2). New York: Free Press.

Mueller, D. (1986). *Measuring social attitudes: A handbook for researchers and practitioners.* New York: Teachers College Press.

Webb, E., Campbell, D., Schwartz, R., & Sechrest, L. (1966). *Unobtrusive measures: Nonreactive research in the social sciences.* Chicago: Rand McNally.

13 Measurement

I n Chapter 12, I discussed various ways of obtaining data. After we administer the questionnaire or interview or collect data from some other source, we are left with a collection of numbers that describe our respondents or other elements of interest. Just what do these numbers mean? How "good" are these numbers as measures of the concepts and variables we are interested in? To answer these questions, we need to review measurement theory.

WHAT IS MEASUREMENT?

Definition: *Measurement* is the assignment of numerals or numbers to objects or events according to rules (adapted from Kerlinger, 1973, p. 427).

Let's take a closer look at this definition. Notice that the definition uses the words *numerals* and *numbers*. Numerals are any symbols that are associated with objects or events but that do not have quantitative meaning; that is, they do not indicate the number of events or amount of a quality. For example, I might "measure" the gender of respondents in my study by assigning a 1 to each male respondent and a 0 to each female respondent.

In this example, 1 and 0 are numerals because they indicate nothing about quantity. They are simply convenient symbols that are used to indicate gender. I could just as easily have used other numerals such as I and II or 111 and 000.

The process of measurement is often confused with the process of quantification. Measurement is any process in which we assign symbols to objects or events, whether or not those symbols have quantitative meaning—that is, whether or not they indicate numerical value. Quantification occurs when we assign numbers, rather than numerals, to objects or events. A number is simply a numeral that has quantitative meaning. For example, I might measure the number of college courses each respondent has completed. Each respondent would be assigned a number, say from 0 to 50, indicating the number of college-level courses completed.

So strictly speaking, measurement is broader than quantification. Quantification is one type of measurement. In practical terms, researchers often do not differentiate between these two processes. That is because numbers are commonly used to measure objects and events in the social sciences, whether or not that measurement is quantitative. The measurement of the variable of *gender* was an example of this. When we measure objects or events, however, we need to be aware of whether the measurement is qualitative or quantitative; that is, we need to be aware of the level of measurement. Levels of measurement are discussed later.

Our definition of measurement also talked about the *assignment* of numerals to objects or events. This assignment of numerals to objects or events defines measurement. What we know as measurement (e.g., assigning 0 to females and 1 to males) is actually a process that involves set theory. When we measure, we are actually dealing with two sets, or collections, of individuals or events. For example, in the measurement of sex, we have two sets, as shown in Figure 13.1.

In this example, we have a rule that assigns each individual in Set A to one numeral in Set B. In set theory, this process of assigning the elements of one set to elements of another set is called *mapping*. In social work research, the rule by which this assignment is made is the operational definition of the variable being measured. In this case, the rule might state, "If the respondent circled *female* on Question 10, assign a 0; if the respondent circled *male,* assign a 1."

Although this example is a simple one, it illustrates the definition of measurement that is applied to every concept and variable that is measured. In social work, it is most common for the members or elements of one set to

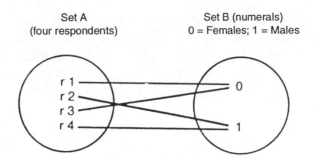

Figure 13.1. The Measurement of Sex: Mapping the Elements of One Set Onto Another

be individuals and for the members of the other set to be numerals or numbers indicating some property of those individuals. But the members of the first set might be groups, families, organizations, or communities rather than individuals.

WHAT IS THE PURPOSE OF MEASUREMENT?

The primary purpose of measurement is to assign numerals or numbers to objects in such a way that the results reflect the true situation in the real world. Another way to say this is that the rules of measurement (assignment) should be accurate.

This seems simple enough. In fact, when we measure variables such as gender, we have some assurance that the rules are accurate because they are easy to specify and to apply. It is easy to tell which of our respondents are male and which are female. Other characteristics that are easy to measure because they involve simple and straightforward rules include age, income, class standing, and race. Generally, these variables have clear and simple operational definitions, so it is easy to specify the rules by which individuals will be assigned to categories of "male-female," "young-old," and so on.

But many variables of interest to us in social work are complex. It is not a simple matter to specify and apply the rules that will allow us to measure variables such as level of motivation, therapist effectiveness, or client compliance. A simple example will illustrate this.

Suppose we are interested in measuring the level of aggression of a group of eight 12-year-old boys placed in a special education class. Suppose, further, that we have designed a special observational inventory that has been used by the boys' teachers to rate the observed level of aggression of each boy. On the basis of these ratings, we assign a score to each boy, with higher scores indicating higher levels of aggression:

Measured scores: 5, 3, 8, 7, 7, 6, 8, 9

Now we have to assume knowledge that we are not likely to have in the real world of social work. Suppose that we have a perfect measure of level of aggression and that we are able to determine each boy's true score. Taking each boy in the same order as before, these scores might be as follows:

True aggression scores: 4, 2, 10, 7, 8, 7, 8, 8

We can see here that we did a fair job of measuring level of aggression:

Measured scores: 1 2 3 4 5 6 7 8 9 10

True scores: 1 2 3 4 5 6 7 8 9 10

We correctly identified boys at the low and high ends of the aggression continuum, and most of the scores were at least in the correct rank order. The "rule" by which we assigned scores to boys, however, was certainly less than perfect.

The question we must ask is this: Is the rule good enough? That is, is the rule accurate enough in assigning scores that measure the true level of aggression of the boys? Ultimately, the accuracy of every measurement is judged in this manner. Although we usually do not have a measure of the true values (as we did in this example), there are procedures that help us to evaluate the accuracy of the measurements—that is, their reliability and validity. (These are discussed in the next chapter.)

I have said that the purpose of measurement is to assign numerals or numbers to objects or events so that the results reflect the real world. We should also note two additional purposes for measurement.

First, measurement adds objectivity and standardization to research. An important characteristic of the scientific method is that each researcher's work can be replicated, and thus verified, by other researchers. Specifying the method of measurement allows different researchers to measure variables in the same way so that their results can be compared. It also takes personal bias and guesswork out of research. For example, if we determined client improvement based solely on the judgment of the client's therapist, we would have no assurance that the results truly reflect the client's status. All therapists tend to rate their work as effective. But with a standardized measurement procedure (e.g., use of a personality inventory or a scale to measure assertiveness), the results are more likely to reflect the client's true situation. We will also be able to compare the results with those of other therapists.

Second, by assigning numerals or numbers, measurement allows us to assess the real world with greater precision. For example, with some types of measurement, we can determine not only if clients are "improved" but whether they are more improved than other clients. In some situations, we can even determine how much clients have improved. We are able to summarize the data, to compare groups of persons or events within the study, or to compare the results with those of others. (For example, the research literature indicates that two thirds of neurotic symptoms improve in time without treatment. A worker might compare his or her own success with clients against this figure.) Finally, the assignment of numerals and numbers allows us to use powerful statistical techniques, such as *t* tests, chi-square, and correlation. These techniques are often used in social work research. (I discuss these techniques in detail in Chapter 16.)

LEVELS OF MEASUREMENT

As we have seen, some variables, such as sex, are measured by assigning numerals—that is, symbols without quantitative meaning. Other variables, such as family income, are measured by assigning numbers—that is, symbols that have quantitative meaning: They indicate quantity. From these examples, we might guess that there are different types or *levels* of measurement that provide different amounts of information about the objects or events being measured.

Social science researchers recognize four levels of measurement (Stevens, 1946). These levels are cumulative in that the amount of information provided by the measurement increases at each level. In fact, each level provides all the information of all preceding levels of measurement, plus some additional information. Figure 13.2 lists the four levels of measurement.

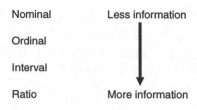

Figure 13.2. The Four Levels of Measurement

It is important to take account of levels of measurement because only certain arithmetic operations can be performed with data at certain levels. For instance, data measured at the nominal level can only be categorized (e.g., into male and female). Even though we may use numerals such as 0 and 1, this level of measurement does not allow us to add, subtract, multiply, or divide. At the other end of the continuum, with data measured at the ratio level (e.g., income) we may perform all of these arithmetic operations.

NOMINAL MEASUREMENT

In this type of measurement, numerals or other symbols are assigned to objects without quantitative meaning. They are simply labels that separate objects or events into mutually exclusive and exhaustive categories. The variable *respondent's gender* is measured at the nominal level. Other variables that are measured at the nominal level are football player numbers, telephone numbers, race, and religion.

Nominal measurement tells us which categories objects or events fall into and nothing more. It tells us nothing about the relative order of categories, how far apart they are, or *how much* of anything they have.

For example, we might measure the religion of respondents by assigning each respondent to one of four categories: Protestant, Catholic, Jewish, and other. We might use the numerals 1, 2, 3, and 4 to indicate these categories. But the essential point is that we cannot rank order the categories. (It makes no sense to say that one religion is greater or better than another.) We cannot make statements about how far apart the categories are. (It makes no sense to say that the difference between Jewish and other is the same as, or different from, the difference between Protestant and Catholic.) We cannot state how much religion a respondent has, based on which category he or she falls into. (If the variable was *intensity of religious beliefs,* we would be able at least to rank order individuals on this variable because this variable is measured at a higher level.)

Nominal measurement is the lowest level of measurement because it provides the least amount of information: It tells us only which categories objects or events fall into.

ORDINAL MEASUREMENT

Variables that are measured at the ordinal level have all the characteristics of nominal measures. In addition, they allow us to order the values of the variable. In other words, we can rank order the values of an ordinal variable on some characteristic or property.

For example, some public opinion polls ask respondents to rank order their preference among a set of items:

The following list represents five different ways to reduce poverty. Place a 1 next to the method that you feel is the best way to reduce poverty, a 2 next to the next best method, and so on. Place a 5 next to the method that you least favor:

_____ Earned income tax credit
_____ Negative income tax
_____ Public assistance grants such as AFDC
_____ Work incentive program
_____ Job training

Ordinal measurement, then, does indicate rank order. But it tells us nothing about how far apart the values or categories are. (It makes no sense to compare the differences between categories.) It tells us nothing about quantity or how much of a characteristic or quality is being measured. (For example, we cannot say that any one method is twice as favored as any other method.)

In this example, the respondent will assign the numerals 1 through 5 to the five values. We can use these numerals to make statements about rank order. For instance, we can state that the method ranked as 5 was less favored than methods ranked as 4, 3, 2, or 1. We could not say, however, that $(5 - 3) = (4 - 2)$ or that the method ranked second is twice as favored as the method ranked fourth. These statements would not make sense.

Therefore, in addition to allowing us to categorize, ordinal measurement also allows us to rank order objects, events, or values. With ordinal

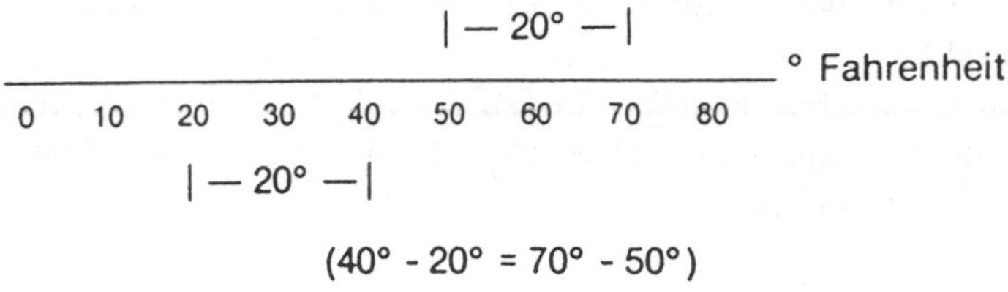

$$| - 20° - |$$

_____ ° Fahrenheit

  0   10   20   30   40   50   60   70   80

$$| - 20° - |$$

$$(40° - 20° = 70° - 50°)$$

Figure 13.3. Illustration of Subtraction Using Interval Measurement

measurement, however, we are not justified in adding, subtracting, multiplying, or dividing.

INTERVAL MEASUREMENT

Interval measurement has all the properties of both nominal and ordinal measurement: categorization and rank ordering. But interval measurement has an additional characteristic: Numerically equal distances on interval measures indicate equal differences in the property being measured.

This characteristic of equal intervals allows us to make valid statements about differences between and among categories or values. In other words, the operations of addition and subtraction make sense. Consider, for example, the variable of temperature level as measured in degrees Fahrenheit or Centigrade. These variables are measured at the interval level. It makes sense, therefore, to say that the difference between a temperature of 40° and a temperature of 30° is 10°. We can also say that the difference between 40° and 20°is the same as the difference between 70° and 50°. Figure 13.3 illustrates this.

An interval scale such as this does not allow us to say that 40° is twice as hot as 20°, because it is not quantities or amounts that are being manipulated but, rather, intervals. Therefore we cannot multiply or divide with an interval measure. In the next section, we will see why the operations of multiplication and division require the highest level of measurement: the ratio level.

RATIO MEASUREMENT

Ratio measures have all the characteristics of nominal, ordinal, and interval measures: categorization, rank order, and equal intervals. They have an important additional characteristic: a natural or absolute zero point. This

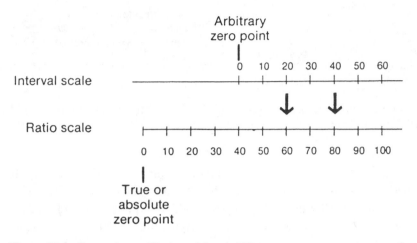

Figure 13.4. Comparison of Ratio and Interval Measures

means that the zero point on a ratio measure corresponds to a total absence of the property being measured.

It is the absolute zero point that makes it possible to meaningfully multiply and divide the numbers used to measure a ratio variable. We can turn again to the temperature example to show why this is so.

We think of temperature as something that we feel. But actually, temperature is a property of matter. It is the extent to which the molecules that make up matter are active, in motion. Fahrenheit and Centigrade measures do not have an absolute zero point because the zero point on these scales corresponds to high levels of molecular activity. The zero points were chosen arbitrarily for convenience. Therefore, the numbers used to measure an interval variable do not indicate the true amount of the property being measured.

But scientists use another measure of temperature that is a ratio measure. On the Kelvin scale, zero degrees corresponds to a total absence of molecular activity and hence a total absence of temperature. It is an absolute zero point. Because the Kelvin scale has this absolute zero point, the numbers used to measure temperature in degrees Kelvin correspond to the actual amount or quantity of temperature. Therefore, with a Kelvin scale it does make sense to say that 40°is twice as warm as 20°.

The fact that an absolute zero point allows us to multiply and divide (that is, to make statements about the amounts of a property) can also be illustrated by comparing a ratio scale with an interval scale. This is shown in Figure 13.4.

Political Identification

		Liberal	Conservative
	Protestant		
Religion			
	Nonprotestant		

Figure 13.5. Example of the Analysis of Two Nominal Variables: Religion and Political Identification

Figure 13.4 shows that the zero point on the interval scale is arbitrary. If we were to state that 40 is twice as much as 20 on the interval scale, we would be mistaken. By referring to the ratio scale, which shows the true value of the property, we see that this is equivalent to saying that 80 is twice 60. That is clearly wrong.

Although most variables in social work research cannot be measured at the ratio level, many can. For example, age is a ratio variable. We can categorize individuals into different age groups (nominal); we can rank order them on the basis of age (ordinal); equal differences on a measure of age correspond to equal differences in the number of years (interval); and the variable of age does have a natural zero point—zero years of age corresponds to the moment of birth. Other ratio variables are income, weight, the number of pages in a book, and number of years of marriage.

THE USES OF LEVELS OF MEASUREMENT

Nominal measurement is the simplest type of measurement: It merely allows us to categorize events or objects. Even so, many of the variables of interest to social work researchers are measured at the nominal level, and these variables can provide us with essential information. Variables such as sex, race, class standing, marital status, religion, and ethnic origin are measured at the nominal level.

Nominal variables are analyzed by counting the number of occurrences in each category or value. Figure 13.5 provides an example of a typical analysis involving two nominal variables. (In Chapter 15, I will discuss data analysis procedures suitable for nominal variables.)

In analyzing social science data, it is common for the researcher to treat an interval or ratio variable as a nominal variable to simplify the analysis. For example, in a study of the effects of retirement, we may have information on the exact age of each respondent (a ratio variable), but for our purposes it may be sufficient to break age into just two categories: under 65 and 65 and older. In the same way, we could take a measure of social class and break it into three categories: lower, middle, and higher.

This process of dividing the values of a variable into two or more groups is called *partitioning*. Partitioning a ratio or interval variable often simplifies the data analysis. It is also possible to cross-partition two variables at the same time, as is illustrated in Figure 13.5.

We should remember that nominal measures may not be added, subtracted, divided, or multiplied. Data analysis procedures appropriate for nominal variables are ones that involve counting the number of cases (frequency) in two or more categories. We can use statistics based on frequencies: percentages, frequency distributions, chi-square, and certain kinds of correlation coefficients. (These will be discussed in Chapters 15 and 16.)

Kerlinger (1973) argues that many of the more complex variables studied in the social sciences are ordinal variables. These include variables such as intelligence, achievement, aptitude, and mental status. Measures of these variables allow us to rank order individuals. For instance, they allow us to identify who is more or less intelligent.

If, indeed, we can measure these variables at a level no higher than the ordinal level, then there are serious limitations on how the numbers derived from these measures can be handled. Let's take a closer look at that.

As we saw earlier, because ordinal scales do not have an absolute zero point, the numbers derived from an ordinal measure do not tell us the true *amount* of the property possessed by the individual or element. Therefore, if intelligence is measured at the ordinal level, then we cannot make a statement such as, "John is twice as intelligent as Mary."

Adding and subtracting amounts of intelligence also makes no sense because the zero point is arbitrary: Different zero points lead to different sums. In Figure 13.6, for example, when we add 4 + 5 on our measured IQ score, we are really adding 2 + 3! From this, it is apparent that adding and subtracting is meaningless without a true zero point. But what is the true or absolute zero point for a measure of intelligence? There probably isn't any absolute zero because it is not possible for any individual to have zero intelligence.

In Figure 13.6, the measured IQ scores are assumed to have equal intervals. If, however, intelligence is measured at the ordinal level, this is not the case because ordinal measures do not have equal intervals. This is another reason

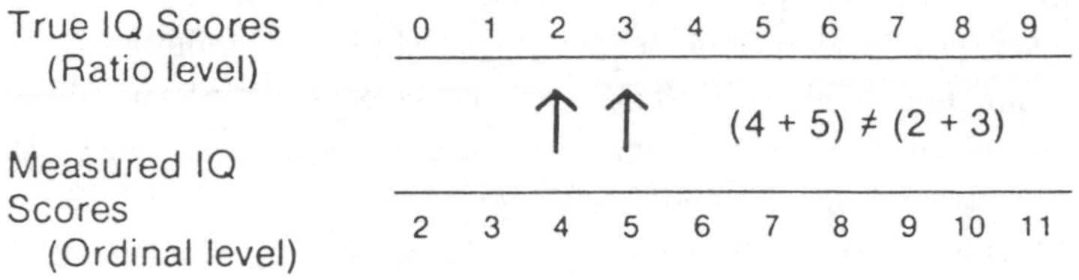

True IQ Scores   0   1   2   3   4   5   6   7   8   9
(Ratio level)
                                ↑   ↑   (4 + 5) ≠ (2 + 3)
Measured IQ
Scores   2   3   4   5   6   7   8   9   10 11
(Ordinal level)

Figure 13.6. Illustration: Arbitrary Zero Points Lead to Different Sums

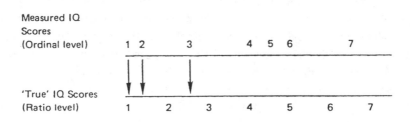

Figure 13.7. Illustration: Absence of Equal Intervals Precludes Adding and Subtracting

why we cannot add or subtract scores of variables measured at the ordinal level. Figure 13.7 illustrates this.

In Figure 13.7, the measured intelligence scores appear to form equal intervals, but in fact they do not. We can use the measured scores to accurately rank order the seven individuals, but we may not add and subtract scores because the intervals between scores are not equal. For example, it would not be accurate to say that the difference between a measured IQ score of 1 and a score of 2 is the same as the difference between the scores of 2 and 3. Scores of 1 and 2 are closer together than scores of 2 and 3.

A number of statistics are used to analyze ordinal data. These statistics rely on rank ordering rather than on adding or subtracting and multiplying or dividing, and they include the median, percentiles, rank order correlation coefficients, and nonparametric (rank order) analysis of variance. These statistics are covered in many introductory statistics textbooks.

I said earlier that Kerlinger (1973) argues that measures of aptitude, intelligence, and so on are ordinal variables. He goes on to point out, however, that in practice, most researchers treat these variables as if they were measured at the interval or ratio levels.

Most studies that use measures such as intelligence, achievement, and aptitude present results in the form of means, standard deviations, *t* tests, and so on. (These statistics are reviewed in Chapters 15 and 16.) To compute these statistics and tests, the researcher must add, subtract, multiply, and divide, and most do this without batting an eyelash! Does this mean that the results of much of social science research are invalid?

Kerlinger (1973) suggests that this is not the case. It is generally understood that many social science measures are, strictly speaking, ordinal measures. In many situations, however, these measures can be assumed to approximate interval or ratio measures so that all arithmetic operations may be used. For example, it has been argued that many attitude scales (see Chapter 12) have at least some type of natural zero point or origin. Consider the five-alternative items that were illustrated in Chapter 12. For each of these items, the respondent circles one of the following alternatives:

Strongly disagree   Disagree   Not sure   Agree   Strongly agree

It can be argued that the middle category represents a natural zero point in that it indicates an absence of agreement or disagreement.

Some researchers also have argued that many ordinal measures have approximately equal intervals. For instance, if there are several measures of a particular variable (say, intelligence) and all these measures have strong linear correlations with each other, it turns out that this is possible only when the intervals are at least approximately equal. (I review linear correlations in Chapter 16.)

The conclusion of all this is that many variables we measure that are, strictly speaking, ordinal measures can in fact be treated as interval or ratio measures without serious error. Most researchers believe that variables such as intelligence, aptitude, achievement, and attitude measures may routinely be treated as interval or ratio variables, unless there is strong evidence to the contrary.

SUMMARY

Social work research would not be possible without measurement. Measurement is the assignment of numerals or numbers to objects and events according to rules. The primary concern in measurement is the quality of

those rules: the extent to which the assigned numerals and numbers reflect the presence of the characteristics we are measuring in the real world. Careful attention to measurement also increases the objectivity, standardization, and precision of the data.

Measurement occurs at four levels: nominal, ordinal, interval, and ratio. It is important to attend to levels of measurement because these levels determine which arithmetic operations are permissible with the data.

Although many social science variables are, strictly speaking, measured at the ordinal level, in many cases we may assume that these measures approximate interval or ratio measurement. This allows us to manipulate the data by using all possible arithmetic operations. Where measures cannot be assumed to be at the interval or ratio level, we are limited to categorization and counting (for nominal measures) and to categorization, counting, and rank ordering (for ordinal variables).

DISCUSSION QUESTIONS

1. In social work research, how is measurement defined?
2. The variable *class standing* has the values freshman, sophomore, junior, and senior.

   a. Use a diagram to illustrate how mapping is used to assign numbers to the values of class standing.
   b. Which of the four levels of measurement applies to this variable?

3. Name two ways in which measurement makes social work research possible.
4. The left column lists the four levels of measurement. The right column lists permissible operations. Match each level of measurement with all the operations corresponding to that level. (Hint: Except for the nominal level, all levels allow for more than one permissible operation.)

Level	*Permissible Operations*
Interval	Categorizing
Nominal	Adding and subtracting
Ratio	Rank ordering
Ordinal	Multiplying and dividing

5. Tom has an IQ score of 75. Dick has an IQ score of 150. Is Dick twice as smart as Tom? Defend your answer.

6. Dr. Freud says, "Ah, vee cannot make the statement about *how much* the patient is in love. Yes? Das is because an individual who has no love at all, such an individual is impossible. I may love you more zen you love me—but how much more? Yavol, this must remain a mystery." Is Dr. Freud correct? Defend your answer.

SHORT ASSIGNMENT

Review recent issues of a journal that publishes social work research articles. (See Box 5.1 for a list of journals.) Find an article that reports on a research study that used at least several dependent variables. For each dependent variable answer the following:

a. How did the researcher operationally define the variable?

b. At what level of measurement did the researcher operationally define the variable?

c. Was the researcher justified in defining the variable at that level of measurement? Explain.

FURTHER READING

Craft, J. L. (1990). *Statistics and data analysis for social workers* (2nd ed.). Itasca, IL: F. E. Peacock. Chapter 2: The Nature of Data.

Stevens, S. S. (1946). On the theory of scales of measurement. *Science, 103,* 677-680.

14 Reliability and Validity of Measurement

I n the previous chapter, I discussed measurement. When measurements are made, it is important to know whether measuring instruments are measuring what they are supposed to measure and whether they are consistent. The former process refers to validity; the latter to reliability.

Keep in mind that reliability and validity are characteristics of operational definitions (discussed in Chapter 2), research designs (discussed in Chapters 7 and 9), and measuring instruments. This chapter discusses the reliability and validity of measuring instruments only (for example, questionnaires, tests, interview schedules, and observations).

Measurement, as defined in the previous chapter, is the assignment of numerals or numbers to objects according to rules. The end product of measurement, then, is a set of numerals or numbers. For example, when an IQ test is administered, it yields a set of numbers, each number representing a person's intelligence score. We ask, How "good" are these scores? or more specifically, How accurately do the scores represent the intelligence of the persons tested? When we ask these kinds of questions about a measuring instrument, we are really asking about its reliability and validity.

WHAT IS RELIABILITY?

Definition: *Reliability* is defined as the extent to which a measuring instrument is stable and consistent.

The essence of reliability is repeatability. If an instrument is administered over and over again, will it yield the same results (assuming that the property being measured has not changed between administrations)?

Why do we need to determine reliability? If the instruments are unstable and give different results even when the property being measured has not changed, we might make the mistake of assuming that some factor other than an unstable test (say, a program to increase academic achievement) caused the change.

Why do we need a measure of reliability? Because in the social sciences, the measurements are imprecise. Whenever we take a series of measurements we are actually measuring a hypothetical "true" score *and* an error component, which may be positive or negative. This can be represented by the following formula:

$$\text{Observed score} = \text{True score} + \text{Error}$$

The error components are referred to as *errors of measurement.* The variance in the observed scores due to these errors of measurement is called *error variance.*

It is virtually impossible to eliminate all of the error. Rather, the goal is to develop instruments that have very small error components. (Some will be slightly positive and some slightly negative, so in the end the observed scores will be very close to the true scores.)

Therefore we can define reliability in another way:

Definition: Reliability is the relative absence of errors of measurement in a measuring instrument.

Several procedures are used to establish the reliability of an instrument. These include the test-retest method, the multiple or alternate forms method, the split-half method, and internal consistency measures.

TEST-RETEST RELIABILITY

The test-retest method consists of using the same set of study participants and readministering the test to them at a different time. Usually, at each administration, a total score is computed for each participant by adding the scores of each item in the instrument or by averaging the items. For instance, the total scores for each participant might look like this:

	Scores	
Participant	*Initial Test*	*Retest*
1	5	6
2	3	4
3	7	7
.	.	.
.	.	.
.	.	.
N	6	8

The next step is to correlate the two columns of scores. The correlation will let us know the degree of association between the scores on the initial test and those on the retest. A high correlation coefficient indicates that participants who score high on the initial test also score high on the retest, and those who score low on the initial test also score low on the retest. This indicates that the instrument is reliable. Test-retest procedures measure reliability in terms of the stability of an instrument.

The biggest advantage of establishing test-retest reliability is that it is a quick, simple, and practical method. The major disadvantage is that the first administration of the test may affect how participants respond the second time they take the test. For example, a test measuring prejudice may increase or decrease participants' level of prejudice. If the test-retest correlation is low, we can't be sure if this is because the instrument is in fact unreliable or if it is because the level of prejudice changed from the first testing to the second.

Another disadvantage of this method of assessing reliability is that if the interval between test and the retest is too short, participants may remember how they responded and try to be consistent. This could lead to a high correlation even though the instrument is not reliable. On the other hand, if the interval between testings is too long, the property being measured might change. In this case, we might get a low correlation even though the instrument is reliable.

The interval between testings should be long enough so that study participants do not remember exactly how they responded the first time but not so long that the property being measured changes. Shorter intervals are appropriate for instruments measuring properties that can change easily, such as feelings and attitudes, and longer intervals are appropriate for instruments measuring relatively stable properties, such as IQ and achievement.

MULTIPLE OR ALTERNATE FORMS AND SPLIT HALF

The multiple- or alternate-forms method of assessing reliability consists of creating two different but equivalent forms of the same instrument and administering both to the same study participants at the same time. Both forms are scored for each participant, and then the scores of one form are correlated with the scores of the other. A high correlation indicates high reliability. The major disadvantage of this procedure is the difficulty in constructing two forms that arc truly equivalent.

If all items on an instrument measure the same characteristic (e.g., intelligence, attitudes toward public assistance, work stress), then the instrument can be split into two halves of equal length. Participants completing the instrument are not aware of the presence of the two halves but take the test as though it is one instrument. Scores for each participant are then computed for each of the two halves, and a correlation coefficient is calculated. Again, a high correlation indicates high reliability. This procedure of assessing reliability is called the split-half method.

INTERNAL CONSISTENCY

Internal consistency measures are used to determine the homogeneity of items. That is, do the items measure the same property? As with split-half procedures, this method is suitable only for instruments that measure a single property. There are various formulas to compute internal consistency, but they all measure the extent to which each item correlates with all other items. One way to evaluate internal consistency is to correlate respondents' scores on each item with every other item and then average all the correlation coefficients.

A common way to assess the internal consistency of an instrument is to compute a measure called Cronbach's alpha (Cronbach, 1951). Cronbach's alpha measures internal consistency by taking random samples of items on the test and correlating the scores obtained from these samples with each other. The average intercorrelation of scores obtained from all possible subsamples of items indicates the test's internal consistency (Kerlinger, 1973, p. 452).

WAYS TO IMPROVE RELIABILITY

As I noted earlier, a reliable instrument is one in which the error variance (variance due to errors of measurement) is low. The general procedure to increase reliability is to minimize the error variance. This can be done by controlling factors that affect the process of measurement.

Ambiguity due to poor wording of questionnaire and interview items increases error variance because respondents interpret the same items differently. In the same way, unclear and poorly defined observational and recording procedures also increase error variance. Therefore, clear and unambiguous wording and clear instructions to observers and recorders enhance an instrument's reliability.

Adding additional items to an instrument may increase reliability, especially if the instrument is short. With only a few items to measure a particular attribute, a chance error of measurement can have a large effect. With more items, the net impact of such an error is reduced because, with more items, each error of measurement is likely to be counterbalanced by another error in the opposite direction. There is, however, a point of diminishing returns in adding items to increase reliability. At some point, additional items no longer enhance reliability.

Reliability can be improved by using clear and standardized instructions and administering the instrument to all participants under standard, well-controlled, and similar conditions. Giving clear, standardized instructions to respondents ensures more consistent responses because the respondents will all be following the same directions. Having all respondents complete an instrument under the same conditions also helps minimize error because certain factors, such as alertness, fatigue, noise level, lighting, and seating arrangements, can introduce unwanted sources of error into a measure.

Care must also be taken to assure the accuracy and completeness of the data. Random investigator error (for example, coding errors, keypunching errors) can be made inadvertently. Therefore, care in each step in the research process must be taken to assure a high degree of reliability.

Social work researchers have available to them a number of standardized instruments that measure attributes such as self-esteem, depression, and life satisfaction. Information regarding the reliability and validity of these measures is available, based on testing with particular groups. If a standardized instrument measures an attribute relevant to the researcher's purpose and if it has been shown to be reliable and valid for the group to be studied, then it is desirable to use the standardized instrument. Fischer and Corcoran (1994) list a number of standardized measures useful to social workers.

WHAT IS VALIDITY?

Definition: The *validity* of an instrument is the extent to which it measures what it is supposed to measure.

Asking the question, Are we measuring what we think we are measuring? is really asking if our measuring instrument is valid. For example, if we administer an IQ test, are we really measuring intellectual ability? Perhaps we are measuring something else, such as reading ability, good test-taking behavior, or familiarity with middle-class concepts.

When physical properties or simple attributes are measured, there is usually no problem in determining validity (for example, measuring length or weight of an object). In social work, however, variables are more difficult to measure. The more indirect the method of measuring variables, the greater the question of validity. For example, income is easy to measure directly, whereas authoritarianism is not. Because many variables of interest in social work are complex or can be measured only indirectly, we are often concerned about the validity of measuring instruments.

There is no one validity. A test or scale is valid for the scientific or practical purpose of its user. Sometimes, we are interested in what a test measures (for example, self-esteem) and, sometimes, in how well a test predicts (for example, occupational ability tests). There are three major types of validity: content, criterion-related, and construct validity.

CONTENT VALIDITY

Definition: *Content validity* is the representativeness or sampling adequacy of the content—the substance, the matter, and the topics—of a measuring instrument.

An instrument has content validity if the content of the instrument is representative of the universe of content of the property being measured. For example, suppose a researcher designs a test to measure the "mental health" of American adults. According to the researcher's theoretical model, mental health is composed of a number of components. These might include absence of pathological symptoms, a low level of current life stress, an adequate social support system, ability to engage in intimate interpersonal relationships, and so on. Theoretically, each component has an infinite number of items that can be used to test that component. A valid test would have a number of items from each of the categories (i.e., it would have items representative of the entire universe of components that define mental health).

Content validity cannot be assessed directly because we never actually know the universe of content. Therefore, content validity is determined by the judgment of the researchers or of experts. When establishing content validity, the universe of content must be clearly defined, the judges or experts assessing the content validity of the instrument must be furnished with specific directions for making judgments, and there must be some method of pooling independent judgments.

CRITERION-RELATED VALIDITY

Definition: *Criterion-related validity* is established by comparing test or scale scores with one or more external variables or criteria known or believed to measure the attribute under question. There is less concern with what the test measures; the real concern is predictive ability.

There are two types of criterion-related validity: concurrent validity and predictive validity.

Concurrent validity refers to the ability of a measure to accurately predict the current situation or status of an individual. It asks how well test results agree with an external criterion currently available. For example, a researcher devises an instrument to identify juvenile delinquents. To establish concurrent validity, the test results could be compared with the current arrest records of respondents.

Predictive validity examines an instrument's ability to predict some future performance or situation. In other words, predictive validity asks how well the instrument agrees with a future criterion. For example, how well does the instrument to identify juvenile delinquency predict future delinquency?

For criterion-related validity, it is necessary that the criterion be independent of the test. The major problem in establishing criterion-related validity is determining the appropriate criterion or criteria. For example, what criterion should be used to validate a measure of caseworker effectiveness or to establish the predictive ability of a test of "family adjustment"?

CONSTRUCT VALIDITY

Of the three major types of validity, the most complex is construct validity.

Definition: *Construct validity* is evaluated by determining the degree to which certain explanatory concepts (constructs), derived from theory, account for performance on a measure.

For example, in evaluating the construct validity of an IQ test, the researcher wants to know if the test measures verbal ability and abstract reasoning. Does it also measure social class membership? The interest is usually in the property being measured (in this example, intelligence) rather than in the test itself.

Studies of construct validity are done to validate the theory underlying the instrument. This is done by seeing whether the instrument confirms or denies hypotheses predicted from a theory based on the constructs.

Let's suppose a researcher creates the construct of affability (the extent to which an individual is sociable and the extent to which he or she shows affection for others). To test the construct validity of a test to measure this variable, the researcher deduces certain relations that should and should not exist between affability and other variables. Thus the researcher expects the measure of affability to correlate highly with tests designed to measure sociability and with objective measurements of cooperation in group tasks. The measure should correlate negatively or not at all with measures of hostility and aggression. These two sets of correlations illustrate two types of construct validity: convergent validity and discriminant validity.

Convergent validity is established when evidence gathered from different sources or in different ways all indicate the same or similar meaning of the construct. Put another way, convergent validity means that different measures of a construct yield similar results. In the example, the construct validation of the instrument to measure affability might find the following to be true (assuming the construct has high convergent validity): The affability instrument correlates highly with an instrument that measures "Good Samaritanism" and with observations of "affectionate" behavior in a group setting.

Discriminant validity refers to the ability to empirically differentiate a construct from other constructs, the ability to predict which constructs will be unrelated to the construct under question, and the ability to determine which groups will differ on the construct. Assuming high discriminant validity, a validation study may find that the affability measure correlates negatively with a measure of hostility (i.e., those who score high on affability will score low on hostility and vice versa) and that members of the National Association of Social Workers score high on affability, whereas members of the Nazi Party score low.

Using different groups that are known to differ on the construct under study is called the *known-groups* approach. With this approach, members of each group are administered an instrument. If the instrument has discriminant validity, the groups should perform differently in the predicted direction.

RELATIONSHIP BETWEEN
RELIABILITY AND VALIDITY

Although reliability and validity have been treated separately, they are related. Reliability is a necessary precondition for validity, but validity is not necessary for an instrument to be reliable. Thus it is possible for an instrument to be reliable but not valid. It is, however, impossible for an instrument to be valid but not reliable.

A rifle and target analogy can be used to illustrate the relationship between reliability and validity. In this analogy, the rifle represents an instrument—for example, a scale to measure a characteristic such as intelligence, self-esteem, or psychosocial adjustment. A familiar pattern of concentric circles serves as a target. The bull's-eye of the target represents the concept we are attempting to measure with the instrument. Shots on the target represent the scores obtained on the instrument.

How good is our rifle? That is, how reliable and valid is our instrument? Figure 14.1 illustrates an instrument that is neither reliable nor valid. The "shots" or scores are scattered: The instrument is not consistent or reliable. In addition, the shots have not hit the bull's-eye: The instrument does not actually measure the intended concept. It is not valid.

Figure 14.2 shows a pattern of clustered shots. The "rifle" or instrument is consistent; it is measuring the same thing each time. It is reliable. The shots,

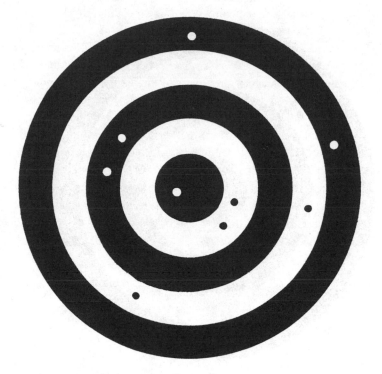

Figure 14.1. Rifle Neither Reliable nor Valid

however, are not on the bull's-eye, indicating that whatever is being measured is not the intended concept. It is not a valid measure.

Finally, Figure 14.3 illustrates a rifle or instrument that is both reliable and valid. Not only are the scores clustered, but they are all within the bull's-eye— that is, the scores measure the intended concept.

SUMMARY

Measurement of variables is essential to the research process. We want measuring instruments to be accurate, and we want to minimize the amount of error in measurements. Therefore, it is important to assess the reliability and validity of measuring instruments. Reliability refers to the extent to which an instrument is stable and consistent, and validity refers to the extent to which

Figure 14.2. Rifle Reliable but Not Valid

*an instrument measures what it is supposed to measure. Reliability is com-
monly assessed by test-retest, alternate forms, split-half, or internal consistency methods. There are various kinds of validity, including content validity,
criterion-related validity (which includes concurrent and predictive validity),
and construct validity. Reliability is a necessary precondition for validity.*

CASE STUDY

Within the past two decades, programs to train adults how to be more
assertive have become popular. The success of these programs has been

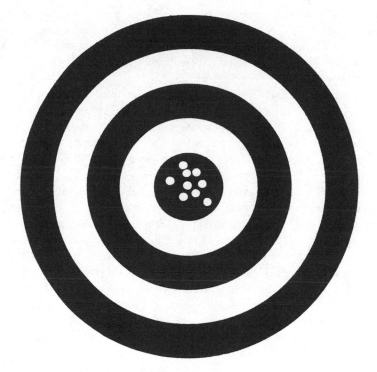

Figure 14.3. Rifle Both Reliable and Valid

measured in a number of ways, but perhaps the simplest and most common method of assessment is the assertion inventory.

An assertion inventory is a questionnaire with a set of items describing typical assertive situations (for example, situations in which the respondent is called on to make a request). For each item, the respondent is asked to make some response, such as an indication as to how likely the respondent is to handle that situation well. Responses to all items are then summed or averaged to give a total score that represents the respondent's level of assertiveness.

Rathus (1973) describes the development of an assertion inventory for a college-age population. In his review of the literature on the assessment of assertiveness, he identifies two earlier studies that developed assertion measures, but these were inadequate. One was badly outdated (the situations were no longer relevant), and the other was an instrument whose purpose was primarily to measure traits other than assertiveness.

He notes that several behavior therapists evaluated the success of their assertion training by asking their clients a series of questions, but none of them had developed a quantifiable assertion inventory (one that would yield a numerical score) or one that was standardized (tested on a large group of people and appropriate for general use).

Rathus assembled a list of social situations common to adult men and women. These were derived from the assertion measures described earlier and from diaries kept by a group of college juniors and seniors, as requested by the author. In these diaries, students recorded situations in which they would have liked to exhibit more assertive behavior. These items were used to construct a 30-item inventory. Typical items were, "I have hesitated to make or accept dates because of 'shyness,' " and "I have avoided asking questions for fear of sounding stupid." The respondent was asked to rate each item from a +3 (*very characteristic of me, extremely descriptive*) to –3 (*very uncharacteristic of me, extremely nondescriptive*).

The purpose of the study described in Rathus's article was to establish the reliability and validity of this instrument, the Rathus Assertiveness Schedule (RAS). Rathus provided evidence that this instrument had test-retest and split-half reliability and construct (convergent and discriminant) and predictive validity.

To determine the test-retest reliability of the RAS, Rathus asked 68 undergraduates to complete the instrument twice, with test administrations 8 weeks apart. This interval was long enough so that at the second testing, respondents were unlikely to remember their responses from the first testing, but it was not so long that their level of assertiveness was likely to have changed. The correlation (r) between respondents' first and second RAS scores was .7782, which indicates a moderate level of reliability. It indicated that the RAS has good stability over time.

Next, Rathus asked each of 18 students to give the test to three or four acquaintances off campus. Unlike the first group, which was of college age, the group of 67 acquaintances who completed the RAS ranged in age from 15 to 70 years. Using this more diverse group, the author was able to establish the validity and reliability of the RAS for a more general population (although Rathus could not claim that he had tested the validity of the RAS for the adult population as a whole because adults identified by college students are hardly a representative sample of the general population).

For each of the 67 acquaintances, Rathus computed an RAS score based on the even items and a corresponding score based on the odd items. The correlation (r) between the two split halves was .7723, indicating that the RAS items had moderate homogeneity—that is, all items tended to measure the same characteristic consistently.

To establish construct validity, Rathus compared evidence from the RAS scores of the 67 acquaintances with other independent data. He asked the 18 college students who had identified these acquaintances to rate each of them on a 17-item schedule based on the semantic differential scale. Two typical items were the following:

Bold____: ____: ____: ____: ____: ____: Timid

Confident ____: ____: ____: ____: ____:____: Uncertain

The college student placed a check mark indicating his or her best description of the acquaintance, and for each item the acquaintance received a score from −3 to +3. Rathus then did a "factor analysis" of these scores. Factor analysis is a complex statistical procedure, but in simple terms it tells the researcher which items are highly related—that is, it groups items into factors. In this way, Rathus determined that assertiveness was made up of five factors: boldness, outspokenness, assertiveness, aggressiveness, and confidence.

Rathus then computed correlations between the RAS scores of the 67 acquaintances and the student raters' impressions of their personality traits on the 17 semantic differential items. The RAS scores correlated significantly with each of the five items on the semantic differential that made up the assertiveness factor. This was evidence in support of the convergent validity of the RAS. That is, the results of the RAS tended to agree with independent raters' impressions.

With one exception, RAS scores were not significantly correlated with any of the other 12 (nonassertiveness) items of the semantic differential. This was evidence for the discriminant validation of the RAS. In other words, Rathus established that the RAS was related to personality characteristics associated with assertiveness but not related to other personality characteristics.

Finally, Rathus collected data to establish the predictive validity of the RAS. This time, he asked 47 college women who had completed the RAS to describe how they would react in five common situations calling for assertive behavior. For instance, they were asked, "You are seated at a restaurant counter, waiting for service. The waitress begins to serve someone who came in after you, a couple of seats away. What would you do?"

Respondents' responses were recorded on audiotape and rated by trained judges who did not know the respondents and did not know their scores on the RAS. The response to each situation could be rated from a 1 (indicating poor assertion) to 5 (indicating appropriate assertion), and a total rating was obtained by adding the ratings across all five situations. To ensure that the judges' ratings were reliable, pairs of judges rated the same audiotapes. The interrater reliability (r) between these two ratings was .9382, indicating a very high rate of agreement between judges.

As a test of predictive validity, Rathus then correlated the 47 college women's RAS scores with the judges' ratings of the audiotaped responses in which the women predicted their behavior in assertive situations. The correlation was a moderate .7049. This means that there was moderate consistency between what the RAS told us about a respondent and impartial others' impressions of the respondents' reports about how they would behave in situations calling for assertion.

The RAS has been shown to have acceptable reliability and validity, it is appropriate for a diverse adult population, and it is quick and easy to administer. For these reasons, it has become a popular way to measure assertiveness.

DISCUSSION QUESTIONS

1. What does it mean to say that a test or instrument is reliable?
2. What does it mean to say that a test or instrument is valid?
3. Name four methods for assessing the reliability of a measuring instrument.
4. Name three major methods for assessing the validity of a measuring instrument.
5. What is the difference between concurrent and predictive validity?
6. What is the difference between convergent and discriminant validity?
7. An instrument may be reliable but not valid. However, an instrument cannot be valid and not reliable. Explain why.

SHORT ASSIGNMENTS

1. Study the following assertions and decide in each case whether the assertion refers to reliability, validity, or both. For each item, name the type of reliability or validity.

   a. The test was given twice to the same group. The correlation between the scores of the two administrations was .90.
   b. Four teachers studied the items of the test for their relevance to the objectives of the curriculum.
   c. The items on the Family Functioning Scale appear to be representative of all the factors that define good family functioning.
   d. The academic aptitude test correlates well with students' grade point average.
   e. The mean difference on the prejudice assessment between the skinheads and the pacifists was significant.

f. Mothers' scores on the instrument were highly correlated with subsequent child neglect.

2. Imagine you are a researcher interested in studying social anxiety—that is, discomfort felt by some people in social situations. In particular, you are interested in learning about the relationship of social anxiety to a much-studied psychological characteristic called *locus of control*. Locus of control refers to individuals' beliefs that they control the events that affect them. Suppose that you have constructed a new instrument that you call the Social Anxiety Assessment and that you have access to your study participants' scores on a well-validated locus of control measure. Describe all the steps you will take to ensure the validity of your Social Anxiety Assessment. Pay particular attention to construct validity. (Hint: Before you assess any measure for validity, you must first determine if the measure is reliable.)

FURTHER READING

Carmines, E. G., & Zeller, R. A. (1979). *Reliability and validity assessment.* Beverly Hills, CA: Sage.
Litwin, M. S. (1995). *How to measure survey reliability and validity.* Thousand Oaks, CA: Sage.

15 How to Analyze Data

So far, we have talked about how to collect data through the use of questionnaires, interview schedules, and other instruments and how to ensure that those data are reliable and valid. But once we have the data, what do we do to answer the research questions? That is the purpose of data analysis.

DATA ANALYSIS

What is data analysis? In simple terms, it is the process by which we take a large set of numbers and reduce it to a smaller set of numbers. The data we collect from our instruments are "raw data." They are usually a set of many numbers that are not too useful in their raw form. To get an idea about trends in the data, about differences between groups, and so on, we must reduce that collection of numbers into a smaller set of numbers that will answer the research questions.

For example, if we had studied the social service needs of a group of families, we would have asked each family in the study to report its family income. We could present these data in their raw form by simply reporting the annual income for each family:

$12,220
$15,000
$8,900
$10,900
$15,500
$8,350

This presentation, however, is not too helpful. It does not give us a good summary of family income, and it would be difficult to compare these six families with other families or with local or national poverty levels.

A more useful way to present the data would be to compute a *statistic* such as a mean or median. The mean is computed by summing all incomes and dividing by the number of incomes. That would tell us that in this study, the mean or average income was $11,812. Another common way to report income is to compute the median. This is done by rank ordering the incomes and taking the middlemost income (if there are an odd number of incomes) or the mean of the two middlemost incomes (if there are an even number of incomes, as in this example). For these six families, the median income is $11,560.

When we conduct a research study, we need a data analysis plan. This plan should be formulated as soon as we have finalized the data collection instruments: our questionnaire, interview schedule, or observational inventory. It is tempting to wait until the data are in before we actually decide how we will analyze them, but there are two reasons why this is not a good idea.

First, if we allow collected data to determine which data analysis procedures we will use, we are violating the scientific method. If we are testing hypotheses, we will get a fair test of them only when the data analysis procedures are determined before the data are collected. Otherwise, we may deliberately select the analysis procedure that is most favorable to the hypotheses, putting ourselves in a situation where it would be difficult to show that the hypotheses are wrong.

The second reason for planning the data analysis before we collect the data is that this plan often reveals important omissions or oversights. When we actually sit down to plan the analysis, we sometimes realize that an important variable has been left out or that we need to have a more precise measure of a particular variable to test the hypotheses. When these issues are identified before data collection, it is possible to modify the data collection instruments appropriately.

I recommend another step that is helpful in ironing out the wrinkles in a data analysis plan. After the data collection instruments are drafted but before the data are collected, it is useful to make up a mock set of data and to carry out a test analysis. If the plan is adequate, we should be able to make up one mock data set that confirms the hypotheses and another one that does not.

This process will also help to clarify how each item in the questionnaire or other instrument will be handled in the data analysis: How will a number be assigned to the various responses? Will the questionnaire item be combined with other items in computing a score? Which of the independent and dependent variables will be measured with which items? We can also plan tables and figures ahead of time so that when the data analysis is done, all we will have to do is plug the appropriate numbers into their correct positions in those tables and figures.

We can now complete the correct order of research steps that we began in Chapter 2:

1. Formulate a theory.
2. State hypotheses (for descriptive research: state research questions). (These first two steps may be dropped if the study is exploratory.)
3. Create operational definitions for study concepts and variables.
4. Determine data collection procedure (e.g., questionnaire).
5. Create a data analysis plan.
6. Collect data.
7. Analyze data.
8. Interpret data and present results.

TYPES OF DATA

There are a variety of ways in which data may be analyzed and presented. But before we discuss these ways, we need to distinguish between two types of data: continuous and categorical.

Definition: *Continuous* data measures are those that can take on any whole or decimal value within a given range—for example, age, height, and weight.

Definition: *Categorical* data measures are those that can take on only a limited number of values within a given range—for example, number of clients in caseload, family size, and social class.

Some data analysis procedures are appropriate for categorical data. (Examples are frequency distributions and crossbreaks, which I discuss later. In

	Low Stress (levels 1–3)	High Stress (levels 4–7)
Subject 1	23	46
2	18	22
.	.	.
.	.	.
.	.	.
.	.	.
n	12	31
	$\overline{X}_L$	$\overline{X}_H$

Figure 15.1. Days of Hospitalization for Low- and High-Stress Patients (Stress Measured on *DSM-IV*).

NOTE: "Levels of stress" treated as a categorical; "number of days of hospitalization" treated as a continuous variable.

general, categorical measures are associated with frequencies—that is, with analyses that involve counting the number of persons or events in categories.) Other data analysis procedures are appropriate for continuous data. (Examples that are discussed in the next chapter are correlation and *t* tests.)

To simplify an analysis, it is often useful to treat a continuous measure as if it were a categorical measure. For example, even though we have information on the exact age of each respondent in the study, we may choose to classify respondents into the three categories of young, middle-aged, and old. Although we lose some information in the process, this does make a data presentation, particularly a figure or graph, easier to follow. (This process is similar to the one in which ratio or interval data are treated as nominal or ordinal data. See Chapter 13.) It is appropriate to present a continuous measure in the form of categories. We should, however, avoid the temptation to repeatedly recategorize the measure until the results agree with our expectations. This dubious procedure "stacks the deck" in our favor, thus violating the scientific requirement that our methods must be capable of showing that the hypotheses are wrong (see page 29).

Figure 15.1 is an example of an analysis in which one variable is treated as categorical and one as continuous. The example is taken from a student who did her field placement in a psychiatric hospital. As part of her training, she learned about the *Diagnostic and Statistical Manual (DSM-IV)*, which includes a scale to measure the stress level of patients. The Psychosocial Stressors Scale assigns a whole number score from 1 to 7 to indicate the current level of stress, with higher numbers indicating higher levels.

		Stress	
		Low (1-3)	High (4-7)
Length of Hospital Stay	Less than one month		
	One month or longer		

Figure 15.2. The Effect of Level of Patient Stress at Admission on Length of Hospitalization. (Stress was measured on *DSM-IV*.)

The student reasoned that because stress is an important determinant of recovery from mental illness, patients with high levels of stress are likely to be hospitalized for longer periods of time. Her hypothesis, then, was that for patients on her ward, as the level of psychosocial stressors (as measured at admission) increases, the length of hospitalization will increase. In Figure 15.1, the level of stress is treated as a categorical variable, and the number of days of hospitalization is treated as a continuous variable.

Figure 15.1 allows us to compare the mean number of days of hospitalization for the low-stress and the high-stress group. These means are indicated by $\overline{X}_L$ and $\overline{X}_H$.

Suppose the student had decided to treat both variables as categorical. This would involve converting the dependent variable, days of hospitalization, into a limited number of categories. When converting a continuous variable, such as this one, into a categorical variable, the researcher must determine where to place the cutoff points between the groups. In Figure 15.2, the cutoff point was 1 month. If the variable is to have two values or categories, it is customary to place the cutoff point at the mean or median, which ensures that cases will be distributed across both categories; that is, we won't have categories with very few or no cases. If the variable is divided into three or four categories, we can determine cutoff points by dividing the distribution into thirds or fourths.

TYPES OF ANALYSES

FREQUENCY DISTRIBUTION

A frequency distribution is used to describe a set of values on a single variable, for instance, the number of students who received various IQ test scores or the number of families who belong to different ethnic groups. It gives us a "picture" of the distribution of values on a variable. That is, it tells us if the values tend to "pile up" in the low, high, or middle end of the distribution or if there are many individuals or elements that have a particular value (such as many individuals who are 65 years old).

A typical frequency distribution includes a column of values and, next to it another column, labeled f (for "frequency"), that indicates how many individuals or elements are associated with each value. The number of values in a variable may be quite large. For instance, imagine a frequency distribution that summarizes the ages of all individuals who live in your town or city. The list of ages will probably have about 100 numbers in it, all the way from 0 (newborns) to those who are 100 years old.

There are some problems with this kind of frequency distribution. For one thing, it will be spread out over several pages, making it hard to read. Also, once we go over the age of 80 or so, there will probably be a lot of values (in this case, ages) that have a low or zero frequency. That is inefficient because a lot of space is taken up to give us very little information. In such a long distribution, it will also be difficult to get a clear picture of the age distribution: what the most common age levels are and whether there are more young, old, or middle-aged people.

For all these reasons, when we have a large number of values in a variable, we use a *grouped frequency distribution*. Table 15.1 is an example of such a distribution.

By grouping values of the age variable, Table 15.1 provides a concise and easy-to-read picture of this distribution. We find that the clients of the Senior Service Center are spread across a wide age range from the young-old to the old-old, with clients predominating in the young-old range (61 to 79 years old).

One of the first requirements for a grouped frequency distribution is that we figure out the *interval width*—that is, what range of values should be included in each group. In Table 15.1, the interval width is 5 years. (For example, the second group includes all those who are 61, 62, 63, 64, and 65 years of age.)

How do we determine the interval width for a frequency distribution? A good method is to find the difference between the highest and lowest values on the variable and divide that by the number of intervals we want. If that number turns out to include a fraction, we round it to the nearest whole number. A typical grouped frequency distribution should include 7 to 10 groups of values. If we want to highlight certain parts of a distribution or if

TABLE 15.1 Example of a Grouped Frequency Distribution: Age of Senior Service
Center Clients ($N = 200$)

Age	f	Percentage	Cumulative Percentage
Less than 61	24	12	12
61-65	42	21	33
66-70	58	29	62
71-75	36	18	80
76-80	22	11	91
81-85	14	7	98
Over 85	4	2	100

we need to show a more detailed breakdown, we may use narrower intervals
and more groups. But in general, it is best to keep the number of groups limited
so that the distribution is easy to read.

A good frequency distribution will show a fairly even spread of scores
across all groups and will avoid listing values that have zero or very low
frequencies. For example, in Table 15.1, the groups could have been extended
beyond age 85: 86 to 90, 91 to 95, and 96 to 100. But notice that we had only
four individuals in these three categories. We would have been adding three
lines to the frequency distribution without adding much additional information. Because the purpose of the grouped frequency distribution is to summarize information, we would have been defeating our purpose.

Many variables have distributions similar to this age distribution. That is,
there tend to be very few cases at the extremes—the low end and the high end
of the distribution. For this reason, it is often helpful to use open-ended end
points, in this case, "less than 61" and "over 85." In addition to making the
distribution more concise, these end points also allow the distribution to meet
one of the requirements for any good frequency distribution: that its values
be exhaustive. In other words, every individual in the sample is included in
the frequency distribution.

It is also necessary for the intervals in the frequency distribution to be mutually
exclusive. In other words, it should be clear that each individual is counted in one
and only one group of values. For example, if two adjoining intervals were
described as 61 to 65 and 65 to 70, individuals who were exactly 65 years of age
would be counted twice. Mutually exclusive intervals ensure that each individual
is counted only once, so that when we add up the numbers in the f column, the
sum represents the total number of individuals or elements in the sample.

Table 15.1 also includes two columns commonly found in grouped frequency distributions. The numbers in the percentage column indicate the percentage of the total sample that falls into each age interval: 12% are less than 61; 21% are 61 to 65; and so on. This simple percentage is computed by dividing the total sample size (*N*) into the number of individuals in each age interval.

The cumulative percentage figures are computed by adding the simple percentage in each interval to the percentages of all preceding intervals. This is a useful figure because it tells us, at each age level, what percentage of the sample is that age or younger. For example, 33% are 65 or younger, and 62% are 70 or younger.

MEASURES OF CENTRAL TENDENCY AND VARIABILITY

A frequency distribution gives us an idea of how values are distributed on a particular variable. To describe distributions more precisely, however, we need statistics that summarize distribution characteristics. These statistics also help us to compare distributions.

Two types of statistics are used to describe distributions: measures of central tendency and measures of variability.

Measures of *central tendency* tell us where the most typical or "average" value lies. The three most common measures of central tendency are the *mean, mode,* and *median.* The mean is a statistic that is commonly known as the average. As we said earlier, it is computed by summing all scores and dividing by the number of scores. The formula for computing the mean is this:

$$\overline{X} = \frac{\sum X}{N}$$

where $\overline{X}$ is the mean, $\sum X$ is the sum of scores, and *N* is the number of scores.

The mode is the score or category with the highest frequency. In Table 15.1, the modal category is 66 to 70 years of age.

As I stated earlier, the median is computed by rank ordering the scores and taking the middlemost score if there are an odd number of scores. If there are an even number of scores, the median is the mean of the two middle scores.

Each of these measures of central tendency represents a different way of describing the most "typical" score or the "center" of the distribution. The

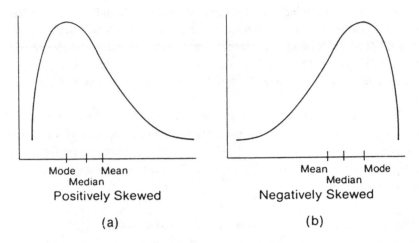

Figure 15.3. Illustration of a Positively Skewed and a Negatively Skewed Distribution

mode represents the most frequently occurring score or value. The mean is the most common way of measuring the center or average of a distribution, and it is usually the most useful because it is used in many statistical applications (as I will illustrate in the next chapter). When the scores in a distribution tend to pile up at either the positive or the negative end, however, the mean may be misleading as a description of the center of the distribution.

In a *positively skewed* distribution (Figure 15.3a), there are a greater number of scores at the lower end of the distribution. The mean is somewhat deceptive as a measure of the center of the distribution because it is pulled toward the tail—that is, toward the higher scores.

For instance, the distribution of family income is positively skewed because many families have lower incomes, whereas a few have very high incomes. The presence of just a few multimillionaires, however, inflates the mean. Therefore, the mean income gives an unrealistically high picture of what the average income is like.

A better measure of average income, and one used more commonly, is the median. By definition, half of all incomes are above the median and half below, so the median gives us a better sense of average income. The same principle applies to a negatively skewed distribution (Figure 15.3b). So in general, the median is a preferable statistic to describe the average value or score in a highly skewed distribution.

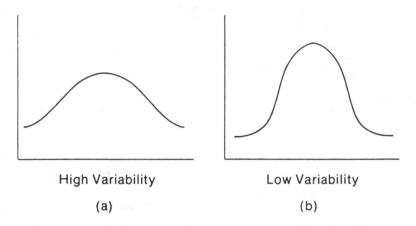

High Variability   Low Variability

(a)   (b)

Figure 15.4. Illustration of Distributions With High and Low Variability

Measures of *variability* tell us if the values are very spread out (i.e., if there are widely different scores) or if they are close together (i.e., if most scores are similar to one another). Figure 15.4a illustrates a distribution with widely spread scores (high variability). A distribution with scores that do not vary greatly (low variability) is illustrated in Figure 15.4b.

The simplest measure of variability is the *range.* It is computed simply by taking the difference between the highest and the lowest scores or values. It gives us a rough idea about the distribution of scores. For instance, a distribution of the ages of clients in an agency may reveal that the agency serves clients ranging in age from 65 to 90, a range of 25 years.

A more common measure of variability, and one that gives us more information, is the *variance.* The distribution in Figure 15.4a has relatively high variance; that in Figure 15.4b has relatively low variance. The "fatter" or more spread the distribution, the higher the variance. It is computed with the following formula:

$$S^2 = \frac{\sum (X_i - \overline{X})^2}{N - 1}$$

In this formula, S^2 is the variance, X_i is the individual score, $\overline{X}$ is the mean of all scores, and $(X_i - \overline{X})^2$ instructs the researcher to find the difference between a score and the mean and to square that difference. The Σ indicates that this process

TABLE 15.2 Percentage of Clients Rated as Improved at Follow-Up (Example of a Quasi-One-Dimensional Table)

Treatment Condition	Percentage	n	Percentage Not Improved
Child adolescent program	78	30	(22)
Family therapy	69	26	(31)
Control group	14	32	(86)

is to be repeated for each score and that all the squared difference scores are to be summed. This sum is then divided by 1 less than the number of scores.

Because the variance is based on *squared* differences, it will tend to be larger than the scores from which it is computed. For convenience and ease of understanding, we can bring the variance down to the same scale as the original scores by taking its square root:

$$s = \sqrt{s^2}$$

The square root of the variance, symbolized by the lowercase letter *s*, is called the standard deviation. In addition to being on the same scale as the original scores, it is also used in many statistical applications.

QUASI-ONE-DIMENSIONAL TABLE

Frequency distributions summarize information about a single variable. But often, we are interested in the relationship between two or more variables. The quasi-one-dimensional table gets its name from the fact that it appears, at first glance, to present information about a single variable. But, in fact, the quasi-one-dimensional table is a simple way to present the relationship between two variables.

Table 15.2 illustrates a quasi-one-dimensional table. The last column of figures (those enclosed in parentheses) should not be included in the table because they can easily be computed from the percentage column by subtracting the percentage improved from 100%. By eliminating figures that can easily be computed from other figures in a table, we create a simpler and easier to read presentation.

At first glance, Table 15.2 looks like a frequency distribution. It is not a frequency distribution, however, because it summarizes the relationship between two variables: treatment condition and number of clients rated as improved.

By the way, note that the second column of figures is labeled *n*. This letter is commonly used to represent the number of individuals or elements. It may refer to the number of individuals in a sample, in a table, or in a grouping within a table. Sometimes the capital letter *N* is used to indicate the number of individuals in the total sample, and the lowercase letter *n* is used to indicate the size of a subgroup within a sample or a table. This is the case in Table 15.2.

MULTIDIMENSIONAL TABLES

Two- and three-dimensional tables are often used to summarize the relationship between two variables or the relationships between three variables. They are appropriate for categorical variables or for continuous variables when they are treated as categorical variables. They are also referred to as *crossbreaks* or *contingency analyses.*

By definition, each variable must have at least two categories. So the simplest multidimensional table will have two variables, each of which is divided into two categories or values. This is called a 2×2 table. By extension, it is possible to have tables that are 2×3 or 3×3 or 3×4 and so on. Every table will have a number of cells. Data are summarized by counting the number of persons or elements that fall into each cell.

A number of rules should be followed when constructing multidimensional tables:

1. Categories should be set up so that they test a research hypothesis or a research question. In other words, the table should be relevant to the purpose of the study. Figure 15.2 is an example of a table that relates directly to a hypothesis.
2. Categories must be exhaustive. That is, every element in the sample must fit into the table.
3. Categories must be mutually exclusive. That is, every element in the sample must fit into one and only one cell.
4. Each variable should be treated as a separate dimension.

A common error among beginning students is to place two variables on a single dimension. Figure 15.5 illustrates this.

Because socioeconomic status (SES) and sex are treated as a single dimension (they are both placed on the horizontal dimension), the table in Figure

| | | Socioeconomic Status (SES) and Sex | | | |
		Low SES	High SES	Male	Female
Attitude Toward the Mentally Ill	Favorable				
	Unfavorable				

Figure 15.5. Attitudes Toward the Mentally Ill, by Low- and High-Status Males and Females (Illustration of an Incorrect Table in Which SES and Sex Are Treated as a Single Dimension)

| | | **Low SES** | | **High SES** | |
		Male	Female	Male	Female
Attitude Toward the Mentally Ill	Favorable				
	Unfavorable				

Figure 15.6. The Effect of Socioeconomic Status (SES) and Sex on Male and Female Attitudes Toward the Mentally Ill (Example of a Correct Table)

15.5 is not mutually exclusive. Each person in the sample will be counted twice. For example, a low-SES male with a favorable attitude will be counted once in the "low-SES-favorable" cell and again in the "male-favorable" cell. The result will be a table in which N will be twice as large as the number of people in the sample.

Figure 15.6 presents a correct version of this table. Because there are three variables in this table (it is a $2 \times 2 \times 2$ table), in principle we need three dimensions: length, height, and depth. Ideally, the table should be presented in the form of a three-dimensional cube. Unfortunately, the technology of holograms has not yet arrived, so we have to settle for ordinary two-dimensional paper. Figure 15.6 shows how three dimensions (variables) are presented on two-dimensional paper. One variable (in this case SES) is twice subdivided into the values of another variable (in this case sex).

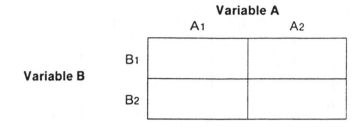

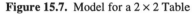

Figure 15.7. Model for a 2 × 2 Table

How many categories (values) can we have for each variable in a table? And how many variables can we include in a single table? There are limits on the number of variables and categories because tables become hard to understand when there are too many cells.

In general, crossbreaks should be limited to two- or three-variable tables. With more than three variables, it becomes difficult to see the relationships between variables. If we are interested in looking at relationships between more than three variables, we should break the hypotheses or research questions into a series of two-variable or three-variable statements and use a table for each statement. In statistics courses, students learn more sophisticated analysis procedures, such as multiple regression and canonical correlation, which are especially designed to summarize multivariable relationships.

The number of categories or values for each variable should always be fewer than eight. We can, of course, reduce the number of categories by "collapsing" across categories. (In Figures 15.1 and 15.2, we did this for the variables of level of stress and days of hospitalization.) For example, instead of having six age categories, we may decide to have just three: young, middle-aged, and old.

Collapsing or reducing the number of categories is done to avoid table cells with zero or very low frequencies (counts). Such tables are hard to interpret, they waste space, and they present problems when we want to apply statistical tests because these tests often assume that each cell has at least a frequency of 5. We do lose some information when we collapse categories. But sometimes that is necessary because the number of cells in a table increases very rapidly as we increase the number of categories for each variable. For example, a 2 × 2 × 2 table has 8 cells; a 3 × 3 × 3 table has 27 cells.

Figures 15.7 and 15.8 are models that we can use for two- and three-dimensional tables in which each variable has two categories. These models can be expanded when variables have more than two categories.

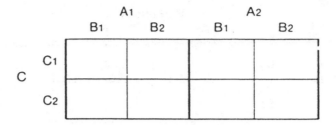

Figure 15.8. Model for a 2 × 2 × 2 Table

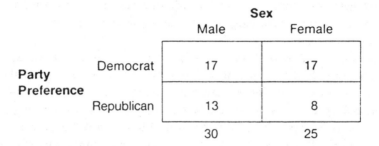

Figure 15.9. Political Party Preference of Males and Females in Social Work Class (*N*s)

There are other rules for constructing multidimensional tables. The independent variable or variables are usually placed at the top of the table and the dependent variable is placed at the side. The first step in building a table, of course, is to set up and label the categories, as illustrated in the preceding models. Then we will need to count the number of individuals or elements in each cell. Figure 15.9 depicts the results of a survey on political party preference conducted in a social work class of 55 students.

Note first of all that the independent variable, sex, is placed at the top of the table. Also, the column totals (30 and 25) are placed outside the table. These totals are called *marginals.*

The purpose of this table is to show if there is a relationship between sex and political party preference. That is, do men and women in this social work class differ in their party preference? An equal number of males and females prefer the Democratic party. But because there are an unequal number of men

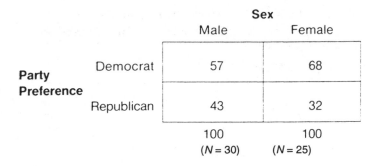

		Sex	
		Male	Female
Party Preference	Democrat	57	68
	Republican	43	32
		100	100
		(*N* = 30)	(*N* = 25)

Figure 15.10. Political Party Preference of Males and Females in Social Work Class (Percentages)

and women, this does not give us a good overall indication of whether the sexes differ in their party preference.

To better "see" the relationship between variables in a crossbreak, it is useful to compute percentages. Again, there is a rule for doing this. The percentages should be computed *from* the independent variable, *across* the dependent variable. Because the independent variable is on top, this means that percentages should be calculated down the columns, one column at a time. Figure 15.10 shows the result.

Percentages were calculated by dividing the number in each cell by the total number in that column. So, for example, in the upper left cell, 17/30 = 57%. In Figure 15.10, the relationship between sex and party preference becomes clear. Only 57% of males but 68% of females prefer the Democratic party. On the whole, women are more likely to support the Democratic party.

In this analysis, we could report both the frequencies and the percentages in each cell. This is sometimes done by placing the cell frequencies in parentheses, with a note indicating that this is where the *n*s appear. The table will be easier to read, however, if we present it as in Figure 15.10. In this example, the marginal *N*s were given. An interested researcher could easily reconstruct the cell frequencies from this information.

What if we had placed the dependent variable, party preference, at the top of the table and computed percentages from the dependent variable across the independent variable, sex? (I have done this in Figure 15.11.) This is not necessarily an error, although it is customary to do these computations in the opposite order, as in Figure 15.10. By placing party preference at the top and

Party Preference

		Democrat	Republican
	Male	50	62
Sex	Female	50	38
		100	100
		(*N* = 34)	(*N* = 21)

Figure 15.11. Sex of Democrats and Republicans in Social Work Class (Percentages)

computing percentages down the columns, however, we get a table that gives us a different picture. The interpretation of the data is somewhat different.

Compare the interpretation of Figure 15.11 with that of Figure 15.10. In Figure 15.11, we would conclude that among students preferring the Democratic party, there are equal numbers of men and women, whereas among students preferring the Republican party, almost two thirds are men.

In Figure 15.10, there appears to be a relationship between the variables of sex and political party preference: Females seem to prefer the Democratic party. But do they? Is the difference between the males and females large enough for us to conclude that it is significant? In the next chapter, I will explain what researchers mean when they say a relationship between variables is statistically significant. At this point, I will note that chi-square (χ^2) is the most common statistical test applied to crossbreak data. In the next chapter, I will show how to use it to determine if the relationship between two variables is significant.

GRAPHS

The sage who commented that a "picture is worth a thousand words" would have appreciated research graphs. By "painting" the relationship between variables, graphs are an efficient way to summarize information. They help us to see trends in the data and to describe complex relationships in a simple-to-understand form.

Each graph has two axes. The horizontal or *X-axis* depicts the values of the independent variable, whereas the dependent variable is plotted on the vertical or *Y-axis*. For example, the relationship between age and health status can be depicted as in Figure 15.12.

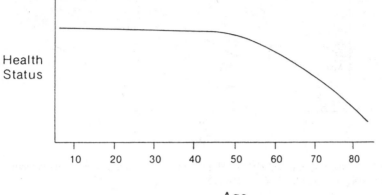

Figure 15.12. The Relationship of Age to Health Status

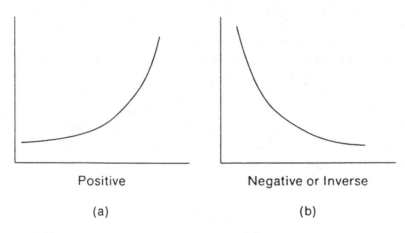

Figure 15.13. Positive and Negative Relationships Between Two Variables

Figure 15.12 shows that health status remains fairly constant through the life cycle but begins to deteriorate at around age 50. From there, it declines gradually with increasing age.

In a two-variable relationship, when one variable increases consistently as the other variable increases, we say that we have a *positive relationship*. When one variable increases consistently as the other variable decreases, we have a

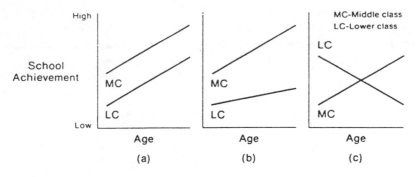

Figure 15.14. Three Hypothetical Relationships Between Age and School Achievement for Lower-Class (LC) and Middle-Class (MC) Students

negative or *inverse relationship.* Figure 15.13 illustrates a positive and a negative relationship.

Graphs are particularly useful for describing relationships between three variables. Figure 15.14 describes hypothetical relationships between the three variables of age, school achievement, and social class of students.

When we attempt to give verbal descriptions of the relationship in each graph, we realize how handy graphs are. For Figure 15.14a: For both lower-class and middle-class students, the level of achievement increases consistently with age, and at the same rate for lower-class and middle-class students. The achievement level of lower-class children, however, is always lower than that for middle-class children, and the difference in achievement is equal across all age groups.

SUMMARY

Data analysis is the process by which a large set of numbers is reduced to a smaller set of numbers to make sense out of the data we have collected. The types of analyses we can perform are constrained by the nature of the data—whether they are continuous or categorical. All continuous data, however, may be treated as categorical.

Individual variables are summarized by using a frequency distribution and described through measures of central tendency and measures of variability. Measures of central tendency tell us where the most typical or "average" value of the distribution lies. They include the mean, mode, and median. Measures of variability tell us if the scores in a distribution are close together or spread apart. They include the range, variance, and standard deviation.

We can use a quasi-one-dimensional table or a crossbreak to present the relationship between pairs of variables. Data can also be presented visually in the form of graphs.

DISCUSSION QUESTIONS

1. Why is data analysis needed?
2. In order, name all the steps in the research process.
3. What is the difference between categorical and continuous data measures? Give examples of each.
4. Why are continuous measures sometimes treated as categorical measures? Give an example.
5. Match each item in Group A with its definition in Group B.

Group A	Group B
Measures of central tendency	
• Mean	• Difference between lowest and highest score
• Median	
• Mode	• Middlemost (or average of two middlemost) scores
	• Average score
Measures of central variability	
• Range	• Average squared deviation of scores from the mean
• Variance	
• Standard deviation	• Square root of the average squared deviation of scores from the mean
	• Most frequently occurring score

6. What is a positively skewed frequency distribution?
7. Create an empty 2×2 table to show the relationship between living arrangement (alone or with others) and self-perceived health (poor or good).
8. Create a line graph that shows the hypothetical relationships between three variables: age, income, and education. (Hint: Treat education as a categorical variable with these values: "completed high school" and "less than high school completion.")

SHORT ASSIGNMENT

In the following, I have presented data on four variables taken from a hypothetical study of parental stress and child abuse. Organize these data into contingency tables to answer each of the following questions. Be sure to give each table a title and to label all variables and values appropriately:

a. What is the relationship between caretakers' relationship to child and history of abuse?
b. What is the relationship between parents' rating of parental stress and history of abuse?
c. What is the relationship between worker's rating of parental stress and history of abuse?
d. What is the relationship between caretakers' relationship to child and history of abuse, controlling for worker's rating of parental stress? (Hint: Construct a table to show the relationship between the first two variables, *only* for parents who were rated low stress by the worker. Repeat *only* for parents who were rated high stress by the worker.)

Caretakers' Relationship to Child[a]	History of Abuse[b]	Parents' Rating of Parental Stress[c]	Worker's Rating of Parental Stress[c]
B	Y	L	L
B	N	L	L
B	N	H	H
F	Y	H	H
F	Y	L	H
F	Y	H	H
B	N	L	L
F	Y	H	H
F	Y	H	H
B	N	L	L
B	Y	L	L
B	N	L	L
B	Y	H	H
F	Y	H	H
B	N	L	L

a. B = birth parents; F = foster parents.
b. Y = yes; N = no.
c. H = high; L = low.

FURTHER READING

Graft, J. L. (1990). *Statistics and data analysis for social workers* (2nd ed.). Itasca, IL: F. E. Peacock.
Zeisel, H. (1957). *Say it with figures.* New York: Harper & Row.

16   Statistical Hypothesis Testing

$\mathbf{I}$n the previous chapter, we looked at three types of analyses:

1. A description of a single variable. We can describe the variable by computing a measure of its central tendency, such as the mean. Or we can describe its variability by computing the variance or standard deviation.
2. A comparison of two or more groups to see if they are different. For instance, in Figure 15.1, we compared the mean number of days of hospitalization for two groups: a low-stress and a high-stress group of patients.

When comparing groups such as these, the mean value for each group is most commonly used. By extension, we could compare more than three groups. For example, we could compare the mean number of days of hospitalization for three groups: low, medium, and high stress. Or we could compare the effects of three or four or any number of treatment programs on the mean length of hospitalization. In this case, we would have as many groups as there were treatment programs.

3. A description of the relationship between two variables. For example, Figure 15.10 described the relationship between sex and political party preference. In this example, both variables were categorical. We might also be interested in describing the relationship between two continuous variables, such as age and school achievement in Figure 15.14.

USING SAMPLES TO INFER
POPULATION CHARACTERISTICS

There are times when our interest is limited to the particular group of people in our study: the sample. In these situations, the sample and population are one and the same. For example, I might be interested in examining the relationship of school achievement to age in my school only, where I have data for all students. The U.S. Census is a common example of a situation in which I measure every person or element in the population. For example, the government is able to publish a correct figure for the median income of all U.S. families based on information from all families (there will, of course, be some missing respondents).

But in most social work research, we measure only a sample, and the purpose of the effort is to make some statement about the population. Typically, the sample consists of a relatively small number of individuals or cases, and the purpose in measuring the sample is to make inferences (guesses) about characteristics of the entire, much larger, population. Therefore, when we do one of the three analyses summarized earlier (description of a single variable, a comparison of groups, or description of a relationship), we have completed only the first step.

The next step is to answer the question, Is what we found in our sample true for the population? In other words, if we measured the entire population would our findings be the same? The purpose of this chapter is to describe a commonly accepted research method for answering this question: statistical hypothesis testing.

Let's look at this question specifically for each type of analysis:

1. For a description of a single variable: Is the mean value of the variable in the sample the same as it is in the population? For example, if the mean income of families in the sample is $10,000, is that also the mean income for all families in the population?
2. For a difference between groups: If the groups in the sample differed, do those groups also differ in the population? For example, if low-stress patients in the sample have fewer days of hospitalization, is that also true for all psychiatric patients?
3. For a description of a relationship: If variables are related in the sample, are they also related in the population? For example, if women in the sample are more likely to prefer the Democratic Party, is that also true for women in the United States as a whole?

TABLE 16.1 Summary of Types of Analyses and Corresponding Test Statistics and Null Hypotheses

Type of Analysis Question	Test Statistic	Null Hypothesis
a. Is the sample mean different from the population mean (one-sample t test)?	$t = (\overline{X} - M)/SE$	$\overline{X} = M$
b. Is there a difference between the means of groups (two-sample t test)?	$t = (\overline{X}_1 - \overline{X}_2)/SE$	$M_1 = M_2$
c. Is there an overall difference between the means of three or more groups (F test)?	$F = MS_{bg}/MS_{wg}$	$M_1 = M_2 = M_3 = \ldots$
d. Is there a relationship between two categorical variables (chi-square test)?	χ^2	χ^2 pop. $= 0$
e. Is there a relationship between two continuous variables (r test)?	r	$r_{pop.} = 0$

NOTE: $\overline{X}$ = sample mean; M = population mean; SE = standard error; MS_{bg} = mean square between groups; MS_{wg} = mean square within groups; χ^2 = chi-square; r = correlation coefficient.

When we measure characteristics of the sample—such as a mean or standard deviation—these measures are called *statistics*. A statistic is measured from our sample to make a guess about the corresponding measure in the population. The corresponding population measure is called a *parameter*.

For example, when we measure the average number of days of hospitalization in our sample, that is a statistic ($\overline{X}$). We measure that statistic to make a guess about the average days of hospitalization in the population. That is a parameter. To show that it is different from the sample statistic, in this chapter, I have indicated the population mean with the capital letter M.

When we describe a sample by computing a statistic (such as $\overline{X}$ or s) we are using *descriptive statistics*. These statistics describe characteristics of the sample.

But as I said, statistics are usually measured so that we can make a guess or *inference* about the "true" value of that number in the population. When we use sample statistics to make inferences about population parameters, we are using *inferential statistics*. Four common inferential statistics are t, F, chi-square (χ^2), and r. Table 16.1 lists each statistic and the type of analysis with which it is associated.

TESTING THE MEAN VALUE OF A SINGLE VARIABLE
(ONE-SAMPLE *t* TEST)

In a recent editorial in the student newspaper, the editor-in-chief (a physical education major) accused social work students of being "below average in intelligence." The nerve! As the head of the Social Work Student Association, you decide to do a bit of research to determine if this is true. You find a standardized intelligence test on which you know the mean score among all those who have taken the test is 100. You manage to get a sample of 500 social work students from all over the country to take the test to see if their scores, on average, are in fact below 100.

When you compute the mean score for your sample of students $(\overline{X})$ you find that it is 99. Does that mean that the student editor was right?

You measured the mean intelligence of a sample of social work students to see if the mean intelligence level of all social work students was below 100. But you know that because every measure includes some random error (see Chapter 14) it is unlikely that your sample mean will be exactly 100, even if that was in fact the population mean.

You might reason as follows: Let me be an optimist and start off with the assumption that the average intelligence of the 500 social work students in my sample is equal to the population mean of 100. I'll call this the *null hypothesis:*

$$H_0: \overline{X} = M = 100$$

If my sample mean comes out "pretty close" to 100, I'll just say that my assumption must be correct. I wouldn't want to reject it (and conclude that social work students are below average) if my sample mean is close to 100.

The problem is, how do we know how much "pretty close" is? If our sample mean is 98 or 99 it may be reasonable to assume that H_0 is true. But what if the sample mean is less than 98? How much less than 98 does it have to be before we can say that H_0 is unreasonable?

To answer that question, statisticians have developed procedures for evaluating inferential statistics. Let's call a statistician. The statistician would evaluate our data as follows:

I'll start out by testing the same hypothesis as our social work student: the null hypothesis that the population mean is 100. If that is true, then the difference between my sample mean and the population mean of 100 should be small. The *t* test will give me a guideline as to when the difference between $\overline{X}$ and *M* is large enough so that I can reject H$_0$. I compute it as follows:

$$t = (\overline{X} - M)/SE$$

SE stands for standard error. It is a measure of how much variability there is in the intelligence scores of the students. If *t* is small enough, I can accept the null hypothesis and conclude that the intelligence of social work students is no different from the average intelligence of 100. If *t* is large (and negative), I must reject the null hypothesis and conclude that the average intelligence of social work students is less than 100. To tell what value of *t* will result in a rejection of the null hypothesis, I have to consult a *t* table.

If my obtained *t* value[1] is greater than the tabled value, that means that if the true population mean (*M*) was 100, then the chances of getting the mean I did are less than 5 in 100. That's not likely. So I have to reject H$_0$ and conclude that social work students are of less than average intelligence.

But if my obtained *t* value is *less* than the tabled value, this means that in 95 out of 100 cases I could have gotten that *t* value if the population mean were 100. Therefore, it is reasonable to not reject H$_0$ and conclude that the average intelligence of social work students does not differ from 100.

You should note that all the inferential test statistics described in this chapter require certain *assumptions*. These assumptions must be met to use these tests in a valid manner. You can learn more about these tests and their underlying assumptions by consulting any standard textbook on social science statistics, such as Hays (1973).

To use the preceding one-sample *t* test, we must assume that either the sample is moderately large (50 or greater) or that the variable—in this case intelligence—is normally distributed in the population (Hays, 1973, p. 393). A normal distribution is one that is not skewed; that is, an equal number of individuals lie below and above the mean, and the distribution looks like a bell (see p. 308 in Chapter 15).

A *t* table is provided at the end of this book. To read the proper value from the *t* table, we need three pieces of information:

1. The degrees of freedom, indicated by *df* in the table. It is the total number of subjects minus the number of groups. In this case, it is 499.
2. Whether the test is one-tailed or two-tailed. A one-tailed test is used for a directional hypothesis. In this case, the hypothesis is directional or one-tailed because we specified that social work students were *less* intelligent than average.

A nondirectional two-tailed test would have specified simply that social work students differed from the average—they could be higher or lower.

3. The probability level. This specifies the chances that we would be wrong if we rejected H_0. By convention, we select a probability level of .01 or .05; that is, if our obtained t value meets or exceeds the tabled value, then the chance that we could reject H_0 and be wrong would be less than 1 in 100 or 5 in 100.

Entering the t table at 499 *df* for a one-tailed test at a probability of .05, we read a t value of 1.645. If our obtained t value meets or exceeds this, we must reject H_0 (at the .05 level) and conclude that social work students are less intelligent than average. The corresponding value for a probability level of .01 is 2.326. In other words, to establish that there are even fewer chances of rejecting H_0 when it is true, we need to have an even larger obtained t value.

By the way, we should be pleased to learn that when our social work student computed the t value based on the sample of social work students, the t value was well below the tabled critical value of 1.645. The student then was able to accept the null hypothesis as reasonable: Social work students are not less intelligent than average.

THE LOGIC OF STATISTICAL HYPOTHESIS TESTING

I have just illustrated the logic of hypothesis testing for the first type of analysis listed in Table 16.1—description of a single variable. Although five different tests are described in this table, the logic of hypothesis testing is always the same. It is as follows:

1. State H_0, the null hypothesis (the hypothesis of no difference).

(Following the types of analyses listed in Table 16.1:

a. To determine if the mean value of a single variable differs from a specified mean value, H_0 states that the sample mean is no different from the population mean.

b and c. To test the mean difference between two groups or between three or more groups, H_0 states that the population means are equal.

d and e. To test the relationship between two categorical or two continuous variables, H_0 states that the population parameters are equal to zero.)

2. Compute the test statistic based on sample data.
3. Compare the test statistic to a tabled value.
4. If the test statistic meets or exceeds the tabled value, reject H_0. Conclude that there is a difference or that the population parameter is not zero.

When H_0 is rejected, we say that our finding is *statistically significant.* Our result may be statistically significant at the .05 or the .01 *level of significance,* depending on which of these two tabled values has been met or exceeded. This means that, based on our obtained data, a difference or statistic that large could have been obtained only 5 or 1 out of a 100 times if H_0 were true. Therefore, the chances of being wrong in rejecting H_0 are quite small.

MEAN DIFFERENCE BETWEEN TWO GROUPS
(TWO-SAMPLE *t* TEST)

To illustrate this type of analysis, let us assume that we have been asked to evaluate the effects of an income subsidy program. Under this program, families who fall below the poverty line are provided with a cash grant. The agency for which we are evaluating the subsidy program is concerned that it may provide a work disincentive: If families know they will receive a subsidy when their income falls, they may work less.

We decide to use a posttest-only control group design. We randomly assign low-income families to experimental and control groups. Experimental group families receive the income subsidy, whereas control group families do not. The work history of the head of household is monitored for all families during and after the program. In determining if the program results in a work disincentive, we analyze the number of days of full-time employment in both groups.

Our test statistic is

$$t = \frac{\overline{X}_C - \overline{X}_E}{SE}$$

The numerator (top number) represents the difference in the mean number of days of full-time employment in the two groups. The denominator is the standard error, a measure of the variability within both groups.

We compute the appropriate degrees of freedom. We have already decided before data collection that we want to use a one-tailed test, because any difference between the two groups should be in only one direction: The experimental families may work less due to the work disincentive of the subsidy. We also decide on a significance level: .01 or .05.

The null hypothesis is that there is no difference between the means of the two groups. That is, if we can imagine an entire population of families, the average number of full-time work days will be the same for families receiving the subsidy and for those not receiving it. Because of random error, of course, we don't expect the sample means to be exactly equal, even if the hypothetical means were equal.

We enter the t table and note the critical value at which H_0 must be rejected. If our obtained t value exceeds the tabled value, we reject H_0. Assuming that experimental families worked less, we conclude that this difference was statistically significant: The income subsidy program did produce a work disincentive. If our obtained t value is less than the tabled value, we conclude that the difference in number of days worked was not significant: The income subsidy program did not produce a work disincentive.

As I noted earlier, all inferential test statistics can be used only when certain assumptions have been met. The assumptions that underlie the two-sample t test are a bit more demanding than those for the one-sample t test (Hays, 1973, p. 393). First of all, the two-sample t test I have described here is only for use with two *independent* groups. This means that each group—in the preceding example, the income subsidy group and the control group—must be selected independently.

If the size of your sample is large (say, 100 or more persons or cases), you do not need to worry about additional assumptions, because violating these assumptions will not invalidate your test.

But what happens if your sample size is smaller? In this case, there are two additional assumptions of concern: the *normal-population* and the *homogeneity-of-variance* assumptions. The normal-population assumption requires that the population variable (in our example, the number of days worked) be normally distributed. As before, however, if the size of the two sample groups is moderately large (over 50), this assumption can be disregarded. The homogeneity-of-variance assumption requires that the variables in the population have equal variances (see p. 309 in Chapter 15 for an explanation of variance). In practice, if the sample variances of the two groups are similar or if the sizes of the two groups are equal, then we don't have to worry too much about this assumption either. Thus, when comparing the means of two groups with a t test, you should try to use large samples and to ensure that the sizes of the comparison groups are equal.

MEAN DIFFERENCE BETWEEN MORE THAN
TWO GROUPS (*F* TEST)

What if the income subsidy program mentioned earlier used three rather than two groups? For example, we may have had two experimental groups and one control group. The first experimental group would have a regular income subsidy, and the second would have a subsidy only after meeting a minimum work requirement (i.e., they would be required to work a minimum number of days before qualifying for the subsidy). The control group would be as before. For each group, we would compute the mean number of days worked. How can we tell if there is an overall difference between all three means?

For situations such as this, in which we are comparing the means of more than two groups, statisticians have developed an extension of the *t* test: the *F* test.

The *F* test is computed by this formula:

$$F = MS_{bg}/MS_{wg}$$

MS_{bg} stands for mean square between groups, and MS_{wg} stands for mean square within groups. The computational formulas for these statistics can be found in any statistics textbook. But as is the case for the other test statistics, today's accessibility to computers makes it unlikely that you will ever have to compute these statistics by hand. Instead, a conceptual explanation will suffice.

Both the *F* test and the *t* test (the latter is just a special case of the *F* test) have a numerator and a denominator. The numerator is a measure of differences between groups. In the case of the two-sample *t* test, it is simply the difference between the means. In the *F* test, its computation is more complex, but it is just a measure of the overall difference between the means. The greater their difference, the larger the MS_{bg}.

The denominator is based on the variance of scores *within* each group. If the within-group variance is high, the denominator (*SE* or MS_{wg}) is large.

A large test statistic (and hence a significant difference) occurs when the between-group differences are large relative to the within-group differences. Therefore, if the differences between means are large and the variance within each group is small, the test statistic is likely to show that the differences are statistically significant. It is also true that if the variance within the groups is small, a relatively small difference between means will result in a significant test statistic. If the variance within the groups is large, you will require a larger difference between means for the test statistic to be significant.

The assumptions for a valid use of the F test are the same as those for the two-sample t test. That is, we assume that each of the groups was selected independently of the others. Also, if we use small samples, we may need to be concerned with the normal-population assumption; and if, in addition, our groups are of very unequal size and their sample variances differ, we may need to modify or abandon the F test (Hays, 1973, pp. 410, 467). These issues are discussed more fully in most social science statistics texts.

RELATIONSHIP BETWEEN TWO CATEGORICAL VARIABLES (CHI-SQUARE)

In Chapter 15, I presented a 2×2 table that examined the relationship of sex to the political party preference of a group of social work students. Figure 15.10 showed that women in the sample were more likely than men to favor the Democratic party. But we were left with the question as to whether this difference was statistically significant: That is, among all social work students in the United States, are women more likely to support the Democratic party?

In crossbreak analysis, as in the other analyses presented so far, we are faced with the question, How large a difference do we need to call that difference statistically significant? In the analyses presented earlier, we used a t or an F test statistic to answer that question. The test statistic that will tell us if the relationship in a two-dimensional crossbreak is statistically significant is called χ^2 or chi-square.

Let's use the same example as in Figure 15.10 but change the numbers so that the relationship between the variables of sex of student and political party preference will become clear. The null hypothesis is that there is no relationship between the variables. In our example, this means that knowing the sex of the student will tell us nothing about how likely that student is to prefer one political party over the other. Or to put it another way, if there is no relationship between the variables, males and females will be equally likely to favor either party. This is illustrated in Figure 16.1a. Notice that exactly half of both the males and females favor each party.

Figure 16.1b illustrates the opposite situation: There is a perfect relationship between the variables. In this situation, knowing the sex of the student

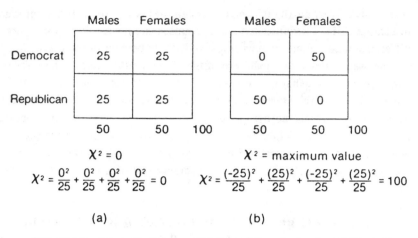

$X^2 = 0$ X^2 = maximum value

$$X^2 = \frac{0^2}{25} + \frac{0^2}{25} + \frac{0^2}{25} + \frac{0^2}{25} = 0 \qquad X^2 = \frac{(-25)^2}{25} + \frac{(25)^2}{25} + \frac{(-25)^2}{25} + \frac{(25)^2}{25} = 100$$

(a)   (b)

Figure 16.1. Political Party Preference of Males and Females in a Social Work Class, Illustrating No Relationship (a) and a Perfect Relationship (b). (Table values indicate Ns.)

gives us complete information about that student's party preference: All the women favor the Democratic party and all the men favor the Republican party.

Chi-square is computed in such a way that its value is zero when there is no relationship between two variables (Figure 16.1a), and its value is at a maximum when there is a perfect relationship (Figure 16.1b). Therefore, the null hypothesis of no relationship is

$$H_0 : \chi^2 = 0$$

The formula for computation of the chi-square test statistic is

$$\chi^2 = \sum \frac{(O - E)^2}{E}$$

O stands for the observed score, which is the actual frequency in each cell. E is the expected frequency—that is, the frequency that would be expected if there was no relationship between the variables. In this example, the expected frequency is 25 in each cell, because there are 50 males and 50 females, and if there is no relationship between the variables (Figure 16.1a), half of each group will favor each party.

By the way, an easy way to figure out the expected frequencies is to note all the marginals—the totals outside the table. Then for each cell, multiply its corresponding row and column marginals and divide by the total frequency in the table. For Figure 16.1a, each cell's expected frequency is (50 × 50) / 100 = 25.

As indicated in Figure 16.1, when there is no relationship, the value of chi-square is zero. When there is a perfect relationship, the value of chi-square is at its maximum—in this case, 100.

The degrees of freedom for chi-square are not dependent on the number of respondents, as they were for the *t* test and *F* test. They are dependent only on the number of rows and columns in the crossbreak:

$$df = (r - 1)(c - 1)$$

where r = the number of rows, and c = number of columns.

For the data in a 2 × 2 table, $df = 1$. As before, we enter a table of critical values for chi-square, with the *df* and level of significance. (A table of chi-square values is provided at the end of this book.) We must also determine if the test is one-tailed (directional) or two-tailed (nondirectional). Assuming that our hypothesis did not specify which sex preferred which political party, in this case we would use a two-tailed test.

From the table, we find that we require a chi-square value of 3.84 for the relationship to be significant at the .05 level. At the .01 level a chi-square of 6.64 is required.

Clearly, the chi-square value of zero (Figure 16.2a) is not significant; the chi-square value of 100 (Figure 16.2b) is significant at a probability level of .01. In the latter case, this means that if sex and party preference were not related in the population, the chance of getting a relationship (chi-square value) as large as we did is less than 1 in 100. This is very unlikely. Therefore we reject the null hypothesis of no relationship. We conclude that sex and party preference are in fact related. The relationship is statistically significant.

We should note a limitation in the use of the chi-square test statistic. The probabilities in the table of critical values for chi-square are based on the assumption that none of the table cells has zero or very low frequency. When this occurs, the probabilities are not accurate. As a general rule, you may not use the chi-square statistic when in a 2×2 table the expected value is less than 5 in one or more cells, *or*

in a larger table, more than 20% of the cells have expected values less than 5.

There is an additional assumption that applies when the sample is relatively small—say, fewer than 100 individuals or cases. With such small samples, we must assume that the variable is normally distributed in the population (Hays, 1973, p. 443).

RELATIONSHIP BETWEEN TWO CONTINUOUS VARIABLES (*r*)

In Figure 15.14 in the previous chapter, we illustrated the relationship between age and school achievement. Presumably, as age increases, the level of achievement should increase. In other words, as the first variable increases, the second variable also increases. As illustrated in Figure 15.13a, this is a positive relationship.

A graph is a useful way to depict this relationship. But from the graph, it would be difficult to determine, overall, *how much* Variable 2 increases as Variable 1 increases. In addition, it would be difficult to compare two graphs illustrating two different relationships and to tell which of the pairs of variables has a stronger relationship.

There is a statistic commonly used to measure the degree to which two continuous variables are related. It is symbolized by the lowercase letter *r* and is called the Pearson product-moment correlation coefficient (usually referred to as the correlation coefficient).

The correlation coefficient can vary from a maximum of +1.00 to a minimum of −1.00. It may also have a value of 0. Figure 16.2 illustrates these three possibilities.

The value of *r* that we usually obtain in our samples is almost never exactly 0, +1.00, or −1.00. Because of random error, even if the variables are perfectly correlated in the population, sample *r*s tend to be in between these values.

A positive correlation indicates that high scores on Variable 1 are paired with high scores on Variable 2 and that low scores on Variable 1 are paired with low scores on Variable 2. For example, age and number of health problems tend to be positively correlated: Persons at higher ages tend to have a larger number of health problems; persons at lower ages tend to have a lower number of health problems.

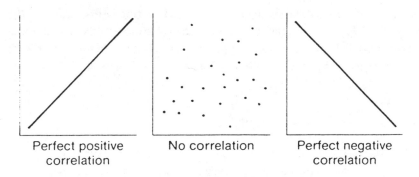

Figure 16.2. An Illustration of Positive, Negative, and No Correlation

A correlation of zero or close to zero indicates that there is no relationship between two variables. As one variable increases, the other variable is just as likely to increase or decrease. Knowing an individual's score on one variable tells us nothing about that individual's score on the other variable. For example, there is no correlation between the size of one's feet and one's IQ score.

A negative correlation indicates that *high* scores on Variable 1 are paired with *low* scores on Variable 2 and vice versa. For example, age and number of years of formal education are negatively correlated. Because older people had fewer educational opportunities in their youth, we find that as age increases, the amount of formal education decreases. Older people have fewer years of formal education than do younger people.

Like the other test statistics, *r* can be used to test the statistical significance of relationships. The null hypothesis is that the correlation of the two variables in the population is zero. If the *r* we obtain in our sample is sufficiently large, then it is unlikely that the population *r* is zero. In this case, we reject H$_0$ and conclude that the relationship between the variables is statistically significant.

How large must *r* be to reject H$_0$? As before, we refer to a standard table of critical values for *r*. (A table of *r* values is provided at the end of this book.) Instead of entering the table with degrees of freedom, we enter with the sample size and the desired level of significance (.01 or .05). If the *r* we obtained in our sample meets or exceeds the tabled value of *r*, we conclude that the relationship between the two variables is statistically significant.

As was the case for the inferential test statistics discussed earlier, the use of the *r* statistic to make an inference about the relationship between two population variables is dependent on one important assumption. We assume that the relationship between the two variables is normally distributed in the population. If it is not, we can still compute the value of r and use it to describe the relationship between the two sample variables. But we should not then use this value of r to make an inference about the relationship between the variables in the population (Hays, 1973, p. 668).

CORRELATION VERSUS CAUSATION

We must observe another caution when we interpret a finding that two variables are correlated. A strong correlation between two variables does not necessarily mean that one variable *caused* the other. For example, a researcher may find that high levels of air pollution are strongly correlated with high levels of reported spouse abuse; in other words, compared to communities with good air quality, those with poor air have higher rates of reported spouse abuse. We may be tempted to conclude that breathing polluted air *causes* people to become violent and thereby leads to higher rates of spouse abuse. This is not the case.

In reality, both air pollution and spouse abuse are the result of the urban environment. Urban living causes air pollution, and rates of reported spouse abuse are higher in urban areas because urban areas (compared with rural areas) are rich in social services—such as shelters, abuse hotlines, and specially trained police units—that encourage victims to report.

Although social work researchers often find correlations between variables, in most instances, it is difficult or impossible to prove that these variables cause one another. When are researchers justified in concluding that Variable A causes Variable B? Only when they can show that three conditions are met. First, the cause must precede the effect in time. Second, when the two variables are measured they must be positively correlated. Finally, the researchers must show that it is not possible to *explain* the relationship between the two variables by introducing a third variable—such as rural-urban location in the example above. (The process of testing relationships by introducing a third variable was discussed at length in Chapter 8.)

PRACTICAL VERSUS STATISTICAL SIGNIFICANCE

In the test statistics presented in this chapter, we have shown how the size of the test statistic (which is computed from the sample) can be used to make inferences about whether differences or relationships exist in the population.

If the test statistic is sufficiently large, we reject the null hypothesis of no difference and conclude that the difference does exist in the population or that the relationship is different from zero in the population.

It is important to understand that test statistics tell us about probabilities and not about how strong the relationship is between two variables. This is an important point because it turns out that we can often get a statistically significant result simply by increasing our sample size. For example, in the table of critical values for *r,* as the sample size increases, we find a decrease in the level of the *r* test statistic that is required for significance. Because of this, when we have a large sample, even very weak relationships (say, an *r* of less than 0.1 or a small difference between two means) will be statistically significant.

This is not a problem as long as we understand what tests of significance mean. If the test is statistically significant, that means that the chances of there being no difference or no relationship in the population are quite small. Therefore, it is very likely that there is a relationship or a difference in the population. Even small differences or relationships can be statistically significant.

The implication here is that statistical significance may not be the only criterion by which we need to judge research findings. We may also need to consider practical significance. For example, consider the income subsidy program used to illustrate the *t* test for the mean difference between two groups. If the sample size had been large, we may have found that a very small difference in the number of days worked by experimental and control families (say one-half of a day) was statistically significant. But from a policy point of view, a difference this small may not be of practical significance.

Tests of statistical significance *are* useful because they provide a standard by which the work of different investigators can be compared; ideally, they will all use the commonly accepted criterion of a probability level of .05 or .01.

Tests of statistical significance also give us a useful way to *interpret* our results, and they tell us how often we are likely to be incorrect in our conclusions. (If we have done our work properly, we should make the wrong conclusion only 1 or 5 times out of 100.) In the *application* of research findings, however, it may be important to consider practical as well as statistical significance.

SUMMARY

In most research studies, we measure characteristics of a sample of individuals, families, groups, or organizations. These sample values (statistics) are used to make inferences about the corresponding values (parameters) in the population. We might measure a single value or the difference between groups, or we might measure the relationship between two or more variables. In each case, statistical hypothesis testing is used to determine if the sample values are indicative of real differences in the population. If our statistical test achieves a minimum critical value, we can say with some confidence that the value or difference we obtained in the sample is significant. Although statistical hypothesis testing provides a standard by which to judge research results, in the application of those results we must consider practical as well as statistical significance.

CASE STUDY

This study (Marcenko, Spence, & Rohweder, 1994) sought to answer the research question, "What differences exist between poor inner-city mothers who abuse alcohol or drugs, and those who do not?"

According to the researchers, the problem of substance abuse among pregnant women should be of increasing concern to social workers. The effects of substance abuse on the mother and child can be catastrophic. The child may be physically and developmentally harmed. Chemically dependent mothers face a variety of problems that severely impair their ability to parent—problems such as lack of emotional stability and lack of basic resources, such as adequate housing, clothing, and nutrition. Ominously, substance abuse among mothers is strongly associated with neglect and abuse of children.

Because social workers see many poor pregnant women in prenatal clinics, they need to be well informed about the psychosocial characteristics and needs of these women, particularly those who abuse drugs and alcohol. The purpose of this study, then, was to identify these characteristics and needs. Armed with this knowledge, social workers will be better able to identify risk factors for maternal substance abuse and focus on those resource needs that are most crucial to these expectant mothers.

The study was set in an outpatient obstetrics clinic in an inner-city hospital. The researchers selected 225 pregnant women from this clinic. These women were selected because they had one or more risk factors associated with child maltreatment—lack of social support, HIV infection, history of domestic violence, or other factors.

Independent Variable: Presence or Absence of Current Substance Abuse. The researchers interviewed each of these women using the Addiction Severity Index (ASI), a validated interview schedule that had originally been developed for male veterans with substance abuse problems. Women in the sample were classified as having a history of substance abuse if they reported on the ASI that they had (a) ever been treated for addiction to alcohol or drugs, (b) used drugs in the past 30 days, or (c) been bothered by substance abuse problems in the past 30 days. Based on these criteria, 52 (23%) of the 225 women in the sample were categorized as having a history of substance abuse.

Dependent Variables. The researchers asked each of the women about any history of abuse (for example, whether they had been abuse victims or if they maltreated their children) and about their needs for resources and services (for example, transportation, housing, and food). These pregnant women were also asked if anyone in the family had a substance abuse problem, if the pregnancy was planned, how happy they and their significant others were about the pregnancy, and how much support they expected from others after the birth.

STATISTICAL HYPOTHESIS TESTS

The data analysis presented by the researchers illustrates many of the topics covered in this chapter. They analyzed both categorical and continuous variables and employed two of the test statistics reviewed earlier: the *t* test and chi-square test. The tests summarized next follow from the research question cited at the beginning of this case study. To simplify the presentation, I will refer to the women who abused alcohol or drugs as "abusers" and those who did not as "nonabusers."

Because the researchers did not explicitly state their hypotheses, all of their tests were nondirectional. (Another way to state this is that the tests were two-tailed.) That is, rather than predicting, for example, that abusers had *lower* expectations for support from others, they simply tested to see if abusers and nonabusers differed in their expectations of support.

Example of a t Test

Using a *t* test, the researchers found that the abusers were older than nonabusers. They reported their test statistics as follows:

Mean age of abusers = 27 years
Mean age of nonabusers = 22 years
$t(223) = 6.11$
$p < .001$

In other words, the abusers were on average 27 years old and the non-abusers 22 years old. The researchers tested the null hypothesis that there was no difference in age between the abusers and nonabusers in the population from which the sample was drawn.

We can see from the results of the test that the null hypothesis was rejected: The difference in age between the two groups in the sample (a difference of 5 years) was large enough that it is unlikely that we would have found this difference if the null hypothesis were true. The p value of less than .001 means that, given the observed difference between the two groups, if we reject the null hypothesis we are likely to be wrong less than $1/1000$ of the time! (That is what p < .001 means.) Therefore, the researchers could be confident in rejecting the null hypothesis and concluding that women who abused drugs were, on average, older than women who did not.

The test statistic was reported as $t(223) = 6.11$. The number 223 in parentheses refers to the degrees of freedom. As I explained on page 326 of this chapter, the degrees of freedom are computed by subtracting the number of groups (in this case, 2), from the total number of subjects (in this case, 225).

The t value of 6.11 was computed using the formula on page 328. Referring to the "Critical Values of t" table at the end of this book, we can see that a test with 223 degrees of freedom will need to yield a t value of at least 3.291 to be significant at the .001 level. (This test is two-tailed because the researchers predicted that the two groups of women would differ in age, but they did not specify which group would be older.) The obtained t of 6.11 exceeds that; therefore, the researchers were correct in concluding that their test was significant at the .001 level.

Example of a Chi-Square Test

The researchers sought to find out if abusers and nonabusers differed in how likely they were to know how their family felt about the pregnancy. If abusers were less likely to know their families' feelings, this would be an indicator that they were estranged from their families and lacked family support. As the researchers learned in their literature review, this was a common characteristic of mothers who maltreated their children.

The result of the data analysis indicated that abusers were, in fact, less likely to know their families' feelings about the pregnancy. The researchers reported their test statistic as follows:

$$\chi^2 (1, 225) = 18.52$$
$$p < .001$$

The numbers in parentheses indicate the degrees of freedom and total sample size, respectively. The p value indicates that the null hypothesis of no

TABLE 16.2 Example of a Chi-Square Test: Knowledge of Substance-Abusing and Nonabusing Pregnant Women Regarding Knowledge of Their Families' Feelings About The Pregnancy

| | Group | | |
	Abusers	Nonabusers	Totals
Mother Knows of Family's Feelings About Her Pregnancy			
Knows	31 (60%)	150 (87%)	181
	$EF = 41.8$	$EF = 139.2$	
Does Not Know	21	23	44
	$EF = 10.2$	$EF = 33.8$	
Totals	52	173	

$$X^2 = \frac{(31 - 41.8)^2}{41.8} + \frac{(150 - 139.2)^2}{139.2} + \frac{(21 - 10.2)^2}{10.2} + \frac{(23 - 33.8)^2}{33.8}$$

$$X^2 = 18.52$$

NOTE: EF = Expected frequency.

relationship was rejected. Therefore, the researchers were correct in concluding that abusers were less likely than nonabusers to know their families' feelings about the pregnancy.

In their article, the researchers did not present the crossbreak table that was used to compute the chi-square value for this test. This is not surprising. As in many research articles, the authors presented quite a number of statistical tests. There would not have been enough room to provide the crossbreak table for every chi-square test.

They did, however, follow a good research practice: They reported enough information in the article so that I was able to reproduce their analysis in greater detail. This analysis is presented in Table 16.2. (As I stated in the first chapter on the scientific method, researchers conduct their work in such a manner that others may reproduce their work, subjecting it to an independent test.)

The data presented in Table 16.2 follow the conventions I discussed in this chapter and in Chapter 15. The independent variable is placed at the top of the table and the dependent variable at the left side. In the cells, I have shown the frequency or count (number of women who fell into each category) and percentages computed down the columns.

As we can see, abusers were considerably less likely (60%) than nonabusers (87%) to know their families' feelings about the pregnancy.

The statistical test summarized in Table 16.2 confirms that this difference is statistically significant. The expected frequencies (*EF*s) indicate the counts that would have appeared in the cells if there was *no relationship* between the independent and dependent variables. They were computed by multiplying the two marginals (outside the table) for each cell and dividing that product number by the total number of women (225). The computations for the chi-square statistic follow the formula given on page 332 of this chapter.

This study illustrates the use of statistical tests to draw conclusions from data. These tests enabled the researchers to draw a number of important conclusions from their data. They concluded that, compared with pregnant women with no substance abuse problems, those who do abuse have a greater need for basic services and resources, such as transportation, housing, and health care. They have less family support and fewer expectations that friends or family will provide support after they give birth. They are more likely to have lost contact with their families, to have been abused as children or adults, and to have delayed prenatal care.

Although these findings are not optimistic, they do identify areas for needed social work intervention.

DISCUSSION QUESTIONS

1. Why do social work researchers use samples to determine population characteristics?
2. What are the five types of statistical tests reviewed in this chapter? For each test, what are the assumptions that must be met to use the test in a valid manner?
3. Using a pretest-posttest control group design, a social work researcher tests the difference between an individual counseling program and a group counseling program in reducing anxiety.

   a. What is the independent variable?
   b. What is the dependent variable?
   c. State the null hypothesis.
   d. If the researcher compares the mean anxiety level of participants in the two programs, what test statistic will he or she use?
   e. What items of information does the researcher need to determine if this test statistic is significant?

4. Name two test statistics that can be used to determine if the relationship between two variables is significant. When these test statistics are computed, what is the null hypothesis?
5. Explain the difference between practical and statistical significance.

SHORT ASSIGNMENT

Review recent issues of a journal that publishes social work research articles. (See Chapter 5 for a list of journals.) Find an article that reports on a research study that employs one or more of the test statistics discussed in this chapter: *t* test, *F* test, chi-square test, or *r* test.

a. What are the independent and dependent variables in this study?
b. What is the research question addressed by the statistical test used by the researcher?
c. What is the null hypothesis for this statistical test?
d. What is the result of this statistical test? (For example, "The test is significant at the .05 level of probability.")
e. How would you interpret this result? (For example, "The two groups of mothers did not differ in child-rearing skills," or "Intelligence and social skills are not correlated in the population of adolescents.")
f. If the researcher reported a statistically significant result, was this result also of practical significance?

NOTE

1. In this example we are using the absolute *t* value, that is, we disregard the negative sign.

FURTHER READING

Besag, F. P., & Besag, P. I. (1985). *Statistics for the helping professions.* Beverly Hills, CA: Sage.
Graft, J. L. (1990). *Statistics and data analysis for social workers* (2nd ed.). Itasca, IL: F. E. Peacock.
Weinbach, R. W., & Grinnell, R. M., Jr. (1995). *Statistics for social workers* (3rd ed.). White Plains, NY: Longman.

17 Computer Uses

A re computers smart? There is so much talk today about the wonderful things computers do, we might think that computers are like very intelligent people. It would be more correct to say that a computer is like a clerk who is extremely fast and accurate.

A computer is an electronic machine that performs large numbers of calculations very quickly—adding, subtracting, calculating, rearranging. Computers are useful because of their incredible speed and accuracy. For example, if an airline kept each of its thousands of reservations on index cards, imagine how long it would take for the reservations clerk to locate a reservation; or if a bank computed compound interest on savings accounts by hand, imagine how long it would take to update each account. Computers are ideal for sorting through lists and doing complex or repetitious calculations that it would take humans many hours to perform.

Social work agencies also need computers. Even a small agency that serves only a few clients must store and manipulate hundreds and thousands of pieces of information—for example, demographic information on each client, such as service need, income, age, sex, and address, and information needed for case records, such as client goals. The agency also needs to maintain its financial records and issue a weekly payroll. Computers have become indispensable for these tasks.

Just a few short years ago, most social workers had little contact with computers. Computers were large and expensive devices that needed to be maintained in special temperature- and humidity-controlled environments. They were practical only for the largest organizations—universities and large businesses. But with today's advances in miniaturization, most of the functions of these *macrocomputers* (large computers) can now be performed by small *personal computers* (also called *desktop computers*).

A word of caution: Because computer technology changes at a rapid pace, in this chapter I can give you only a general overview of some of the most important features of computers and computer programs. By the time you read this, some of the details of operating computers probably will have changed. But reading this chapter will give you a good idea of what you can accomplish with computers. Using your computer effectively will require that you get more specific information about its operation. You can get this by reading the *documentation* (written instructions) that you received with your computer or program. In addition, many computer programs come with tutorials and help functions that provide basic instruction.

A basic personal computer, small enough to fit on an office desk, can now be purchased for under a $1,000. Information that was formerly stored on large, expensive magnetic disks can now be stored on an inexpensive *diskette,* about the size of an index card, or on a *CD-ROM,* which is very much like a music compact disk that you buy at a record store.

Today, because of the changes in the accessibility of computers, virtually every agency uses computers, and many social workers use computers routinely. For example, many social workers use computer programs for the following tasks: entering and updating case records, monitoring client progress and use of services, editing written reports, and billing. Computers are even used to administer and score tests given to clients to assess their mental health. They have been used to train social workers in counseling skills.

Today, many social workers have linked their personal computers to *computer networks.* A network is a large collection of computers at diverse sites linked together by telephone. There are many computer networks all over the world, often sponsored by governments, universities, research centers, and private groups. The Internet is a network of individual networks all over the world (Marine et al., 1994).

By linking our personal computers into these networks we can gain access to a wide variety of databases. For example, by "signing on" to a network we can search for a book or journal article within a regional library system. We

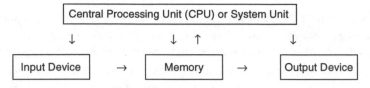

Figure 17.1. Basic Components of a Computer

can "download" (copy into our computer) data from a research study and obtain information about a topic of interest, such as social services in Europe or the latest information on psychotropic drugs. There is almost no limit to the amount and types of information we can obtain. We can also join an electronic "bulletin board," called a BBS (bulletin board system). By signing on to a BBS we can send and receive electronic messages to and from our BBS "address." We can also have live "on-line" conversations or "chats" (send and receive typed communications) with colleagues from across the world.

Although new computer users may feel intimidated at first, they soon find that computers are an invaluable resource. I wrote this book entirely on a personal computer using a word processor (more on that later). I was delighted to have the help of the computer in composing, revising, and storing the text.

WHAT IS A COMPUTER?

Every computer consists of four basic components. These are illustrated in Figure 17.1.

Input devices allow the user to communicate with the computer (Table 17.1). The user may enter data, commands, or a set of instructions (called a program) into the computer by typing the information onto a keyboard, very much like the keyboard on a typewriter.

Other information may be entered into the computer by using a pointing device: a mouse, track ball, or pointer. With the mouse (or other pointing device), the user is able to move an arrow or other symbol to any location on the display screen. With this function, the user locates an item (word, box, or picture) on the computer screen by moving the mouse and then "selecting" the item by "clicking" or pressing a button on the mouse. Information entered by keyboard and mouse may be entered directly into the computer.

TABLE 17.1 Typical Input and Output Devices on a Personal Computer

---

Keyboard (input only)

Mouse, track ball, or pointer (input only)

CD-ROM (currently available for input only)

Diskette (input or output)

Hard disk (input or output)

Printer (output only)

Display or monitor (output)

Scanner ("scans" material into the computer)

Modem (transmits data to and from the computer, usually via telephone line)

Sound card and speakers (output only)

As of this writing, some types of information also can be entered into the computer by "reading" it from a hard disk (a series of storage platters within the computer or attached to it). Information can also be read into the computer by inserting a diskette or CD-ROM into a special slot in the computer. CD-ROMs store enormous amounts of information. For example, several encyclopedias are now available on CD-ROM (an entire set of volumes fits onto one CD-ROM). A scanner is a machine that looks like a small photocopier. The user can feed a printed page, design, or photograph into the scanner, which converts the page into digital information for storage in the computer. Information can also be sent to (or from) a computer by a modem. The modem is a device that allows computers to send and receive data, usually over telephone lines.

The computer uses an *output device* to communicate the results of its operations to the user (Table 17.1). For example, after performing statistical tests on a set of data, the computer will print the results of those tests for the user. Most commonly, the results will be printed to a display or monitor (a device similar to a small television screen) or to a printer. Results may also be printed to a diskette or hard drive for storage. As of this writing, multimedia personal computers come equipped with a sound card and speakers that allow the computer to output a full range of sounds, including speech and music.

The printer is a machine that prints output onto sheets of paper. The paper copy it produces is called a "hard copy," compared with the "soft copy" produced on the monitor or display. A hard copy is useful if we want to store the output separately from the computer. I used a printer to generate the printout in Figure 17.4.

The *memory* is used by the computer to store input information. When the computer performs calculations, it needs a place to store intermediate results; these are also stored in memory. The memory is divided into a large number of cells or locations. So, for example, when the computer calculates the average of a series of numbers, it adds the numbers, one at a time, to a memory location. It uses another location to store the result (the average).

The *central processing unit (CPU)* or *system unit* is the brain of the computer. It serves as a master control, issuing instructions to all other parts of the computer. For example, it tells the input devices when and where to place information into memory, and it tells the output devices when to output information from memory. It interprets the program, which is a set of instructions written in a computer language by the user and entered through an input device. It also performs all operations and calculations on the data.

A computer is composed of two types of elements. First, there are the machines themselves (for example, the CPU and the input and output devices). These are called *hardware.* Second, instructions are written by people and entered into the computer through input devices. These instructions tell the various parts of the computer what to do. They are called *software.*

Early computers were difficult to use because little software was available to help untrained users communicate with the computer. Instructions had to be entered in long strings of digits and numbers and, later, in highly technical computer language. Today's computer—particularly the personal computer that students are likely to use—relies on a much simpler *user interface.*

THE USER INTERFACE

The user interface refers to the way in which the computer communicates with the user. As of this writing, two types of user interfaces are gaining popularity on personal computers. The first type is the *pull-down menu.* With this type of user interface, a *menu bar* appears at the top of the display screen, with a list of possible commands. For example, the word processing program I am using to write this book displays the following menu bar:

FILE EDIT SEARCH LAYOUT MARK TOOLS FONT GRAPHICS HELP

When the mouse is used to click (select) one of these menu items, an additional set of items "pops down" onto the screen. So, for example, if I use the mouse to select the EDIT command, additional commands pop down. These include MOVE, COPY, PASTE, DELETE, and others. I can then use the mouse to click on any of these command items.

The second type of user interface that is currently popular is the *graphic user interface* (GUI). In this system, the monitor screen displays a collection of pictures called *icons,* each representing some program or item that may be selected. You will be familiar with GUIs if you use a Macintosh computer or Windows software on your IBM-compatible personal computer.

Icons that perform various functions are pictured within *windows.* The window is a box on the display screen that contains the files for a particular software application or files that contain other information. For example, several types of programs may be installed in a personal computer: the system that operates the basic functions of the computer, a word processor, a statistical analysis program, and so on. (These are described later.) Each program or *application* appears in a separate box. By clicking the mouse in various locations on the screen, the user can open and close windows for the various programs. The user can also shrink or expand the size of each window or even overlap windows. This allows the user to run more than one application at a time and to transfer information from one application to another.

USING THE COMPUTER TO ANALYZE DATA: STATISTICAL PACKAGE FOR THE SOCIAL SCIENCES (SPSS)

In Chapter 16, I discussed several of the statistical tests commonly performed on data from social work research studies. Usually, these computations are done by computer. The speed and accuracy of computers make them ideal for data analysis tasks.

Many software programs perform statistical analyses. These software programs are designed to perform a large variety of complex tasks with just a few commands. The most popular of these statistical software programs is the Statistical Package for the Social Sciences (SPSS). This program is capable of generating a wide variety of types of data analyses, including the analyses I described in Chapter 16: descriptive statistics and inferential statistics, such as t tests, F tests, correlations, and chi-square tests (Abouserie, 1992).

In Figure 17.2, I have listed a typical SPSS program. This program is designed to generate frequency distributions and simple descriptive statistics

```
DATA LIST / STUDNO 1-2 CLASS 3 SEX 4 VOLUN 5 GPA 6-8 (2).
VARIABLE LABELS STUDNO 'STUDENT ID NUMBER'
                /CLASS 'CLASS STANDING'
                /VOLUN 'VOLUNTEER EXPERIENCE'
                /GPA 'GRADE POINT AVERAGE'.
VALUE LABELS CLASS 1 'FIRST YEAR' 2 'SECOND YEAR'
             /SEX 0 'FEMALE' 1 'MALE'
             /VOLUN 0 'LESS THAN 1 YEAR'
             '1 A YEAR OR MORE'.
FORMATS  GPA (F3.2).
MISSING VALUE CLASS SEX VOLUN (9) GPA (9.99).
BEGIN DATA.
01101346
02201301
03110999
04201400
END DATA.
FREQUENCIES GENERAL=CLASS TO VOLUN
            /STATISTICS MINIMUM MAXIMUM MODE.
FREQUENCIES GENERAL=GPA
            /STATISTICS MEAN MEDIAN MODE RANGE STDDEV.

FINISH.
```

Figure 17.2. SPSS Program to Generate Frequency Distributions for Grade Point Average Study

for the data set presented in Figure 17.3. Let's review each of the lines in the SPSS program in Figure 17.2.

The first 10 lines of the SPSS program are *data definition* lines. They provide basic information about the variables in the data set.

The DATA LIST line lists all the variables in the analysis and their locations. In this program, there are five variables. The first variable is called STUDNO and is represented in columns 1 and 2 of the data set. CLASS, the second variable, is represented in column 3, and so on. The final variable, GPA, is represented in columns 6 to 8. The numeral 2 in parentheses indicates that this variable has two decimal places.

On the DATA LIST line, the variable names are limited to just eight characters. With such short variable names, the meaning of each variable may not always be clear. The purpose of the next line, VARIABLE LABELS, is

			Columns				
Student Number		Class Standing	Sex	Volunteer Experience		GPA	
1	2	3	4	5	6	7	8
Student 1 0	1	1	0	1	3	4	6
Student 2 0	2	2	0	1	3	0	1
Student 3 0	3	1	1	0	9	9	9
Student 4 0	4	2	0	1	4	0	0

Figure 17.3. Data Set With Data for Four Students

to provide lengthier labels that describe the variables in more detail. For example, STUDNO stands for "STUDENT ID NUMBER." The variable label will appear in the final results every time its associated variable appears.

The VALUE LABELS line allows us to provide labels for the values of the variables. For example, the variable SEX has two values: 0 indicates female, and 1 indicates male. In the final results, the value labels will appear alongside each value.

The VARIABLE LABELS and VALUE LABELS cards are optional. We should include them, however, whenever the meaning of variable names and values may not be clear. This makes the final printout of results easy to interpret, particularly if we put it away and come back to it later when we have forgotten the meaning of the variable names and values.

The FORMATS line tells the SPSS program that the variable GPA is three columns wide and has two decimal places. If no FORMATS line were included, the program would assume that all of the variables are whole numbers (no decimals).

In almost every study, we will have missing data. This may be due to the failure of a subject to complete a questionnaire item or respond to an interview question. Or it may be due to coding error. The MISSING VALUE line tells the computer that for the CLASS, SEX, and VOLUN variables, the numeral 9 is entered in the database to indicate a missing value. For the GPA value, the number 9.99 indicates a missing value.

As you can see in Figure 17.2, the BEGIN DATA and END DATA lines come immediately before and after a series of numbers. These numbers are called a *data set*. In this case, they represent the questionnaire responses of four students, as indicated in the data set in Figure 17.3.

In every quantitative research study, information collected about subjects is entered into a data set. The data set follows a standard format. In research studies, data sets are organized into two-dimensional tables, as illustrated in Figure 17.3.

The rows of the data file represent *cases*. Usually, the case is an individual. In this example, the case is a student; that is, each case or row represents the data for one student. Here, we have only eight columns of information for each student, but some systems allow for 120 or more columns. Where there is a lot of information per case, there may be two or more lines for each case.

Variables appear as columns or groups of columns. A column or group of columns that represents a single variable is called a *field*.

The numbers in the body of the data set are called *data values*. They represent the student ID number, class standing, sex, volunteer experience, and grade point average (GPA) for each student.

In our example, the first variable, student ID number, takes up the first two columns. This is the first data field. Possible data values range from 00 to 99.

The next field is defined by column 3, and it is used to enter the student's class standing. It is coded 1 for first-year students and 2 for second-year students.

Column 4 is the field used to code the student's sex: 0 for female and 1 for male.

Students who have at least a year of volunteer experience in a social work agency receive a code of 1 in the next data field (column 5); those who do not are coded 0.

Finally, columns 6 through 8 compose a three-column data field in which the student's GPA is coded. GPA is entered to the nearest 100th. It is not necessary to allow a column for the decimal place, because the FORMATS line (described earlier) will tell the computer to insert the decimal point after the first digit.

In the SPSS program illustrated in Figure 17.2, it is crucial that all data values between the BEGIN DATA and END DATA lines appear in the correct columns (as defined by the DATA LIST line) and that no blank lines appear between the BEGIN DATA and END DATA lines.

The next four lines in the SPSS program (after END DATA) are *task definition* lines. They provide instructions that guide the analysis of data. This program includes two FREQUENCIES lines. The first line asks SPSS to generate simple frequency distributions for the variables CLASS, SEX, and VOLUN, along with the minimum and maximum values of these variables and their modes. These statistics are appropriate for categorical variables. The second FREQUENCIES line asks SPSS to generate a simple frequency distribution for the variable GPA. Because this is a continuous variable, it makes sense to ask SPSS for a different set of statistics—in this case, the mean, median, mode, range, and standard deviation.

When this program is run on SPSS, we obtain a printout of results. This printout is reproduced in Figure 17.4.

```
DATA LIST / STUDNO 1-2 CLASS 3 SEX 4 VOLUN 5 GPA 6-8 (2).
VARIABLE LABELS STUDNO 'STUDENT ID NUMBER'
                /CLASS 'CLASS STANDING'
                /VOLUN 'VOLUNTEER EXPERIENCE'
                /GPA 'GRADE POINT AVERAGE'.
VALUE LABELS   CLASS 1 'FIRST YEAR' 2 'SECOND YEAR'
                /SEX 0 'FEMALE' 1 'MALE'
                /VOLUN 0 'LESS THAN 1 YEAR' 1 'A YEAR OR MORE'.
FORMATS    GPA (F3.2)
MISSING VALUE CLASS SEX VOLUN (9) GPA (9.99).
BEGIN DATA.
END DATA.
```

4 cases are written to the compressed active file

This procedure was completed at 12:52:40

```
FREQUENCIES GENERAL=CLASS TO VOLUN
             /STATISTICS MINIMUM MAXIMUM MODE
```

***** Memory allows a total of 17873 Values, accumulated across all Variables.

There also may be up to 2234 Value Labels for each Variable.

Page 3　　　　　　　　　　SPSS/PC+　　　　　　　2/12/95

CLASS　　　CLASS STANDING

Value Label	Value	Frequency	Percent	Valid Percent	Cum Percent
FIRST YEAR	1	2	50.0	50.0	50.0
SECOND YEAR	2	2	50.0	50.0	50.0
	Total	4	100.0	100.0	

Mode　1.000　　Minimum　1.000　　Maximum　2.000

* Multiple modes exist. The smallest is shown.

Valid cases　4　Missing cases　0

Page 4　　　　　　　　　　SPSS/PC+　　　　　　　2/12/95

SEX

Value Label	Value	Frequency	Percent	Valid Percent	Cum Percent
FEMALE	0	3	75.0	75.0	75.0
MALE	1	1	25.0	25.0	25.0
	Total	4	100.0	100.0	

Figure 17.4. Output of SPSS Analysis in Grade Point Average Study

(continued)

Mode   .000   Minimum   .000   Maximum   1.000
Valid cases   4   Missing cases   0

Page 5   SPSS/PC+   2/12/95
VOLUN   VOLUNTEER EXPERIENCE

				Valid	Cum
Value Label	Value	Frequency	Percent	Percent	Percent
LESS THAN 1 YEAR	0	1	25.0	25.0	25.0
A YEAR OR MORE	1	3	75.0	75.0	75.0
		---------	-------	-------	
	Total	4	100.0	100.0	

Mode   1.000   Minimum   .000   Maximum   1.000
Valid cases   4   Missing cases   0

Page 6   SPSS/PC+   2/12/95
This procedure was completed at 12:52:50
FREQUENCIES GENERAL=GPA
            /STATISTICS MEAN MEDIAN MODE RANGE STDDEV.
***** Memory allows a total of 17873 Values, accumulated across
      all Variables.
      There also may be up to 2234 Value Labels for each Variable.

Page 7   SPSS/PC+   2/12/95
GPA GRADE POINT AVERAGE

				Valid	Cum
Value Label	Value	Frequency	Percent	Percent	Percent
	3.01	1	25.0	33.3	33.3
	3.46	1	25.0	33.3	66.7
	4.00	1	25.0	33.3	100.0
	9.99	1	25.0	Missing	
		---------	-------	-------	
	Total	4	100.0	100.0	

Mean   3.490   Median   3.460   Mode   3.010
Std dev .496   Range   .990
* Multiple modes exist. The smallest value is shown.
Valid cases   3   Missing cases   1

Page 8   SPSS/PC+   2/12/95
This procedure was completed at 12:52:56
SET PRINTER OFF

Figure 17.4. Continued

OTHER SOFTWARE

In the not too distant past, computers were useful only to those with extensive training in programming languages. But today there are thousands of "user-friendly" software packages. They are user-friendly in that they are easy to learn and they give a lot of good directions when mistakes are made. Many of the most popular software packages used in social work agencies and business and commercial settings can be learned in just a few hours.

This section gives brief descriptions of three types of software packages that are likely to be of use in social work agencies: word processors, database managers, and spreadsheets.

I have room here to give only an overview of each type of software. Once we have decided on a particular type of software, we will have a choice among several different packages. How do we decide which one to choose? One way is to get recommendations from a friend or instructor or refer to one of several computer magazines that review software. Most universities and some computer stores have personal computer libraries where users can try out various software packages before purchase.

WORD PROCESSORS

Word processors are designed to help the writer produce text material. They manipulate letters, words, sentences, and larger blocks of text.

All word processors have an edit or insert mode. While in this mode, users enter text from the keyboard, just as they would from a typewriter.

The great advantage of a word processor is that it allows us to *compose* text electronically. (The text appears on the display or monitor screen as you enter it onto the keyboard.) Then we can make any changes we like. We can use our mouse to select from a pop-down menu (see above) to insert, delete, modify, replace, rearrange, and so on until the text is just right. At that point, we can save the text file or send it to a printer.

The advantages of electronic composition are enormous. It lets us "cut and paste" text without the bother of scissors and glue. This is done by "blocking" pieces of text and copying or moving them from one location to another. We can create alternative versions and decide on the best one. Almost instantly, we can substitute one word or phrase for another. For example, we can update a text file by asking the computer to substitute the year 1996 wherever the year 1995 appears. Or we can send individually printed form letters to hundreds of addresses, with the names and addresses individualized. This saves many hours of retyping.

We can also locate words or phrases by asking the editor to "find" a string of characters. This saves the time of searching through lengthy texts. By entering a series of formatting instructions, we can instantly change margins and tabs, switch from single to double space, and make other formatting changes.

To facilitate entry of text from the keyboard, a number of functions are represented by keys on the keyboard. For example, an INS key allows the user to insert characters or text into already entered text. A DEL key deletes one letter at a time. Up, down, right, and left arrows control the movement of a cursor, making it possible to position the cursor at any point in the text. The cursor is an electronic pointer, usually a flashing underline, that indicates the current position of the computer "brain." Users employ position keys or a pointing device, such as a mouse, to place the cursor at the point at which they would like to enter or change text.

Other keys or the mouse move the cursor to the beginning or end of the file, to the top or bottom of each "page," or to the beginning or end of a line. These functions allow the user to position the cursor very quickly. They also make it possible to browse through pages of text with great speed.

Many word processors allow us to alter the size of the type, use regular or boldface type, underline words, and use superscripts and subscripts. Most word processors will check the text for proper spelling. Misspelled words are "flagged," and a "dictionary" is used to help us find the correct spelling. Given all these capabilities, word processors have become a popular tool for writers in every field.

DATABASE MANAGERS

A database manager is a program that allows us to record and manipulate almost any list of data. Like a word processor, it can be used in any setting. How might a social worker use a database manager? Table 17.2 reproduces a report that was produced on a popular database manager program.

Table 17.2 was used by a social worker to organize data on a client caseload for a 1-month period. It took the worker less than 5 minutes to enter the data on 10 clients and generate this report. Let's take a closer look at how this database was created, and how it can be used to organize information about clients.

The user clicked the mouse to select the FILE command word that appeared at the top of the display screen. From a number of command words that popped

TABLE 17.2 A Report Produced Using a Database Manager

			CLIENT LIST FOR MAY 1995		
NAME	*SEX*	*AGE*	*COUNTY*	*NUMBER OF CHILDREN*	*INCOME*
ABELS, MARY	F	39	CLACKAMAS	3	19,800
ALBERTS, LORETTA	F	64	CLACKAMAS	3	13,000
BARGER, CLINT	M	27	MULTNOMAH	2	31,000
BEAUMONT, CLARA	F	47	MULTNOMAH	3	15,400
CARUTHERS, PENNY	F	19	WASHINGTON	1	3,400
PAULUS, MARILYN	F	54	CLACKAMAS	5	17,600
SMITH, MARY	F	30	MULTNOMAH	2	13,200
STEVENS, BARBARA	F	42	WASHINGTON	1	15,600
TREVINSKY, PETER	M	41	WASHINGTON	2	23,000
ZWEIG, MARK	M	19	MULTNOMAH	0	9,800
TOTAL				22	

down onto the screen, the user then selected CREATE. At a prompt, the user then entered the name of the new database file to be created: CLIENT LIST.

The computer then prompted the user to enter the "structure" of the file. One at a time, the social worker entered each data field, specifying its width, field name, and field type (C for character or N for numeric):

```
WIDTH,NAME,TYPE
15,NAME,C
1,SEX,C
2,AGE,N
10,COUNTY,C
1,CHILDREN,N
7,INCOME,N
```

(This step is equivalent to the DATA LIST card in the SPSS program listed in Figure 17.2.) These commands established the structure of the file. The social worker then entered the data. For each case or client, the program prompted the user to enter the data:

```
CASE 0001:
NAME: _____
SEX: _
```

```
AGE:__
COUNTY: _____
CHILDREN: _
INCOME: _____

CASE 002:
NAME: _____
: : etc.
```

After all data were entered, the user selected a DISPLAY ALL command from the menu bar to display all the cases in the file CLIENT LIST. Then, additional menu bar commands were used to locate and correct errors in the data:

EDIT, DELETE, REPLACE, and LOCATE

The command REPORT allowed the social worker to create Table 17.2. The social worker used one command to sort the cases into alphabetical order by clients' last names. Additional commands provided the report heading, the variable headings, the column spacings, and the number of children.

Database managers are useful because they allow us to "query" the database. That is, we can ask questions of the data and get immediate answers. For example, we can ask the program to display the data presented in Table 17.2 for only those clients who reside in Washington County.

The kinds of question we can ask are almost limitless. We might ask the program to display all clients under the age of 30 or all female clients below a specified income.

The program will also do calculations for us. We can ask it to compute the average age of clients or the number of clients with incomes over $10,000. With larger databases, it would take many hours of work to answer these queries if a database program were not available. Clearly, database management by computer is a valuable aid to the social worker and to the agency.

SPREADSHEETS

A spreadsheet is a two-dimensional table used to summarize financial data. Spreadsheet software has been used primarily in the business and financial world to produce items such as balance sheets, income statements, and

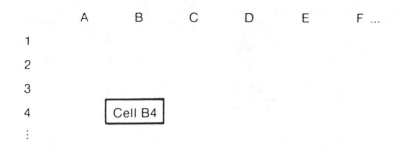

Figure 17.5. The Structure of a LOTUS 1-2-3 Spreadsheet

operating plan forecasts. These programs also can be useful in social work agencies, particularly for the preparation of budgets and other financial statements.

A popular spreadsheet program is LOTUS 1-2-3. This is a sophisticated program with user options that allow us to construct spreadsheets with great efficiency.

The basic format of LOTUS 1-2-3 is a "worksheet" that is displayed on our monitor screen. The worksheet consists of "cells" defined by columns labeled A, B, C, . . . and rows labeled 1, 2, 3, . . . Thus each cell is identified by a letter and number, as illustrated in Figure 17.5.

To make it easier to construct, rearrange, and print worksheets, LOTUS 1-2-3 provides a large number of commands. Each command can be selected with the mouse from a pop-down menu. For example, when the LOTUS 1-2-3 program is called, the following menu bar appears at the top of the screen:

WORKSHEET RANGE COPY MOVE FILE PRINT GRAPH DATA QUIT

Using the WORKSHEET command, the user enters information into the cells. Each cell may be located by "pointing" to the cell with a pointer that moves up, down, and sideways, controlled by the mouse or by position keys on the keyboard.

Three kinds of information may be entered, as illustrated in Table 17.3. We may enter a number, such as $500; we may enter a label, which generally serves as a column or row heading, such as Jan., Feb., and Mar. Finally, we may enter a "formula." This is where LOTUS becomes really useful. For Cell B4 (Table 17.3), we did not enter a dollar amount; rather, we entered the

TABLE 17.3 Illustration of Worksheet Entries Using LOTUS 1-2-3

	A	B	
1	Jan	$500	
2	Feb	$400	Entry in cell B4: "+B1+B2+B3"
3	Mar	$500	
4	Quarterly total	$1,400	

formula "+B1+B2+B3," which instructed the program to add the contents of these three cells and place the result in Cell B4. The advantage of entering a formula is that whenever the individual monthly figures are updated, the quarterly total in cell B4 will automatically be updated.

Social workers often face the task of drafting, reviewing, or supervising budgets. Proposals to United Way and other funding sources usually require detailed budgets. Computer spreadsheet programs are useful tools for drafting and revising such budgets. Table 17.4 presents a spreadsheet that was prepared using LOTUS 1-2-3.

Of the 48 entries in the spreadsheet in Table 17.4, only 11 were entered as dollar amounts. For the first year of the budget, we entered each person's salary. Year 2 salaries were computed by formula so that they reflected a 6% increase over the first year's salary. To compute indirect costs, LOTUS automatically multiplied each year's total personnel costs by 23%. All totals were calculated by user-entered formulas that added the appropriate cells.

LOTUS 1-2-3 makes this draft budget easy to revise. When individual Year 1 entries are revised, LOTUS will automatically make the appropriate changes to bring the entire spreadsheet up to date.

Because spreadsheet software programs are used primarily in business settings, they have often been overlooked by social work agencies. They can, however, be powerful tools for the collection, presentation, and analysis of financial and other data in social work settings.

In recent years, several manufacturers have developed software programs that perform multiple functions: word processing, database management, and spreadsheets. They can be purchased at lower cost than separate programs, and they allow the user to combine functions and exchange data from one type of program to another.

TABLE 17.4 A Budget Prepared Using LOTUS 1-2-3

DRAFT BUDGET FOR HOME HEALTH CARE PROJECT			
	Year 1	*Year 2*	*Total*
Personnel			
Project director	$43,000	$45,580	$88,580
Project coordinator	31,500	33,390	64,890
Nurse	27,000	28,620	55,620
Social worker	27,000	28,620	55,620
Secretary	19,450	20,617	40,067
TOTAL PERSONNEL	147,950	156,827	304,777
Supplies			
Office supplies	5,400	5,400	10,800
Nursing supplies	12,500	12,500	25,000
Postage	565	565	1,130
Telephone	800	800	1,600
TOTAL SUPPLIES	19,265	19,265	38,530
Travel			
For patient visits	8,400	8,904	17,304
Conferences	1,200	12,000	2,400
TOTAL TRAVEL	9,600	10,104	19,704
Indirect costs (23% of personnel)	34,029	36,070	70,099
GRAND TOTAL	210,844	222,266	433,110

SUMMARY

A computer is a sophisticated machine that performs calculations with great speed and accuracy. It consists of a central processing unit or system unit, memory, and input and output devices. With the recent development of small, inexpensive personal computers and user-friendly programs, millions of individuals and groups now have access to computer technology.

Users communicate with personal computers through user interfaces that rely on a mouse or other pointing device and on pop-down menus or pictures called icons. Various types of software are useful to social workers. These include statistical analysis packages, word processors, database managers, and spreadsheet programs.

DISCUSSION QUESTIONS

1. Define each of the following terms:

   a. Macrocomputer
   b. Personal computer or desktop computer
   c. Diskette
   d. CD-ROM
   e. Modem
   f. Computer network
   g. Internet
   h. BBS

2. What are the four basic components of a computer?
3. Give an example of two input devices and two output devices.
4. In your program or agency, what devices are used for data input? What devices are used for output of results?
5. What is a mouse? How is a mouse used with pop-down menus or icons?
6. What is the difference between software and hardware?
7. What are the functions of each of the following types of software?

   a. Statistical analysis program
   b. Word processor
   c. Database manager
   d. Spreadsheet

SHORT ASSIGNMENT

1. Familiarize yourself with the computer facilities in your university or agency. Answer the following questions:

   a. Do you need an account to use the computer? If so, how is one obtained?
   b. Where are the computers located and when are they available?
   c. What type of user interface is employed? What steps will bring you to the display screen with the commands or icons used to run the programs?
   d. What software programs are available to you? Where can you get help in using them? Is written documentation available?

e. How is a printout of results obtained?

2. If you have a statistical analysis package available to you, duplicate the analysis illustrated in Figure 17.4. Note: To gain access to the program, you will need to use commands that are specific to your computer. The commands in your statistical analysis program may also differ from the example in this chapter. Learn the relevant commands and generate a printout that provides the same information as that in Figure 17.4.

FURTHER READING

Butterfield, W. H. (1995). Computer utilization. In R. L. Edwards & J. G. Hopps (Eds.), *Encyclopedia of social work* (19th ed., Vol. 1, pp. 594-613). Washington, DC: National Association of Social Workers Press.

Weitzman, E. A., & Miles, M. B. (1995). *Computer programs for qualitative data analysis: A software sourcebook.* Thousand Oaks, CA: Sage.

Also see the journal *Computers in Human Services,* published by the Haworth Press, 10 Alice Street, Binghamton, NY 13904-1580.

APPENDIX A

Guidelines for Preparing Research Proposals

Whether your research proposal is to be part of a grant application, a thesis, or a class assignment, you may use the following guide. The items that follow are outlined according to the usual sections of a research proposal and are intended as a guide for the beginning proposal writer and as a checklist for those who are more experienced.

The Problem

Things to include:

Introduction
Statement of the problem and its scope
Background about the problem and purpose of the study
Rationale and importance of doing the study
Objectives of the study
Hypotheses to be tested or research questions to be answered

Questions to ask yourself:

Is there a concise statement of the purpose of the research?

364

Does the problem statement convince the reviewer of the value of the proposed research?

Has the problem been shown to be relevant for people in other settings?

Has the problem been defined specifically enough so that the reader will understand what the proposed research study includes and what it leaves out?

Are the objectives specific, clear, and achievable?

Do the hypotheses or research questions clearly flow from the problem statement?

Review of the Literature

Things to include:

Demonstration of mastery of the literature in the field

Presentation of pertinent research to acquaint the reader with existing knowledge on the subject

Discussion of the proposed study in relation to the current literature

A discussion of the conceptual or theoretical framework of the study

A bibliography of the sources cited

Questions to ask yourself:

Have primary as well as secondary sources been reviewed?

Do the references cited relate directly to the research problem?

Has the conceptual or theoretical base for the study been clearly described? Have you explained how the conceptual base for the study is related to the research problem?

Is there a complete listing of all the sources cited?

Methodology or Procedures

Things to include:

A description of the population and sample

Research design

Data collection methods and instruments

Data analysis procedures

Work plan (a list of tasks and the dates by which they will be completed)

Deliverables (a list of products that will be delivered to the funding agency or evaluator)

Questions to ask yourself:

How was the population defined and what sampling method was employed?

Have the independent and dependent variables been clearly identified and operationally defined?

Have possible problems related to internal and external validity been addressed?

Have the measuring instruments been found to be reliable and valid for the intended purpose? If instruments will be constructed for the research, how will their reliability and validity be established?

Have methods for data collection been clearly specified?

Are the data analysis procedures appropriate for testing the stated hypotheses or answering the research questions?

Is the amount of time allocated for each task adequate?

Personnel

Things to include:

A list of all staff involved in completing the research study, along with specific job descriptions for each position

If appropriate, a list of ancillary personnel (e.g., advisory committee members, consultants) and their responsibilities

Vitae of key staff

Questions to ask yourself:

Is the staffing adequate to complete the research study?

Do the staff have the necessary qualifications and research experience to complete the study?

Budget

Things to include:

All costs for personnel and consultants, including fringe benefits

The percentage of time that each person will be working on the research study

All anticipated expenses for equipment, supplies, postage, travel, photocopying, utilities, rent, data processing, and any other essential items

Any indirect costs for conducting the project (costs that the university or sponsoring agency charges for allowing use of their facilities)

Questions to ask yourself:

Are all necessary budget items included?

Is the budget adequate to complete the project in the manner intended in the proposal?

APPENDIX B

Guidelines for Critique of a Social Work Research Study

Conceptualization

1. Is there a theory underlying the research questions? Is there a clear and explicit connection between the theory, earlier findings, and the purpose of the present study?
2. What are the research hypotheses?
3. Enumerate all the independent and dependent variables in the study.
4. Is there an adequate (i.e., reliable and valid) operational definition for each of these variables? Can you suggest better or alternative ways to operationally define any of these variables?

Sample

1. What is the population from which the sample is drawn (or does the sample represent the entire population)?
2. Have the researchers explicitly defined the procedures by which individuals or other elements have been selected for inclusion in the sample? Are sampling procedures appropriate to the nature and limitations of the study? How do limitations of the sampling procedures affect the external validity of the results?

Research Design

1. What research design is employed? Draw a schematic of the design using Campbell and Stanley (1963) notation. Is this an appropriate design? Which of the factors of internal and external validity might be uncontrolled? Specifically, how could these factors affect the results?
2. Is a nonexperimental research design used? How are relationships between variables determined? Are these procedures adequate?

Reliability and Validity of Dependent Variables

1. Are the assessment measures reliable and valid? What procedures, if any, could have been employed to establish the reliability and validity of the assessment measures?
2. If interviews or questionnaires were used, were these adequate? Are there additional sources of data that could be used?

Data Presentation

1. Were data analyzed appropriately?
2. Do the conclusions follow logically from the data analyses? Are the data sufficient to warrant the conclusions? Are they presented in sufficient detail? Given the data presented, would you modify or change the conclusions? If so, how and why?

Ethics

1. Does this research meet acceptable standards of ethics? If no, which procedures were objectionable? How could the study be modified so that the research questions would be answered without violation of ethical principles?

APPENDIX C

Presenting Data in Tables and Figures

In Chapters 15 and 16, I discussed a variety of ways in which data can be analyzed and presented. Once we have completed the data analysis, we need to present our findings in the form of a research report or journal article. There are three ways in which we can present the data: (a) in narrative form in the text of our report, (b) in tables, or (c) in figures.

Very simple data analyses (such as a comparison between two means) can be presented in the text. But when the data presentation is complex or when it would be difficult to follow trends or understand the results, a table or figure should be used.

Tables

Use a table to present numerical data. Follow these guidelines:

1. Be conservative in selecting the data you wish to present. In many studies, researchers collect more data than they will want to present in a single report. Present only those data that are important *and* directly related to the purpose of the research.

2. Use a table to present data in which relationships would not be readily apparent if the data were presented in the text.

TABLE C.1 Geographic Distribution of African American and White Respondents in Metropolis

| | *Geographic Location* | | | | | |
| | | | *North* | *South* | | |
Race	*Northeast*	*Southeast*	*Central*	*Central*	*Western*	*Total*
African American	4	8	13	18	19	62
White	10	6	9	10	5	40

Consider this data summary:

The number of African American respondents from the northeast section of the city was 4; from the southeast, 8; from north central, 13; from south central, 18; and from the western section of the city, 19. The number of white respondents from the northeast section of the city was 10; from the southeast, 6; from north central, 9; from south central, 10; and from the western section of the city, 5.

A tabular presentation of these data will be more efficient and will help the reader to compare the various groups. This can be seen in Table C.1.

3. A table should not be used merely to repeat what is in the text of your report. The text should refer to every table and its data. The text, however, should merely highlight the table. In the text, you should discuss trends, unexpected results, or other noteworthy features of the tables.

4. Each table should stand on its own; that is, it should make sense to the reader without reference to the text. The reader should not have to go back to the text to understand the table. This can be accomplished by using a good descriptive title as well as notes or subheadings to explain abbreviations, italics, parentheses, and units of measurement.

5. Every table should include a title at the top. The title should be brief but explanatory. A good title uses a telegraphic style but includes enough information so that the reader can readily understand the purpose of the table. Consider these examples:

Too telegraphic: Relationship Between Treatment and Outcome

Too detailed: Mean Client Satisfaction Ratings on Forms 1, 2, and 3 of Clients Receiving Task-Centered, Crisis Intervention, and Behavior Modification Therapy [This title duplicates information in the headings of the table.]

Good title: Mean Satisfaction Ratings of Clients Receiving Different Therapies

6. An identical column or row of figures should not appear in two tables. Combine tables that overlap.

7. To make it easier to compare tables, be consistent in format from table to table. That is, be consistent in the use of terminology, subheadings, units of measurement, and placement of numerals.

8. Express numerical values only to the number of significant digits that the accuracy of the measurement justifies or that makes sense. For example, it is not helpful to know that each worker saw an average of 5.3354 clients; 5.3 will do. Do not change the unit of measure in a column or row. Indicate the unit only once; for example, for percentages, do not repeat the percent sign (%) after each number.

9. Unless you have a specific purpose in mind, you should not include columns or rows that could easily be calculated from other columns or rows.

10. Use an asterisk in the body of the table and a note at the bottom to indicate significance level. The following notations are commonly used:

$*p < .05$
$**p < .01$

11. Use a footnote to avoid repetition in a table:

Poor:

Group	$\overline{X}$	n
1	5.4	15
2	2.6	15
3	1.3	15

Better:

Group	$\overline{X}$
1	5.4
2	2.6
3	1.3

NOTE: $n = 15$ for each group.

12. A table should not include more than three variables or dimensions—for example, a crossbreak of race, sex, and marital status.

13. A table should not have an excessive number of "empty" or zero cells. If this happens, consider reducing the number of categories or values in your variables.

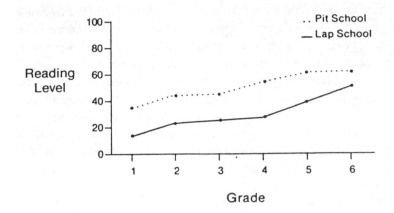

Figure C.1. Reading Levels of Children at Two Elementary Schools

14. The size of the table should not exceed one 8 ½" × 11" sheet of paper. If possible, the table should be presented upright rather than sideways so that the reader will not have to turn the report on its side to read the table.

Figures

Use a figure to present data in the form of graphs, charts, illustrations, and photographs. Follow these guidelines:

1. Graphs, charts, illustrations, and photographs should be used to present, in a concise way, findings that would otherwise have to be presented in a lengthy discussion or findings that would be difficult to explain in narrative form. Include a figure only if it extends, clarifies, or supplements the text. It should not repeat the text. All figures in the report should be referred to in the text.

2. For a graph, use heavy lines for the horizontal and vertical axes. Place the independent variable on the horizontal axis and the dependent variable on the vertical axis. Each axis must be labeled. The label should indicate the variable being presented and the units in which it is measured.

3. All numbering and lettering should be horizontal.

4. Do not include so much data that the figure is hard to decipher. As a general rule, do not include more than four curves in a line graph. Use separate geometric forms, such as squares or triangles, to indicate points on the graph.

5. In choosing appropriate scales for the axes, make sure the plotted curves span the entire graph with no large empty spaces. Indicate scale values by grid marks placed on each axis at the appropriate intervals.

6. Each figure should include a title at the bottom. In choosing a title, follow the rules for titling tables.

Figure C.1 is an example of a well-presented figure.

Four Steps to Writing a Research Report

Below, I present a four-step plan for writing and disseminating a brief research report. Follow the hints. As you write, make sure you can answer each of the following questions.

Step 1: Plan the Content of Your Report

HINT: Use one sentence to summarize the central statement made by your report. Write it down. Keep referring to it.

Is there a clear purpose statement within the first two pages?

Is there a good rationale for the stated purpose of the report or the research?

Does the author's purpose make sense in terms of previous work done by others? Is previous work adequately summarized and reflected in the report?

Does the Method section provide enough detail for the reader to understand what follows? Are all concepts and variables defined clearly? Will the reader understand how each variable was measured and computed?

Are the same terms used to describe particular variables and concepts throughout the report?

AUTHOR'S NOTE: Adapted from Berger, R. M. (1991). Four steps to getting your paper published. *Child and Youth Care Forum, 20*(3), 211-214. Reprinted with permission of Human Sciences Press.

Is there substance? Does the author present adequate and convincing documentation or arguments to back up the report's contentions?

Is the topic appropriate for the intended readership of the report?

Step 2: Plan the Form of Your Report

HINT: Write an outline of the report before and then again after you have written it. Use the outline to explain to a listener what each section of the report accomplishes. Does it make sense?

Is the report well organized? Are topics in correct order? Do they follow logically one from the other? Are there appropriate transitions? Does the author avoid needless repetition?

Is the writing grammatically correct?

Are the style and presentation appropriate for the intended readers?

Does the author follow elements of good style? For example, does he or she avoid overuse of passive voice, vary sentence length and structure, use parallel sentence structure, avoid excessive qualifiers, and avoid idiosyncrasies of style that interfere with effective writing?

Are verbs used in the appropriate tense? Generally, use past or present perfect for Literature Review and Method sections, past to describe Results, and present tense to discuss Results and present Conclusions.

Is the writing clear, or is reading the report like taking a Rorschach (ink blot) test?

Can the report be made shorter and still successfully achieve its purpose?

Does the author avoid wordiness? For example, "It is interesting to note that without exception all the students seemed to be bored."

Does the author avoid awkward wording? For example, "Student needs speak to counseling professionals' importance."

Is the title concise but descriptive?

Are subheadings used to guide the reader?

Are introductory and concluding paragraphs informative? "Tell 'em what you're gonna tell 'em; then tell 'em; then tell 'em what you told 'em."

Are tables and figures well constructed? Can they be interpreted without reference to the text? Does the text supplement rather than repeat information in the tables and figures?

Step 3: Plan the Process of Writing Your Report

HINT: If the way in which you write feels uncomfortable, try new ways.

As you work from your outline, write in relatively small blocks of time (one half to one hour). Research shows that those who write in small blocks of time are more productive and creative writers.

Always write in the same physical setting. Write in a place where you know you won't be disturbed.

Do you procrastinate? Then make an appointment with yourself for writing sessions. Treat this as seriously as you would any important appointment.

Are you a perfectionist, constantly stopping to correct your writing? Then start by writing small amounts "freely," without making any corrections. Put your writing away. Later go back and edit.

Are you "blocked"? Then start with "spontaneous writing": Write whatever comes into your mind. Don't censor. The content does not matter. After a while, write whatever comes to mind about a particular topic. Eventually, you will be able to write from your outline.

Are you impatient? Put your writing away for a couple of days. Then go back and read your copy with a fresh perspective.

Step 4: Plan a Strategy for Disseminating Your Report

HINT: Take as much care with the steps that follow the writing of your report as you did with the writing itself.

Find two colleagues who will read your report and give you useful comments. If possible, choose colleagues who are experienced writers. Also, solicit feedback from your agency director or your instructor. Carefully consider the comments of all these persons.

Present a verbal summary of your report in a special or regularly scheduled meeting at your agency, or present the summary in class. Present your report to a community agency or board. Make typed copies of the report available to others. (Note: You will be able to present your research in greater detail in a written report.)

Create overheads or posters based on tables and figures in your report. Use these when presenting a verbal report of your research.

Consider submitting your report to a journal, newsletter, or other publication.

Ensure that your report meets all the length, format, style, and referencing requirements of the publication.

Review recent issues of the publication. Given the form and content of your report, is it the kind of report this publication is likely to publish? If the publication is a professional journal, check the journal's "Information to Authors" (in an issue or obtainable from the editor) to see if your topic is likely to be of interest. For information about the journal, you can also check *An Author's*

Guide to Social Work Journals by Henry N. Mendelsohn (1992) and published by the National Association of Social Workers Press.

If the publication has an editorial board, check the affiliations of its members as listed in a recent issue. Try to take their perspective in evaluating your report. For example, a practitioner's perspective will differ from that of a faculty member. Social workers, psychologists, and sociologists use different jargon. Are you speaking to your audience in terms it understands?

Submit a clean, crisp, and typed copy; double-space all text, including references.

Further Reading

Beebe, L. (Ed.). (1993). *Professional writing for the human services.* Washington, DC: National Association of Social Workers Press.

STATISTICAL TABLES

TABLE T.1   Random Number Table

53706	22285	80527	52917	83170	61000	70742	24925	63365	77507
63848	17393	61768	72149	39081	65323	20995	07050	35757	17743
49794	68434	23328	35968	64105	12369	44054	10329	08839	19929
90016	10178	41106	40295	58710	96164	43461	65043	00759	90018
09736	13510	03995	17560	85072	54892	18712	48031	04448	42147
39497	71929	86048	89768	69874	41270	67419	52451	11370	31625
89115	97651	07196	43914	90402	01461	89910	73400	48587	22465
95773	49371	78114	80790	79650	88107	02218	87515	41451	03018
11707	37312	67035	08583	57289	72198	63455	11680	22850	88820
05771	32200	94306	77682	57601	37141	85135	43856	35195	51303
06791	60096	15902	61122	93508	32460	19749	23930	05464	85836
49506	49283	76273	17988	63809	09659	94585	59000	20134	76792
27518	95592	63431	19306	65614	12294	76115	28657	28665	60712
68439	03629	20333	93218	90361	46364	74320	87522	06047	22376
74828	89659	95799	51072	07087	81144	14884	14216	07181	28423
35153	23195	97394	88983	99290	81183	15243	62227	70968	92604
48634	82399	59382	51456	04912	03844	54950	46138	34393	48215
52597	66444	92752	85002	19123	99561	05333	61034	55327	15313
62037	07589	30631	68211	35632	87078	04638	68423	32331	18983
32282	82566	27174	21599	48405	04097	97354	38100	79198	75534
03116	15532	27695	97126	21216	90261	22127	24684	15037	59657
84320	22336	53634	00347	23652	49270	85431	93805	19619	63466
59902	82564	16047	72241	47055	67544	18282	98202	61147	82603
53989	19584	37741	39782	31311	57068	32521	00874	21436	61469
39771	54955	03622	47129	16284	63246	18504	10364	50555	54619
16990	10247	75400	01445	81637	00452	58598	55825	26661	86666
25223	62311	31067	02631	16098	56474	29011	62962	09203	15182
10778	19971	19853	73705	70162	14449	45306	54572	05208	47133
43770	56555	23578	62861	45140	90889	78076	93604	41554	88802
94006	18507	77401	59884	39787	53068	21099	61647	35416	58327
93900	88973	06933	49764	37608	92136	26326	82330	91341	45662
11107	63380	51549	78045	67709	22058	63634	99014	92169	79318
63468	03489	78317	52418	37335	56317	53415	38138	46737	80573
79565	72464	15472	83225	40253	82290	52678	13020	31744	90865
66341	58142	64681	84402	00463	01309	02106	83237	90154	00893
67205	87816	35226	20020	01754	85895	46393	45336	27038	23093
19730	10171	63972	82265	89081	91651	24210	66749	48405	45019
84139	80212	99510	64787	40432	24319	10354	57376	26341	87082
88652	14588	61513	27100	25232	80356	88968	64195	87541	88248
41917	21970	64809	82897	09464	42183	12577	41783	69774	62085
96519	32713	81681	37556	86646	35147	05451	01030	69605	48538
93963	16862	57638	83267	29095	92588	10446	74698	15760	77471
10976	75246	39956	95737	59958	90498	17237	60906	07561	37932

SOURCE: Copyright 1987: Raymond M. Berger, California State University, Long Beach.

TABLE T.2 Critical Values of χ^2

		Level of Significance for a One-Tailed Test				
df	.10	.05	.025	.0	1	.005
		Level of Significance for a Two-Tailed Test				
df	.20	.10	.05	.02	.01	.001
1	1.64	2.71	3.84	5.41	6.64	10.83
2	3.22	4.60	5.99	7.82	9.21	13.82
3	4.64	6.25	7.82	9.84	11.34	16.27
4	5.99	7.78	9.49	11.67	13.28	18.46
5	7.29	9.24	11.07	13.39	15.09	20.52
6	8.56	10.64	12.59	15.03	16.81	22.46
7	9.80	12.02	14.07	16.62	18.48	24.32
8	11.03	13.36	15.51	18.17	20.09	26.12
9	12.24	14.68	16.92	19.68	21.67	27.88
10	13.44	15.99	18.31	21.16	23.21	29.59
11	14.63	17.28	19.68	22.62	24.72	31.26
12	15.81	18.55	21.03	24.05	26.22	32.91
13	16.98	19.81	22.36	25.47	27.69	34.53
14	18.15	21.06	23.68	26.87	29.14	36.12
15	19.31	22.31	25.00	28.26	30.58	37.70
16	20.46	23.54	26.30	29.63	32.00	39.29
17	21.62	24.77	27.59	31.00	33.41	40.75
18	22.76	25.99	28.87	32.35	34.80	42.31
19	23.90	27.20	30.14	33.69	36.19	43.82
20	25.04	28.41	31.41	35.02	37.57	45.32
21	26.17	29.62	32.67	36.34	38.93	46.80
22	27.30	30.81	33.92	37.66	40.29	48.27
23	28.43	32.01	35.17	38.97	41.64	49.73
24	29.55	33.20	36.42	40.27	42.98	51.18
25	30.68	34.38	37.65	41.57	44.31	52.62
26	31.80	35.56	38.88	42.86	45.64	54.05
27	32.91	36.74	40.11	44.14	46.96	55.48
28	34.03	37.92	41.14	45.42	48.28	56.89
29	35.14	39.09	42.69	46.69	49.59	58.30
30	36.25	40.26	43.77	47.96	50.89	59.70
32	38.47	42.59	46.19	50.49	53.49	62.49
34	40.68	44.90	48.60	53.00	56.06	65.25
36	42.88	47.21	51.00	55.49	58.62	67.99
38	45.08	49.51	53.78	57.97	61.16	70.70
40	47.27	51.81	55.76	60.44	63.69	73.40
44	51.64	56.37	60.48	65.34	68.71	78.75
48	55.99	60.91	65.17	70.20	73.68	84.04
52	60.33	65.42	69.83	75.02	78.62	89.27
56	64.66	69.92	74.47	79.82	83.51	94.46
60	68.97	74.40	79.08	84.58	88.38	99.61

SOURCE: Table T.2 is taken from Table III of Fisher & Yates; STATISTICAL TABLES FOR BIOLOGICAL, AGRICULTURAL AND MEDICAL RESEARCH. Published by Longman Group UK., 1974. We are grateful to the Longman Group UK Ltd., on behalf of the Literary Executor of the late Sir Ronald A. Fisher, F.R.S. and Dr. Frank Yates F.R.S. for permission to reproduce Table III from *Statistical Tables for Biological, Agricultural and Medical Research 6/e (1974)*.
NOTE: The obtained value of χ^2 is significant if it is greater than or equal to the value listed in the table.

TABLE T.3 Critical Values of *r*

n	.05	.01	n	.05	.01
03	.997	.999	38	.320	.413
04	.950	.990	39	.316	.408
05	.878	.959	40	.312	.403
06	.811	.917	41	.308	.398
07	.754	.874	42	.304	.393
08	.707	.834	43	.301	.389
09	.666	.798	44	.297	.384
10	.632	.765	45	.294	.380
11	.602	.735	46	.291	.376
12	.576	.708	47	.288	.372
13	.553	.684	48	.284	.368
14	.532	.661	49	.281	.364
15	.514	.641	50	.279	.361
16	.497	.623	55	.166	.345
17	.482	.606	60	.254	.330
18	.468	.590	65	.244	.317
19	.456	.575	70	.235	.306
20	.444	.561	75	.227	.296
21	.433	.549	80	.220	.286
22	.423	.537	85	.213	.278
23	.413	.526	90	.207	.270
24	.404	.515	95	.202	.263
25	.396	.505	100	.195	.256
26	.388	.496	125	.170	.230
27	.331	.487	150	.159	.210
28	.374	.478	175	.148	.194
29	.367	.470	200	.138	.181
30	.361	.463	300	.113	.148
31	.355	.456	400	.098	.128
32	.349	.449	500	.088	.115
33	.344	.442	600	.080	.105
34	.339	.436	700	.074	.097
35	.334	.430	800	.070	.091
36	.329	.424	900	.065	.086
37	.325	.418	1000	.062	.081

SOURCE: From IX of James E. Wert, Charles O. Neidt, and J. Stanley Ahmann, *Statistical Methods in Educational and Psychological Research* (New York: Appleton-Century-Crofts, 1954). Reprinted by permission of Appleton & Lange.
NOTE: The obtained value of *r* is significant if it is greater than or equal to the value listed in the table.

TABLE T.4 Critical Values of *t*

| df | Level of Significance for One-Tailed Test | | | | | |
	.10	.05	.025	.01	.005	.0005
df	Level of Significance for Two-Tailed Test					
	.20	.10	.05	.02	.01	.001
1	3.078	6.314	12.706	31.821	63.657	636.619
2	1.886	2.920	4.303	6.965	9.925	31.598
3	1.638	2.353	3.182	4.541	5.841	12.941
4	1.533	2.132	2.776	3.747	4.604	8.610
5	1.476	2.015	2.571	3.365	4.032	6.859
6	1.440	1.943	2.447	3.143	3.707	5.959
7	1.415	1.895	2.365	2.998	3.499	5.405
8	1.397	1.860	2.306	2.896	3.355	5.041
9	1.383	1.833	2.262	2.821	3.250	4.781
10	1.372	1.812	2.228	2.764	3.169	4.587
11	1.363	1.796	2.201	2.718	3.106	4.437
12	1.356	1.782	2.179	2.681	3.055	4.318
13	1.350	1.771	2.160	2.650	3.012	4.221
14	1.345	1.761	2.145	2.624	2.977	4.140
15	1.341	1.753	2.131	2.602	2.947	4.073
16	1.337	1.746	2.120	2.583	2.921	4.015
17	1.333	1.740	2.110	2.567	2.898	3.965
18	1.330	1.734	2.101	2.552	2.878	3.922
19	1.328	1.729	2.093	2.539	2.861	3.883
20	1.325	1.725	2.086	2.528	2.845	3.850
21	1.323	1.721	2.080	2.518	2.831	3.819
22	1.321	1.717	2.074	2.508	2.819	3.792
23	1.319	1.714	2.069	2.500	2.807	3.767
24	1.318	1.711	2.064	2.492	2.797	3.745
25	1.316	1.708	2.060	2.485	2.787	3.725
26	1.315	1.706	2.056	2.479	2.779	3.707
27	1.314	1.703	2.052	2.473	2.771	3.692
28	1.313	1.701	2.048	2.467	2.763	3.674
29	1.311	1.699	2.045	2.462	2.756	3.659
30	1.310	1.697	2.042	2.457	2.750	3.646
40	1.303	1.684	2.021	2.423	2.704	3.551
60	1.296	1.671	2.000	2.390	2.660	3.460
120	1.289	1.658	1.980	2.358	2.617	3.373
∞	1.282	1.645	1.960	2.326	2.576	3.291

SOURCE: Richard P. Runyon and Audrey Haber, *Fundamentals of Behavioral Statistics,* 2nd ed. (Reading, MA: Addison Wesley Publishing Co., 1974). Table T.4 is taken from Table III of Fisher & Yates; STATISTICAL TABLES FOR BIOLOGICAL, AGRICULTURAL AND MEDICAL RESEARCH Published by Longman Group UK., 1974. We are grateful to the Longman Group UK Ltd., on behalf of the Literary Executor of the late Sir Ronald A. Fisher, F.R.S. and Dr. Frank Yates F.R.S. for permission to reproduce Table III from *Statistical Tables for Biological, Agricultural and Medical Research 6/e* (1974).
NOTE: The obtained value of *t* is significant if it is greater than or equal to the value listed in the table.

TABLE T.5 Critical Values of *F* (at the 5% and 1% significance levels)

(df Associated With the Denominator)		1	2	3	4	5	6	7	8	9
					(df Associated With the Numerator)					
1	5%	161	200	216	225	230	234	237	239	241
	1%	4052	5000	5403	5625	5764	5859	5928	5982	6022
2	5%	18.5	19.0	19.2	19.2	19.3	19.3	19.4	19.4	19.4
	1%	98.5	99.0	99.2	99.2	99.3	99.3	99.4	99.4	99.4
3	5%	10.1	9.55	9.28	9.12	9.01	8.94	8.89	8.85	8.81
	1%	34.1	30.8	29.5	28.7	28.2	27.9	27.7	27.5	27.3
4	5%	7.71	6.94	6.59	6.39	6.26	6.16	6.09	6.04	6.00
	1%	21.2	18.0	16.7	16.0	15.5	15.2	15.0	14.8	14.7
5	5%	6.61	5.79	5.41	5.19	5.05	4.95	4.88	4.82	4.77
	1%	16.3	13.3	12.1	11.4	11.0	10.7	10.5	10.3	10.2
6	5%	5.99	5.14	4.76	4.53	4.39	4.28	4.21	4.15	4.10
	1%	13.7	10.9	9.78	9.15	8.75	8.47	8.26	8.10	7.98
7	5%	5.59	4.74	4.35	4.12	3.97	3.87	3.79	3.73	3.68
	1%	12.2	9.55	8.45	7.85	7.46	7.19	6.99	6.84	6.72
8	5%	5.32	4.46	4.07	3.84	3.0	3.58	3.50	3.44	3.39
	1%	11.3	8.65	7.59	7.01	6.63	6.37	6.18	6.03	5.91
9	5%	5.12	4.26	3.86	3.63	3.48	3.37	3.29	3.23	3.18
	1%	10.6	8.02	6.99	6.42	6.06	5.80	5.61	5.47	5.35
10	5%	4.96	4.10	3.71	3.48	3.33	3.22	3.14	3.07	3.02
	1%	10.0	7.56	6.55	5.99	5.64	5.39	5.20	5.06	4.94
11	5%	4.84	3.98	3.59	3.36	3.20	3.09	3.01	2.95	2.90
	1%	9.65	7.21	6.22	5.67	5.32	5.07	4.89	4.74	4.63
12	5%	4.75	3.89	3.49	3.26	3.11	3.00	2.91	2.85	2.80
	1%	9.33	6.93	5.95	5.41	5.06	4.82	4.64	4.50	4.39
13	5%	4.67	3.81	3.41	3.18	3.03	2.92	2.83	2.77	2.71
	1%	9.07	6.70	5.74	5.21	4.86	4.62	4.44	4.30	4.19
14	5%	4.60	3.74	3.34	3.11	2.96	2.85	2.76	2.70	2.65
	1%	8.86	6.51	5.56	5.04	4.70	4.46	4.28	4.14	4.03
15	5%	4.54	3.68	3.29	3.06	2.90	2.79	2.71	2.64	2.59
	1%	8.68	6.36	5.42	4.89	4.56	4.32	4.14	4.00	3.89
16	5%	4.49	3.63	3.24	3.01	2.85	2.74	2.66	2.59	2.54
	1%	8.53	6.23	5.29	4.77	4.44	4.20	4.03	3.89	3.78
17	5%	4.45	3.59	3.20	2.96	2.81	2.70	2.61	2.55	2.49
	1%	8.40	6.11	5.18	4.67	4.34	4.10	3.93	3.79	3.68
18	5%	4.41	3.55	3.16	2.93	2.77	2.66	2.58	2.51	2.46
	1%	8.29	6.01	5.09	4.58	4.25	4.01	3.84	3.71	3.60
19	5%	4.38	3.52	3.13	2.90	2.74	2.63	2.54	2.48	2.42
	1%	8.18	5.93	5.01	4.50	4.17	3.94	3.77	3.63	3.52
20	5%	4.35	3.49	3.10	2.87	2.71	2.60	2.51	2.45	2.39
	1%	8.10	5.85	4.94	4.43	4.10	3.87	3.70	3.56	3.46

(continued)

TABLE T.5 Critical Values of F (at the 5% and 1% significance levels)

(df Associated With the Denominator)		(df Associated With the Numerator)								
21	5%	4.32	3.47	3.07	2.84	2.68	2.57	2.49	2.42	2.37
	1%	8.02	5.78	4.87	4.37	4.04	3.81	3.64	3.51	3.40
22	5%	4.30	3.44	3.05	2.82	2.66	2.55	2.46	2.40	2.34
	1%	7.95	5.72	4.82	4.31	3.99	3.76	3.59	3.45	3.35
23	5%	4.28	3.42	3.03	2.80	2.64	2.53	2.44	2.37	2.32
	1%	7.88	5.66	4.76	4.26	3.94	3.71	3.54	3.41	3.30
24	5%	4.26	3.40	3.01	2.78	2.62	2.51	2.42	2.36	2.30
	1%	7.82	5.61	4.72	4.22	3.90	3.67	3.50	3.36	3.26
25	5%	4.24	3.39	2.99	2.76	2.60	2.49	2.40	2.34	2.28
	1%	7.77	5.57	4.68	4.18	3.86	3.63	3.46	3.32	3.22
26	5%	4.23	3.37	2.98	2.74	2.59	2.47	2.39	2.32	2.27
	1%	7.72	5.53	4.64	4.14	3.82	3.59	3.42	3.29	3.18
27	5%	4.21	3.35	2.96	2.73	2.57	2.46	2.37	2.31	2.25
	1%	7.68	5.49	4.60	4.11	3.78	3.56	3.39	3.26	3.15
28	5%	4.20	3.34	2.95	2.71	2.56	2.45	2.36	2.29	2.24
	1%	7.64	5.45	4.57	4.07	3.75	3.53	3.36	3.23	3.12
29	5%	4.18	3.33	2.93	2.70	2.55	2.43	2.35	2.28	2.22
	1%	7.60	5.42	4.54	4.04	3.73	3.50	3.33	3.20	3.09
30	5%	4.17	3.32	2.92	2.69	2.53	2.42	2.33	2.27	2.21
	1%	7.56	5.39	4.51	4.02	3.70	3.47	3.30	3.17	3.07
40	5%	4.08	3.23	2.84	2.61	2.45	2.34	2.25	2.18	2.12
	1%	7.31	5.18	4.31	3.83	3.51	3.29	3.12	2.99	2.89
60	5%	4.00	3.15	2.76	2.53	2.37	2.25	2.17	2.10	2.04
	1%	7.08	4.98	4.13	3.65	3.34	3.12	2.95	2.82	2.72
120	5%	3.92	3.07	2.68	2.45	2.29	2.18	2.09	2.02	1.96
	1%	6.85	4.79	3.95	3.48	3.17	2.96	2.79	2.66	2.56

SOURCE: Merrington, M., and Thompson, C. M. Tables of percentage points of the interval beta (F) distribution, *Biometrika*, 1943, *33*, 73-88, by permission of the editor.

References

Abouserie, R. (1992). *Statistical methods for educational and psychological research: Basic concepts and guide to data analysis using SPSS/PC+ 4.01.* Cardiff, Wales: University of Wales, College of Cardiff, School of Education.

American Psychiatric Association. (1994). *Diagnostic and statistical manual of mental disorders: DSM-IV* (4th ed.). Washington, DC: Author.

American Psychological Association. (1994). *Publication manual of the American Psychological Association* (4th ed.). Washington, DC: Author.

Annas, G. J., & Grodin, M. A. (Eds.). (1992). *The Nazi doctors and the Nuremberg Code: Human rights in human experimentation.* New York: Oxford University Press.

Applebaum, R., Seidl, F. W., & Austin, C. D. (1980). The Wisconsin community care organization: Preliminary findings from the Milwaukee experiment. *The Gerontologist, 20*(3), 350-355.

Ashford, J. B. (1994). Are traditional empirical research methods inherently biased against people of color? No. In W. Hudson & P. S. Nurius (Eds.), *Controversial issues in social work research* (pp. 29-34). Boston: Allyn & Bacon.

Atherton, C. R., & Klemmack, D. L. (1982). *Research methods in social work.* Lexington, MA: D. C. Heath.

Baltes, P. B., & Labouvie, G. J. (1973). Adult development of intellectual performance: Description, explanation, and modification. In C. Eisdorfer & M. P. Lawton (Eds.), *The psychology of adult development and aging.* Washington, DC: American Psychological Association.

Barlow, D. H., & Hersen, M. (1984). *Single-case experimental designs: Strategies for studying behavioral change.* New York: Pergamon.

Beebe, L. (Ed.). (1993). *Professional writing for the human services.* Washington, DC: National Association of Social Workers Press.

The Belmont report: Basic ethical principles and their application (Video recording). (1987). Bethesda, MD: National Library of Medicine.

Berger, R. M. (1984). *Gay and gray: The older homosexual man.* Boston: Alyson. (Reprinted from University of Illinois Press, 1982, Urbana-Champaign)

Berger, R. M. (1986). A better recipe for social work practice models. *Social Casework, 67*(1), 45-54.

Berger, R. M. (1988, April 28). Common paths: Helping clients to survive a loss. *Social Work Today,* pp. 14-17.

Berger, R. M. (1991). Four steps to getting your paper published. *Child and Youth Care Forum, 20*(3), 211-214.

Berger, R. M., & Anderson, S. (1984). The in-home worker: Serving the frail elderly. *Social Work, 29*(5), 456-461.

Berger, R. M., & Kelly, J. J. (1995). Gay men. In *Encyclopedia of social work* (19th ed., pp. 1064-1075). Washington, DC: National Association of Social Workers Press.

Berger, R. M., & Piliavin, I. (1976a). The effects of casework: A research note. *Social Work, 21*(3), 205-208.

Berger, R. M., & Piliavin, I. (1976b). A rejoinder by Berger and Piliavin. *Social Work, 21*(5), 349, 396-397.

Berger, R. M., & Rose, S. D. (1977). Interpersonal skill training with institutionalized elderly patients. *Journal of Gerontology, 32*(3), 346-353.

Bergin, A. E., & Garfield, S. L. (1994). *Handbook of psychotherapy and behavior change* (4th ed.). New York: John Wiley.

Bieber, I. (1965). Clinical aspects of male homosexuality. In J. Marmor (Ed.), *Sexual inversion: The multiple roots of homosexuality* (pp. 248-267). New York: Basic Books.

Blenkner, M., Bloom, M., & Nielsen, M. (1971). A research and demonstration project of protective services. *Social Casework, 52*(8), 483-499.

Bloom, M., & Fischer, J. (1982). *Evaluating practice: Guidelines for the accountable professional.* Englewood Cliffs, NJ: Prentice Hall.

Botwinick, J. (1978). *Aging and behavior* (2nd ed.). New York: Springer.

Bourne, L. E., Jr., & Ekstrand, B. R. (1982). *Psychology: Its principles and meanings* (4th ed.). New York: Holt, Rinehart & Winston.

Campbell, D. T., & Stanley, J. C. (1963). *Experimental and quasi-experimental designs for research.* Chicago: Rand McNally.

Carstensen, L. L., & Erickson, R. J. (1986). Enhancing the social environments of elderly nursing home residents: Are high rates of interaction enough? *Journal of Applied Behavior Analysis, 19*(4), 349-355.

Conoley, J. C., & Kramer, J. J. (Eds.). (1989). *The tenth mental measurements yearbook.* Lincoln: University of Nebraska Lincoln, Buros Institute of Mental Measurements.

Cook, T. D., & Campbell, D. T. (1979). *Quasi-experimentation: Design and analysis issues for field settings.* Chicago: Rand McNally.

Coon, D. (1983). *Introduction to psychology: Exploration and application* (3rd ed.). St. Paul, MN: West.

Cronbach, L. J. (1951). Coefficient alpha and the internal structure of tests. *Psychometrika, 16,* 297-334.

Deimling, G. T., & Bass, D. M. (1986). Symptoms of mental impairment among elderly adults and their effects on family caregivers. *Journal of Gerontology, 41*(6), 778-784.

Denzin, N. K., & Lincoln, Y. S. (1994). Introduction: Entering the field of qualitative research. In N. K. Denzin & Y. S. Lincoln (Eds.), *Handbook of qualitative research* (pp. 1-18). Thousand Oaks, CA: Sage.

Drew, C. J. (1980). *Introduction to designing and conducting research* (2nd ed.). St. Louis, MO: C. V. Mosby.

Edinberg, M. A. (1985). *Mental health practice with the elderly.* Englewood Cliffs, NJ: Prentice Hall.

Fischer, J., & Corcoran, K. (1994). *Measures for clinical practice* (Vols. 1 & 2, 2nd ed.). New York: Free Press.

Flick, U. (1992). Triangulation revisited: Strategy of validation or alternative? *Journal for the Theory of Social Behaviour, 22,* 175-198.

Fontana, A., & Frey, J. H. (1994). Interviewing: The art of science. In N. K. Denzin & Y. S. Lincoln (Eds.), *Handbook of qualitative research* (pp. 361-376). Thousand Oaks, CA: Sage.

Frank, A. (1993). *Diary of a young girl.* New York: Bantam.

Freud, S. (1920). *A general introduction to psychoanalysis.* New York: Liverright.

Freud, S. (1933). *New introductory lectures on psychoanalysis* (W. J. H. Sprott, Trans.). New York: Norton.

Glaser, B. G., & Strauss, A. L. (1967). *The discovery of grounded theory: Strategies for qualitative research.* Chicago: Aldine de Gruyter.

Goldfarb, A. I. (1962). Prevalence of psychiatric disorder in metropolitan old age and nursing homes. *Journal of the American Geriatrics Society, 10*(1), 77-84.

Goldzieher case raises ethical storm. (1971, October 11). *Behavior Today.*

Guba, E. G., & Lincoln, Y. S. (1994). Competing paradigms in qualitative research. In N. K. Denzin & Y. S. Lincoln (Eds.), *Handbook of qualitative research* (pp. 105-117). Thousand Oaks, CA: Sage.

Haefele, J. W. (1962). *Creativity and innovation.* New York: Reinhold.

Hays, W. L. (1973). *Statistics for the social sciences* (2nd ed.). New York: Holt, Rinehart & Winston.

Hersen, M., & Barlow, D. H. (1976). *Single case experimental designs.* New York: Pergamon.

Homans, G. C. (1965). Group factors in worker productivity. In H. Proshansky & L. Seidenberg (Eds.), *Basic studies in social psychology* (pp. 592-604). New York: Henry Holt.

Hudson, W. (1981). Clinical measurement package for social workers. Reprinted in R. M. Grinnell (Ed.), *Social work research and evaluation.* Itasca, IL: F. E. Peacock.

Humphreys, L. (1970). *Tearoom trade: Impersonal sex in public places.* Chicago: Aldine-Atherton.

Janesick, V. J. (1994). The dance of qualitative research design. In N. K. Denzin & Y. S. Lincoln (Eds.), *Handbook of qualitative research* (pp. 209-219). Thousand Oaks, CA: Sage.

Joint Commission on Mental Illness and Health. (1961). *Action for mental health.* New York: Science Editions.

Julian, J., & Kornblum, W. (1983). *Social problems* (4th ed.). Englewood Cliffs, NJ: Prentice Hall.

Kastenbaum, R., & Candy, S. E. (1973). The 4% fallacy: A methodological and empirical critique of extended care facility population statistics. *International Journal of Aging and Human Development, 4*(1), 15-22.

Kazdin, A. (1982). *Single-case research designs: Methods for clinical and applied settings.* New York: Oxford University Press.

Kerlinger, F. N. (1973). *Foundations of behavioral research* (2nd ed.). New York: Holt, Rinehart & Winston.

Lash, T. W., & Sigal, H. (1976). *State of the child: New York City.* New York: Foundation for Child Development.

Leitenberg, H. (1973). The use of single-case methodology in psychotherapy research. *Journal of Abnormal Psychology, 82*(1), 87-101.

Lewis, O. (1968). *La vida.* New York: Vintage.

Liebow, E. (1967). *Tally's corner: A study of Negro streetcorner men.* Boston: Little, Brown.

Lofland, J. (1971). *Analyzing social settings: A guide to qualitative observation and analysis.* Belmont, CA: Wadsworth.

Marcenko, M. O., Spence, M., & Rohweder, C. (1994). Psychosocial characteristics of pregnant women with and without a history of substance abuse. *Health and Social Work, 19*(1), 17-22.

Marine, A., Kirkpatrick, S., Neou, V., & Ward, C. (Eds.). (1994). *Internet: Getting started.* Englewood Cliffs, NJ: Prentice Hall.

Marlow, C. (1993). *Research methods for generalist social work.* Pacific Grove, CA: Brooks/Cole.

Masters, W., & Johnson, V. (1966). *Human sexual response.* Boston: Little, Brown.

McCain, G., & Segal, E. M. (1969). *The game of science* (2nd ed.). Belmont, CA: Brooks/Cole.

Mendelsohn, H. N. (1987). *A guide to information sources for social work and the human services.* Phoenix, AZ: Oryx.

Mendelsohn, H. N. (1992). *An author's guide to social work journals* (3rd ed.). Washington, DC: National Association of Social Workers Press.

Milgram, S. (1963). Behavioral study of obedience. *Journal of Abnormal and Social Psychology, 67,* 371-378.

Milgram, S. (1965). Some conditions of obedience and disobedience to authority. *Human Relations, 18,* 57-76.

Murray, C., & Herrnstein, R. J. (1994, October 31). Race, genes and IQ: An apologia. *New Republic,* pp. 27-37.

National Association of Social Workers. (1994). *NASW code of ethics.* Washington, DC: Author.

National Commission for the Protection of Human Subjects of Biomedical and Behavioral Research. (1978a). *The Belmont report: Ethical principles and guidelines for the protection of human subjects of research* (DHEW Publication No. OS 78-0012). Washington, DC: Government Printing Office.

National Commission for the Protection of Human Subjects of Biomedical and Behavioral Research. (1978b). *Special study: Implications of advances in biomedical and behavioral research.* Washington, DC: Government Printing Office.

New Republic. (1994, October 31). [Special issue on race and IQ]

Penslar, R. L. (1993). *Protecting human research subjects: Institutional Review Board guidebook* (U.S. Department of Health and Human Services, Public Health Service, National Institutes of Health, Office of Extramural Research, Office of Protection from Research Risks). Washington, DC: Government Printing Office.

Pincus, A., & Minahan, A. (1973). *Social work practice: Model and method.* Itasca, IL: F. E. Peacock.

President's Commission on Mental Health. (1978). *Report to the president* (Vol. 1). Washington, DC: Government Printing Office.

Rathus, S. A. (1973). A 30-item schedule for assessing assertive behavior. *Behavior Therapy, 4,* 398-406.

Reinharz, S. (1992). *Feminist methods in social research.* New York: Oxford University Press.

Renzetti, C. M. (1992). *Violent betrayal: Partner abuse in lesbian relationships.* Newbury Park, CA: Sage.

Renzetti, C. M. (1995). Studying partner abuse in lesbian relationships: A case for the feminist participatory research model. *Journal of Gay and Lesbian Social Services, 3*(1), 29-42.

Robertson, I. (1981). *Sociology* (2nd ed.). New York: Worth.

Rosenberg, M. (1965). *Society and the adolescent self-image.* Princeton, NJ: Princeton University Press.

Rosenberg, M. (1968). *The logic of survey analysis.* New York: Basic Books.

Rosenblatt, A., & Kirk, S. A. (1981). Cumulative effect of research courses on knowledge and attitudes of social work students. *Journal of Education for Social Work, 17*(2), 26-34.

Rosenthal, R., & Jacobson, L. (1968). *Pygmalion in the classroom.* New York: Holt, Rinehart & Winston.

Rubin, A., & Babbie, E. (1993). *Research methods for social work* (2nd ed.). Pacific Grove, CA: Brooks/Cole.

Schneebaum, T. (1988). *Where the spirits dwell: An odyssey in the New Guinea jungle.* New York: Grove.

Schuster, C. S., & Ashburn, S. S. (1980). *The process of human development: A holistic approach.* Boston: Little, Brown.

Selltiz, C., Wrightsman, L. S., & Cook, S. W. (1976). *Research methods in social relations* (3rd ed.). New York: Holt, Rinehart & Winston.

Simon, B. K. (1970). Social casework theory: An overview. In R. W. Roberts & R. H. Nee (Eds.), *Theories of social casework.* Chicago: University of Chicago Press.

Sohng, S. S. (1994). Are traditional empirical research methods inherently biased against people of color? Yes. In W. Hudson & P. S. Nurius (Eds.), *Controversial issues in social work research* (pp. 22-26). Boston: Allyn & Bacon.

Stake, R. E. (1994). Case studies. In N. K. Denzin & Y. S. Lincoln (Eds.), *Handbook of qualitative research* (pp. 236-247). Thousand Oaks, CA: Sage.

Stein, H. D. (1969). *The crisis in welfare in Cleveland.* Cleveland, OH: Case Western Reserve University.

Stevens, S. S. (1946). On the theory of scales of measurement. *Science, 103,* 677-680.

Strauss, A., & Corbin, J. (1994). Grounded theory methodology: An overview. In N. K. Denzin & Y. S. Lincoln (Eds.), *Handbook of qualitative research* (pp. 273-285). Thousand Oaks, CA: Sage.

Suchman, E. A. (1967). *Evaluative research: Principles and practice in public service and social action programs.* New York: Russell Sage.

Swigonski, M. E. (1994). The logic of feminist standpoint theory for social work research. *Social Work, 39*(4), 387-393.

Thomas, S. B., & Quinn, S. C. (1991). The Tuskegee syphilis study, 1932 to 1972: Implications for HIV education and AIDS risk education programs in the black community. *American Journal of Public Health, 81*(11), 1498-1505.

U.S. Congress, Joint Economic Committee, Subcommittee on Fiscal Policy. (1972). *Issues in welfare administration: Welfare—An administrative nightmare* (Studies in Public Welfare, Paper No. 5). Washington, DC: Government Printing Office.

Van Maanen, J. (1988). *Tales of the field: On writing ethnography.* Chicago: University of Chicago Press.

Vidich, A. J., & Bensman, J. (1960). *Small town in mass society.* Princeton, NJ: Princeton University Press.

Warheit, G. J., Bell, R. A., & Schwab, J. J. (1979). *Needs assessment approaches: Concepts and methods.* Washington, DC: Government Printing Office.

Webster's new world dictionary of the American language (College ed.). (1964). Cleveland, OH: World.

Weinberg, M. S., & Williams, C. J. (1975). *Male homosexuals: Their problems and adaptations.* New York: Penguin.

Glossary

AB Design A type of **single-subject research** design. The researcher records a behavior during a baseline phase (A) and also during a subsequent intervention or treatment phase (B).

ABAB Design A type of **single-subject research** design. The researcher records a behavior during a baseline phase (A) and also during a subsequent intervention or treatment phase (B). The researcher continues to record the behavior during a return to the baseline phase (A) and then a return to the treatment phase (B). See **reversal design** and **withdrawal design.**

Abstract Indexes that provide brief descriptions or summaries about the contents of books, articles, and other sources (e.g., *Social Work Abstracts*).

Accidental Sample A type of **nonprobability sample** in which subjects are recruited for study as they become available or because they are conveniently accessible to the researcher.

Anonymity Research subjects are *anonymous* when their participation in a study and their responses to it cannot be identified by anyone, including the researcher. For example, a questionnaire is anonymous if it is picked up in a public location and returned without the subject's name or other information that could be used to identify the subject. See **confidential.**

Antecedent Variable In analyzing the relationship between two variables, researchers may find that a third variable precedes the original variables. This third variable is called an *antecedent variable*.

390

Asymmetrical Relationship A type of two-variable relationship in which it is clear that one variable came first. For example, in a study of the effect of gender (first variable) on career choices (second variable) of men and women, it is clear that gender led to career choice and not the other way around.

Available Materials Data that have been gathered by persons other than the researcher, usually for purposes other than research. For example, available materials include census data, motor vehicle or birth registrations, newspapers, institutional records, personal documents such as letters and diaries, and archives.

Back Translation A procedure to ensure that a test, questionnaire, or interview schedule is translated correctly into another language. The original instrument is translated into a new language. Then the translated instrument is translated back into the original language by a new person or group. Finally, the back-translated version is compared with the original version, and discrepancies are resolved.

Bibliography A list of books, journals, reports, and other materials on a single topic.

Brainstorming A psychological technique to help people generate new and creative ideas. Using this technique, individuals generate as many ideas as possible about a topic, without evaluating the appropriateness of these ideas.

Bulletin Board System (BBS) A service provided by a **computer network.** Users can leave, send, and receive messages (e-mail) and hold live online conversations with other users.

Case Study The intensive study of a single individual, family, group, or other social grouping. One type of **qualitative research.**

Categorical Data Data that can take on only a limited number of values within a given range. For example, caseload size, race, and social class are categorical data.

CD-ROM Compact disk-read only memory. A small round platter (similar to a music CD) that stores data for input into personal computers.

Chi-Square A statistic that is used to determine if there is a statistically significant relationship between two **categorical variables.**

Cluster Sample A type of probability sample in which the researcher divides a population into successively smaller subunits or clusters. Then within each cluster, a random sample is drawn. The clusters are often based on successively smaller geographic units—for example, regions, states, counties, and school districts.

Computer Network A collection of computers linked by telephone or other device. The network may be located in one site (for example, an office or university) or at various locations around the world.

Concept A word, term, or symbol that describes what otherwise different things have in common.

Conceptual Scheme A collection of related concepts. For example, the systems approach in social work is a conceptual scheme. When a conceptual scheme is developed through reasoning, logic, or research, it may be called a **theory.**

Concurrent Validity The ability of a measuring instrument to accurately predict the current situation or status of an individual. See **criterion-related validity.**

Confidential Research subjects' participation in a study and their responses to it are *confidential* if they can be individually identified by the researcher (for example, by name), but the researcher pledges not to reveal this information to anyone outside the research setting. See **anonymity.**

Construct Validity (of measuring instruments) A complex form of validity that is evaluated by determining the degree with which certain explanatory concepts derived from theory account for performance on a measure. Two types of construct validity are **convergent validity** and **discriminant validity.**

Content Validity (of a measuring instrument) The representativeness or sampling adequacy of the content—the substance and the topics—of a measuring instrument.

Contingency Analysis or Crossbreak A type of analysis in which two or three **categorical variables** are presented in a two- or three-dimensional table. For example, a contingency analysis might be represented by a table with two rows representing gender (male and female) and two columns representing race (African American and Caucasian). The cells of the table contain counts of the number of individuals in each category.

Continuous Data Data that can take on any whole or decimal value within a given range. For example, age, height, and income are continuous data.

Convergent Validity A type of **construct validity** of measuring instruments. Convergent validity is established when evidence gathered from different sources or in different ways all indicate the same or similar meaning of the construct.

Correlation Coefficient (*r*) A statistic used to determine the strength of relationship between two continuous variables. This statistic is called the Pearson product-moment correlation coefficient.

Cost-Benefit Analysis A type of **program evaluation** that uses a comparison of costs and benefits to determine the net benefit of a program.

Criterion-Related Validity (of measuring instruments) The predictive ability of a measuring instrument based on comparing the instrument's scores with one or more external criteria. There are two types of criterion-related validity. See **concurrent validity** and **predictive validity.**

Cronbach's Alpha A measure of the internal consistency of a measuring instrument. See **internal consistency measure.**

Cross-Sectional Research Design A type of research design in which individuals of varying ages are all measured at one point in time. See **longitudinal design.**

Culture "Learned ways of life, which are modified and passed on from one generation to the next" (Robertson, 1981, p. 53). Culture includes the material aspects of a society, such as tools and clothing, as well as nonmaterial aspects, such as language, customs, and rituals. See **race** and **ethnicity.**

Data Analysis The process by which a large set of numbers is reduced to a smaller set of numbers to make it more understandable.

Database Manager A computer program that stores, organizes, and analyzes a set of information. For example, a social worker in private practice might use a database manager to store and analyze information about clients, such as name, age, address, family situation, diagnosis, number of sessions completed, and billing information.

Demographic Variables Variables that describe basic characteristics about the persons or events under study. Typical demographic variables include age, race, income, and marital status.

Dependent Variable In a relationship involving two or more variables, a variable that comes after the independent variable.

Descriptive Research A type of research that seeks to describe a group of persons, families, organizations, communities, events, or other phenomena rather than to test hypotheses about them.

Descriptive Statistics Statistics that describe characteristics of a sample of individuals or cases. See **statistic.**

Directory A list of organizations, agencies, or persons. For example, the *Foundation Directory* lists government and charitable foundations.

Discriminant Validity A type of **construct validity.** Discriminant validity refers to the ability of a measuring instrument to differentiate a construct from other constructs, to predict which constructs will be unrelated to the measured construct, and to determine which groups will differ on the construct. See **known-groups approach.**

Documentation In the computer field, documentation refers to instruction manuals for the use of software programs. These may be available as pamphlets or written manuals. Or they also may be included in the software program itself, to be read on the computer display.

Double-Barreled Question A type of poorly worded interview or questionnaire item in which a respondent is asked two questions simultaneously.

Duration Recording A method of recording observed behavior in which the observer records how long a specified behavior occurs. Used in **single-subject research.**

Elaboration A procedure often used to study relationships between variables in **survey research.** Using elaboration, the researcher studies the relationship between two variables by introducing a third variable (**test factor**).

Ethnicity The cultural characteristics of a group. These include "language, religion, national origin, dietary practices [and] a sense of common historical heritage" (Robertson, 1981, p. 282). See **culture** and **race.**

Ethnography A written description of a culture or some aspect of a culture. For example, ethnographies have been used to study foreign cultures and domestic subcultures, such as lower-class Puerto Ricans. Ethnography is a type of qualitative research. See **fieldwork** and **participant observation.**

Ex Post Facto Research A type of research that studies events that occurred in the past. Ex post facto research is often associated with **survey research.**

Exhaustive Categories A scheme for categorizing phenomena is exhaustive if every phenomenon can be placed into a category.

Experimental Research A type of research in which the independent variable is manipulated by the researcher; that is, the researcher assigns individuals or study units to comparison groups or determines who will and will not experience an intervention.

Experimental Research Design A research design that consists of groups formed by the researcher using random assignment.

External Validity A characteristic of research designs that relates to the **generalizability** of observed effects. Questions of external validity ask, "To what other groups of people, families, organizations, and so on can the observed effect be generalized?" and "With what other treatment variables and outcome variables will this effect hold true?" See **internal validity.**

Extraneous Variable In analyzing the relationship between two variables, researchers may find that this relationship is due to a third variable. This third variable is called an *extraneous variable.* See **spurious relationship.**

F Test In inferential statistics, a test to determine if the overall mean difference between three or more groups is statistically significant.

Field In computer programs, a column or group of columns that represent data on a single variable. For example, a database manager program may have a field for clients' gender, another for age, and so on.

Fieldwork A method for collecting observations for an **ethnography.** Fieldworkers study people in their natural settings. For example, a fieldworker may live with a primitive culture during the period of observation and data collection.

Fixed-Alternative (or Closed) Item A type of questionnaire or interview question in which the respondent chooses from two or more predetermined alternatives. See **open-end item.**

Frequency Distribution A type of data analysis used to describe a set of values on a single variable. The values are listed in a column on the left, and the number of cases that fall into each of the values is listed on the right. For example, a frequency distribution might summarize the number of individuals who fall within each of several levels of social class. See **grouped frequency distribution.**

Frequency Measure A method of recording observed behavior in which the observer counts the number of times a behavior occurs within a given time period. Used in **single-subject research.**

Funnel Question A type of interview or questionnaire item that begins with a broad question and then "funnels" into more specific questions on the same topic.

Gender Identity The self-perception of being male or female.

Generalizability The extent to which a study's findings hold true for persons, situations, locations, independent and dependent variables that were not included in the study. In most situations, researchers favor studies with findings that are generalizeable to a wide variety of persons, situations, and so on. See **Interaction of Selection and X.**

Grounded Theory An approach to qualitative research developed by sociologists for the study of complex social phenomena. Grounded theory researchers use in-depth interviews, observations, and other means to collect data. They then generate explanatory theory from the data.

Grouped Frequency Distribution A type of frequency distribution in which the values of a single variable are grouped into intervals. For example, a grouped frequency distribution of the age of clients in a social work agency might list the number of clients who are under 18 years old, aged 18 through 28, 29 through 39, and so on. See **frequency distribution.**

Handbook A volume or set of volumes that provide an overview of a particular topic area.

Hardware Machinery that makes up a computer or computer network—for example, the central processing unit, display, and printer. See **software.**

History A factor of internal validity. History refers to events other than the experimental variables that occur during the course of the study and that may affect the outcome.

Hypothesis A guess about the nature of the relationship between two or more variables.

Independent Variable In a relationship involving two or more variables, the variable that is presumed to come first.

Index A list of books, journals, and other sources in a particular area—for example, the *New York Times Index,* which helps to locate newspaper articles.

Inferential Statistics Statistics that are used to make inferences about population parameters. Examples of statistics are t, F, χ^2, and r. See **parameter** and **statistic.**

Informed Consent A basic principle of all ethical standards for research participation by human subjects.

Institutional Review Board (IRB) A committee of persons who review proposals for research studies to ensure that the studies meet ethical guidelines. IRB review and approval is required for research conducted at most universities, hospitals, research centers, and other institutions.

Instrumentation A factor of internal validity. Instrumentation occurs when the calibration or accuracy of a measuring instrument changes over time.

Intact Groups Design A research design in which comparison groups are already formed—for example, a design that compares the clients of two agencies.

Interaction of Selection and X A factor of external validity. The interaction of selection and X occurs when the results of a research study are applicable only to the particular persons and situation studied—that is, when results are not **generalizable** beyond the study.

Interaction of Testing and X A factor of external validity. The interaction of testing and X is a problem when the experience of taking a test sensitizes or in some other way changes the way a subject responds to an experimental treatment.

Internal Consistency Measures Measures used to determine the homogeneity (similarity) of items on a test or measuring instrument that is designed to measure a single characteristic, such as depression or self-esteem.

Internal Validity A characteristic of research designs. A research design that is internally valid establishes that the experimental treatment did lead to an observed effect with the particular subjects studied at the time the effect was measured. See **external validity.**

Internet A worldwide network of computer networks.

Interval Measurement The third highest level of measurement. In interval measurement, the variables being measured provide all the information of nominal and ordinal variables. In addition, in interval measurement, numerically equal distances indicate equal differences in the property being measured.

Interval Recording A method of recording observed behavior in which the observer records whether a specified behavior occurs within each of many time intervals. Rather than counting the number of times the behavior occurs, the observer records whether the behavior occurred at all in each interval. Used in **single-subject research.**

Intervening Variable In analyzing the relationship between two variables, researchers may find that a third variable intervenes between the two. This third variable is called an *intervening variable.*

Interview A face-to-face situation in which an interviewer asks questions of one or more interviewees. See **structured interview** and **unstandardized interview.**

Intrasession History A factor of internal validity. Intrasession history refers to a research design with two or more groups in which an event or events occur within one group but not another. This event may affect the way a group responds to the experimental treatment.

Known-Groups Approach A procedure to determine the **discriminant validity** of a measuring instrument. For example, the discriminant validity of an instrument to measure "authoritarianism" might be established by showing that members of the Nazi Party score high on this instrument, whereas members of the National Association of Social Workers score low.

Levels of Measurement Variables are measured in different ways that provide varying amounts or levels of information. There are four levels of measurement: **nominal, ordinal, interval,** and **ratio.**

Longitudinal Design A type of research design in which a single group of individuals is measured repeatedly over time. See **cross-sectional research design.**

Maturation A factor of internal validity. Maturation refers to "processes within the respondents operating as a function of the passage of time per se (not specific to the particular events), including growing older, growing hungrier, growing more tired and the like" (Campbell & Stanley, 1963, p. 5).

Mean The sum of a group of scores divided by the number of scores.

Measurement The assignment of numerals or numbers to objects or events according to rules. The primary purpose of measurement is to assign numerals or numbers in such a way that we have accurately described some aspect of what we are studying.

Measures of Central Tendency Measures that describe the most typical or "average" value of a **frequency distribution.** The most common measures of central tendency are the **mean, median,** and **mode.**

Measures of Variability Measures that describe the dispersion of values in a **frequency distribution**—that is, how "spread out" the values are. The most common measures of variability are the **range, variance,** and **standard deviation.**

Median In a **frequency distribution** with an odd number of scores, the median is the middlemost of the ranked scores. In a frequency distribution with an even number of scores, the median is the mean of the two middlemost of the ranked scores.

Mode In a **frequency distribution,** the mode is the most frequently occurring value, score, or category.

Mortality A factor of internal validity. Mortality occurs when subjects drop out of comparison groups so that the comparability of the groups is compromised.

Multiple or Alternate Forms Reliability A type of reliability of measuring instruments. A measuring instrument has multiple or alternate forms reliability if simultaneous administration of equivalent instruments to a single group of respondents yields a consistent result.

Multiple-Baseline Design A type of **single-subject research** design. The researcher records a behavior during a baseline phase (A) and also during a subsequent intervention or treatment phase (B). Then the A and B phases are repeated by applying the intervention to two or more new behaviors, subjects, or settings.

Multiple-Treatment Interference A factor of external validity. Multiple-treatment interference occurs when the researcher's attempt to evaluate the effect of a treatment is clouded by the effect of a previous treatment.

Mutually Exclusive A scheme for categorizing phenomena is mutually exclusive if every phenomenon can be placed in one and only one category.

Needs Assessment A type of **program evaluation** designed to determine the type and extent of services needed and how services are used.

Negative Relationship A negative relationship occurs between two variables when, as one variable increases, the other consistently decreases.

Nominal Measurement The lowest level of measurement, in which numerals are assigned to objects without quantitative meaning. For example, gender (male and female) is measured at the nominal level.

Nonequivalent Control Group Design A type of research design in which two groups are compared by testing both groups before and after an intervention, treatment, or event. In this design, the groups are not formed by random assignment.

Nonexperimental Research A type of research in which the independent variable is not manipulated by the researcher; that is, the researcher is not able to determine which individuals or study units will be exposed to the events being studied. For example, a study comparing the reactions of males and females is a type of nonexperimental research.

Nonprobability Sample A type of sample that does not use random sampling.

Nonproportional Stratified Sampling A type of stratified sample in which the researcher selects an equal number of elements for each group or in which elements are selected in numbers that do not reflect their proportions in the population. For example, even though foreign-born persons may compose only 10% of a given population, a researcher interested in a comparison of native and foreign-born persons may select equal numbers of each. See **stratified (random) samplin.**

Null Hypothesis In inferential statistics, the hypothesis of no difference. Specifically, the null hypothesis states that the sample mean is no different from the population mean or that there is no difference between or among populations means or that the population parameter is equal to zero.

Nuremberg Code A set of standards to guide the ethical behavior of scientists who conduct biomedical research. The Nuremberg Code was written as a result of the trials of Nazi war criminals after World War II.

One-Group Pretest-Posttest Design A research design in which one group is tested before and after an intervention, treatment, or event.

One-Sample *t* Test A statistical test to determine if a sample mean is significantly different from a presumed population mean. For example, a one-sample *t* test might be used to determine if an observed mean IQ score of 98 is significantly different from the presumed mean score of the population, which is 100.

One-Shot Case Study A research design in which a single individual, family, group, community, or other unit is studied at one point in time.

One-Tailed Test A statistical test used to evaluate a directional hypothesis—that is, a hypothesis that specifies the direction in which two or more variables differ. For example, a one-tailed test would be used to evaluate the hypothesis that social workers are more liberal than physicists.

Online Public Access Catalog (OPAC)   A computerized library catalog. This is a modern version of the old "card catalog."

Open-End Item   A type of questionnaire or interview question in which respondents are free to respond in their own words. See **fixed-alternative (or closed) item.**

Operational Definition   A way of defining a concept or variable that specifies what activities or operations we need to perform to measure the concept or variable.

Ordinal Measurement   The second highest level of measurement. In ordinal measurement, the variables being measured provide all the information of nominal variables, and, in addition, the values of the variable can be rank ordered.

Paradigm   A set of basic beliefs about the nature of the world and the individual's place in it. The **scientific method** and **positivism** are paradigms.

Parameter   A measure that describes some aspect of a **population.** See **statistic.**

Participant Observation   A method used by ethnographers to collect data about a social phenomenon. The participant observer lives with or has extensive contact with study subjects and participates in their day-to-day activities. Associated with **fieldwork.**

Partitioning   The process of dividing the values of a variable into two or more groups.

Placebo   An inert substance or treatment that is administered to a comparison group to evaluate the effectiveness of a drug or treatment beyond those effects due to the subject's expectations of improvement.

Population   The collection of all individuals, families, groups, organizations, communities, or events that we are interested in studying.

Population Element   Each unit (individual, family, etc.) of a population.

Positive Relationship   A positive relationship between two variables occurs when, as one variable increases, the other variable also increases consistently. See **negative relationship.**

Positivistic Research   An approach to social science research that relies on several assumptions. These include the assumptions that there is an independent and objective reality and that researchers can study phenomena without bias. See **quantitative research.**

Posttest-Only Control Group Design   A research design in which an experimental treatment is administered to one of two randomly formed comparison groups and both groups are tested after the treatment.

Predictive Validity The ability of a measuring instrument to predict some future performance or situation. See **criterion-related validity.**

Pretest-Posttest Control Group Design A research design in which an experimental treatment is administered to one of two randomly formed comparison groups and in which both groups are tested before and after the experimental treatment.

Probability Sample A type of sample that uses random sampling in at least one stage of the sampling process.

Program Evaluation A type of research that uses social science research methods to evaluate a social service program.

Proportional Stratified Sampling A type of stratified sample in which the number of elements sampled in each subgroup is proportional to the representation of that subgroup in the population. For example, if women compose 50% of the population, then the researcher will select a number of women so that they make up 50% of the sample. See **stratified (random) sample.**

Purposive Sample A type of **nonprobability sample** in which the researcher hand-picks subjects for study based on theory or on the researcher's expert opinion.

Qualitative Research An approach to research that relies on general and narrative descriptions rather than on numbers and statistics. Qualitative research attempts to measure the full complexity of social phenomena and to capture the perceived meanings of those studied. Often seen as an alternative to **positivistic research.**

Quantitative Research An approach to research that relies on studying phenomena through the use of numerical means. Often associated with **positivistic research.**

Quasi-Experimental Research A type of research that approximates an experimental design. Most quasi-experimental designs use comparison groups that are not formed by random assignment. See **experimental research.**

Questionnaire A self-administered set of questions or items in written form.

Quota Sample A type of **nonprobability sample** in which the researcher establishes quotas for recruitment of subjects into the sample so that the sample will be similar to the population on selected characteristics.

Race "The genetically transmitted physical characteristics of different human groups" (Robertson, 1981, p. 281). See **culture** and **ethnicity.**

Random Assignment to Groups A situation in which every member of a sample has an equal chance of being assigned to any one of two or more comparison groups.

Random Sample (or Simple Random Sample) A type of sample in which every element in the population has an equal chance of being selected for the sample.

Random Sampling A procedure for drawing a sample from a population so that every element in the population has an equal chance of being selected for the sample.

Range In a **frequency distribution,** the difference between the highest and lowest scores or values.

Ratio Measurement The highest level of measurement. Ratio variables have all the characteristics of **nominal, ordinal,** and **interval** variables. In addition, ratio variables have a "zero point" that corresponds to the total absence of the property being measured.

Reactive Arrangements A factor of external validity. Reactive arrangements occur when the setting of the study is artificial or different from what occurs routinely. Studies that occur in unusual settings produce results that are not **generalizable** to routine or real-world settings.

Reciprocal Relationship A type of two-variable relationship in which the variables influence each other, but it is impossible to tell which came first.

Reliability The extent to which an operational definition, a questionnaire, test, interview schedule, or other instrument is stable and consistent.

Reliable Operational Definition An operational definition that is replicable. That is, two researchers working independently, from the operational definition, will both measure the same concept or variable in exactly the same way.

Representative Sample A sample that is similar to the population from which it was drawn, on the characteristics under study.

Reversal Design A type of ABAB **single-subject research** design in which the treatment is applied to an alternative but incompatible behavior in the third (A) phase. See **ABAB design.**

Sample A portion of a population selected for study.

Scale A special type of **fixed-alternative** questionnaire or interview item. A scale is a set of items to each of which an individual responds by expressing degrees of agreement or disagreement or some other type of response. See **summated rating scale.**

Scientific Bias The tendency for scientists to allow personal preferences to influence the research process.

Scientific Method The philosophical basis for social science research methods. The scientific method requires that the scientist be systematic, use control to understand the relationships between events, and consider only propositions that can be tested objectively.

Selection A factor of internal validity. Selection occurs when subjects in comparison groups differ on characteristics related to the dependent variable. For example, an age difference between two groups might cloud a comparison of the way the two groups react to a social work intervention.

Serials A librarian's term for journals, magazines, and newspapers.

Sexual Orientation An individual's preference for sexual and affectional relationships with persons of the same sex, opposite sex, or both sexes.

Single-Subject Research A type of research in which a single individual or case is studied by repeatedly observing or measuring that case over time.

Social Desirability Bias A type of bias in interview and questionnaire items in which the item is worded in such a way that the respondent is likely to respond in a socially desirable way (e.g., in a way that denies racial prejudice).

Software The instructions that make computers run. See **hardware.**

Solomon Four-Group Design A research design that uses four comparison groups formed by random assignment. Two of the groups receive an experimental treatment, and two do not. Two groups are tested both before and after the experimental treatment, while the other two groups are tested only after the treatment.

Split-Half Reliability A type of reliability. It applies to measuring instruments that are designed to measure a single characteristic, such as depression or self-esteem. Split-half reliability is determined by splitting an instrument into two halves of equal length and then correlating scores based on the two halves. A high correlation indicates good split-half reliability. See **internal consistency measures.**

Spreadsheet Program A computer program that enters financial data into cells in a 2-by-2 table.

Spurious Relationship In analyzing the relationship between two variables, researchers may find that this relationship is due to a third variable. Then the original relationship between the two variables is said to be *spurious.* See **extraneous variable.**

Standard Deviation In a **frequency distribution,** the square root of the **variance.** A measure of the "spread" of scores or values.

Static Group Comparison A research design in which a group that has experienced an intervention, treatment, or event is compared with a group that has not. In this type of design, the groups are not formed by random assignment.

Statistic A measure that describes some aspect of a **sample** of individuals or cases. See **parameter.**

Statistical Package for the Social Sciences (SPSS) A popular computer program for statistical analysis of data.

Statistical Regression A factor of internal validity. Statistical regression refers to the fact that whenever a group is selected because of very high or very low scores, when the group is retested, on average, the retest scores will be closer to the mean.

Statistical Significance In inferential statistics, a criterion that must be met to reject the **null hypothesis.** This criterion is normally set at a level of .01 or .05. For example, if the difference between two sample means is statistically significant at the .01 level, we can conclude that the chances of finding the observed difference in means, if the two population means were equal, is less than 1 in 100.

Stratified (Random) Sample A type of sample in which the researcher divides the population into subgroups or strata by population characteristics, such as race, income, and sex. Then a simple random sample is drawn from the population within each subgroup or stratum.

Structured (or Standardized) Interview A type of interview in which the specific wording and order of questions is predetermined and standardized for all interviewees.

Summated Rating Scale On a questionnaire or interview schedule, a set of scale items, all of which are weighted equally and to each of which the respondent responds with degrees of agreement or disagreement or some other response. An individual's score on a summated rating scale is the sum or average of scores across the scale. See **scale.**

Survey Research A type of research in which a large number of persons or other units respond to a questionnaire or interview.

Symmetrical Relationship A type of two-variable relationship in which neither variable influences the other. The two variables tend to occur together but do not cause or influence each other.

Systematic Sample A type of probability sample in which the first element is chosen from the numbers 1 through K and subsequent elements are chosen at every Kth interval. For example, a researcher may select every 100th name in a phone book for inclusion in the sample.

Test Factor A variable that is used to study the nature of the relationship between two other variables. For example, the researcher may examine the relationship between level of stress and self-perceived health separately for males and females (gender). In this case, gender is a test factor. See **elaboration.**

Testing A factor of internal validity. Testing occurs whenever performance on a test is affected by having taken a previous test.

Test-Retest Reliability One type of reliability of measuring instruments. A measuring instrument has test-retest reliability if a repeat test yields a consistent result (assuming that the property being tested has remained the same).

Theory An explanation of some aspect of the world. A theory is a set of interrelated concepts, definitions, and propositions that presents a systematic view of phenomena by specifying relations between variables, with the purpose of explaining and predicting.

Two-Sample *t* Test In inferential statistics, a test to determine if the difference between the mean values of two groups is statistically significant.

Two-Tailed Test A statistical test used to evaluate a nondirectional hypothesis—that is, a hypothesis that does not specify the direction in which two or more variables differ. For example, a two-tailed test would be used to evaluate the hypothesis that social workers and physicists differ in their level of social concern (without specifying which group has higher social concern).

Unobtrusive Measures Techniques for observing and recording human behavior without the knowledge of those being observed.

Unstandardized Interview A type of interview in which the general nature of the questions is specified in advance, but the specific questions are not.

User Interface A software program used by a computer to communicate with a user. A typical user interface on a personal computer will employ pop-down menus, icons (pictures that can be "selected" with a mouse), and windows.

Valid Operational Definition An operational definition that measures a concept or variable in such a way that it reflects the "true" meaning of the concept or variable.

Validity (of measuring instruments) The extent to which a measuring instrument measures what it is supposed to measure.

Variable A concept that can take on two or more **exhaustive** and **mutually exclusive** values. For example, the concept **gender** is also a variable because it can take on the values "female" and "male."

Variance A measure of the "spread" of scores or values in a **frequency distribution.** See **standard deviation.**

Withdrawal Design A type of ABAB **single-subject research** design in which the treatment is withdrawn in the third (A) phase. See **ABAB design.**

Word Processor A computer program for the entry and editing of text.

X-Axis The horizontal axis of a graph. It usually depicts the values of the **independent variable.**

Y-Axis The vertical axis of a graph. It usually depicts the values of the **dependent variable.**

Index

About the Author

Raymond Mark is an educator and scholar with more than 15 years of teaching experience in social work. He earned his B.A. in Psychology (summa cum laude) at the State University of New York at Stony Brook (1972) and his MSSW (1973) and Ph.D. (1976) at the University of Wisconsin—Madison. He is widely published in social work and has served on the editorial boards of *Social Work* and *Behavioral Group Therapy*. He is the recipient of the Humanitarian of the Year Award of the Dade County (Florida) Coalition for Human Rights (1979) and of the Evelyn Hooker Research Award (1982).